INDIGENOUS ARCHIVES

INDIGENOUS ARCHIVES

THE MAKING AND UNMAKING OF ABORIGINAL ART

EDITED BY DARREN JORGENSEN AND IAN MCLEAN

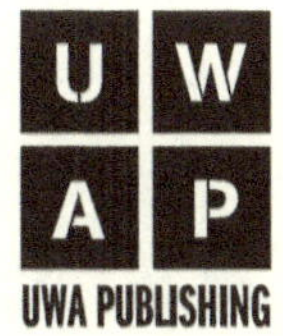

First published in 2017 by
UWA Publishing
Crawley, Western Australia 6009
www.uwap.uwa.edu.au

UWAP is an imprint of UWA Publishing
a division of The University of Western Australia

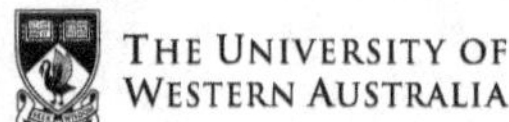

A full Cataloguing-in-Publication entry is available from the National Library of Australia.

Typeset by J&M Typesetting
Printed by Lightning Source
Cover image: Brook Andrew, *I Split Your Gaze*, ink jet print, 108 by 100cm, 1997.
Image courtesy the artist, Tolarno Galleries, Melbourne and Galerie Nathalie Obadia, Paris and Brussels.

CONTENTS

PREFACE

Darren Jorgensen and Ian McLean

Because a society archives what it considers to be its most significant things, the archive reveals what and how a society thinks, and the values by which it lives. Thus the archive is what Foucault dubbed a 'truth regime': its function is to produce truth – or determine what is true. As the touchstone for authority (truth), the archive is the guardian of ideology and the central site of power. This is what Foucault, who made the archive his field of study, meant by reminding us of the ancient aphorism that 'knowledge is power'. He coined the term 'knowledge/power' to indicate that each is one and the same: knowledge produces power and power produces (or delimits) knowledge.

Foucault's historical studies are based on the assumption that each society and culture is differentiated by a particular truth regime as revealed in its official archives – as if, like a fingerprint, the archive is an identity marker. This scenario is complicated in the modern state as it consists of many competing interests each with its own specialised archives. In his later writing Foucault developed a keener sense of the continuous flux of power, characterising it as a distributive, networked and relational economy in which, despite being increasingly governmentalised or regulated by the state, various truth regimes (or archives) are engaged in constant struggle: dominant groups 'together with the resistance and revolts which that domination comes up against'.

However, beneath this turbulence, Foucault – ever the structuralist – detected a deeper, more steady current: 'a massive and universalizing form, at the level of the whole social body'. This 'locking together of power relations'[2] occurs in the common ground between these competing groups (or archives), making 'visible those fundamental phenomena of "domination"' that comprise the over-arching truth regime or official archive that sets the ideology of our times. In this Foucauldian spirit, we have compiled a selection of essays that work with varying purposes across different types of archives, ranging from those held by state museums to those in Aboriginal art centres. They address Indigenous Australian art through archives of all kinds, but these archives are all of a kind: each is a voice in the struggles that produce power in 'the whole social body'. Together their essays touch on the turbulence that makes up the 'massive and universalizing form' of The Archive. Working within this turbulence, they cannot help but affirm its power, to demonstrate just how essential archives are to the functioning of contemporary Aboriginal Australian art. As Indigenous artists authorise themselves through The Archive, the Aboriginal art world authorises its auctions, exhibitions and writings with certificates and signatures, dates and names. Archives carry with them an authority that art alone does not. So it is that our contributors have reason to consult and defer to The Archive, to elucidate the very specific information it holds, to use it as a toolbox for research, or to treat The Archive as a subject in its own right.

In conceptualising this book we were well aware of the so-called 'archival turn' in contemporary art. Inaugurated by Appropriation Art in the late 1970s and early 1980s, and since then a feature of much contemporary art, it inevitably frames the essays in *Indigenous Archives*. Thus they address questions that inexorably flow from a turning: What does it mean for art to turn to The Archive? In what sense is art archival? What is it about The Archive that it can turn art? Towards what in art is The Archive being turned, and what is it about The Archive that art might turn on it? The bigger question, which Nikolas Kompridis points out in his rumination on the aesthetic turn in politics (and from which we directly purloined the aforementioned questions), is how do we judge the many turns – the ideological, the linguistic, the aesthetic, the material – that afflict our times? Are they a matter of fashion, or if they collectively point to some larger underlying turn, which of them matters the most? 'Turns', writes Kompridis, 'can be overturned – some more easily than others', and he argues, 'if we are to speak confidently' on the matter, 'we must show that this turn involves a consequential change in our understanding of', in this case, art. He suggests that the more meaningful the turn the more substantial and long-lived must be the relation of its terms, such that the turn in question may in fact be one of many returns.[3]

Australia was the site of the first archival turn in contemporary art. It was a defining characteristic of the Papunya Tula painters who initiated the Aboriginal contemporary art movement. In what was perceived at the time as a contentious and dangerous move, they revisited their archives as a means to create a modern art that spoke to their contemporary political concerns. This occurred shortly after the 1967 Referendum and in the midst of Land Rights demands, that is, in what was also a decisive turn in the Australian polity towards Aboriginal politics. Thus in Australia the archival turn in contemporary art was also an Indigenous turn. This is further underlined by the archival turn that occurred in white Australian art later in the 1970s and the 1980s with Appropriation Art. Two of its key artists, Tim Johnson and Imants Tillers, also turned towards Papunya Tula painting in their appropriations, as if emulating not just the look but also the form and content of the art.

In Australia Indigenous artists and scholars have used photographs, ceremonies and files to change our understanding of art, its histories and properties. In what has become the most classic example, featured on the cover of this book, Brook Andrew's *I Split Your Gaze* (1997) dusts off an ethnographic photograph of an Indigenous man, to split his image that splits the viewer's gaze looking at him. *I Split Your Gaze* is contemporary with Jacques Derrida's *Archive Fever* (1996), and both deconstruct The Archive's authority to recreate the turmoil by which archives are constituted and reconstituted. For Derrida, archives enact a concealment rather than a revelation. In the process of concealing its items, The Archive conceals itself, gathering itself against an outside by which it also defines its difference. Paradoxically, it is the outside to which The Archive defers, in a doubled movement by which The Archive is both constituted and is exposed to its own undoing.

More than ten years after its exhibition, Djon Mundine and Fiona Foley complained that Andrew had not consulted with the descendants of the archival photographs that he had used to create I Split Your Gaze.[4] For Mundine and Foley, Andrew had skipped a crucial archival protocol, one that differentiates the Indigenous Archive from its outside. But the scandal of Andrew's work is greater than this. For if, as Derrida argues, The Archive's authority crucially depends upon forgetting, upon a historical amnesia, the power of the archival photograph signals the trauma that brought about the forgetting in the first place. *I Split Your Gaze* produces a new historical trace upon this trauma of the old, working not to reveal this man's place in Australian history but concealing it, in the process deconstructing the possibility of archival truth itself.

Contrast Andrew's photo-compositions with his contemporaries, with Leah-King Smith's 1991 *Patterns of Connection* series and Brenda Croft's 1998 *In My Father's House.* The first sees archival photographs of Indigenous people through a fish-eye lens, and like Andrew recreates their heroic place in history with a layered looking. The second series also writes over photographs, these being Croft's family archive that have come to symbolise the personal histories of many Indigenous Australians. While trauma is written into the distance of the fish-eye and the writing over Croft's family, Andrew's photo-compositions make it uncertain whether the image stands for a traumatic history at all.

Paralleling the work of artists, Australian art history has seen its own archival and Indigenous turns. Vivien Johnson undertakes a dogged archival journey in *Once Upon a Time in Papunya* (2014), in the process overhauling the history of painting at Papunya in 1971. Crucial to Johnson's chronology is the label on a box of slides, through which she argues for a 'School of Kaapa', a group of figurative works on board that preceded, and were independent of, the 'School of Bardon' that has become the origin story of contemporary art in the Western Desert.[5] These figurative works create a stylistic bridge between the 'painting men' who had gathered around Bardon, and the naturalism of Albert Namatjira, the celebrated landscape painter, whose style Kaapa also appropriated. All of this rests upon an archival reading, a reading of the writing on a box of slides.

Other signs of this archival and Indigenous turn appeared when a box of paintings stored in a New York university gallery were discovered to be a lost collection of Noongar paintings from the 1940s. The return of this collection to Perth led to a series of exhibitions and the ongoing creation of an archive around this col-lection.[6] Also in Western Australia, ceremonial archives were used to resolve a debate over the origins of a group of so-called 'Bradshaw' rock paintings in the Kimberley. The publication of *Gwion Gwion: Secret and Sacred Pathways of the Ngarinyin Aboriginal People of Australia* (2000) illuminates the ceremonial and cultural context of the Gwion Gwion. Here one archive conceals another, rock art concealing ceremony and ceremony concealing rock art, to create The Dreaming Archive, an assemblage of enunciations and metaphysics, ceremonies and representations, that determine the possibilities of what can be said and done. While the turbulence of modern history shapes archives of the nation state, the repository of The Dreaming Archive is situated in deep time, its epochs glacial rather than centurial, its enunciations multidimensional rather than polemic.

Indigenous Archives is framed by contemporary archives that authorise and govern Aboriginal contemporary art and debates around it, and is haunted by both this Dreaming Archive and the deep-rooted archival impulse it represents –what Derrida describes as a pathology to order the world in one way or another. McLean's Introduction anatomises this tendency, this gaining power over things by ordering them, while Jorgensen's Afterword tracks the shifting identity of The Dreaming Archive within Aboriginal art centre archives.

Indigenous Archives is an outcome of an Australian Research Council project to investigate the uses of remote archives for scholarly research,[7] and of a symposium in Alice Springs in 2014 that addressed remote art centre archives.[8] The first of four sections considers the limits of such archives for the art historian. Each essay is based on PhD research projects by art historians working with remote art centre archives in their investigation of a particular artist. Two essays draw on the relatively elusive and partial archives of a place, Utopia, that lacked a proper art centre. Anne Marie Brody, whose professional work as a curator with Utopia artists from the beginning of the art movement there has given her unique insights into the art, and analyses the significance of Rodney Gooch's archive of the artists' work that he developed while acting as their field worker. While undertaking her dissertation on Emily Kame Kngwarreye, Chrischona Schmidt was confronted with the lack of a complete archive of the artist's work. Her essay considers the issues of working with partial archives spread across the country in galleries, art museums and other places, and the problems she encountered in developing her own archive of Kngwarreye's work. Suzanne Spunner guides us through the complexities and controversies of provenance in Rover Thomas's art through the evaluation of archival evidence – what it can reveal and also what it might not reveal. She draws on the Waringarri Arts archives and also considers the archives of other people for whom Thomas worked. Alec O'Halloran shows how even one of the most substantial and complete art centre archives, that of Papunya Tula, presents problems for the art historian seeking to write a biography of one of its original painters, Mick Namarari Tjapaltjarri. The lesson of this section is that The Archive is not sacrosanct. Rather, it is an incomplete document that requires – indeed only gains its power – through extensive hermeneutical revision. In other words, behind The Archive is the archivist, the interpreter and organiser of The Archive.

Having established the importance of the archivist in the first section, the second section comprises essays that develop various arguments about Indigenous art from art centre archives. While, as in the first section, these writers build out from existing archives, their examination is instrumental rather than hermeneutical – they make use of archives for larger ends rather than reflect on their limits. John Kean also works with the Papunya Tula archive in his essay on the early life and art of Johnny Warangula Tjupurrula, supplementing it with the examination of private archives, weather records, diaries and photographs. Philippa Jahn also uses art centre archives to flesh out the place of an artist within a regional history. She examines the ways in which the choices of Kalumburu artist Mary Puntji Clement reflect the regional politics of northern Australia. Sadly, as this book was going to print, Clement passed away, leaving us many wonderful paintings from an all too brief career. After Jahn documents her life and what is now her legacy, Darren Jorgensen uses the archives of Kayili Artists to work out what Jackie Giles and Ngipi Ward have in common, and how their work embodies a general 'style' that grew out of this desert outstation.

The third section examines the ways in which contemporary artists have built their own archives, beginning with an examination of two examples of remote artists who have sought, in their art practices, to archive local histories. Emilia Galatis examines Warakurna history paintings and Robert Lazaras Lane investigates Wukun Wanambi's archival, multi-media art. John Dallwitz, Janet Inyika, Susan Lowish and Linda Rive take us through the Ara Irititja archive of Ngaanyatjarra, Pitjantjatjara, Yankunytjatjara speakers, a digital repository whose accessible, multi-media model is now being adopted by Indigenous communities in other parts of Australia.[9] Ara Irititja functions like an Anangu Google, but one that allows its contributors to upload content while holding ceremonial knowledge in confidence. 'It can hide things if necessary, and then bring them back later. The Ara Irititja computer is clever like a dingo', says Wilton Foster.[10] This is true not only of secret-sacred content, but of anthropological archives, including many photographs, that have been imported into Ara Irititja, reproduced from one archive into another. Here the photographs become part of a living archive, as Ara Irititja allows its users to add to the information around them, to name their subjects and places. Using examples from her experience curating and collaborating, Margo Neale proposes a 'third archive' that lies in the country itself, and in the minds of the Elders.

Indigenous Archives makes a decisive shift in the fourth section to highly urbanised centres. Four essays by seven authors bring different perspectives to bear on the work of seven artists who aim to decolonise existing museum archives developed in the colonial period. Jessyca Hutchens investigates the different strategies of decolonising the museum that arose from the art residencies of Christian Thompson and Julie Gough in British institutions that hold Aboriginal materials from the nineteenth century. Odette Marie Kelada and Genevieve Grieves trace the various ways in which artists Vernon Ah Kee and Yhonnie Scarce adopt archival strategies to invert the legacies of colonialism. Khadija von Zinnenburg Carroll argues that this return to archives by Indigenous artists – she examines the work of Brook Andrew, Daniel Boyd and Julie Gough – is necessarily anachronic in order to maintain its deconstructive edge. Jane Lydon analyses how Vernon Ah Kee, Brenda Croft, and Christian Thompson use historical photographs to deconstruct existing histories and their archives, and reconstruct new ones. The fourth section concludes with Brook Andrew and Katarina Matiasek's travelogue into the colonial archives of the Austrian anthropologist Rudolf Pöch – what might be considered the diary of an excursion into an existing archive in preparation for creative research.

Arguably these seven artists can only deconstruct the archive by, in turn, becoming archivists. The same is true of academics, who have long been compelled to work with archives – to either affirm or deconstruct them – so that they are able to authorise what they say, or in Foucault's terms to place statements in relation to each other. Yet as this volume shows, the logic of such authorisations and relations are not only academic. The recursive logic of The Archive, which embeds knowledge in relations, is a universal activity that occurs in all cultures. This is because The Archive, as the site of ideology and power, produces social order and the culture that constitutes it. Thus its recursive logic is also at work in the compulsions of artists and Indigenous communities, and is tied less to any one logic than it is to the contingencies of history and subjectivity. The Archive relies upon archives that are idiosyncratic and political, and dependent upon technologies and powers. They envisage modes of relation while overwriting other modes of relation. *Indigenous Archives* examines the various ways in which archives and archivists have made, and are remaking, Aboriginal identities and histories.

Finally, this volume is dedicated to one of our authors who may not live to see this book in print, the community leader and political campaigner Janet Inyika, in whom we lose a living archive of both the Pitjantatjara Lands and Australian history.

Notes

1 R. Bell, 'Bell's Theorem: Aboriginal Art – it's a white thing!', 2002, viewed 23 January 2016, <http://www.kooriweb.org/foley/great/art/bell.html>.
2 M. Foucault, 'The Subject and Power', *Critical Inquiry,* vol. 8, no. 4, 1982, pp. 777–95 at 795.
3 N. Kompridis, 'Introduction: Turning and Returning: The Aesthetic Turn in Political Thought', in N. Kompridis (ed.), *The Aesthetic Turn in Political Thought*, Bloomsbury, London, 2014, pp. xiv–xxxvii at xiv–xv.
4 F. Foley, 'When the Circus came to Town', *Art Monthly Australia*, no. 245, 2011, pp. 5–7; D. Mundine, 'Nowhere Boy', *Artlink*, vol. 30, no. 1, 2010, pp. 18–22.
5 V. Johnson, *Once Upon a Time in Papunya*, University of New South Wales Press, Sydney, 2014, pp. 11–43.
6 These exhibitions include Koolark Koort Koorliny (Heart Coming

Home) and Revel Cooper both at the John Curtin Gallery in 2014, and Bella Kelly at the Vancouver Arts Centre in Albany in 2016.

7 ARC project number DP110104509 Mobilising Remote Aboriginal Art Centre Records for Art History.

8 Art Centres Art Histories Symposium, Alice Springs, 4 September 2014.

9 For example, at the Mowanjum Art and Culture Centre, viewed 3 March 2016, <http://www.slwa.wa.gov.au/for/indigenous_australians/storylines>.

10 Why is Ara Irititja Important? needs underscore under the 'r' of Ara.

Indigenous Archives

1

INTRODUCTION: CONVERGENT ARCHIVES

Ian McLean

> **Arch**: from Latinised form of Greek *arkh-*, *arkhi-*, 'first, chief, primeval', comb. form of *arkhos*, 'chief'; with derivatives *arkhe*, 'rule, beginning', and *arkhos*, 'ruler'.

The gathering of curiosities is an age-old human habit – we are the bowerbirds of the primates. The gathering already is a consigning, which as Derrida reminds us literally means 'gathering together signs'. He characterised this act as one 'of assigning residence' – an archiving or arranging of these propitious signs into 'a single corpus…a synchrony in which all the elements articulate the unity of an ideal configuration'.[1] In Australia the shaman did it for tens of thousands of years in secret caves, whereas systematically arranging curiosities into a cabinet was a characteristic archival act of the European Renaissance. Buttressing the arrangement with an arsenal of tabulated and catalogued data, a meta-archive, is a symptom of modernity. But driving this evolution of archive types is an archetypal impulse. The wise ape, *Homo sapien*, is sometimes called *homo aestheticus*, but why not *homo archivist*? This upright primate made its monumental mark on the world because of its ability to order its curiosities into a type of language that animated the things of world, bringing them into being. The archive has a divine status: through it the world is written into existence.

Thus we should not be surprised that Derrida's *Archive Fever: A Freudian Impression* (1995) opens with a concerted attack on the work of the archive. Following his familiar strategy, Derrida warns against the ways in which authority is so omnipresent (universal) that its power is embedded in language: 'The meaning of "archive" comes to it from the Greek *arkheion*: initially...the residence of the superior magistrates, the *archons*, those who commanded'; *Arkheion* is in turn derived from '*Arkhe*', which names at once the '*commencement*' and the '*commandment*': it creates and commands.[2] From this Derrida makes three closely related accusations against the archive: it enacts a 'patriarchic' politics 'without which no archive would ever come into play or appear as such', its documents 'state the law: they recall the law and call on or impose the law', and they do this from a specific place.[3] Thereby an otherwise invisible law is embodied (in the archons) and physically manifested (in the archive). In short, the archive and its archons spin a magic that gives the spirits a powerful presence. If human funerary rites are designed to send ancestral spirits away so that their ghosts won't return to haunt present generations, the archive calls them back to aid in the political demands of the day.

These claims, which for Derrida state the obvious, are quickly asserted as a sort of rallying call before mounting his main attack of deconstructing the 'patriarchive' through a 'project of general archiviology'[4] – i.e. to unpack the archive by tracing and pinpointing its genealogy, its ancestral history. Thus archiviology is not concerned with the archive's manifestation in the actual institutions of the law or its changing forms in the modern world, but with its founding in the metaphysical underworld. Derrida digs around in Hades for the archetypal ur-archive. Having declared his position, Derrida hurriedly – on the second page of his article – segues into the domains of mythology and Freudian psychoanalysis in order to investigate how the 'irrepressible force and authority of transgenerational memory' is passed down via the ghosts of ancestors, as if 'an ancestor can speak within us' and we too can 'speak…in such an "unheimlich", "uncanny" fashion, to his or her ghost'.[5]

The dream world, which is where Freud conducted most of his research, is the river Styx across which ancestral ghosts traditionally journey from the spirit world to that of the living. Freud began writing *The Interpretation of Dreams* in late 1895, coincidentally at the very moment that Spencer and Gillen introduced the pivotal Indigenous concept that they – following Gillen's discussions with Arrernte shamans and ceremonial leaders – translated as 'Dreamtime'. 'Dreamtime' takes this name because, as in other cultures, the visitations of spirits generally occur in the dark, unpredictable crosscurrents of dreams. Like Freud, Dante and numerous shamans before him, Derrida crosses the river Styx as if the archetypal archive is wrought in dreaming's inferno of the unconscious, and – and here his reference is also Freud – its origins are biological rather than cultural, let alone political.

In fact archiviology can push back beyond the origins of biology (of organic life and its spirits) to the very formation of the laws that govern our physical universe, as if the impulse to archive – to order information – haunted our universe from its beginnings and is impressed in the very atoms from which the molecules of our DNA are made. In our universe's dark regions are archived its own creation – ghostly echoes of the big bang – which scientists are in the process of decoding by creating their own mirror archive of data, a mirror of a mirror.

The archive always comes after the big bang: it is a second order. More than a regulating commentary on something other that preceded it, the archive seeks to resurrect this prior other as if in its ghostly remnants the fiery forces that brought it into being can still be traced and mined. Thus the archive is like a magical glass that, as in a séance, ghosts appear to reveal their secrets.

By their very nature ghosts cannot be touched. Leaving no impression and passing through things, they are mere shadows of their former lives, only appearing like images on a screen. As much as the archive purports to catalogue the hidden order of things, something secret, mysterious and unknowable remains. The archival impulse is never satisfied. Like a photograph its ancestral resurrections always fail: the subject remains an image; the ghostly ancestral realm persists. Thus for all the marvellous scientific revelations of late, the big bang still is the stuff of myth and enduring mystery.

Animating every archive is a secret past. The issue is one of form not content. It is not a matter of what the secret actually is but its intractable ghostly form: no matter how much the archive renders visible or public, how much data it pulls into the public domain or how many photographs we compile, an invisibility endures. Thus the archive is founded by a fundamental lack, which is why desire – the archive's subjects are objects of desire – is a fundamental drive of the archive. Only the ghost whisperer – the archon or shaman – can mediate this desire. Hence the pivotal factor in archiviology is not the ancestor or its ghost, but the ghost whisperers – the archons. Their unique ability to converse with ghosts makes them the guardians of the law and the keepers of its place and its secrets. 'They are also accorded the hermeneutic right and competence. They have the power to interpret the archives'.[6] No wonder the archon is the principal target of Derrida's critique.

In their 'archive fever', says Derrida, the archons aim to 'bring to light a more originary origin than that of the ghost…a more archaic impression…which is almost no longer an archive', but instead 'confuses itself with the pressure of the [ancestral] footstep which leaves its still-living mark on a substrate, a surface, a place of origin'. The archon dreams of cataloguing that 'instant when the printed archive is yet to be detached from the primary impression in its singular, irreproducible, and archaic origin', as if this originary moment, this commencement, is a law, a commandment. At this point the archive seeks to be its subject (what it archives), 'an archive which would in sum confuse itself with the *arkhē*... An archive without archive'.[7] This delusion is the symptom of archive fever.

Archive fever infects traditional Indigenous societies, which are societies beholden to the ghosts of their ancestors and take their law from the places in which they walked. In retracing their footsteps the shaman establishes the *sensus communis* of the Indigenous world. This retracing is authorised by the archive of ancestral signs at his command. The shaman is the classical archon whose ability to converse with ancestral ghosts unlocks the 'archontic power' (as Derrida called it) of the archive.

Like the big bang, when the ancestors returned into the earth after their wanderings, creating the hills, rivers and waterholes that are the bones and lifeblood of the country, they made a living-evolving memorial or museum of their escapades. To those who still feel this ancestral pulse – this *tjukurrpa* (Dreamtime or Dreaming) – the lie of the land and its ecosystems echo ancestral events. However, this echo is just the surface inscriptions of a deeper script, screening from view the animating forces or 'archontic power' of the country.

Country is there in the open to be read by those with eyes, but within its folds and crevices are secret places that only initiated men can visit; and in these secret places are secret caves in which secret objects with esoteric signs are carefully wrapped and stored.

These are generally ancestral relics saturated with the origin of things – indexes for the ancestors' footsteps. The most important part of the archive, they are the keys that unlock its workings and call forth the ancestors. Only the archons or shamans can unlock this 'archontic power'. This dangerous activity requires the careful management of the archive. Like a nuclear power plant, some of its power is released into the public realm to abet current needs but its blinding furnace must be obscured, kept secret and secure in the private domain or all hell will break loose. This is why nuclear plants are closely guarded secretive places. The shaman's hermeneutic task is not just to plumb the ancestral secrets in the archive but also to be their keeper.

The archon's command, which for Derrida is the ultimate command, lies in *his* hermeneutic rather than political or military power. In calling forth and conversing with ghosts so that he might release some of their ancestral power into the public domain, the archon fulfils the political function of the archive to provide the 'institutional passage from the private to the public'. However, Derrida added, this 'does not always mean [the passage] from the secret to the nonsecret'.[8] The ghost whisperer's job is, through *his* hermeneutic skills, to police the threshold between the secret and non-secret in ways that maintain rather than subvert this difference.

If the archon's command is not political, there can be no political power without control of the archive and its archons. This is why today Indigenous activists focus so much attention on controlling the modern archive of their cultures, as if it is the only way to wrestle back political advantage. However, controlling the archive is not the same as being its archon. Moreover, while the modern archive and the shaman's archive are each expressions of the archetypal archive (phenotypes of the same genotype), each has radically different procedures and categories. This is not unusual, which is why on first encountering another's archive we are invariably bewildered, like Foucault's uneasy laughter on reading 'a certain Chinese encyclopedia': 'In the wonderment of this taxonomy', he ruminated, 'is demonstrated…the exotic charm of another system of thought…[and] the limitation of our own'.[9] This ordering of things – 'the pure experience of order and of its modes of being'[10] – is, said Foucault, the beginning and ending of all knowledge. We only truly know about other cultures through the taxonomies with which they order their world, no matter how strange and foreign they may appear. And the often stark silhouette of this strangeness is the best means we have of knowing our own culture, its limits and oddities.

Convergent Archives

Perhaps the different archives of the world can be broken down into a sort of language tree – a network of relations – but their radically shifting categories are exceedingly difficult to map. Instead they appear, as they did to Foucault, as utterly different paradigms with no relation to the other. An archive readily incorporates anything whenever or wherever it was made if it meets the criteria of the archive. The things we now know as art previously lived a different life in other worlds where a dissimilar epistemology ordered the ruling archive. For example, ecclesiastical archives made certain objects visible as icons, whereas the art archive made these same objects, taken from the altars of churches and rehoused in the white walls of the art museum, visible as art.

The step from secret esoteric designs in the service of ancestral ghosts and shamans to art in the service of aesthetics, curators and art centre managers, was a paradigmatic shift radically altering the nature and function of ostensibly the same objects. Yet on remote Indigenous communities some of the most celebrated contemporary artists move between both paradigms without a blink of the eye. What does it say about the convergence between these radically different archives when the same person can be a successful contemporary artist in his day job at the community art centre and a shaman working similar signs in ceremonies at night?

From the time they encountered the modern archive Indigenous people were keen to engage it because they knew, from their own archival practices, that it was the power behind modernity and its objects that they desired. Even first-contact Indigenous people were keen to give their stories, often illustrated with artworks, to the archives of anthropologists and missionaries. William Barak's art-making is probably a direct outcome of his role as a close and committed informer for the anthropologist A. W. Howitt, whereas Albert Namatjira's watercolours are a direct result of his desire to participate in the modern art market on its terms.

Thus the Western archive stimulated the production of modern Indigenous art – art calibrated to the needs of the art archive rather than the shaman's ghost whispering. Further, since the beginning of their contact with Western art forms, Indigenous artists have never hesitated to appropriate them into their archival practices. 'That print', Bede Tungutalum said to me a few months ago while strumming his guitar at a party in a print studio in Port Kembla where he was resident artist, 'has a song. I'll sing it to you'. It was the story of the ancestor Murtankala and her daughters Wurupurungala and Murupiyamkala (similar to the Yolngu story of the Wagilug and Djan'kawu sisters) who created the features of the landscape and gave birth to the tribes, but it was sung country and western style. As Bede made clear to me that night, this print was a contemporary (i.e. living) archive of ancient ancestral stories. Subsequently bought by Sydney's Museum of Contemporary Art, it will be duly photographed and catalogued in its art archive as an original work of art by Bede, as it will also, no doubt, be catalogued in the archive of the Duck Point print workshop and the Tiwi Design art centre, which Bede founded with Giovanni Tipungwuti in 1969. Indigenous art, which began as an archive, is now destined to be archived in Indigenous art centres as well as far off Western institutions.

In the current enthusiasm for cultural convergence we should not lose sight of the radical differences being obscured in the archival blurring that occurs in the production of Indigenous contemporary art. If the shaman's archive archives ancestral origins, what does the modern archive archive? The shaman's archive became the subject of a modern archive, such that the ancestral subject of the Indigenous archives disappeared from view or, once removed, were sublimated into the modern archive. Where the shaman looking at *his* archived signs – say a group of *tjurungas* – saw ancestral ghosts, the modern archivist looking at her archive of the same *tjurungas* saw artefacts or perhaps even art.

The art archive is a quintessentially modern epistemology that bends things to its order: ritual objects became art, artists rather than ancestral beings or their incarnations create the art, and art curators and critics, not shamans, mediate their meaning and function. The cultural convergences of colonialism swirl in its powerful transcultural currents, but a shared archival impulse fuels this convergence. Thus Western interest in archiving Indigenous culture was not just due to the political machinations of the immense Imperial archive designed to regulate the British Empire that was established in nineteenth century. It also expressed the deeper drive of an archetypal archival impulse.

Little need was felt to archive Australian Indigenous culture during the early phase of colonialism, as it was not seen to be in any way providential. Only in the latter half of the nineteenth century, with the ascent of social evolutionism that believed primitive cultures held secrets about the origins of Western modernity, did the race begin to archive Indigenous things. Driving this Western archival impulse was a deep yearning for 'a more archaic impression'. A similar drive was evident in Western modernism, which also got underway at this time. Its search for originality made its adherents particularly interested in the Indigenous curios that colonists retrieved from shamanistic rituals. Thus in the late nineteenth century there began a convergence of Indigenous and Western archival impulses, each lusting after an archive that confused 'itself with the *arkhē*'. Both took their bearings from an ultimate primeval origin as if caught by the allure of an unattainable ancestral secret. In this respect the modern art archive has all the characteristics of the archetypal archive, as if Indigenous shamans didn't have to become modern; they already were modern.

The shaman was also modern in the sense that he located the ancestral imprints in his archive not just in iconographic signs but also in aesthetic affects. The shaman's work of revelation and concealment with the documents of his archive is primarily conducted in a performative mode: it lies in the evocations of rhythm and patterns through art, dance and music. The European Enlightenment called such evocation aesthetics, a notion that became central to modern ideology but which its philosophers never fully grasped and which its archives have never successfully tabulated, except to occasionally reduce it to a style or even an ethnic sensibility that would provide the basis for a *sensus communis*.

Aesthetics, the science of feeling, refers to a sensibility that discerns underlying energies that animate the sensible world – what Western modernist critics called 'significant form', by which they meant something akin to the music of the spheres. Kant, the most important philosopher of aesthetics, argued that aesthetic sensibility, like other faculties, would in its most disinterested mode – a mode that was true to its own logic or operational structure rather than simply following external (e.g. utilitarian) preferences – reflect a universal and therefore quasi-objective judgement, as opposed to the sort of subjective taste that generally prevailed in public opinion. In thus providing the basis for a fully public rather than just private taste, aesthetic sensibility could underwrite a cosmopolitan *sensus communis* that overcame individual, tribal or national prejudices. Aesthetic experience or fine art had become a definitive hallmark of modern art by the turn of the twentieth century, and also a modern conduit of transculturation.

The notion of aesthetic experience became important in modernity because it provided a means of conceiving a *sensus communis* that was true to the workings of individual sensibility rather than imposed from above or outside individual experience, yet conjoined rather than divided individuals. As conceived by Kant, aesthetic experience is essentially anthropocentric: in prioritising the individual's experience, fine art becomes an index of the human subject's freedom – embodied in the genius artist – rather than ancestral presence. In short, fine art displaces ancestral presence into significant form. Thus modern aesthetics effectively relocated the presence of the ghost into fine art and that of the shaman into the artist. The secret did not so much disappear – it wasn't foreclosed, to use the language of psychoanalysis – but repressed in the idea of fine art or significant form.

Aesthetic affects also provided a primary means by which the shaman hid the ancestral secrets of his archive in full view, thus ensuring the safe passage of its power into the public domain. The Yolngu, for example, called a particular optical aesthetic affect *Bir'yun*. After consulting his informants in 1937, the anthropologist

Donald Thomson described *Bir'yun* as 'the flash of light – the sensation of light that one gets and carries away in one's mind's eye, from a glance at the *likanbuy miny'tji* [paintings that are ancestral manifestations]', or as Howard Morphy put it: '*Bir'yun* is the shimmering effect of finely cross-hatched paintings which project a brightness that is seen as emanating from the wangarr [ancestral] being itself'.[11] Here, indeed, is an archive [the shaman's catalogue of signs] that confuses itself with the *arkhē* [the ancestor].

This convergence of Indigenous shamanism and Western modernist art in the realm of aesthetics was imperfect, as the ancestral content of the shaman's archive had been sublimated in the art archive. In its most ideal form, the art archive completely aestheticises its objects of desire. In actuality this was rarely the case, as despite Kantian theory and the rigour of critics such as Clement Greenberg, many moderns inclined to the spiritualist or metaphysical content of the shaman's aesthetic practices. The 'flash', said Martin Heidegger, is a universal sign of ancestral intervention:

> In the flashing glance and as that flash, the essence, the coming to presence, of Being enters into its own emitting of light. Moving through the element of its shining, the flashing glance retrieves that which it catches sight of and brings it back into the brightness of its own looking.[12]

Rather than the disinterested terms of Kantian philosophy that sought to engage the logic of significant form, many modernists understood the aesthetic aims of their abstract art in spiritual terms that resonated with shamanism. From the other side, as if sensing this convergence, Indigenous shamans pushed their optical aesthetic affects towards a modernist purpose, in much the same fashion that Michael Fried claimed American colour-field painters did in the 1960s – what he called a 'purely visual or optical mode of illusionism' that conjured 'a depth of field or space accessible to eyesight alone'.[13] In doing so, Indigenous shamans slipped almost unnoticed into the shoes of contemporary artists, transferring their shamanistic practices to that of art.

This transformation has often been charted in the evolution of Papunya Tula paintings. As if caught between two archives – those of shamanism and art – the early Papunya painters were driven by a deliberate duel between the shaman's secrecy and the purely aesthetic demands of the art archive, as if they believed in calling up the ancestors through the appropriate iconography would augur well in their assault on the white artworld. However, this pushing against ancestral secrecy produced considerable anxiety in other Indigenous communities.[14] This anxiety continues to haunt remote Indigenous art, resulting in the prohibition of iconography that references the shaman's archive. The prohibition means that these days Indigenous artists opt for the purely aesthetic domain of the modern archive, and simply 'make their art flash'. As in Western contemporary art, aesthetics is no longer a tool to mediate the secret and the public in cementing ancestral connections, but a means of making art.

A similar transition from ancestral impressions to fine art occurred in the Western world some 500 years earlier, and was also instigated by contact with exotic cultures, and in particular with the so-called 'curios' of nature and culture discovered there. This is how Indigenous objects first caught the eye of Western modernists. Curios are things that strike our eye, spark our mind, and ignite desire (in bookseller's catalogues 'curious' once referred to texts with erotic content) because they are extraordinary in some way – an excessive shine, a peculiar shape, a wildness or seductive charm. Like *Bir'yun*, the flash of the curio confuses itself with the *arkhē*.

A curio is anything out of the ordinary. From the Latin *extra ordinem*, the extraordinary is 'out of order' – an *atopos* or unplaced thing. It is a mystery, perhaps providential or auspicious, perhaps forbidden, taboo or secret, perhaps a magical relic, a sign of the divine, a message from the gods or a remnant of their being that is both alluring and dangerous.

When things appear out of place our lack of knowledge is revealed. In sensing another order we are made uneasy. The archive is our cure. Giving the curio a place and order settles the existential dread we have of ghosts and brings them under our command, be it through shamans or fine art. Thus curiosity brings out the curator in us. Our instinct is to pocket the curio – to remove it from the world and add it to our collection or cabinet. Fitting it into the existing order of our archive, we simultaneously tame and capitalise on its wildness. From the Latin *curiosus* 'careful, diligent; inquiring', and *cura* 'care', curiosity has the same etymological roots as curate and also cure or heal. The curator makes sure that nothing is out of order.

Western picture making was rerouted in the modern era via the Renaissance 'cabinet of curiosities' into the spectacular archives of scientific illustration and the shimmer of fine art. These storage cabinets in which curios from around the world were ordered, archived and displayed, gave birth to the modern art museum. Princes and scholars were the initial creators of 'cabinets of curiosities' – Leonardo and Dürer each had a cabinet – but they ultimately descend from the collections of ecclesiastical relics and the sacred stones stored by Indigenous shamans in their private abodes.

Like the secret cave and the inner sanctum of the cathedral, the prince's curiosity cabinet was an *arkheion*, a place in which power was centred: indeed the centre of the centre. The art museum is a place in its own right but usually situated in an existing precinct of power. The National Gallery of Australia is adjacent to the High Court and in a precinct of government ministries over which looks the houses of Parliament, in the front of which is a Western Desert design of a waterhole, designed by the Warlpiri ceremonial leader Michael Nelson Jagamara – a former buffalo shooter and drover, and son of the powerful Warlpiri shaman, Hitler Tjupurrula. This *curious* convergence of Western and Indigenous histories and archives at the *arkheion* of the Australian nation state became a symbol of Australia's hopes and aspirations as a nation at the turn of the twenty-first century. This same convergence is now well and truly embedded in the prominence of the Indigenous contemporary art movement in the nation's art world, as if the constitution of the nation state, founded 115 years ago on the idea of a white Australia, has become irrelevant to its future.

The Indigenous Contemporary Art Archive

The Indigenous contemporary art movement is a direct outcome of the new government-subsidised, Indigenous-run art centres established in the 1970s and 1980s, of which Papunya was the first example when it was incorporated in 1972. From the beginning the modern archive played a central role in the work of the art centre, and was instrumental in shifting its product from being catalogued in art museum archives from 'primitive art' to 'contemporary art'.

When Geoffrey Bardon initially galvanised the painting movement at Papunya in mid-1971, he immediately felt the urge to archive the men's painted scraps of board. No doubt the artists' fevered desire to tell him the stories of their paintings contributed to this urge, though as his writings attest, Bardon had his own fever. So too did 22-year-old Felicity Wright when, some fifteen years later, she was appointed to establish the first official art centre at Yuendumu. One of her priorities was to establish a systematic photographic archive of the work produced, and this is now standard practice. Today the most sophisticated procedures are brought to bear on the archiving of Indigenous art in Australia's state fine-art museums.

The archiving of Indigenous contemporary art in art centres follows many of the standard procedures of the modern art archive but it also added a new feature. This additional element was a parallel textual documentation of the story that the painting told, for these artists specialised in history paintings. This document, got directly from the artist's mouth, was like an artist's statement. Used as a written certificate that accompanied the painting and a copy kept in the art centre, it is in some respects the love child of the shaman's and anthropologist's archives, both of which were more interested in the didactic story rather than poetic or aesthetic features of the artwork. The document's abbreviated descriptions are the surface movements of the darker whisperings and knotty hermeneutics that originate in the very different epistemology of shamanistic practices, but its form mimics the written text of Western archival practices. Perhaps Indigenous artists got the idea from making drawings for anthropologists, though illustrated bibles and biblical teaching aids that missionaries used could also have been models. Either way, the artists considered this written document an essential feature of the work, as if its text authenticated or authorised the image.

The art centre certificate was part of a modern Indigenous archival impulse that began in the 1960s – modern in the sense that Indigenous painters sought to incorporate their ancestral stories in Western archives, as occurred for example at mission churches in Millingimbi, Yirrkala and Yuendumu. The same men behind the church at Yuendumu were also behind the Yuendumu men's museum that opened in 1971, which was an Indigenous-driven hybrid archive based on Indigenous and Western models that housed secret artefacts and murals to be looked at or engaged aesthetically, but also, for a while at least, to be used in ritual ceremonies. In the 1980s as the contemporary art movement began to take off and an art centre was established at Yuendumu, the museum fell into disrepair. The shaman was no longer needed.

In Yirrkala the art centre includes a museum in which a history of modern Yolngu art is displayed, including its origin works – the church panels and a replica of the bark petition from 1963 (also a text work) – and employs several Indigenous archivists who busy themselves archiving every document they can lay their hands on from existing archives, as well as making their own photographic records of new ceremonies. However, left out of this modern archive at Yirrkala are the secret sacred ceremonies, as if a clear distinction has been drawn between the shaman's archive and the modern one maintained at the art centre.

A primary duty of the art centre manager is archivist. She photographs each work produced in the art centre, and enters its details into a digital archival software program especially developed for art centres. Yet she would hardly seem a shaman. Does she dance with ancestral ghosts or deal in secrets? Who then is the archon of the art archive? Where are its ghosts and secrets?

The art archive that administers Indigenous contemporary art, and is the subject of the essays in this book, has its own ghosts and secrets that are embedded in its formative structures. The origin of the art archive can be traced to Vasari's *Lives* (1550), which put the artist and his (there are no women artists in Vasari's archive) inventive imagination – which Vasari called *disegno* – centre stage. While, in a nod to the ecclesiastical authorities of the day that ruled with an iron fist,[15] Vasari ascribed the origins of *disegno* to 'Almighty God…the Divine Architect of time and of nature' – as if God was the first artist – Vasari's focus is the art and not its divine origins. He effectively transforms the artwork from an archive of ancestral secrets and creations into something created by mortal artists. In the art archive the artist has ancestral status. He authors the work, and his name, person and life stories are the central feature of the archive – a direct substitution of the lives of the ancestors that concern the shaman's archive.

If the lives of the ancestors are documented in the lie of the land, Vasari had to rely on 'the tales of old men and from various records and writings, left by their heirs a prey to dust and food for worms',[16] records kept in churches, castles and town halls of transactions between artisans and patrons, and the remembered chatter collected from the oral archive of gossip. The place of his archive is the book, thus removing its documents from their place of origin, for example church murals, to the text's narrative. These fragmented tales, woven into a narrative of cultural renaissance (the second coming of classical authority) and historical destiny, was reproduced in many editions and distributed across Europe, effectively establishing a global vector for the archive and a new art world that would come to have universal aspirations. Vasari's paradigm of *disegno* underpinned the pedagogy of the new academies of the Enlightenment – the first art centres – which produced their own archives, some of them becoming magnificent collections and art museums.

At first technological limits restrained the art archive. While the book was Vasari's cave, he couldn't actually collect the objects of his desire in the book. Most of them were on church walls in Tuscany and even further afield. As his paradigm quickly took hold across Europe, increasing its geographical reach, the archive was increasingly unable to contain its subject except in a virtual way. This explains why easel paintings, which hardly existed before the birth of the art archive, quickly became the dominant art form, and a virtual world of reproductions suddenly proliferated from the widespread copying of paintings, plaster casts of sculptures and prints of artworks. In locating the art archive in the book and text-based narrative, Vasari had condemned its subject, art, to become like the book: something easily reproducible. Only with the invention of photography did the fine art archive gain real traction. In one space, be it the limited space of a book or that larger space we art historians once called the slide library – since made redundant by Google – the art of the world could be easily assembled, juxtaposed and mapped into a structure, system or language that made from art its own self-sufficient narrative, a *tjukurrpa*. The art archive had come of age.

Photography was also a boon for the modern archive more generally. Being 'simultaneously the documentary evidence and the archival record', as if 'the camera is literally an archiving machine', the photograph is the privileged form of the modern archive in all its forms. The photograph sparked, said Okwui Enwezor, an 'archival madness, a "burning with desire" to transpose nature into a pictorial fact', and, he should have added, artworks.[17] The pioneering German art historian Aby Warburg exemplified this modern archival madness in his *Mnemosyne Atlas*, in which he vainly sought through a complex cartography of black and white photographs to map from the babel of images over the ages a history of human cosmology would, in revealing its own archetypal logic, would finally articulate its soul. Contemporary artists, including Indigenous ones, have taken this approach to heart, either in soul-searching explorations or to open the modern archive up to its own logic.[18] Today, Enwezor argued, 'we witness firsthand how archival legacies become transformed into aesthetic principles'.[19]

The photographic reproduction is the actual archival object of the art archive and the larger modern archive of which it is part. Increasingly the actual or original object is out of reach of researchers, who must make do with photographic simulations. Like the ancestral ghost, the photograph is only a trace, an echo of the original. Thus the photographic archive requires an archon whose privileged access to the original underpins *his* hermeneutic authority. The artist, as the privileged ancestral origin of art-works, is seizing this role, but in doing so encountering the same 'indeterminate zone' of secrets, ghosts and elusive origins as the shaman. So too do other aspiring archons of the art archive – the art historian, curator and art centre manager – each beavering away as if the archive can provide 'a suture between the past and present',[20] origin, and trace: 'an archive which would in sum confuse itself with the *arkhē*...An archive without archive'.[21]

Notes

1 J. Derrida, 'Archive Fever: A Freudian Impression', *Diacritics,* vol. 25, no. 2, 1995, pp. 9–63 at 10.
2 ibid., p. 9.
3 ibid., p. 10.
4 ibid., p. 26.
5 ibid., p. 27.
6 ibid., pp. 9–10.

7 ibid., p. 61.

8 ibid., p. 10.

9 M. Foucault, *The Order of Things: An Archaeology of the Human Sciences*, Vintage Books, New York, 1994, p. xv.

10 ibid., p. xxi.

11 H. Morphy, *Ancestral Connections: Art and an Aboriginal System of Knowledge*, University of Chicago Press, Chicago, 1991, p. 194.

12 Quoted in S. Eldin, *Mapping the Present: Heidegger, Foucault and the Project of a Spatial History*, Continuum, London, 2001, p. 75.

13 M. Fried, 'Jules Olitski (1966–67)', *Art and Objecthood*, University of Chicago Press, 1998, pp. 132–47 at 139.

14 V. Johnson, *Once Upon a Time in Papunya*, University of New South Wales Press, Sydney, 2010.

15 Pope Paul III established the Roman Inquisition – which famously tried Galileo in 1633 – in 1542, eight years before the publication of the first edition of Vasari's *Lives*.

16 G. Vasari, *Lives of the Most Eminent Painters, Sculptors and Architects*, trans. Gaston Du C. De Vere, 10 vols, Macmillan and Co. and the Medici Society, London, 1912.

17 O. Enwezor, 'Archive Fever: Photography between History and the Monument', *Archive Fever: Uses of the Document in Contemporary Art*, International Center of Photography, London, 2007, pp. 11–51 at 11–12.

18 H. Foster, 'An Archival Impulse', *October*, vol. 110, 2004, pp. 3–22.

19 Enwezor, 'Archive Fever: Photography between History and the Monument', pp. 21–2.

20 ibid., p. 47.

21 Derrida, 'Archive Fever: A Freudian Impression', p. 61.

PART 1:
LIMITS TO ARCHIVES

2

REFLECTIONS ON THE RODNEY GOOCH FILES

Anne Marie Brody

1

Rodney Gooch (1949–2002) had a fifteen-year association with the Utopia art movement, in the course of which he gathered an important archive. Today his name is well known in art circles as a major provenance for the paintings of Emily Kame Kngwarreye, although he was also instrumental in developing and promoting the solo careers of many other Utopia artists. However, the content of his archive foreshadows a reputation as much defined by his involvement with the wider Utopia collective as with its major stars. When as manager of CAAMA (the Central Australian Aboriginal Media Association) Shop, Gooch first introduced acrylics on canvas to the Utopia batik artists just before Christmas in December 1988, he galvanised the community and facilitated the biggest transition in Utopia art since Jenny Green and Julia Murray introduced batik a decade earlier and established the Utopia Women's Batik Group.

Not one to mark time, Gooch quickly followed up this inaugural painting survey – A Summer Project – with other innovative projects in different media and formats.[1] Between late 1988 and early 1991, when he left CAAMA, Gooch coordinated several community-wide art surveys. In this period he worked with extended family groups of Utopia artists in ways that were for the time unique, in large-scale projects that became archives in their own right, virtually overnight – such was the rare concentrate of information they contained. This was before the Aboriginal art boom of the 1990s when contemporary art was limited to a handful of central desert communities and published information was scarce – particularly so for the Utopia region. The archival potential of some of the Gooch CAAMA/Utopia projects was further consolidated when they were sold intact as 'collections'.[2]

Amongst the largest of the projects that followed the acrylic-on-canvas survey of 1988–89 was one in watercolours (1989), which resulted in eighty-six works by seventy-seven artists and another in woodcuts, The Utopia Suite (1989), involving seventy artists.[3] Gooch also experimented with different support formats, commissioning a body paint project in ovals (1989–90) and adding a circular stretcher to the traditional mix of squares and rectangles. In an edgier move, and with a nod towards the precedent of Michael Nelson Tjakamarra's 1989 painted BMW, he introduced wrecked car doors, bonnets, boots and hubcaps as art media.[4]

Gooch also enthusiastically encouraged artists to develop themes that they had initiated themselves such as the camp scenes and sculpture that emerged in 1989 at Ngkwarlerlaneme. There were other themes he put forward such as 'abstracts' and children's Altyerre (Dreaming stories). Almost back-to-back, these projects over two years provided Utopia with continuous jolts of creative energy and a major profile in the art market. Even so, from the appearance of her first painting, the urban fine art market mainly had eyes for Emily Kame Kngwarreye, and her name continues to lead an art story that outgrew Utopia.

There were three stages to Rodney Gooch's relationship with Utopia art and artists and the archive that grew up around it. The first lasted for just over three years, beginning in late 1987 when the Utopia Women's Batik Group (UWB) came under the umbrella of CAAMA Shop in Gap Rd, Alice Springs.[5] This was an art, craft and music outlet initially set up by Gooch and colleagues in the early 1980s to support Aboriginal music. In mid-1991 Gooch left CAAMA and established a new relationship with the Utopia art movement when he set up his own company, Mulga Bore Artists (MBA), named for a community on Woodgreen Station, today known as Atartinga PL. During this phase, which lasted until the end of the decade, Rodney Gooch dealt with a smaller group of artists. Then, around 2000, he set up another business, his last, called Red Dirt Art, which operated on a smaller scale again until his death in August 2002.

By dint of his wide experience in various kinds of work and small businesses, Rodney Gooch was also a seasoned record keeper. He was very conscious of the importance of documenting the art he handled and left a comprehensive archive. This consists of artwork files, certificates, invoices, photographs, press clippings and the various ephemera and correspondence relating to the business he conducted with Utopia artists. In 1998 Gooch donated a substantial part of his personal art collection – itself an idiosyncratic archive of Utopia art – to the Riddoch Art Gallery in Mt Gambier, South Australia. When he died in 2002, the balance of his collection went to the Flinders University Art Museum (FUAM) in Adelaide whilst his art and business files stayed with his estate and executor, his nephew Marc Gooch.[6]

Gooch kept his archive close. Moving when and where he did, his files remain relatively intact having survived some challenging circumstances in his life. Chief among these was his relocation to Perth in December 1991 for health reasons. Coming as it did only six months after he had left CAAMA to establish Mulga Bore Artists, this move abruptly disrupted Gooch's future plans for working with Utopia artists. However, and notwithstanding his conviction that the move was permanent, it proved very temporary. Homesick in no time, he and his partner, Alice Springs artist Robert Cole,[7] were back in their country after nine months. Gooch had spent much of his time in Perth flying back and forth to Alice Springs commissioning paintings, sculpture and batik. Amongst the wide spectrum of commissions were major works, notably by Kngwarreye for his Sydney agent, Christopher Hodges, as well as tourist entry paintings and artefacts for a handful of Perth retail outlets. The climax of the year was a thirty panel commission executed in December from which Kngwarreye's twenty-two panel *Alhalkere Suite* (1993), now at the National Gallery of Australia, was selected for the inaugural Clemenger Contemporary Art Award at the National Gallery of Victoria.[8]

For most of 1993, Rodney Gooch and Robert Cole lived and worked in Alice before moving onto a 5-acre block just outside of town, a peaceful spot where Gooch built a house and office that was, in fact, a shed. His nephew, Marc Gooch, joined him there, helping with the art business and the property. After two unsettled years, Rodney Gooch once again had a garden, space to run his business and a permanent headquarters for his files, art collection and miscellany of 'treasures'.

2

Unlike the majority of art communities across Central Australia, Utopia is distinguished by its lack of an arts centre and, by corollary, a central archive. Recently looking again at Gooch's files, I was vividly reminded of their importance to any history of Utopia art. But even though they reference many key moments – particularly in the early stages and include lots of 'firsts' – the full Utopia story resides with the many agents who came to deal with Utopia artists after the inaugural painting phase initiated by Gooch at CAAMA.

Thus the complete Utopia archive is a dispersed entity, housed in known and unknown places, in filing cabinets with variable contents. Due to the Aboriginal art market's requirement for a specific kind of documentation, a certificate with a code, story and photo of the work are probably the common thread stringing this archive together.

The central and most valuable component of Rodney Gooch's Utopia archive is the (approximately) 210 artists' records filed in individual manila folders. Each folder, containing photographs and codes of paintings and sculptures, is numbered and ordered by skin group in Gooch's handwriting. Whether they contain one photograph or several, they tell a valuable story – even if sometimes only the minimal one that some artists may have done no more than a single painting for Gooch. Although the folders are not all perfectly consistent and ordered inside, they represent a considered system that Gooch clearly invested a lot of time in – a substantial and organised effort.

Gooch's artists' files were not just passive record keeping for its own sake; they were also an important means to an end. One purpose was to engage artists by providing them with the means to review their work via the photographic record (this was the pre-digital era). Another point of making records accessible to artists was so they could track the sales of their paintings. Gooch hoped that his files would involve artists more in their own careers and give them an idea of how the art world worked – in mid-1991, this kind of approach was probably quite radical. He was also optimistic that this method would reduce an artist's frustration with the process if he were able to 'demonstrate' through documentation the status of a work on consignment.

Towards the end of the nineties Gooch began travelling more, occasionally visiting Adelaide for medical treatment and to see his family. He also travelled overseas and made plans to write a book about Utopia. Thus it transpired that in 1999 he recalled the box of negatives and prints that he had sent me a couple of years earlier for my research and safekeeping. He never did write his own account of Utopia art, and the whereabouts of this part of his archive is currently not known. However, it is highly likely that these pictorial records – envelopes full of MBA photos – are all reproduced in the archive in Marc Gooch's possession, such was the multiplicity of spare photos at his disposal. Whilst the negatives remain missing, the prints he sent me were clearly not the only copies he had. This is also the likely case with another 'missing' part of the archive, the CAAMA Shop lever-arch files. These volumes, always fascinating to revisit on trips to Alice Springs, have also become separated from his archive.

Gooch took a copy of these binders with him when he left CAAMA. They contained duplicate CAAMA certificates filed in chronological order by code, and detailed all the paintings, sculptures and artefacts handled by CAAMA Shop from 1989 to early 1991. Catalogued as they came in, each work was assigned an item number followed by a dash and the month and the year. The resulting sequences provided an invaluable snapshot of the time and its emergent art history. To my surprise, when I recently did a deeper audit of Gooch's artists' files, I discovered that many contained photographs from this period: if an artist had painted something in those CAAMA years then photos of those paintings are probably in their file. I found all of Kathleen Petyarre's 1989 works in her folder. So, even though the 'original' CAAMA Shop files can't be found, it seems that the images and history they contained might well be embedded in Gooch's archive courtesy of his ample supply of 'spares'.[9]

For many years, photography was a core and costly part of Gooch's record keeping and marketing strategy for paintings and sculpture. Multiple prints were made of each work and at least two certificates with photos were made for each painting, one for the client and one for the files. Additional sets of photographs were sent around to collectors, agents and galleries. Hence, if there were to be any major gaps in Gooch's artist files, it would be theoretically possible to track down sets of photos in the hands of third parties and fill them in. But at first glance this does not seem necessary and it may well be a long time before research into Utopia art will be ripe for that level of drilling down. In mid-1995, Gooch switched to Polaroids and the era of multiple prints was over.

3

When the Department of Aboriginal Affairs (DAA) formally handed over management of the Utopia Women's Batik (UWB) group to CAAMA (and Gooch) in January 1988,[10] there was no art centre on Utopia. Moreover, unlike the cultural landscape of the desert today, in the late 1980s funded art centres were thin on the ground. From 1977, the Utopia women had produced extraordinary batik in their camps adapting bush infrastructure and utilising improvised equipment – all managed by a succession of dedicated drive-in-drive-out art advisors. They transformed traditional Indonesian batik methods, working on cloth stretched over their knees and heating wax in old hubcaps or saucepans over campfires.

Gooch instantly fell for the magic of the silks and soon lengths of exuberant fabric began to transform CAAMA Shop, adding a rich overlay to its more traditional fare. Before batik, the Shop had mainly retailed works by Alice Springs 'town' artists alongside Hermannsburg watercolours and topped up occasionally with paintings by bush artists who were visiting town for various reasons. It also sold Aboriginal music cassettes and a range of artefacts – beads, carvings and boomerangs.

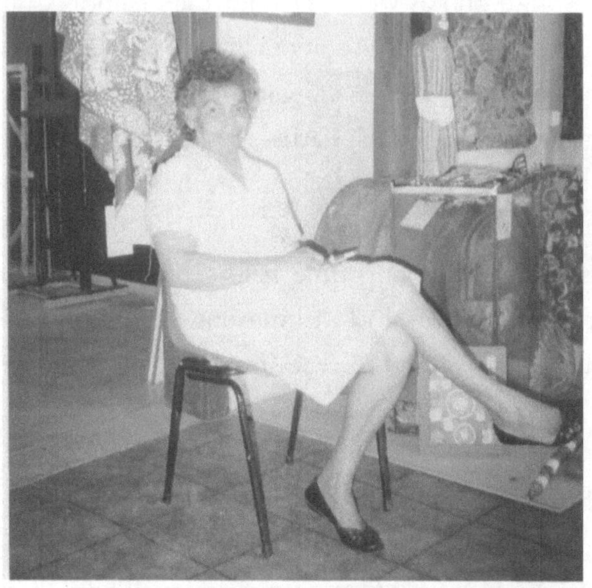

Figure 2.1: Doris Stuart, Rodney Gooch's Assistant, in CAAMA Shop, c. 1989

Before the 1990s' boom when galleries began to proliferate in Alice Springs, Papunya Tula Artists (PTA) and CAAMA Shop were the town's key outlets for Aboriginal art. They were not art centres but Aboriginal retail businesses with Indigenous boards. With CAAMA Shop taking on the Utopia Women's Batik Group (UWB), the two organisations began to have a lot more in common. Both now represented large constituencies of artists living in remote communities to the west and east of Alice Springs. Resourcing them with art materials involved covering vast distances. At 250 kilometres east and west, Utopia and Papunya were roughly the same distance from Alice Springs, although the more remote destinations of PTA's fieldworkers – Kintore and Kiwirrkurra – were much further. At this period, the Utopia artists were living in eight family-centred communities spread across an 1,800 square kilometre area. For both organisations, fieldwork bush trips consumed a lot of time, energy and resources.

Much that has been written assumes that Gooch was an art coordinator who lived on the community. One writer refers to 'Gooch's tenure as Art Advisor at Utopia'.[11] This was not so. Although he took on a community of artists, he was not a community-based art coordinator. Moreover, not only was he based in Alice Springs, Gooch was careful when he was out bush not to form partisan alliances in his interactions with the family networks of Utopia artists. He once mentioned to me that he had resisted invitations to camp with one family or another in order to avoid any perception of favouritism. In the context of working on such delicate terrain, an art centre and residence might well have provided him with some neutral ground on Utopia itself. As it turned out, the length of the journey to and from Alice and the number of camps to be visited often required an overnight stop but the site he chose to camp was far from everyone – a place he called his 'bush office' on the banks of the Sandover River, just over the border of Utopia on Ammaroo Station. He would often, while the light held out, study the works he had picked up during the day.

Rodney Gooch was a frequent visitor to Papunya Tula Artists in Todd Mall and was on excellent terms with its manager, Daphne Williams. He was also an occasional collector of PTA work and so was familiar with their operation and systems. And he would have known that, with a floating population (similar to PTA's) of between eighty to 100 artists, he was going to need to set up similar systems of his own.

With the UWB on board, Gooch looked to Papunya Tula Artists certainly as a role model and also a potential competitor. In some notes he drafted in 1990,[12] Gooch indicates his respect for

PTA and his intention to avoid any potential conflict over market share. Reflecting on the recent development – when the Utopia artists began to paint on canvas – he stated his belief that the key to avoiding such conflict resided in taking a different 'creative' direction to PTA and its artists:

> The backbone to the Aboriginal art movement is Papunya Tula Artists, central desert neighbours to Utopia with a large percentage of Utopia's Anmatyerre people related to the Papunya Tula artists. Having both community organisations competing for the traditional Aboriginal art market could lead to some unrest; consequently the move for Utopia artists to express themselves as individuals has been a strong one.[13]

4

In the late 1980s and early 1990s, collectors – institutional and private – and the art market were confronted with new movements and developments that had the shallowest histories. Although Utopia batik originated in the late 1970s – earlier than most desert painting movements and only eight years after the first boards were being painted at Papunya – these eastern desert artists lacked archival visibility perhaps because the batik medium, being regarded as craft, did not lend itself to documentation in the way that paintings did. When in early 1988 Gooch commissioned an inclusive community batik project to which the artists gave the name 'A Picture Story', he was in a sense starting from scratch. In commissioning the project, he invited the artists of the UWB to produce a work that would tell him (and us) who they were.

In a sale negotiated by Gooch's first agent, the artist (and later gallerist) Christopher Hodges, The Robert Holmes à Court

Collection[14] acquired 'A Picture Story'. This project collection of eighty-eight batiks came with the caveat that the buyer would help profile the group through exhibition and publication. This resulted two years later in a book that aimed to provide a benchmark reference point for Utopia art. The content of *Utopia – A Picture Story* was anchored around a photographic portrait of each artist, a bilingual text setting out the iconography of each piece alongside a relatively large format image of each work.[15] There were four categories of personal information: artist, group (language), camp (residence) and country (patrilineal). And although this information was basic, the work itself and the story texts that accompanied it reverberated with connections between families, stories and country.

Prior to this, the point-of-sale documentation of batik had been relatively straightforward. Batiks didn't have certificates, although a tag or ticket was generally attached to the fabric. Buyers of Aboriginal art and craft wanted something apart from the receipt, and the tag was a simple form of documentation. In the beginning, Gooch did not photograph batik, something that he later told me he regretted. However, by the second half of 1988, batik started to become a routine part of his photography. It was also in this period that he commissioned a number of very large batiks, including several 10 x 1 metre works, one of which was done by Emily Kame Kngwarreye.

Also belonging to this period is a rare image of a batik that Gooch himself photographed out bush. The size and fluidity of the piece made the task difficult, so why did he attempt it? It does not seem to have been for identification, as it is impossible to read in any detail on the flat. It seems that he took the photo because everyone, including himself, was so proud of the work. Beneath the batik there is a dog taking advantage of the instant shelter – a pointer to the harshness (for all) of bush conditions. On the ground, to the left of the child in the front, is Gooch's black briefcase with its bright red and yellow CAAMA sticker. This housed his cheque book and was therefore the most essential piece of equipment he took on bush trips. The briefcase was also the first base repository for his artwork documentation – if he took down any information about the work, it went in there. In his files is a loose photograph of the same batik taken in front of CAAMA Shop but at an angle that yields slightly more information.

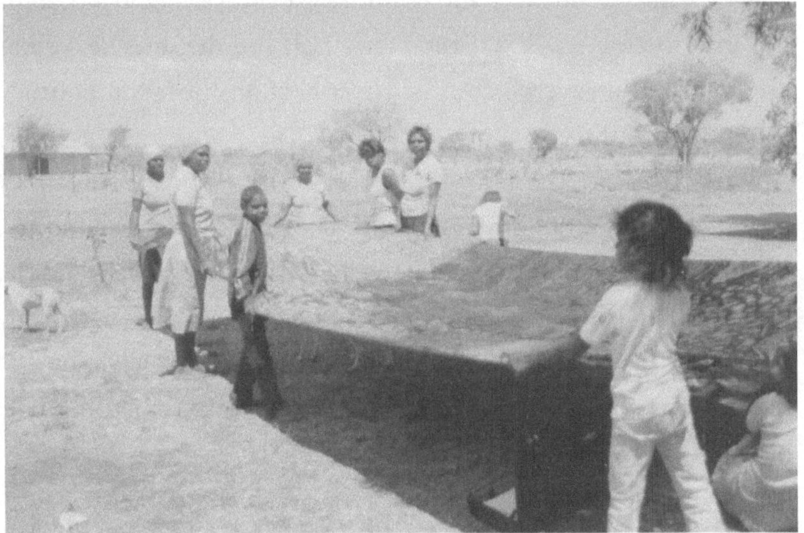

Figure 2.2: Antarrengenye artists and children holding batik, 1988.

Gooch himself doubted that any comprehensive pictorial history of Utopia batik would ever eventuate since many of the pieces sold would have been used and worn as shirts, sarongs, tablecloths and scarves rather than treasured as works of art. There are around eight batiks by Emily Kngwarreye in public collections but, in contrast to the magnitude of her painting *oeuvre*, there are no published estimates of how much batik she might have done over the ten or so years that she worked in the medium.

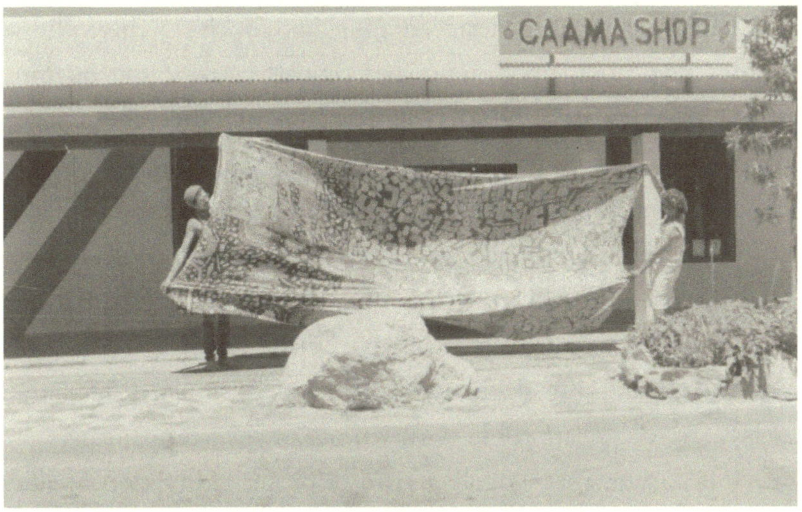

Figure 2.3: Rodney Gooch and CAAMA Shop Assistant, Doris Stuart, holding up an Antarrengenye batik, 1988.

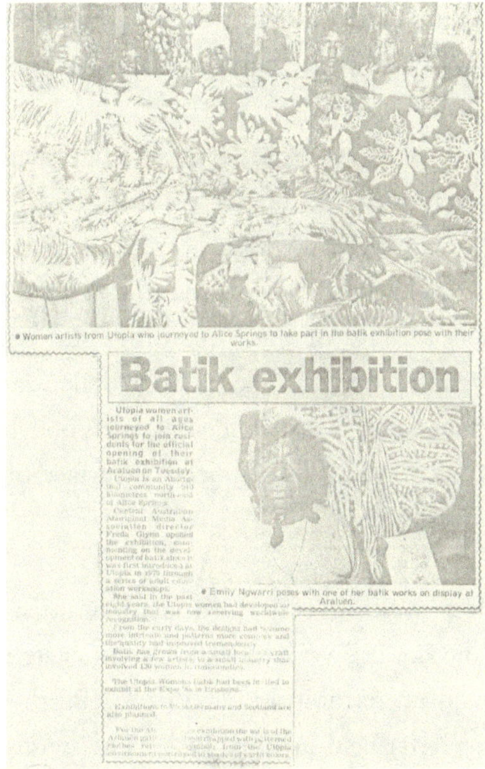

• Women artists from Utopia who journeyed to Alice Springs to take part in the batik exhibition pose with their works.

Batik exhibition

Utopia women artists of all ages journeyed to Alice Springs to join residents for the official opening of their batik exhibition at Araluen on Tuesday.

Utopia is an Aboriginal community [illegible] kilometres north-east of Alice Springs.

Central Australian Aboriginal Media Association director Freda Glynn opened the exhibition, commenting on the development of batik since it was first introduced at Utopia in 1975 through a series of adult education workshops.

She said in the past eight years, the Utopia women had developed an industry that was now receiving worldwide recognition.

From the early days, the designs had become more intricate and patterns more complex and the quality had improved tremendously.

Batik has grown from a small [illegible] craft involving a few artists, to a small industry that involved 130 women [illegible].

The Utopia Women's Batik had been invited to exhibit at the Expo '88 in Brisbane.

Exhibitions to [illegible] Germany and Scotland are also planned.

[illegible]

• Emily Ngwarri poses with one of her batik works on display at Araluen.

Figure 2.4: Press clipping from the Centralian Advocate, *November 1987.*

A photocopy of a news clipping in Gooch's archive shows Kngwarreye posed in front of her draped batik at the opening of a Utopia batik exhibition at Araluen in November 1987.[16] Kngwarreye was no doubt chosen to be front of house on account of her age and charisma rather than for her austere batik which contrasts dramatically with the 'appealing' floral designs behind – they couldn't be more different. This is an occasion when a certificate with a photo would have been extremely valuable – especially since the tantalising detail we can see of the open grid design clearly shows a relationship with Kngwarreye's later paintings.

It is possible that Gooch, a great respecter of traditional values and seniority, put Kngwarreye forward for the press photograph. His views on her status are reflected in a story annotation on a CAAMA painting certificate written in April 1990 when Emily was on the point of immense fame. He introduces her as:

> …the oldest artist at Utopia and an important woman in the ceremonial life of her country. She paints the various Dreamings and then according to the sacred significance she will either cover them with a few or many dots. A few of the Dreamings she will reveal or partly reveal are the Mountain Devil Lizard, Emu, Snake Vine, Sand Goannas, Perenties, Woollybut Grass or Grass Seeds which only touch the surface of her rich cultural background.[17]

Not long after writing this certificate, Gooch interviewed Kngwarreye and Louie Pwerle to obtain 'artist's statements' for their forthcoming joint exhibition at PICA (Perth Institute for Contemporary Arts) held in June 1990. The words that resulted have undergone numberless iterations in publications, certificates and websites. By May, a few weeks later, Gooch was using the 'new' story on his certificates.

With the assistance of Kathleen Petyarre translating, Emily was asked to explain the stories to her paintings, and she replied,

> Whole lot, that's all, whole lot, Awelye (my dreaming), Arlatyeye (Pencil Yam), Arkerrthe (Mountain Devil Lizard), Ntange (Grass Seed), Tingu (A Dreamtime pup), Ankerre (Emu), Intekwe (favourite food of emus, a small plant, Atnwerle (green been) and Kame (Yam seed), that's what I paint, whole lot. That's my name Kame (pronounced CAAMA).[18]

And this is how the 'whole lot' story became 'law' for Kngwarreye's paintings. And, as for the note on pronunciation of the artist's bush name, Kame – this was Gooch's spirited comment on the various claims of 'ownership' that some dealers tried to exert over Emily.

5

Gooch created a CAAMA Shop artwork certificate when Utopia made the transition from batik to canvas. It looked quite different to the Papunya Tula certificate, a key feature being the inclusion of a photograph of the painting – PTA did not include a photograph. Although Gooch wanted a photo on the certificate, he was against the increasingly entrenched practice of photographing artists with their paintings. There were a number of reasons why he adopted this position.

One consideration was that photography in general was not common on Utopia in this period: he did not want to expose the artists to unwanted photography. Many women were reluctant initially to have their photo portraits taken for publication in *Picture Story*, and some even trembled with apprehension in front of the camera. This aversion to being photographed gradually changed to the extent that today it is just routine. However, back then when it became the practice for dealers to include a photo of the artists with their artwork on the certificate, Gooch was dismissive. He thought the assumption that the person holding the painting had executed it to be a simplistic and inadequate proof of authenticity – and one that was in any case inappropriate for a sophisticated fine art market. So he typically photographed artworks separately back in town at CAAMA Shop or in his backyard with various personnel co-opted to hold the paintings. The photos were then stapled or glued to the certificate. He wrote the code on the photograph so that it matched the certificate.

Such photographs, particularly of works by Kngwarreye, are today often visually scanned as much for the residual information they contain as for the work featured. Similarly, dealers' photographs of Emily in painting camps, surrounded by her own paintings – often in different styles – may also carry a lot of 'surplus' information.

6

In early 1989, when the CAAMA-Utopia enterprise was poised to head in a major new direction, something totally unforeseen by Gooch began to unfold on Delmore Downs, the pastoral property neighbouring Utopia. By the time the new media experiment in acrylics on canvas, A Summer Project, went on exhibition at the S. H. Ervin Gallery in Sydney on 14 April 1989, Emily Kngwarreye and other Utopia artists had started painting for Donald and Janet Holt on Delmore Downs.[19] Their start-up operation paralleled CAAMA's in scale and Donald Holt has written that: 'in some months more than 300 paintings were purchased from a total of 138 artists'.[20] It would be an understatement to say that Gooch was disappointed, his idealism sorely dented as his fledgling strategies for Utopia art were about to come under extreme market pressure. He just had to live with the reality; the horse had bolted. But it would be two more years before he left CAAMA to set up his own business.

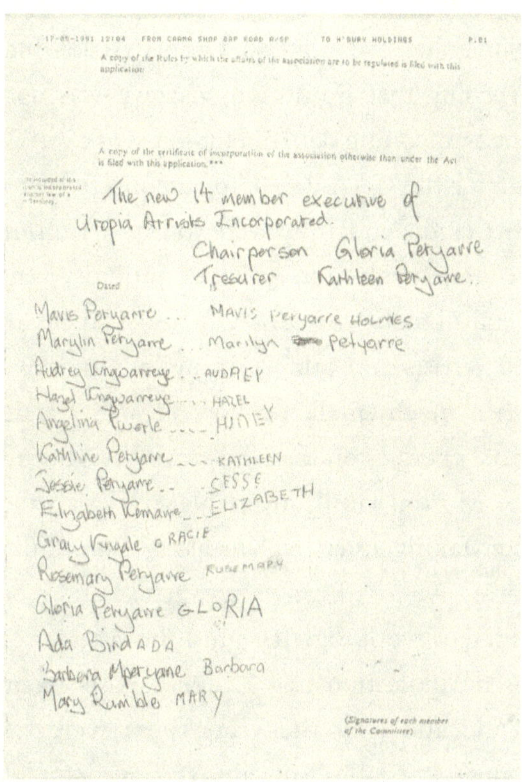

17-05-1991 12:04 FROM CAAMA SHOP BAP ROAD A/SP TO H'BURY HOLDINGS P.01

A copy of the Rules by which the affairs of the association are to be regulated is filed with this application

A copy of the certificate of incorporation of the association otherwise than under the Act is filed with this application.***

The new 14 member executive of
Uropia Arrists Incorporated.
Chairperson Gloria Petyarre
Tresurer Kathleen Petyarre.

Dated

Mavis Petyarre ... MAVIS Petyarre Holmes
Marylin Petyarre ... Marilyn Petyarre
Audrey Kngwarreye ... AUDREY
Hazel Kngwarreye ... HAZEL
Angelina Pwerle ... HINEY
Kathline Petyarre ... KATHLEEN
Jessie Petyarre ... JESSE
Elizabeth Kemarre ... ELIZABETH
Gracy Kngale GRACIE
Rosemary Petyarre ROSEMARY
Gloria Petyarre GLORIA
Ada Bird ADA
Barbara Mpetyane Barbara
Mary Rumble MARY

(Signatures of each member of the Committee)

Figure 2.5: Utopia Artists Incorporated, fax, May 1991

Gooch did this for a variety of reasons, some to do with how the art business sat within CAAMA itself and others to do with the gradual opening up of Utopia art to all-comers.[21] Before making the final decision about his future with CAAMA, Gooch set up a new Utopia co-op as a bulwark against the tide of independent dealers entering the community. In early April he wrote to Anthony and Beverly Knight at Alcaston Gallery envisioning the venture as a 'warehouse where anybody can buy', adding that the artists 'understand the co-op is theirs & they have to keep control'.[22] He expressed frustration with the developing situation on Utopia, and whilst ambivalent about his own continued involvement thought CAAMA should 'umbrella (the co-op's) administration'.[23] Over a month later, he sent me a list of the new 14-member executive of Utopia Artists Incorporated.[24] It is not surprising that Emily Kngwarreye was not a signatory given that the burgeoning demand for her work was a chief part of the 'problem' for the CAAMA–Utopia collective. It is likely that Emily and her extended family were too busy running their own 'co-op' to become involved in a new community venture.

In the end Gooch left CAAMA and had his new business, Mulga Bore Artists, up and running by mid-1991. He now worked with a much smaller cohort of artists and focused his entrepreneurial energies on the Bird family at Mulga Bore/Akaye Soakage; the Morton family from Ngkwarlerlaneme; and three of the Hunter family sisters at Kurrajong Bore: Suzy, Jessie and Annie Petyarre. Even so, Emily Kngwarreye and Rodney Gooch would continue to work together until the last year of her life.

There is no indication that Utopia Artists Incorporated got off the ground and over the years there were several unsuccessful attempts at establishing an art centre on Utopia.[25] But in the end this desert community – perhaps taking the lead from Kngwarreye – has remained self-managing to a greater extent than any other remote community. Whilst there are many reasons to admire such agency, it is ironic that this independence has disadvantaged Utopia artists in some sectors of the marketplace. This is because art centre representation today is an essential cachet for participating in key indigenous 'industry' events, such as Desert Mob held annually at the Araluen Art Centre in Alice Springs.

7

Gooch devised a new certificate for Mulga Bore Artists. He continued his CAAMA cataloguing system with some modifications and followed the same coding principle – number/month/year. He tweaked the 'blurb' on the 'Aboriginal Art of the Centre' section, making it less 'folksy'. At the bottom of the sheet he signed and dated the document under a new header titled 'certification' – a field that had not been on the CAAMA certificate. What the signatory – usually but not always himself – certified was that the work of art on the certificate was 'an original and genuine work of Australian Aboriginal Art using modern materials'. Gooch knew that it was a potential minefield to certify that the work on the certificate was by a particular artist, although this is what most certificates do state. Below his signature and the date, he inserted a new field to do with copyright. In respect of the eternal triangle of artist, agent and collector, the new Mulga Bore Artists certificate better reflected the requirements of the times.

There were other differences between the CAAMA and the MBA certificates. Gooch changed the format so that the photo had its own place on the certificate and did not obscure any information – which it did in the CAAMA certificate, where it masked the dimensions of the work. In both formats the key header fields were the catalogue number and the dimensions. The CAAMA document had a field labelled 'site' next to the title of the work and this has resulted in some confusion. Some auction entries assume that it refers to either the site of the painting, the artist's birthplace or Dreaming country.[26] However, apart from an occasional lapse, Gooch chiefly uses the 'site' field to indicate place of residence – where he picked up the work – and by implication where it was most likely (but not necessarily) painted. With few exceptions, Soakage Bore, Kngwarreye's primary place of residence in the CAAMA years, is the site name entered on the majority of her certificates.

Gooch dropped the 'site' field off the MBA certificate altogether – perhaps because artists were beginning to be highly mobile and many, including Emily, frequently brought their paintings in to him. Initially, for Gooch, noting the site as place of residence was of great use in creating a socio-cultural map of the artists in terms of their camps, family relationships and Dreamings. Residence is also of art historical interest when considering aesthetic relationships and influences. However, it seems that the omission of this field from the MBA certificate says more about the practicalities of obtaining the information than doubts about its relative importance.

8

Rodney Gooch was not Emily Kngwarreye's only agent. Virtually from day one (give or take a few months) Kngwarreye began to paint for the Holts, pioneering the way that most Utopia artists 'traditionally' work with multiple dealers today. Kngwarreye's high status in the art world rapidly attracted many agents and commissioners and, as a consequence, her *oeuvre* is parsed into the multiple provenances that shaped it. Of these agents, Rodney Gooch was one of the few to have worked with Emily Kngwarreye throughout most of her painting career. He is the acknowledged source of her first painting on canvas, *Emu Woman* 1988–89, although not her last as, out of a concern for her health, he stopped commissioning work several months before she died.

Kngwarreye, however, continued to paint for other agents and produced some extraordinary work in the final months of her life after Gooch had stepped back.

Emily Kame Kngwarreye's *oeuvre* is generally cited as between three and four thousand works – a seemingly cavalier margin for a painter who worked for less than a decade. The numbers are sometimes put another way: one for every day of her eight-year career,[27] but the arithmetic never quite adds up. Whilst I am not yet in a position to be definitive about the Gooch provenance works, I expect the count to be well under 1,000 paintings. Along with firming up the numbers, a sequential catalogue of Gooch provenance works holds the promise of deeper insight into Kngwarreye's practice. To date, her paintings have been presented in broad stylistic and thematic sequences – such as awelye, colourism, seeds, yam, and body lines. An examination of her production at a micro level may reveal more about how she worked not only for one agent but also for all of them, sometimes on the same day. And documenting even one of her lineages – my undertaking with Gooch provenance works – should shed more light on the rampant speculation surrounding her *oeuvre* in the mid-1990s, in particular the rumours of copies and fakes. Perhaps, with more insight into how she worked, there will be less at issue than people once thought.

9

Rodney Gooch's archive is the key but not exclusive resource in my endeavour to produce a Kngwarreye *catalogue raisonné* for works with his provenance. However, his Emily Kngwarreye records are not a complete and closed resource – there are some gaps for which I have sourced supplementary images, data and history provided by his closest associates.[28] And although my research focus is on Gooch's Kngwarreye works from 1988 to 1996, his broader Utopia archive for the same period provides essential and illuminating context. Photographs showing what other artists were producing, especially in 1989, the first year Utopia artists painted on canvas, are an instant reminder of just how much Emily Kame Kngwarreye stood out not only amongst her own Utopia crowd but right across the western desert. Whilst other Utopia artists, notably Kathleen Petyarre, Ada Bird Petyarre, Angelina Pwerle and Gloria Tamerre Petyarre, went on to develop impressive solo careers, 1989 was not their year – but it was Emily Kngwarreye's. That she did not stand out to the sensational degree in the previous decade as a batik artist is but another intriguing aspect of her story.

One purpose of my most recent hunt through Gooch's folders was to look again for his Kngwarreye files, something I had done in previous years without success. That I did not find them finally confirmed in my mind that they have been removed. Fortunately their absence has not disrupted my project since, in 1996, during an earlier phase of looking into Emily Kngwarreye's *oeuvre*, Gooch let me copy the artist's files (records, photos and codes). For back up, I also copied all the Kngwarreye images on his negatives before I returned them in 1999. It now seems quite possible, in the absence of Gooch's original Emily files, that the reconstituted copy of Kngwarreye's CAAMA and MBA records I made two decades ago is, if not unique, at least quite rare.

Because of the artist's great fame, Rodney Gooch's Emily Kngwarreye records may come to be regarded as the most important he created over a working life that involved producing documentation of one kind or another about a great number of artists. In his final years, he clearly felt that his records should transition into a permanent archive and was serious enough to have had 'Utopia Art and Archives' guidelines drawn up – he wanted to do it properly. There is little evidence that Gooch ever found the process of archiving tedious, although there are signs that it became a difficult task at the end of his life when he was trying to finalise the catalogue of his own collection. But whether in the Utopia artists files or his own, there is every now and then a bit of fun such as the annotation below showing that he relished a passing opportunity to set the record straight. In his catalogue sheet for a work titled *Men's Business (Honey Ant and Snake)* (1988) painted by Dean Petyarre, the description says: 'The artist spent a long time on the painting & was offered no more than $30.00 in 6 Shops. Disillusioned he painted no more with any interest & took up football'. This is just the sort of story Rodney Gooch liked to put on a certificate and just the kind of painting he liked to rescue. It is a reminder of our loss that he never did write his own account of Utopia art as he once set out to do. Recently, Doris Stuart, senior Arrernte custodian of Alice Springs and Gooch's great friend and long time CAAMA Shop assistant, recalled old times. In a perfect summation of the era, she laconically declared: 'He got us all moving'.[29]

Notes

1 A. Brody, *Utopia Women's Paintings. The First Works on Canvas. A Summer Project 1988–89, The Robert Holmes* à *Court Collection*, Heytesbury Holdings Ltd., Perth, 1989.

2 The Robert Holmes à Court Collection acquired three of these projects including the first paintings and the watercolours. Prior to that they acquired Gooch's first survey, the batik project '*Utopia – A Picture Story*'.

3 This project was initiated by artist and gallerist Christopher Hodges and his partner, the artist Helen Eager. Hodges established the gallery Utopia Art Sydney in mid-1989.

4 The project resulted in the exhibition Art Cars and the Landscape at William Mora Galleries, Melbourne, in 1990. See M. Boulter, 'Spare-part

Art' in *The Art of Utopia: A New Direction in Contemporary Aboriginal Art*, Craftsman House, Sydney, 1991, pp. 164–5.

5 The Utopia Women's Batik Group (UWB) was established at Utopia in 1978 with Julia Murray as its first coordinator.

6 Marc Gooch and his partner, Janet Pierce, continue to work with Utopia artists through their business Artlore.

7 Robert Cole was born in 1959 in Alice Springs. He died there in November 1994.

8 The inaugural Clemenger Contemporary Art Award was held at the National Gallery of Victoria in February 1993.

9 The artists' files would need to be fully audited to verify this proposition.

10 Rodney Gooch archive. Letter from the Regional Manager, Department of Aboriginal Affairs (DAA), 25 January 1988, confirming management agreements made between the UWB and CAAMA on 16 September 1987.

11 C. Nicholls, 'Ronnie and Co: The making of the Gooch Collections,' in *Gooch's Utopia: Collected works from the Central Desert*, Flinders University City Gallery in collaboration with Riddoch Art Gallery, Mt Gambier, 2008, pp. 32–42 at 41.

12 Rodney Gooch 1990, Draft notes for the publication *Utopia A Picture Story*, R. J. Gooch archive.

13 Ibid.

14 This collection has undergone a number of name changes. This is what it was called when the batik collection 'A Picture Story' was purchased and published.

15 A. Brody, *Utopia. A Picture Story. 88 silk batiks from The Robert Holmes à Court Collection*, Heytesbury Holdings Ltd, Perth, 1990.

16 'Batik Exhibition', *Centralian Advocate*, November 1987, n.p.

17 CAAMA Shop certificate (duplicate) catalogue no. 10-490.

18 CAAMA Shop certificate (duplicate) catalogue no. 22-590.

19 J. Holt, 'Emily Kngwarreye at Delmore Downs 1989–1996', in J. Isaacs (ed.), *Emily Kngwarreye Paintings*, Craftsman House, Sydney, 1998, pp. 148–58 at 150.

20 D. Holt, 'The History of Delmore Gallery', viewed 20 August 2013, <http://www.delmoregallery.com.au>.

21 P. Batty, 'The Gooch Effect. Rodney Gooch and the art of the art advisor', in *Gooch's Utopia: Collected works from the Central Desert*, Flinders University City Gallery in collaboration with Riddoch Art Gallery, Mt Gambier, 2008, pp. 26–31 at 30–1.

22 Rodney Gooch archive, fax to Beverly and Anthony Knight, 9 April 1991.

23 Ibid.

24 Rodney Gooch archive, fax to Anne Brody, Heytesbury Holdings Ltd, 15 May 1991.

25 See C. Schmidt, 'Creating the Archive – Research into the history of the Utopia Art Movement', this volume; also Schmidt, '"I Paint for Everyone" – the making of Utopia art', PhD thesis, Australian National University, Canberra, 2012, pp. 63–72.

26 'Lot 149', *Bonhams Aboriginal Art Auction Monday 28 May 2012*, Bonhams, Sydney, 2012, p. 40.

27 M. Neale, 'Marks of meaning: the genius of Emily Kame Kngwarreye' in M. Neale (ed.), *Utopia: the Genius of Emily Kame Kngwarreye*, National Museum of Australia Press, Canberra, 2008, pp. 217–47 at 217.

28 To date Marc Gooch, Artlore, Alice Springs and Christopher Hodges, Utopia Art Sydney, have greatly assisted my research.

29 Doris Stuart, personal communication, Alice Springs, 2015.

3

CREATING THE ARCHIVE – RESEARCH INTO THE HISTORY OF THE UTOPIA ART MOVEMENT

Chrischona Schmidt

Artists working in the remote Central Desert communities of Utopia have been making art for the commercial art market since the late 1970s. The Utopia homelands are situated about 230 kilometres north-east of Alice Springs and comprise of twenty-one outstations, sixteen of which were inhabited at the time of my doctoral research (2008–12). In my research I focused on the development and history of the Utopia art movement, including significant artists and their *oeuvres*,. as well as how the artists interacted with the art market, for example by means of establishing relationships with art dealers and by working with various organisations. Throughout the history of the art movement there has been no continuous existence of an art centre in the region. In this article I discuss what impact this absence of an art centre means for researching the art of this region.

The discourse about Utopia art focuses on two main tropes: the painter Emily Kame Kngwarreye and her *oeuvre*, and art from Utopia being particularly abstract and gestural. Generally, Kngwarreye's *oeuvre* is discussed in isolation from the art-making in Utopia that surrounded her. She has been portrayed a 'genius' and her work has been compared to Western artists like Gerhard Richter, Jackson Pollock and Claude Monet. Her artworks have often been placed in groups according to style in the way Western artists are.[1] This was particularly the case in the two major retrospectives of her work, in 1998 at the Queensland Art Gallery and in 2008 at the National Museum of Australia. It was notably emphasised in the wall texts of the exhibition, as well as in certain sections of the accompanying catalogues.

In my research, I investigated the four-decade history of the entire Utopia region and not only Emily Kame Kngwarreye and her *oeuvre*. I placed her within a local social and artistic world. By doing so I was able to discover and unveil a very different perspective on the Utopia art movement and its history. All of this research was based on data collected, in particular images of art-works created over forty years, and information elicited through interviews and trips to country during several field research trips to Utopia. Through creating a digital image database I was able to record, sort and compare the images of artworks from Utopia. Thus I identified three main currents in artistic practices in this region: naïve; ritual and abstract. All of these currents coexisted alongside each other from the 1970s onwards and some artists created works in all three currents for different purposes, dealers and markets. In this article, I outline my research methodology and the crucial role the digital image database had in rewriting the history of the Utopia art movement.

Absence of Records

The history of art-making in Utopia is much fractured as various agencies took a role in it over time. Batik-making started in 1976 with Jenny Green through workshops funded by the Department of Education, and from 1986 the Central Australian Aboriginal Media Association (CAAMA) was the organisation through which the Utopia artists worked. In those early years art advisors, first based in the Utopia homelands and later in Alice Springs, would rove around the large area of Utopia and collect the works for sale in Alice Springs and beyond. In 1992 an art centre was established at Ahalper, one of the outstations and a service hub for the homelands[2].

However, much of the history of Utopia's art movement has been determined by private agents rather than publicly sponsored projects and institutions. Around 1988 art dealers began buying artworks directly from Utopia artists. By 1989 Utopia artists were not only painting for Rodney Gooch, who worked with CAAMA, but for other commercial dealers too.[3] The development of the Utopia art movement is intrinsically linked to these relationships with art dealers.

There was consistency in the first period of the art movement when batik was being made, and before painting. In the first period, T-shirts were batiked and sold at football games and other events.[4] Unless the buyer remembered who the artist was or cherished the actual piece, a lot of the batiks would have been worn out, torn and cut up by now, turned into table cloths and curtains for example. Thus not many of the very early batik pieces still exist in their original state. Both Jenny Green and Julia Murray have kept photos of their time at Utopia, when batik-making was being established and started off, from 1976–1982. They have both published articles about their experiences in Utopia and used their photographs on many occasions to illustrate this.[5]

The second phase of the art movement was defined by the expansion of the media being used, especially the shift into painting. It is highlighted by the great sudden interest of commercial art dealers into the region, Rodney Gooch's move to Perth and his subsequent return a year later as a commercial art dealer, and the establishment of an art centre operating out of Ahalper, a women's centre with a focus on batik. During this decade of art centre existence in Utopia, record keeping by the art centre took place, however, most of these records were lost due to a fire in 2002 and the subsequent closure of the art centre.[6] This forced closure led to lengthy court cases. The peak organisation for art centres in the region, Desart Inc, tried to salvage the computers at the art centre in order to get hold of the records; however, the art centre had been hit by a storm and some young people then went in and burnt a lot of the place down. Since 2002 there has been no art centre in the Utopia homelands and artists have been actively working with art dealers in one-on-one relationships, being their own agents.

Thus records of the art movement in Utopia are held by various people, including those who held early workshops and private dealers.[7] This history means that there is not one consolidated archive, in the form of an art centre archive or art centre records, available for the researcher. Yet, in order to write a history of the art-making in the Utopia region, an 'archive' is crucial. A void such as this has made it possible to create chronologies of artists' developments using simply a few works, leaving out others, and thus delineating from that artistic development whole periods in an *oeuvre* of an artist. In summary, this absence of an archive has meant that writings about the history of the Utopia art movement have been shaped by the lack of records and/or access to them.

Creating an Archive – Methodology of an Art History

The fragmented history of the Utopia art movement with its many players means great inconsistencies in terms of record-keeping and databases. In this section, I will expand on my methodology of dealing with this absence of records and creating a digital image database. As I have outlined, locating records for tracing the Utopia art movement was difficult for the early stages; however, the longer the artists were making art with commercial dealers and selling personally to them, the more difficult it became to reconstruct artistic developments over time. The countless numbers of art dealers, collectors and entrepreneurs engaging on a one-on-one basis with the artists since 1989 grew exponentially. At some stages various artists dealt with twenty art dealers if not more at any one time. At the same time artists would have sold artworks to staff at the local clinic, council office and anyone travelling through if the opportunity arose. This led to Rodney Gooch withdrawing himself from working with most Utopia artists and only dealing with a selected group that his nephew Marc Gooch has since narrowed down to only a handful of artists.[8] After having examined the vast networks that Utopia artists established with the art world, I approached the rhizomatic history of this art movement by accessing as many artworks as possible from 1976 onwards. By doing so I aimed at gaining an understanding for the artistic developments in this region and over time.

Firstly, I established which collections held works by Utopia artists and documented these. I travelled across Australia in order to record the Utopia artworks in all of these collections and included over forty public, corporate and private collections in my database. Some of these collections had no digital records of the artworks and asked for the photos that I took to be sent back to them. Secondly, I created a digital database using FilemakerPro and the Cataloguing Cultural Objects Guidelines by the Smithsonian Institute. Thirdly, I entered all records I had collected into the database. Finally, I took this digital image database to Utopia and showed it to everyone who was interested, from five-year-olds to old ladies who had participated in the early batiks in 1976. On one of the five research trips to Utopia I spent over five weeks travelling through the sixteen outstations, talking to people about the digital image database and showing them artworks by themselves and their family members. This led to a variety of reactions: from laughter to crying in front of the screen, from trying to touch the artwork to singing its Dreaming story in front of the laptop; and finally from seeing the artwork again after so many years, they wanted to go to the places depicted and tell me the ancestral stories shown in the paintings, explain to me more about them to connect the artwork, story and country with each other. The digital database, which only included all information accessible about the artworks, such as an image, the artist, year, the medium and technique, and the title according to the collection records, became an important tool to elicit information about the art movement, the artwork and its social history. It inspired many discussions about how artworks had been made, what happened at the time and who was the art coordinator or art dealer to whom the works were then handed. All this information was also collected in the digital image database, creating another layer of knowledge about each work discussed.

Throughout my research I accessed over 5,000 works in various collections. Information was collected from all accessible and available sources including state, corporate and private collections as well as online resources and publications. Additionally, I sighted records of more than 20,000 artworks from various art dealers. However, only a fraction of that was included in the database due to commercial art galleries denying their gallery records being included in the digital image database. While artists and their family members gave me permission to access the works and to record them, gallery owners often declined the request to share their records. This may be connected to the allegedly numerous fakes and frauds of Utopia artists' works being dispersed widely; thus the problem of provenance, which is at the core of an absence of an archive, re-emerges. A number of these commercial dealers were interested in creating their own *catalogue raisonné* of Utopia artists and their *oeuvre*, in particular about artists such as Emily Kame Kngwarreye and Minnie Pwerle. In many interviews that I conducted with commercial art dealers, they expressed the interest and urge to publish their own monographs. Previously published monographs by art dealers range from promotional type books, such as Boomerang Art Gallery's *The Utopia Story* (Fortescue 2008), to Delmore Downs Gallery's book on *Emily Kame Kngwarreye*, published in 1998.[9]

The complexity of the situation at Utopia means that artists have long been denied access to artworks; which, until this research, they had never seen since the moment they were created, and family members were unable to see works created by relatives who have since died. Bringing the digital image database back to Utopia was the first time in most cases that the artists and families had the opportunity to see their artwork again since it had been sold and left the community. By accessing an archive artists can revisit their works, think about them, and discuss them with family, art coordinators and dealers. However, in the absence of an archive artists are left to recollect their works, very rarely able to compare older with new works. It removes the opportunity for the artist to think about his or her works and/or their entire *oeuvre*. Furthermore, it does not allow for the same professional and artistic development as when being able to revisit artworks. Another notable difficulty of denying artists access to their artwork is the impossibility to create a *catalogue raisonné* or to verify the provenance of an artwork. Finally, from a perspective of an Anmatyerr or Alyawarr artist the artworks are an expression of one's *Altyerr* (Dreaming), which is a part of oneself.[10] By painting these stories the artists are giving a part of themselves away, and by never seeing them again and having no access to them, or even an image of them, the relationships between the artists and their interpretations and expressions of country and *Altyerr* are interrupted. This very deep connection between the artists and their artworks explains their strong reactions when seeing them again in the form of a digital image.

The digital image database I created was a catalyst at the same time as being an important tool for the chronological reconstruction of the history of art-making. It became a catalyst to tell stories: stories about everything and anything that was connected in some way or another to the artworks. Hence oral history was the key in reconstructing the history of the art movement and in linking events and artistic developments: I conducted interviews with as many players as possible, from within the community, including artists, their family members, and important stake holders; as well as from outside of the community and within the art world, including art dealers, gallery owners, curators, collectors and auctioneers, as well as former art coordinators in Utopia. Finally, I also interviewed exhibition visitors. Through oral history and interviews I was able to capture the points of view of elderly artists and integrate them into the history before their demise. In many cases these voices had already been lost. For example the late Emily Kame Kngwarreye was hardly ever interviewed, and if, as so often, there was no translator present, the actual communication between interviewer and interviewee was complicated, especially due to Kngwarreye's limited English language skills.[11]

The digital image database was not only enriched through the oral history but also through all other information available about the artworks and the history, such as photos and descriptions of artworks, as well as articles and written encounters between artists and other individuals. Most of these resources I only found through following up on sources, not only in archives and libraries, but also by meeting collectors and them referring me onto other collectors. For example on one occasion I had a chat with someone on a bus in Sydney, who just happened to be a collector of works by Gloria Petyarre. On another occasion I interviewed someone at the National Museum of Australia Emily Kngwarreye retrospective to find out that this woman had bought a batik T-shirt by Emily in the late 1970s, which she still kept at home.

This very open approach to data collection and its inclusion in the database ensured that not only artworks favoured by the media and collectors are part of the reconstruction of the history but that it also included other, less-well-known works. I facilitated an inclusive view of the Utopia art movement: despite being particularly renowned for its abstract and gestural painting, I found that since the beginning three currents existed within the art movement: abstract, ritual and naïve.[12] The fact that abstract art from Utopia has become the commonly known current of art-making says more about the art market and the art world than about the actual 'studio' situation. By entering all records into the database the first chronological and stylistic comparison was made possible. A broader image of Utopia art emerged through the skeleton of this archive, filled with all the information given through many an interview with artists and anyone who participated in some shape or form in the history of the Utopia art movement.

Limitations of an Archive

In all the research conducted I relied on the collector, gallery or art dealer to have recorded and kept the information about the artwork in some shape or form. The more collections I visited and the more information I recorded about artists, their countries and *Altyerr* stories, the more it became apparent that many of the private, public and corporate collections do not hold accurate data for the artworks; or sometimes they only have very limited information about the artwork, its provenance or the year it was created. Often collections had no digital image database themselves or had one with very poor digital image quality. In a few cases this meant that all the images used for the research were returned to the respective collection in order for them to have digital copies of the artworks in their collection. This absence of information and record-keeping around the artworks at the collection level added another layer of difficulty to the research. The limitations of the collections researched are part of the archive created. This archive of Utopia artworks highlights the absence of records throughout the entire history of the art movement; furthermore, it reflects the silence of the artists, as their voices had rarely been included with the artworks. The digital image database enabled me to return the images of the artworks to the artists together with all the information collected. Furthermore, through its comparative abilities I was able to determine three main currents of art-making in Utopia over the past four decades: abstract, ritual and naïve. This is a different analysis to that usually proposed in studies of Utopia work, especially that of Kngwarreye's paintings. In summary, the digital image database was crucial and instrumental in tracing and writing the history of the Utopia art movement of the past four decades.

Notes

1 See C. Schmidt, 'Utopia: The Genius of Emily Kame Kngwarreye', exhibition review, *ReCollections*, vol. 4, no. 1, 2009, viewed 14 February, 2016, < http://recollections.nma.gov.au/issues/vol_4_no1/exhibition_reviews/utopia>; and Margo Neale's discussion of Emily Kngwarreye's 'Colourism' period for the comparison with Monet, in M. Neale, 'Colourism' in M. Neale (ed.), *Utopia: The Genius of Emily Kame Kngwarreye*, exhibition catalogue, National Museum of Australia, Canberra, 2008,

pp. 115–34 at 123. See also Terry Smith, 'Kngwarreye woman abstract painter' in J. Isaacs (ed.), *Emily Kame Kngwarreye Paintings*, Craftsman House, Sydney, 1998, pp. 24–42, and his talk 'Emily Kngwarreye's practice of painting: an international perspective', at the *Emily: 'Why do these fellas paint like me?'* symposium as part of the *Utopia: The Genius of Emily Kame Kngwarreye* opening weekend in 2008. Neale edited three exhibition catalogues about Emily Kngwarreye in 1998, and two catalogues in 2008 for exhibitions in Canberra (ibid.) and Japan. See M. Neale (ed.), *Emily Kame Kngwarreye. Alhakere: Paintings from Utopia*, exhibition catalogue, Queensland Art Gallery, Art Gallery of New South Wales and National Gallery of Victoria, 1998 and M. Neale (ed.), *Utopia: The Genius of Emily Kame Kngwarreye*, exhibition catalogue, National Art Centre and The Yomiuri Shimbun, Osaka and Tokyo, 2008.

2 See C. Schmidt, 'Rodney Gooch's Role and Influence in the Development of the Utopia Art Movement: A History of the Art Movement and Rodney Gooch's Role within it', *International Journal of the Arts in Society*, vol. 5, no. 6, 2011, pp. 149–62.

3 Personal communication with Donald Holt, 2011. Holt started working with male artists from Utopia as early as 1988, and later on worked with female artists.

4 Personal communication with Jenny Green, 2010.

5 J. Green, *Utopia Women, Country and Batik*, Utopia Women's Batik Group, Alice Springs, 1981; and 'Singing the Silk: Utopia Batik', in J. Ryan and R. Healy (eds.), *Raiki Wara – Long Cloth from Aboriginal Australia and the Torres Strait*, exhibition catalogue, National Gallery of Victoria, Melbourne, 1998, pp. 38–49; J. Murray, 'Utopia Batik: The Halycon Days 1978–82', in ibid., pp. 50–5; and J. Murray, 'Drawn Together: The Utopia Batik Phenomenon', in J. Ryan (ed.), *Across the Desert – Aboriginal Batik from Central Australia*, exhibition catalogue, National Gallery of Victoria, Melbourne, 2008, pp. 116–21.

6 Personal communication with Narayan Kozeluh, 2010.

7 An example for this record keeping can be found by Delmore Gallery. This was run by Janet and Donald Holt, who published *Emily Kngwarreye: Paintings*, Craftsman House, Sydney, 1998. This book is the result of their close relationship with Utopia artists. Janet Holt had previously worked for Papunya Tula Artists and was aware of the importance of record-keeping for authenticity purposes and provenance in years to come.

8 Personal communication with Marc Gooch, September 2014.

9 E. Fortescue, *Art of Utopia, Volume 1*, Boomerang Art, Adelaide, 2008; D. Holt and J. Holt, *Emily Kngwarreye*, 1998.

10 *Altyerr* (Anmatyerr) or 'the Dreaming' describes the belief-system and ontology for Indigenous Australians. The country and the people are from the Dreaming. The 'Dreaming may refer both to the specific stories and to the whole creative epoch of which the stories are part' (F. Myers, *Pintupi Country, Pintupi Self: Sentiment, Place, and Politics among Western Desert Aborigines*, University of California Press, Berkeley, 1991, p. 48); see also F. Myers, *Painting Culture – The Making of an Aboriginal High Art*, Duke University Press, Durham, 2002, pp. 118, 361.

11 One of the few examples of Emily Kame Kngwarrye being interviewed with an interpreter present is: M. West, J. Green and K. Petyarr, 'Kathleen Petyarr in Conversation', in H. Perkins (ed.), *One Sun One Moon – Aboriginal Art in Australia*, Art Gallery of New South Wales Press, Sydney, 2007, pp. 210–17.

12 See C. Schmidt, '"I paint for everyone" – The Making of Utopia Art', PhD thesis, Australian National University, Canberra, 2012.

4

THREE CERTIFICATES ARE NOT ENOUGH: ROVER THOMAS AND ART CENTRE ARCHIVES

Suzanne Spunner

Primary research at art centres on provenance can appear quite straightforward. Aboriginal artists in remote areas generally work under the auspices of a local community-owned art centre, and for Rover Thomas that was Waringarri Aboriginal Arts in Kununurra. Rover Thomas began painting in 1983, and soon after, in 1985, Waringarri Arts was founded. Thomas painted for the Waringarri Art Centre from 1986 until 1996, so the art centre records capture his most productive decade. Warmun Art Centre was founded in 1998 in Warmun (or Turkey Creek), the community where Rover Thomas lived; however Thomas died in 1998 and never painted for Warmun Art Centre. He did paint for other agents and individuals who kept records of varying degrees of reliability.

The Waringarri records provide a solid database for researchers. What exactly are these records? They comprise three distinct sets of records and a number of subsets. The first set, the primary records, are two green-coloured Collins nine-column money books headed Waringarri Arts and Crafts Artists Supplies and Stock Book. All the entries are handwritten and stretch over a double opened page as they try to capture the purchase by the art centre of paintings by artists such as Thomas. These records detail how much was paid for it, when it was made, whether it was on canvas board or a canvas, when it was sold and for how much. They also show which canvases, boards, brushes, binders and ochres were supplied at a price noted, to which artist and when. This system assigned a stock number to the support (the canvas or board) and a separate catalogue number to the finished work when it was purchased back by the art centre. At a certain point a new art centre manager decided to simplify things and assign one catalogue number to each work and to begin the numbering system all over again, and then at a later date another manager went back to year zero and started the catalogue numbering again. The stock books are a unique record which yield rich material for research. As well as very specific details about materials, they show who Rover Thomas was painting with at each stage of his career. This can be deduced from records of a buying trip as the art coordinator documents his visit to Warmun/Turkey Creek or Frog Hollow (a nearby community), where, for example, he picked up three Rover Thomas works, two Queenie McKenzies and two Jack Brittens. Financial records of payments to artists and to galleries and daily takings books, cheque accounts, invoices and receipts, as well as correspondence with dealers and galleries, are all there in the archives to forensically track the life of a work.

A certificate of authenticity is generated for each work sold by Waringarri Aboriginal Arts. In its perfect form it has the artist's name, their skin name, bush name, domicile, language, the date the work was painted, the dimensions, the medium and the support, a title for the work and the story explaining the Indigenous significance of the subject matter, the location, dreaming or historical event it depicts. These certificates also contain a schematic representation of the painting with labelled sites or objects marked and a photograph of the work, which could be a Polaroid or an SLR photograph in colour, and a catalogue number. While these records are sometimes comprehensive, they can be as scant as a Polaroid with a catalogue number. These certificates were filed in plastic pockets in large spring folders under the name of the individual artist. So there was a 'Rover Book' and a 'Queenie Book', until 1997, when the manager Kevin Kelly left Waringarri and set up his own art business, Red Rock Art. His successors decided to break up these artists' books and file material in general artists' files in filing cabinets by year, under different headings. In 2002, after five years and more than five different managers, Cathy Cummins was appointed to Waringarri Aboriginal Arts and remains in the position today. Attempts have since been made to reconstitute the individual artists' books, at least for the famous names like Rover Thomas. While I was at Waringarri in 2008, I found various photographs of paintings. Some of them had dimensions written in pen on the back and others had catalogue numbers; some of them went with the certificates in the plastic pockets and some needed a new plastic pocket of their own because they were the only extant evidence of that painting. Cathy Cummins has developed a computer database of artist records, which again, in perfect form, contains: the catalogue number, the medium, the dimensions, the title or location depicted and the story. It also shows that the work was sold and has two blank fields relating to its purchase. There are significant discrepancies between the paper and digital records and there are certificates missing.

Getting the Story – Frances Kofod

Linguist Frances Kofod began her work on East Kimberley languages in 1971. She helped the Indigenous Mirima Council in Kununurra set up the Mirima Dawang Woorlab-gerring Language and Cultural Centre, which produced wordbooks, grammars and dictionaries in Miriwoong, Gajirrawong and Gija for the Kimberley Language Resource Centre. Between 1989 and 2008,

Kofod worked with all of the community controlled art centres in the region – Waringarri Aboriginal Arts in Kununurra, Warmun Art Centre at Turkey Creek and Jirrawun Arts at Kununurra and Wyndham – taking down stories of the paintings from the artists in language. The stories of the paintings constitute an invaluable record. As Kofod comments:

> Some stories often talk about the physical reality of the paint and how it represents the country. They may include dreaming stories, stories that recount the relatively recent history of the invasion by Europeans, and the artists' personal travels in the country as stockmen and women working for the pastoralists.[1]

In 1991, in her role as a language worker contracted by Waringarri Art Centre, Kofod interviewed, transcribed and created the most authoritative oral history of the life of Rover Thomas – effectively the only one. Kofod's records of the stories and sites associated with Rover Thomas paintings formed the basis of an important document generated by Waringarri Aboriginal Arts titled, 'Waringarri Arts: Artist Reference, Artist: Rover Thomas (Roba)'. It was compiled in late 1995 or early 1996 and runs to sixteen pages, is undated, unpaginated and no author is given. For the purpose of citation, I numbered the sixteen pages and called it *Roba: Themes and Stories.* It is a detailed list and contains a description of the themes and topics painted by Rover Thomas with Waringarri Arts, and it is referenced to Waringarri catalogue numbers of paintings, which depict the theme or subject noted. The manager, Kevin Kelly auspiced its production with assistance from Eric Kjellgren, who was then a PhD student and was also helping take down artists' stories for paintings.

Roba: Themes and Stories is arranged in many categories: Country, Dreamings (including, the Goorirr-Goorirr or Krill Krill), Natural events (Sun, Sunrise, Milky Way, Night Sky, Flood), Historical events (including Cyclone Tracy) and man-made features: bridges, crossroads, roads and telephone boxes. 'Country' is the largest category and takes up almost seven pages of the document, followed by 'Dreamings', which covers six pages. The detail within each category is extensive; for instance, under 'Country: Canning Stock Route', ten particular places or sites are described, and under 'Country: Texas Downs', another ten places and sites are described. It is an invaluable resource for understanding what the artist painted freely as opposed to the themes, stories and sites he might have painted under commission from other agents. *Roba: Themes and Stories* also provides a base-line comparison for works attributed to the artist. For example, in 1995 Rover Thomas was brought to Melbourne by Kimberley Art and participated in a Painting Camp in the Dandenongs run by Neil McLeod. Amongst a very large cluster of paintings purportedly produced at this time are eleven Owl paintings, and eight paintings of Willy Willy and Lightning have subsequently appeared; however the Roba document lists only one painting each for Owls and Willy Willy (Miowon) and none at all for Lightning. Dealer Adrian Newstead has been closely associated with Neil McLeod, and Newstead's book *The Dealer is the Devil: An Insider's History of Aboriginal Art* (2014) is an extended defence of McLeod cast within a voluminous history of Aboriginal art.[2]

The Waringarri Records – Ceci n'est pas un cyclone

As an example of just how useful art centre records are, consider the painting *Ngarin Janu Country*, 1988, featured in the *Yiribana* catalogue of 1994.[3] Yiribana is the name for the Indigenous art gallery inside the Art Gallery of New South Wales (AGNSW) and this publication surveys its works. The catalogue is by Margo Neale and edited by Vivien Johnson. *Ngarin Janu Country* is from Waringarri Arts and was purchased by the AGNSW from Aboriginal Arts Australia after it was shown in the 1988 exhibition *Aboriginal Art of the East Kimberley* at Hogarth Galleries, curated by Ace Bourke. The story on the Waringarri Art Centre certificate states:

> Ngarin Janu Country is near the Canning Stock Route. This painting is about the Dreamtime story when the big lake (Ngarin Janu) got flooded. The people who lived there tried to escape the flood, but were drowned when they tried to cross the channel from the sandbar to the big hill (Miwuda). (Waringarri Arts Painting Certificate AP 1691)

The accompanying diagram on the certificate shows the distinctive funnel shape set on the diagonal, a striking feature of the composition, which represents the lake water (Ngarin Janu), and a smaller funnel shape running parallel to the lake on one bank which represents the sandbar where the people tried to cross.

In Roba Themes and Stories, even more details are noted about this site and subject:

> Ngarinjanoo Country: Ngararinjanoo is a lake and swamp with reeds near the CSR between Well 33 and Kintore. This is the artist's father's country. The proper law for this place is called Ngoolooboolbarr. It is associated with mens song and flood dreamings.[4]

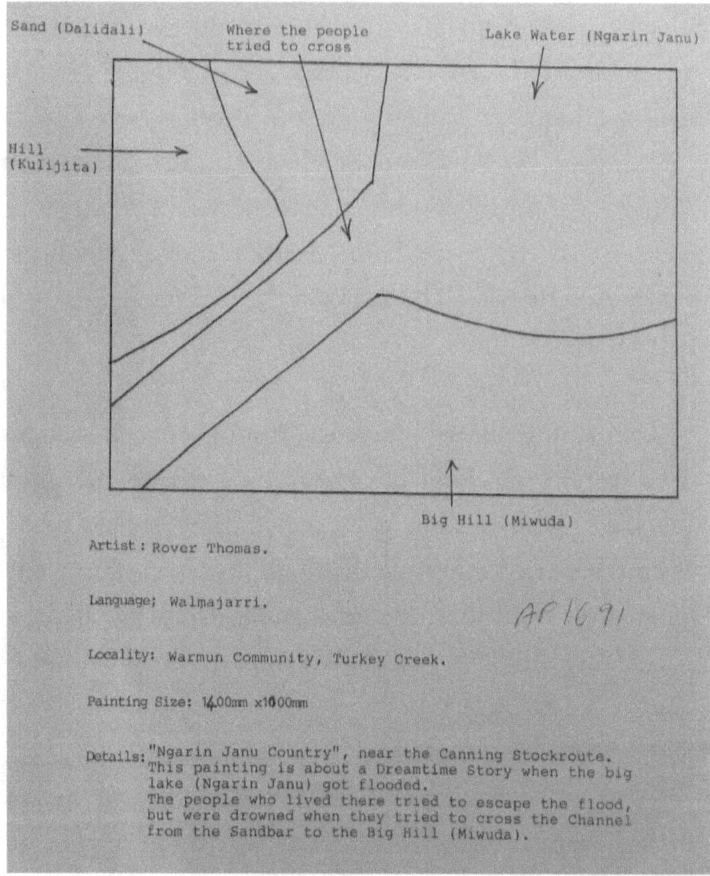

Figure 4.1: Waringarri certificate of Ngarin Janu Country

There can be no doubt what this painting depicts and why it is an important story for Rover Thomas.

Now consider Lot 39 offered by the auction house Lawson-Menzies in November 2007. This painting is called by a similar but significantly different title, *Ngarin Janu Place (Cyclone Tracy)*, 1995, natural earth pigments on linen, 101 cm x 183 cm, Provenance: 'Neil McLeod Fine Art, Private Collection, Vic, sold with original gallery documentation'. Estimate: $60,000–80,000. The image is a simplified single funnel shape running diagonally across the picture plane demarcated by fine white dots. What story has been provided (presumably by Neil McLeod) to the auction house, Lawson-Menzies, to connect Ngarin Janu with Cyclone Tracy? After a preamble about the Krill Krill Dreaming and Cyclone Tracy hitting Darwin and finally petering out at Port Hedland, the purported subject is mentioned:

> In this painting, Cyclone Tracy toward the end of its journey, is transmogrified into one of the Rainbow Snakes – Wungurr, Ungudd or Juntarkal. These Rainbow Snakes imbue the Kimberley landscape with eternal life force.[5]

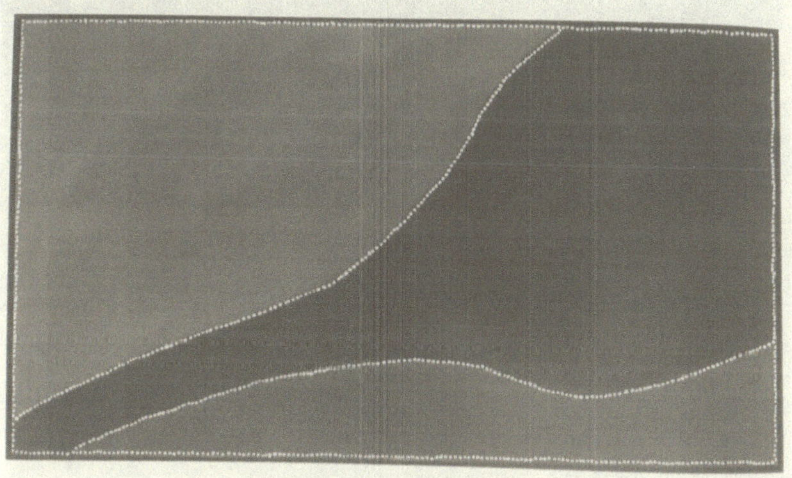

Figure 4.2: Lawson-Menzies catalogue Ngarin Janu Place (Cyclone Tracy)

Who would be convinced by this story? Only somebody who did not know the actual Ngarin Janu story, and whose mind and eyes had been prepared by the *Yiribana* catalogue entry by Margo Neale on *Ngarin Janu*. It is printed as part of a double-page spread with a full-page colour reproduction of the AGNSW-owned painting on the right, and the exegesis on the left, accompanied by a small colour image of another painting by Rover Thomas, entitled *Cyclone* (1994), with no dimensions, material, support, source or provenance cited. There is no indication where *Cyclone* (1994) came from, no proper credit either on the page itself or in the back of the publication listing picture sources.

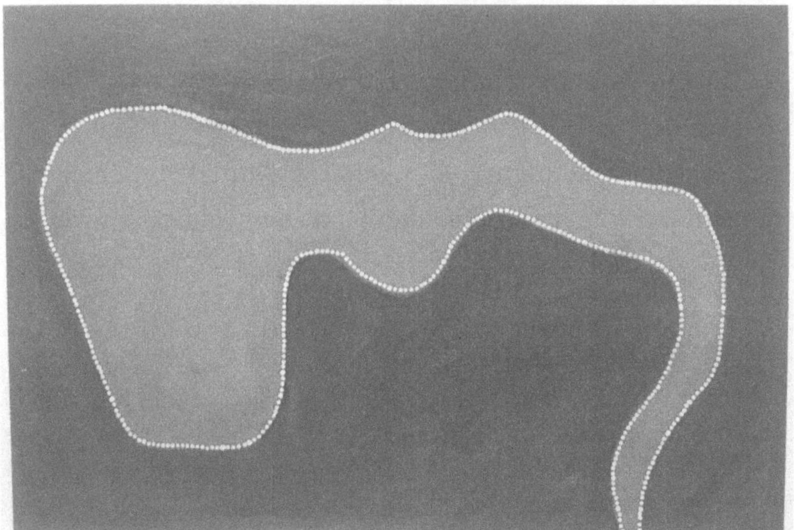

Figure 4.3: Detail of Yiribana *catalogue* Cyclone, *1994*

In the acknowledgments to *Yiribana* Christopher Hodges is mentioned, and it is most likely that this second painting came from Hodges' gallery, Utopia Art Sydney.[6] This is because their first exhibition of Rover Thomas work, *New Paintings: A Solo Exhibition*, was held in 1994, and the painting illustrated clearly relates to another work: *Cyclone* (1996), ochre and synthetic polymer on linen, 78 cm x 57 cm, exhibited by Hodges in the Utopia Art Sydney/Sherman Gallery exhibition 'Rover Thomas Survey Exhibition' in 1997 and illustrated in the catalogue.

I have not been able to locate a checklist of the works from the 1994 exhibition but I do have the checklist for the 1997 exhibition. I do not have confidence in the dates given for these two similar cyclone works, 1994 and 1996, because I found so many inconsistencies around the dates of the recent work in this 1997 exhibition. Dates given on captions in the 1997 catalogue did not agree with the dates given for the same work in the checklist.

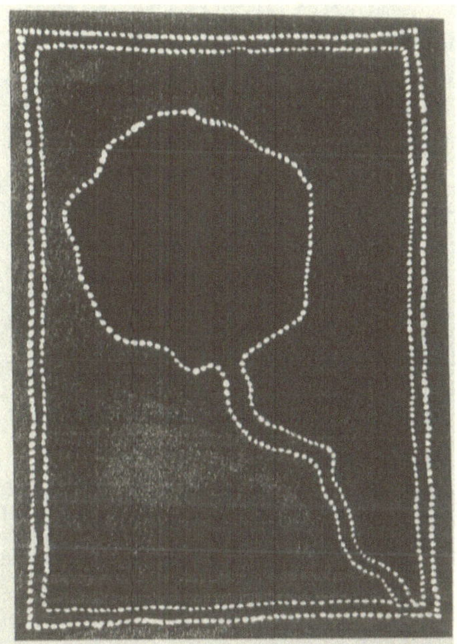

Figure 4.4: Utopia Art Sydney catalogue, Cyclone *(1996)*

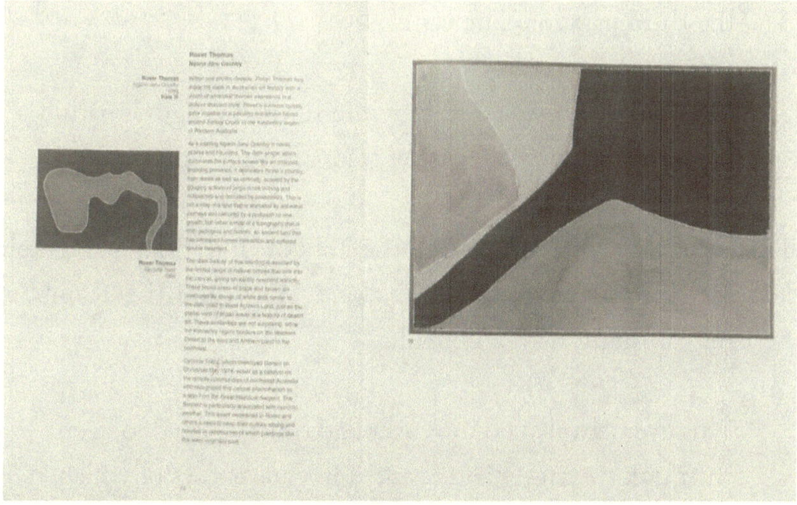

Figure 4.5: Yiribana *catalogue double page*

The *Yiribana* catalogue follows a very consistent format: an AGNSW painting on the right-hand side of the page accompanied by a page of text on the left-hand side and a small supporting colour reproduction of a photograph or another related artwork, establishing for the reader a connection between the AGNSW painting and the accompanying small image. Margo Neale's essay on *Ngarin Janu Country* does not reflect any of the detailed story information documented by Waringarri Aboriginal Arts in relation to this painting. Neale's opening paragraph locates Rover Thomas in the East Kimberley School, and the second paragraph tells us:

> As a painting, *Ngarin Janu Country* is harsh and haunting. The dark shape, which dominates the surface hovers like an ominous brooding presence. It delineates Rover's country from above as well as vertically, scarred by the gouging actions of large-scale mining and massacres and denuded by pastoralists. This is not a map of a land that is animated by ancestral journeys

And the third paragraph, refers to:

> The stark beauty...assisted by the limited range of natural ochres...giving an earthy resonant warmth.

Then for no apparent reason the fourth and final paragraph launches into a discussion of Cyclone Tracy and the Rainbow Serpent, finishing with a flourish:

> This event awakened in Rover and others a need to keep their culture strong and resulted in ceremonies of which paintings like this were originally part.[7]

So now, *Ngarin Janu Country* has nothing to do with the Canning Stock Route, Rover Thomas's father, a terrible flood where many people died, flood Dreamings and proper Men's Law, but it might just have something to do with Cyclone Tracy and is otherwise harsh and haunting and depicts a landscape despoiled by miners and pastoralists. How could this happen? My inference is that the small Cyclone Tracy painting suggested this new and unusual interpretation of *Ngarin Janu Country. Ngarin Janu Place (Cyclone Tracy)* (1995) has not sold and can be seen on the Burrinja Gallery website. The text and story associated with the painting (*Ngarin Janu*) cannot be verified from information located in the Waringarri Aboriginal Arts archives.

Another Willy Willy Formed Over Japan

Rover Thomas produced an untitled painting, known as *Baragoo country, where the dog Killed the emu*, for Waringarri Arts in 1990

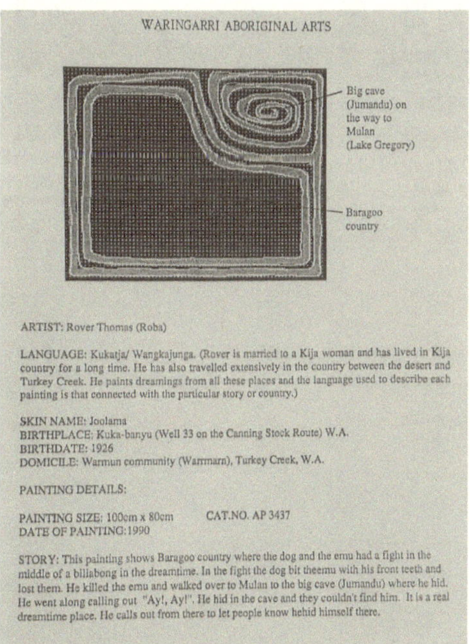

WARINGARRI ABORIGINAL ARTS

ARTIST: Rover Thomas (Roba)

LANGUAGE: Kukatja/ Wangkajunga. (Rover is married to a Kija woman and has lived in Kija country for a long time. He has also travelled extensively in the country between the desert and Turkey Creek. He paints dreamings from all these places and the language used to describe each painting is that connected with the particular story or country.)

SKIN NAME: Joolama
BIRTHPLACE: Kuka-banyu (Well 33 on the Canning Stock Route) W.A.
BIRTHDATE: 1926
DOMICILE: Warmun community (Warrmarn), Turkey Creek, W.A.

PAINTING DETAILS:

PAINTING SIZE: 100cm x 80cm CAT.NO. AP 3437
DATE OF PAINTING:1990

STORY: This painting shows Baragoo country where the dog and the emu had a fight in the middle of a billabong in the dreamtime. In the fight the dog bit theemu with his front teeth and lost them. He killed the emu and walked over to Mulan to the big cave (Jumandu) where he hid. He went along calling out "Ay!, Ay!". He hid in the cave and they couldn't find him. It is a real dreamtime place. He calls out from there to let people know hehid himself there.

Figure 4.6: Waringarri certificate, Baragoo country, where the dog Killed the emu

(Waringarri Arts Archives, 1990, AP 3437). This painting was exhibited in *Turkey Creek Artists* at Dreamtime Gallery Perth in 1990. Works from this exhibition were included in an exhibition that went to Japan, *Western Australian Painting and Ceramics,* Gallery Sanyo, Ginza Chuo-Ku, Tokyo, 5–27 July, 1991.

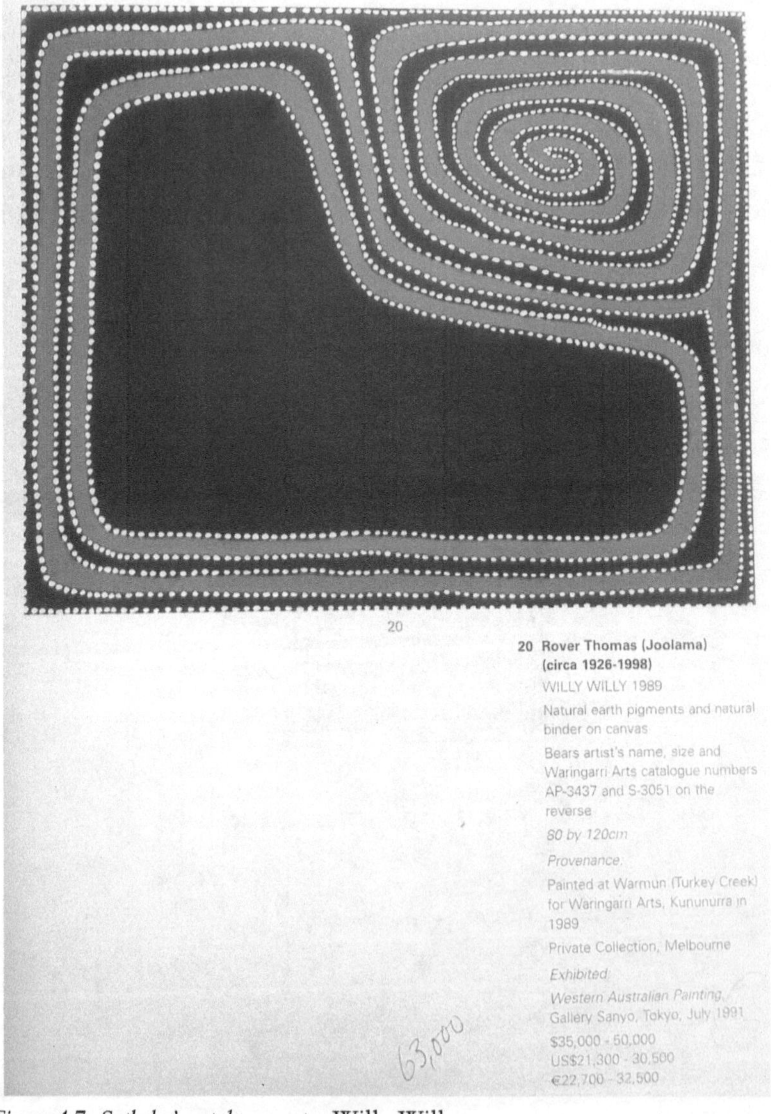

20

20 Rover Thomas (Joolama) (circa 1926-1998)

WILLY WILLY 1989

Natural earth pigments and natural binder on canvas

Bears artist's name, size and Waringarri Arts catalogue numbers AP-3437 and S-3051 on the reverse

80 by 120cm

Provenance:

Painted at Warmun (Turkey Creek) for Waringarri Arts, Kununurra in 1989

Private Collection, Melbourne

Exhibited:

Western Australian Painting, Gallery Sanyo, Tokyo, July 1991

$35,000 - 50,000
US$21,300 - 30,500
€22,700 - 32,500

63,000

Figure 4.7: Sotheby's catalogue entry Willy Willy

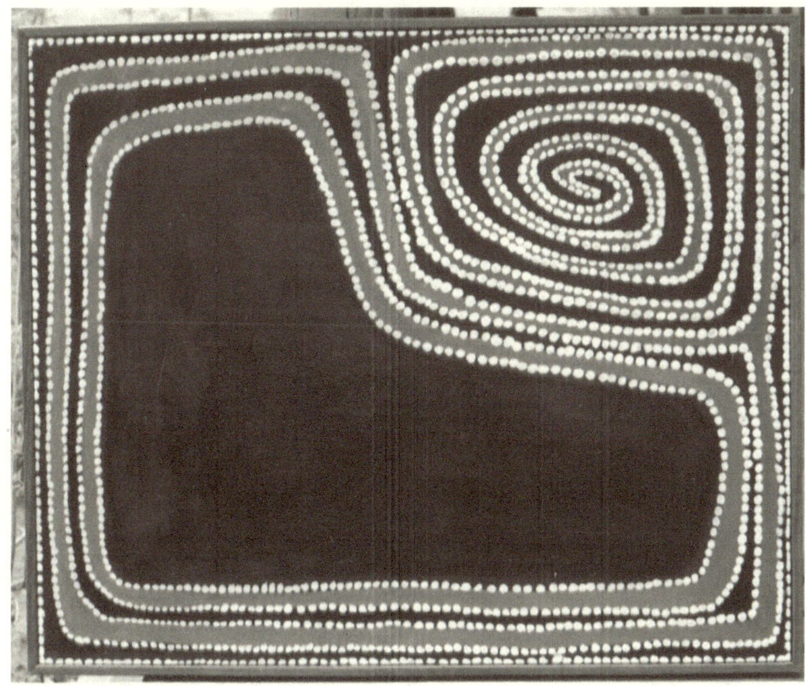

Figure 4.8: Waringarri photograph of AP 3437

In 2000, Sotheby's offered a Rover Thomas painting *Willy Willy* (Thomas, R. 1989), which cited its provenance as Waringarri Arts AP 3437 and looks remarkably like *Baragoo country, where the dog Killed the emu*, and one may wonder why the title has changed; however close examination of the photographs, particularly of the eye of the spiral form, shows it is not the same painting.[8] The provenance notes the Japanese exhibition and its current location in a 'private collection, Melbourne'. So there are two different works with the same Waringarri catalogue number and exhibition history. The second work has a more saleable title and a connection by implication to the National Gallery of Victoria work *Dreamtime Story of the Willy Willy* (1989), but it is a spurious title and the connection misleading as the painting story on the original Waringarri certificate makes clear–the spiral form in the top represents a big cave on the way to Mulan and Lake Gregory, and does not represent a willy willy. At this point the painting remains a mystery and highlights how schematic representations on certificates can be ambiguous and deceptive. If you had only consulted the schematic drawing on the Waringarri certificate against the image in the auction catalogue, you could easily have thought the works were the same, albeit with a new title. Comparing the two photographs showed that something else was happening, which in turn drew attention back to the new title.

Warmun Art Centres: Many and Various

The Warmun Art Centre opened in 1998, the year Rover Thomas died, and he never painted for them, so why should it be considered in any examination of his *oeuvre*? It must be considered because before Warmun Art Centre (WAC) opened, there were two earlier versions, which are frequently glossed as 'Warmun Art Centre' in auction catalogues, and work attributed to Rover Thomas was sourced from them. The first manifestation, which operated in Warmun in 1994, was called Warmun Aboriginal Corporation or Warmun Community Arts, Warmun Community (Turkey Creek) Incorporated. It issued its own certificates and operated under the benign aegis of the Warmun Council. It was organised by Peter Harrison of Kimberley Art gallery in Melbourne and run on the ground by Dave Rock, a community policeman and later an employee of the Warmun Community Council.[9] There is no indication in the Waringarri records that there was any formal or acknowledged relationship with Waringarri Arts. In fact Kimberley Art, which had previously bought from Waringarri Arts, continued to buy from them occasionally.

Kimberley Art sent pre-primed and stretched canvases to Dave Rock who distributed them to the most saleable senior artists: Rover Thomas, Queenie McKenzie, Jack Britten, Hector Jandany, George Mung Mung and Henry Wanambi. Completed work was returned to Dave Rock and then sent on to Kimberley Art in Melbourne.

In 1995, anthropologist Patricia Vinnicombe directed a project with Queenie McKenzie and Warmun women making paintings and recording stories about the community and local sites. Vinnicombe was given permission to photocopy the records of Queenie McKenzie's work, kept by both Waringarri Arts in Kununurra and the 'Warmun Community Co-ordinator' of the paintings sold through the auspices of the community – some fifty-two works during the nine month period from September 1994 to May 1995.[10] Vinnicombe presumably is referring to Warmun Community Arts and Dave Rock, though she does not name them. She does, however, mention connections to a gallery in Melbourne and Paris. Kimberley Art was based in Flinders Lane, Melbourne, and had exhibitions with Galerie Baudoin Lebon in Paris. Vinnicombe remarks: 'The standard of documentation that accompanies the paintings (by Queenie McKenzie) varies from excellent to abysmal, with that from Waringarri Arts being the most comprehensive'.[11]

In November 1995 Dave Rock was leaving Warmun and he facilitated the entry into the community of Maxine Taylor and her partner 'Serge' Terrence Brooks, who had previously run the takeaway fish and chip shop in Wyndham. Warmun Community Council recruited Taylor and Brooks to run the Warmun roadhouse on the Great Northern Highway close to the community, and subsequently Taylor and Brooks began to sell artwork from the roadhouse under the business name Narangunny Art Traders (NAT). Three months later, in early 1996, the Warmun Community Council arranged for Taylor and Brooks to move into the community and live in the old post office, a large elevated dwelling, which in the past had housed the community advisors.[12] Taylor and Brooks ran an 'art centre' from the old post office and prepared the canvases on site for a group of older, saleable artists who came and painted there and were given food and looked after. The work produced for Warmun Traditional Artists and NAT went primarily to Kimberley Art in Melbourne and two Sydney dealers, Adrian Newstead of Coo-ee Art and Christopher Hodges of Utopia Art Sydney. Others who also bought from NAT included dealers such as Indigenart, now Mossenson Gallery in Perth, who were also buying from Waringarri Arts, and Helen Read of Palya Art and the collectors she brought to Warmun on her Digeri Art Tours, among them Colin and Liz Laverty.

The de facto art centre arrangements at Warmun unravelled in October 1997, when Helen Read of Digeri Art Tours/Palya Art sent a letter of complaint to the Warmun Community Council. The incident was 'the catalyst' for establishing the community-owned art centre. Read visited Warmun with a group of art collectors in October 1996 and again in 1997, and when she enquired, Maxine Taylor told Read that the enterprise was a non-profit organisation recognised by the Aboriginal and Torres Strait Islander Commission[13]. Helen Read 'became suspicious when she couldn't locate the enterprise in the ATSIC Visual Arts and Crafts Directory'.[14] Read raised the matter with the Warmun Community Council and the artists, and after a series of meetings in December 1997, it was revealed that: 'Warmun Traditional Arts or Narangunny Art Trader was a private business owned by Maxine Taylor and Terrence Brooks'.[15] Warmun Community Council voted to rescind their arrangements with NAT. Adrian Newstead of Coo-ee Art and Tom Spender of Kimberley Art both submitted letters to the Warmun Community Council supporting

Taylor and Brooks. Christopher Hodges of Utopia Art Sydney and Dianne Mossenson of Indigenart did not. The Warmun Community Council further resolved to set about establishing their own community-owned and community-controlled art centre and wanted the old post office, where Taylor and Brooks had been living and running the art centre, as premises for the new organisation. They were required to vacate the old post office by 30 December.[16]

After Rover Thomas's death, at Warmun at Easter 1998, documents (re)emerged which showed Rover Thomas had signed the rights in his work over to NAT. At least five other 'older painters have signed with Narangunny Art Traders and it has come into question whether the artists fully understood what they were putting their names to'.[17] The artists are said 'to have signed contracts… which now claims exclusive access to all income from works'[18] and 'In Thomas's case the income is substantial'.[19] Furthermore the Rover Thomas agreement was signed both by Thomas and his daughter Jane Yalunga. Freddie Timms acknowledged he painted for NAT but he was suspicious and refused to sign the exclusivity agreement. He spoke to locals who were on the Warmun Community Council about his concerns, in particular how people were paid: 'She (Maxine) just opened the front window and chucked it down from the top and sung "wak wak" that mean crow. I think the old people didn't like it'.[20] In their defence, Taylor and Books argued that: 'The authenticity of the works is fully documented by NAT and recorded by video and photographing the working artists. All of the artists sign their works and they receive 60% of all sales'.[21] When attempts were made to enforce these agreements Waringarri Arts opposed the claim. Maxine Taylor conceded Rover Thomas had suffered from serious illness before he signed the agreement but denied it affected his judgment: 'His mind was as sharp as ever'.[22]

A flurry of legal and press activity ensued about Rover Thomas's health and capacity, and the agreements were not enforced. After Warmun Art Centre (WAC) opened in September 1998, the manager, Anna Moulton, said that Jack Britten continued to paint for NAT.[23] By contrast other senior artists, including Queenie McKenzie and Hector Jandany, were distressed by the way they were treated by NAT and threw their weight behind the new community-owned art centre.

I have not seen the records of these entities and have only seen, in auction catalogues, the works that have appeared on the secondary market, so I am not in a position to comment on their authenticity or the conditions under which they were produced or the remunerations received by the artists. There are grounds for regarding them as a class as problematic; however each work needs to be individually assessed on its merits when it appears. What does concern me more is the blurring of provenance descriptors and the way that the good name and transparent records of the Warmun Art Centre are invoked by these other short-lived entities, to disguise the actual and very unclear nature of their relationship with the artists and to trade off the reputation that WAC and the art centre system have built over many decades.

Caveat Emptor – Check the Catalogue Number

Buyers should check the provenance details carefully whenever 'Warmun Art Centre' is invoked, to ensure they know from whom they are buying. The first indicator is the date; is it before or after 1998 when WAC opened? The next step is to check the catalogue number; Narangunny Art Traders/Warmun Traditional Arts either uses N, NA or NAT as the prefix and the artists' initials as the suffix or some combination; for example NAT 0154 or QM0154 or N0154-QM, whereas Warmun Art Centre uses

WAC as the prefix on its catalogue number and the date of the work as the suffix. When Warmun Art Centre was incorporated in 1998, it was clearly mindful that this could be a problem and described itself as 'Kelarriny Arts – Warmun Art Centre' to distinguish themselves from the previous incarnations. However, within a year of trading this nomenclature had become cumbersome and was abandoned.

In 1999, the year after WAC opened, when Jennifer Isaacs was collecting work for the Gantner-Myer Aboriginal Art Collection, it is clear that she dealt with both entities. In the catalogue, acknowledgments for *Spirit Country*, Isaacs thanks: 'Kevin Kelly formerly of Waringarri Arts and now of Red Rock Art, Kununurra...Maxine Taylor, formerly of Warmun Arts in the Kimberley...Anna Moulton and Jonathon Kimberley of Warmun Arts, Warmun'.[24] Isaacs' descriptor 'Warmun Arts' does not distinguish between these two substantially different entities. Subsequently the approach has been to ignore the previous incarnations in all Warmun Art Centre publications and histories. This has left the field wide open for others to take advantage of the situation and it has not helped buyers of East Kimberley art to make sense of provenance descriptors. When I queried Tim Klingender and Crispin Gutteridge of Sotheby's about their acceptance of this loose Warmun Art Centre descriptor, they replied variously that these entities were the (only) Art Centre at Warmun at the time.[25] This reasoning, while understandable, highlights the problem. Adrian Newstead has consistently promulgated the view that this was the first Warmun art centre with simply a different administrative structure:

> Narangunny Art Traders is the trading name used by Maxine Taylor and Terry Brooks who became the first

> art co-ordinators in the Warmun community in 1997. The art centre under Taylor and Brooks operated as Warmun Traditional Arts until 1999 when a new constitution and incorporation led to the current Warmun Art Centre.[26]

What is an Art Centre and Why Does it Matter?

What is an art centre? It is useful to think in terms of necessary and sufficient conditions. These entities operating in Warmun at the time fulfilled criteria that is necessary for an art centre; they operated in the community, they bought and sold art from the community, money was paid to artists, artwork certificates were issued, artists were looked after and exhibitions were arranged. They did not, however, meet the critical criteria: community ownership and community control, accuracy of records, transparency of financial arrangements and accountability to regulatory third parties. In the study by Felicity Wright, art and craft centres are defined as:

> organisations operating in remote Australia owned and controlled by Aboriginal people. Their principal activity is facilitating the production and marketing of art and craft. A centre may be independently incorporated or auspiced by an Aboriginal company or incorporated association.[27]

Art centres are important because they are 'often the only source of externally generated income in remote communities' and they are 'special cases' and 'not conventional businesses'[28] because they are 'directly accountable to their stakeholders'.[29] Compared to private dealers, where there is 'no transparency', the art centre 'has a set of responsibilities to the artists, the executive, and the Registrar of Corporations'.[30] Art centres are incorporated under the Federal Aboriginal Councils and Associations Act (1974) and 'as such members have a range of legal responsibilities and moral obligations which have a bearing on issues of authenticity'.[31] Art centres provide verifiable documentation.

Art consultant Michael Reid advises collectors to 'look for the community art centre stock numbers on the reverse of the canvas. Having found the stock number it is advised to contact the relevant arts community to cross-reference their sale records with your painting'.[32] Art centre archives are 'an extremely important record of the history and evolution of the art centre, the artists and the wider industry' and have 'implications for the entire industry in the light of current debates about authenticity and provenance'[33].

What are the implications for authenticity and provenance? Consider this example: a Rover Thomas painting was offered at auction by Menzies Art Brands in September 2009 as Lot 142 *Dingo Dreaming*, 1996, natural earth pigments and synthetic binders on linen. Provenance: 'Warmun Traditional Artists, Western Australia, Kimberley Art Gallery, Melbourne, cat KA-RT-0104/96'.[34] It had been previously offered at Lawson-Menzies in May 2005 as Lot 199, when its provenance was described as: 'Warmun Arts Centre, WA, Private Collection, USA'.[35] This is a prime example of provenance blurring; implying it was from the Warmun Art Centre, whereas actually it was from Narangunny Art Traders or Warmun Traditional Arts.

At the time of the 2005 auction Adrian Newstead sent a fax of the Warmun Traditional Artists certificate to Warmun Art Centre asserting its association: 'In 1996 there was definitely an art centre in the Warmun community despite its constitutional change in

2005 17:01 0292515665 LAWSON-MENZIES PAGE 01

Warmun Traditional Artists

Catalogue Number : RT0104

Artist Name : Rover Thomas

Age : 70 years

Language : Lakatja-Wangkagungka

Sub Section : Joolama

Artist Background :

Born in the desert region of the Warburton Ranges, at a place called " Three Wells" on the community of Jigalong, as a young boy Rover hunted and gathered the desert food with his Father and family.
"Gudiyas" (white men) would roam and "take" young boys for work on Kimberley cattle stations, Rover was one of these boys, brought to Texas Downs where he learnt about fencing and droving and here he underwent tribal initiation and was accepted as one of the Kija people of "Warramun" (Warmun).

Artwork Name :"Baba" (Dogs)

Image Id(s) : RT0104

Date Completed : 5/7/96

Size :140/100cm.

Medium : Ochre on Canvas

Artwork Story :

Rover depicts a scene from his days as a desert wanderer, Mother and baby dingoes and the well-worn tracks made as they play and hunt.

COPYRIGHT FOR BOTH PAINTING AND TEXT REMAINS WITH WARMUN ARTISTS AND MAY NOT BE REPRODUCED WITHOUT PERMISSION.

Price : $

Figure 4.9: Faxed certificate sent to Warmun Art Centre

1998'.[36] The certificate attached with the fax is interesting reading. Under the heading 'Artist Background', it claims that Rover Thomas was born at a place called 'Three wells on the community of Jigalong' and taken by 'Gudiyas (white men) as young boy to work on Texas Downs, where he learnt about fencing and droving and…underwent tribal initiation and was accepted as one of the Kija people of Warramun (Warmun)'. This mix of half-truths and complete fabrications is an example of how poor and unreliable the documentation that comes from these sources can be. Warmun Art Centre declined to provide a certificate. The painting did not sell and immediately after, in October 2009, it was offered on the internet auction sites ebay and Gumtree as an:

> amazing work...huge...superb provenance...painted for Warmun Traditional Artists – the predecessor of the Warmun Art Centre (eg. Sotheby's regularly sells Rover paintings from both these organisations). Three certificates (1) Warmum Traditional Artists (2) Lawson-Menzies signed by one of Australia's leading Aboriginal art experts and (3) Kimberley Art, signed by director, Peter Harrison.

Three certificates but not enough, as Adrian Newstead knew. He wanted a certificate from the only certificate-issuing entity with the credibility and authority to implicitly trump the other three, the community owned and operated art centre.

Notes

1 F. Kofod, 'My Relations, My Country – Language, Identity and Land in the East Kimberley of Western Australia', *Proceedings of the 7th Foundation for Endangered Languages Conference*, Broome, 2003, p. 2.

2 A. Newstead, *The Dealer is the Devil: an Insider's History of the Aboriginal Art Trade*, Brandl and Schlesinger, Sydney, 2014.

3 M. Neale, *Yiribana*, Art Gallery of New South Wales, Sydney, 1994, pp. 74–5.

4 This is on page 2 of Roba Themes and Stories (c. 1993).

5 'Lot 39: *Ngarin Janu Place* (1995)', *Lawson-Menzies Catalogue, Aboriginal Art, Sydney 14 November 2007*, auction catalogue, Sydney, 2007, p. 43.

6 M. Neale, *Yiribana*, p. 232.

7 ibid., p. 74.

8 'Lot 20: Rover Thomas, *Willy Willy* (1989)', *Aboriginal Art Auction, Sotheby's, Melbourne, 26 June 2000*, auction catalogue, Sotheby's, Sydney, p. 19.

9 Interview with Tom Spender, Melbourne, 2011.

10 P. Vinnicombe, *Women's Sites, Paintings and Places: Warrmarn Community Turkey Creek (A project with Queenie Mckenzie)*, Aboriginal Affairs

Department, formerly Department of Aboriginal Sites, Western Australian Museum, Perth, 1995–6, p. 2.

11 ibid., p. 3.

12 S. Georgeff, 'Kimberley Painters in Legal Bind', *The Australian*, 14 August 1998, p. 14; J. Healy, 'A Fragile Thing: Marketing Remote Area Aboriginal Art', PhD thesis, The University of Melbourne, 2005.

13 J. Healy, 'A Fragile Thing'.

14 ibid., p. 184.

15 ibid., p. 85.

16 S. Georgeff, 'Kimberley Painters in Legal Bind', p. 14; J. Healy, 'A Fragile Thing', pp. 185–7.

17 S. Georgeff, 'Kimberley Painters in Legal Bind', p. 14.

18 G. Greene, 'Doctors Dispute Agreement signing away artist's rights', *The Age,* 9 June 1998, p. 2.

19 G. Greene, 'Dispute Over Control of Outback Art', *The Age*, 30 May 1998, p. 3.

20 S. Georgeff, 'Kimberley Painters in Legal Bind', p. 14.

21 M. Taylor and T. Brooks, unpublished article sent to *The Age* (then to Jane Yalunga by fax at Warmun), undated, c. June 1998, Warmun Art Centre Archives, Rover Thomas Estate.

22 G. Greene, 'Doctors Dispute Agreement signing away artist's rights', p. 2.

23 A. Moulton, personal communication, Kununurra, 2009.

24 J. Isaacs, *Spirit Country: Contemporary Aboriginal Art*, Melbourne, Hardie Grant Books, 1999, p. 232.

25 T. Klingender, personal communication, 2009; C. Gutteridge, personal communication, 2010.

26 A. Newstead, Aboriginal Art Resource, viewed 29 November 2011, <http://www.aboriginalartresource.com/collecting-aboriginalart/provenance/provenance-index>.

27 F. Wright, *The Art and Craft Centre Story, Volume One Report,* Aboriginal and Torres Strait Islander Commission, Canberra, 1999, p. ix.

28 ibid., pp. 4, 5.

29 ibid., p. 154.

30 ibid., p. 124.

31 K. Dayman, 'Authentication: The role of art centres', *Proceedings of the Art Crime Conference: Protecting Art, Protecting Artists and Protecting Consumer,* Australian Institute of Criminology, Sydney, 1999, p. 3.

32 M. Reid, 'Aboriginal Art', *The Australian Art Market Report*, no. 8, 2003, pp. 22–3.

33 F. Wright, *The Art and Craft Centre Story, Volume One Report,* pp. 91, 175.

34 'Lot 142: Rover Thomas *Dingo Dreaming* (1996)', *Major Fine Art Auction, Menzies Art Brands, Sydney, 23 September 2009*, auction catalogue, Menzies Art Brands, Sydney, p. 127.

35 Lot 199: Rover Thomas *Dingo Dreaming* (1996), *Fine Aboriginal Art, 31 May 2005*, auction catalogue, Lawson Menzies, Sydney.

36 A. Newstead, fax to Warmun Art Centre requesting certificate for painting from Lawson-Menzies on 27 May 2005.

5

NAMARARI AND THE PAPUNYA TULA ARCHIVE: LINKING ART HISTORY AND BIOGRAPHY

Alec O'Halloran

Introduction

In researching the life and art of the accomplished Papunya Tula artist Mick Namarari Tjapaltjarri (c. 1923–98), assembling a *catalogue raisonné* of his work was an essential task. Without it my ultimate aim – a biography of the artist for a doctoral thesis completed in 2013 – would have been impossible. This chapter examines the value and limits of one art centre's archive in assembling a *catalogue raisonné*, and the various ways in which I sought to overcome the limits of the existing archive through my efforts in cataloguing four works. While my analysis may have some general lessons for researchers using art centre archives, each archive is unique, as indeed is each artist whose work it catalogues.

Namarari, a Pintupi man from Australia's Western Desert region, was a founding shareholder of Papunya Tula Artists (PTA) in late 1972 with other senior Aboriginal men at Papunya. Enthusiastically assisted by Geoffrey Bardon and others, Namarari began painting commercially in 1971 and continued until his passing in 1998. His career peaked in the early 1990s when he won three art awards and PTA mounted four solo exhibitions of his work in Melbourne and Sydney.

Like some art historians writing an artist's biography, I never met my subject, Namarari – though this is atypical for recent biographies of Indigenous artists and indeed contemporary artists in general, in which subjects and authors usually collaborate on the project. I did, however, receive vital support from Namarari's relatives, particularly his widow Elizabeth Marks Nakamarra, a Kintore resident. As well, various art centre workers and others who knew Namarari were most helpful, especially PTA staff (working through 1973–98). They were key informants regarding Namarari's life and art, with the majority of their knowledge being 'in their heads' not 'in the archives'. Individuals of particular interest were those who had witnessed Namarari painting. They could comment on his style and techniques and share insights into his character, and therefore offer links between practice and personality. Like many art historians writing an artist's biography, I relied on disparate sources, including oral histories and interviews ('the people who were there'); provenance records, art exhibition and auction catalogues; anthropological studies, language dictionaries and translators' expertise; fieldwork including community and site visits; documents, maps, films and photographs, and access to existing archival and reference materials.

The main archive for my research is that of PTA. However, one of the first lessons I learnt is that archival research requires a triangulation of information gleaned from a variety of sources. Invariably art historians rely on archives that were not established to aid the work of art history. This is the case with the PTA archive, which was established primarily as a record of commercial transactions. This is a record of paintings that entered its business. Each is identified by a short description that identifies the artist, the dimensions of the painting, its subject and (usually) its look – for many years in the form of a diagrammatic sketch. In this respect the PTA archive was no more than a gateway for what was, for me, a much longer journey. Perhaps this is one reason why

I am the first researcher to utilise it for the purposes of preparing a *catalogue raisonné* even though PTA's records go back to 1972.

Because the PTA archive was assembled for reasons quite different from my purposes, I had to supplement its information to construct, in effect, my own purpose-built archive. In this case I had a range of other archives from which to draw, among the most valuable being art auction records through the period 1995–2014. These provide good images of PTA paintings on the secondary market and pre-PTA Papunya paintings with a variety of documentation from various vendors, plus numerous works that Namarari painted for several private dealers, particularly in the 1990s when he became a sought-after artist. Many public and private collections hold Namarari's work and the documentation and images of those paintings is exceptionally helpful in assembling a *catalogue raisonné*. Exhibition catalogues and lists that include Namarari's paintings are another aid in tracing the distribution of paintings. Galleries that regularly displayed his PTA work, notably Gallery Gabrielle Pizzi in Melbourne and Utopia Art Sydney in Sydney in the 1980s and 1990s, were immediate sources of images that were already numbered or could be matched with their unique PTA number and then entered confidently into the database.

The PTA Archive and Mick Namarari

PTA's archival materials are held in its Alice Springs office and at the Art Gallery of New South Wales's Library in Sydney. PTA uses an excellent numbering system for artworks and each Namarari painting has a unique number, using a format introduced by Peter Fannin in 1973 (see Case Two, below).[1] Photographs of paintings were usually not taken so the search continues for images of many works that might be in Australia or overseas. PTA staff recorded a field note in addition to assigning a number when collecting a work, following on from Bardon's annotated diagrams practice.[2] Altogether this formed the basis for issuing a certificate (for the purchaser) for virtually all Namarari's paintings in the period 1973 to 1998. PTA's record for each painting usually includes the site and/or story, dimensions, month/year of production and medium. Archival searches often stimulated follow-up with individuals or organisations to find out more about the production of paintings or annotation details. In several instances minor corrections were possible, such as a painting's number or the identification of a site name. With a dual focus on Namarari's life story and art career I utilised individual artwork records for numerous topics of enquiry, including: the date and place of production; the materials used; subject matter; how the information was recorded and the language/s used; the presence of anecdotes, incidental notes, diagrams or photographs with original records; and later, sales and exhibition history, and so on. Individual records often indicated where a painting was executed, thereby showing where Namarari was living at the time. By linking written records to interview accounts (of Namarari and his relatives, PTA and other community staff) I produced a 'timeline of residency', a key aspect of biographical research. Namarari moved around frequently, particularly through the 1970s and early 1980s. For example, when Namarari resided at the Blackwater, Haasts Bluff and Browns Bore outstations in the early to mid-1970s, his output dropped. Why? Because PTA staff, based in Alice Springs with limited mobility, had difficulty reaching him to provide materials and collect completed work.

Namarari and other PTA artists produced thousands of paintings in numerous locations, beginning with Papunya.[3] The assembly of a *catalogue raisonné* begins with compiling a preliminary list of the artist's paintings in some order. My task was to compile such a list with two objectives at the outset: how many paintings did Namarari do at Papunya during 1971–72, and how many did he produce for Papunya Tula between 1973 and 1998? My research priority is Namarari's pre-PTA paintings at Papunya (1971–72) and his PTA paintings (1973–98). I noted but do not aim to list all the works he did for private dealers and alternate outlets, with the exception of paintings for Geoffrey Bardon because of the relationship they formed in 1971. So it is that I classified Namarari's works with the following provenances:

Papunya, 1971–2

A Stuart Art Centre (SAC) Consignments 1 to 20

A1 In SAC record

A2 Not confirmed in SAC record (usually have a cons. #19 or #20 number)

B Non-consigned paintings

B1 Direct sale by artist to buyer (frequently Bardon)

B2 Sale by agent to third party

Sub-total = 130

1973–98

C Papunya Tula Artists

Sub-total = 591

D Non-PTA

D1a Direct sale by artist

D1b Gift of artist to recipient

D1c Exchange by artist with recipient for goods/services

D2 Warumpi Arts, Papunya

D3a Private dealer/agent

D3b Commercial gallery – Alice Springs

D3c Commercial gallery – metropolitan

Sub-total = unknown

Total of known works = 721

There are numerous sub-sets of Namarari's 1971–72 paintings. His post-1973 paintings are separated into PTA or non-PTA provenance categories. The total of 721 paintings by Namarari for 1971–98 excludes non-PTA works for the period 1973–98 and is not exhaustive because additional paintings from 1971–2 may yet surface. Untraced works are mostly those he sold directly to a buyer for which no written record was made. My research indicates that most of the non-PTA works were produced in and around Alice Springs (especially in the mid-1990s), with fewer at Kintore, Mt Liebig, Haasts Bluff and Papunya.

Many, but not all, of his 1971–2 paintings were consigned from Papunya to the Stuart Art Centre (SAC), a commercial gallery in Alice Springs, with the balance being sold at Papunya. His non-PTA works post-1973 fell into numerous categories. These include direct sales by the artist; a gift from the artist; an exchange by the artist for goods or services; work for another Aboriginal-owned centre at Papunya, Warumpi Arts; paintings for private dealers; and work offered by commercial galleries that was secured by the gallery directly from Namarari or purchased from private dealers and placed in the gallery for sale. There is no formal compilation of paintings that passed directly from the artist to individual recipients and non-PTA outlets. I gathered some stories about such activity for his biography, and some such works have reappeared in auctions.

The Four case studies

Case 1

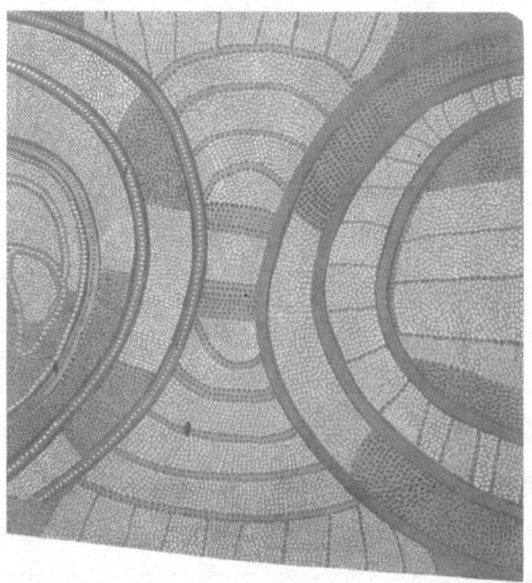

Figure 5.1: Mick Namarari Tjapaltjarri, Kangaroos sleeping, grass in the rocks, *painting #19123A, 1972, synthetic polymer paint on composition board, 53 cm × 46 cm, irregular. © Estate of the artist licensed by Aboriginal Artists Agency Ltd.*

Sotheby's listed this work for sale in its October 2008 Sydney auction (Fig. 5.1).[4] I drew on three main sources of information to investigate this work's provenance: the painting itself, a PTA art adviser, and the PTA archive. The illustrated Sotheby's catalogue entry offered this description of the painting:

> Mick Namarari Tjapaltjarri circa 1926–1998
> Kangaroos sleeping, grass in the rocks
> Bears artist's name 'Mick Jab' (sic) and catalogue number 19123A and inscribed in Peter Fannin's hand 'Kangaroo's Sleeping: Grass in the Rocks – MN' on the reverse.
> Synthetic polymer paint on composition board.
> 57.5 by 54.5 (irregular)

Provenance
Painted at Papunya in September–October 1972
Margaret Carnegie, Melbourne
Gallery Gabrielle Pizzi
Sir James and Lady Cruthers Collection, Perth

My examination of the back of the painting (the typical rough texture of masonite) revealed that the details were written irregularly with some elements 'upside down' or at an angle to the others, and the writing appears to be the handiwork of at least two individuals. The use of masonite sheeting preceded the introduction by Fannin of larger sections of thicker chipboard, which is the subject of Case 2. The actual details on the back of the painting are:

40089679/3PRGK
Kangaroos sleeping: Grass in the rocks MN
Kangaroos sleeping
Grass in the rocks
MICK JAB
19123A

I noted that '40089679/3PRGK' is written on a white label affixed near a corner; the phrases about the kangaroos and grass seems to be written with a black texta pen; the number '19123' and the name 'MICK JAB' are each written in bold using white chalk; and the number '19123' has the capital letter 'A' added in pencil after the '3', so the number then reads as '19123A'. When I approached PTA's art adviser (late 1972 to 1975) Peter Fannin for further information on the painting, he recalled the particular painting and generously responded to my requests. Neither Fannin nor any other source knew what the number '40089679/PRGK' might relate to. This is an extract from Fannin's reply:

> What a superb painting! But the auction blurb-writer wasn't too good…at identifying Peter Fannin's hand. In Sept '72 we were hoping Geoff would return. Consignments were being handled by Pastor Petering, Pat Hogan and Laurie Owens. My era starts with initials and date numbers about November that year. [5]

Fannin also considered the writing on the back of the painting. His reply signals a range of matters, including incidental details of interest to a biographer or historian:

> It is possible that I did indeed get those remarks from Mick – who was my particular friend, and for some reason noted them on the back. Geoff left the artists with huge sheets of masonite and a saw and Laurie was regarding painting as a make-work activity – for which he was paying them a few dollars a board. When I took over I sold these off +/- at cost. I tried to get storys [sic] – but the artists (particularly Kaapa) were keen to press on and get better money being offered by Aboriginal Arts Board under Bob Edwards. [6]

My pursuit of detail is required here because many paintings were produced at Papunya in the 'interregnum' (following Bardon's mid-1972 departure from Papunya) and their provenance can be somewhat clouded. The interregnum period aligns in part with the nineteenth and twentieth final consignments of artworks to the SAC. I was in the process of realising that the SAC record for consignments nineteen and twenty was incomplete. In response to a further enquiry Fannin replied:

> I wouldn't have written 'JAB'. I knew very well that Lurija (I use journalistic 'j' for linguist's 'tj') doesn't use 'B'. Laurie Owens' chalking, I'd say. I'd guess he didn't know that 19…meant a Pat Hogan batch; that he'd seen 19122 on a painting and chalked 19123 on this without realising
> 1) That this implied it was from a consignment or
> 2) That there was already a 19123 (if this is the case).[7]

In relation to painting 19123A Fannin made salient points, including: it was not all his handwriting on the back of the board; Namarari may have told him the painting's story; selling paintings ('boards') was very difficult and resulted in their disposal for a few dollars each; different spelling conventions were used by different white individuals; and the consignment numbering system was not failsafe. Fannin also indicated that a painting may have been assigned a consignment number and sent to Alice Springs, only to be returned to Papunya, unsold. It was then no longer a SAC 'consigned painting' and was added to the mounting 'unsold' pile of boards at Papunya.

If that unsold status applied to painting number 19123A then it may have been painted some months before September/October, remaining at Papunya until consigned to Alice Springs but returned around October/November when Fannin was helping out, thereby inheriting both the Bardon/SAC and the Owens/Petering numbering 'systems'. However, I could not locate the number 19123A anywhere in the SAC records, suggesting that this work did not go into Alice Springs, even though it may have been intended for inclusion in consignment number 19 in 1972. Fannin also provided a timely reminder that some artists (for example Kaapa Tjampitjinpa) were keen on sales (cash income) and less interested in the art adviser's need for information ('annotations') for paintings already completed. Fannin advised me separately about his close friendship with Namarari but could shed no further light on the particular painting 19123A.[8]

And so to the third source of information in this case, the PTA archive. PTA's manager transferred some of its records in Alice Springs to the Art Gallery of NSW to facilitate a digitising process. Among numerous boxes there I found tantalising rough pencil sketches in one of the miscellaneous manila folders.[9] The SAC ledger of consigned paintings from 1971–2 is also there – it is the multi-column stock ledger that Pat Hogan maintained. On a single sheet of paper headed '212' top left and '6/12/72' top right is a rough drawing headed '2 Kangaroos'. It compares favourably with the design in painting 19123A, showing two sets of arced lines with shorter lines connecting them. Another sheet has a similar sketch, headed '16/9/72' and 'Mick Jab' with a title 'Bush Tucker'. It also shows two sets of arced lines joined by short lines. The arcs are labelled as 'tracks of porcupine through bush tucker' and the shorter lines are 'creeks', with a note under the drawing adding 'all rest Bush Tucker'. A third sketch is headed 'Oct 72' top left, with '167' top right and 'Mick Jab.' in the centre top. The drawing again shows two sets of arcs joined by short lines across the intervening space. To one side is another single 'arced line', underneath which is written '2 Kangaroos Sleeping. Bush tucker between creeks'.

Altogether, those sketches offer a compelling case to be associated with the painting 19123A. Given Fannin's input (above), the date of the final sketch (October 1972) and the use of the name

'Mick Jab', it is possibly the (rushed) handiwork of Laurie Owens. There are other drawings in the folder so there may have been an attempt in late 1972 (after Bardon's departure) to make some rough sketches of the unsold paintings stockpiled at Papunya. My lingering doubts were finally dispelled by a search of the PTA records on a subsequent trip to Alice Springs – the research into the painting 19123A had by then been spread over more than a year.

On that visit to PTA's office I made a critical finding. In a multi-columned ledger labelled 'Stock Book 1-4-74',[10] I located many numbered paintings that appeared to fall within the interregnum period.[11] The front of the ledger has a hand-written list of artist's names with their initials adjacent – these initials are used throughout the Stock Book alongside the numbers assigned to particular paintings. Mick Namarari Tjapaltjarri is listed with the initials 'MN'. On page 4 of that Stock Book I found this hand-written entry:

19123A MN Kangaroos

Here was the first original unambiguous identification within PTA's records for the artwork. It confirmed the number, the artist and the subject of the painting. It sustained Fannin's recollections (after a gap of some thirty-five years) and corroborated the information published in Sotheby's catalogue. This work had not been listed in the SAC ledger. The PTA Stock Book indicated that it was indeed sold for 'a few dollars'. Finally, I could confirm the painting 19123A as the work of Mick Namarari, having located pivotal details in the archive concerning its provenance.

A key lesson learned was that pursuing the provenance of a single painting is a profitable way to delve into the archive; one never knows what might be unearthed. Discoveries along the way will undoubtedly help with other forays because the archive has become a more familiar place. In this case, several sources were utilised to pull back the veil that shielded the painting's provenance: the auction catalogue, the front and back of the painting itself, an art advisor, the SAC ledger, pencil sketches and a PTA stock book. Additionally, the research shone some light on how the painting entered the market and confirmed that various individuals were actively involved, thereby supporting Namarari's endeavours to become an income-earning artist at Papunya.

Namarari continued to paint the Two Kangaroo story throughout his career, with nearly forty works identified in PTA's records (1973–98), though the majority were painted between early 1988 and late 1992. The most frequently occurring Two Kangaroo sites in Namarari's paintings are Marnpi and Mintjilpirri, with Watukarri, Ngatuti and Lingakurra on fewer occasions.[12]

Case 2

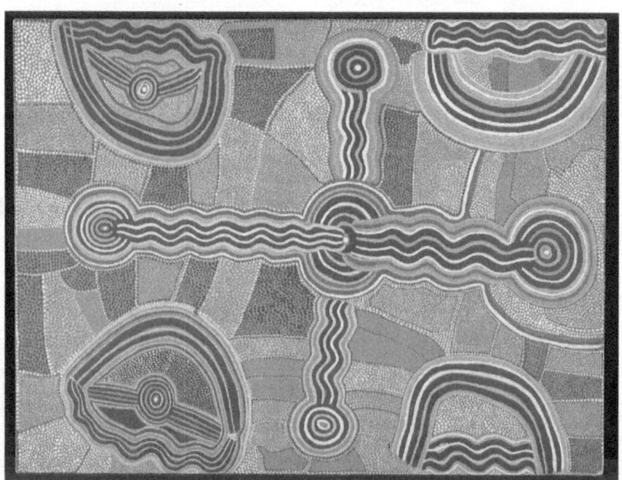

Figure 5.2: Mick Namarari Tjapaltjarri, Mingarjara corroboree or Possums come home, *MN731154, 1973, synthetic polymer paint on chipboard, 123 cm × 91 cm. © Estate of the artist licensed by Aboriginal Artists Agency Ltd.*

Early in Fannin's employment he introduced larger boards ('chipboard') to PTA's artists, only one of which has been located as the work of Namarari (Fig. 5.2). In 1973 he also instituted a new (and excellent) numbering system, which PTA staff use to this day. The format takes the artist's initials, the year and month of production, and adds a final number. For example, the painting here, 'MN731154', is by Mick Namarari (MN), from 1973 (73), in the month of November (11), and is one of at least fifty-four (54) paintings documented that month. All Namarari paintings produced under the PTA banner are documented using that system.[13]

This late 1973 example has been held in the Australian Museum (AM) collection since 1978 and has not been exhibited. The Australian Museum Card states its title (as above) and adds that it is a 'Ground painting on chipboard', with dimensions of 123 x 91 cm.[14] However, the AM card offers no further description of Namarari's intricate design of roundels, spherical objects, interconnecting wavy lines and dotted infill. The impressive composition is carefully executed with fine line work and dotting throughout. The palette extends the so-called traditional colours (black, white, red and black) and includes matt black, translucent black, white, red and translucent red, light pink and mid-pink, mid-yellow and bright yellow, yellow-orange and bright orange, olive green, light brown and brown-black and grey. The dotted infill comprises asymmetrical neat patches in a single layer of dots in various colours that are usually bordered with a single line of white dots.

Once again I sought extra information from Peter Fannin, PTA's first art adviser. In our interviews and correspondence he informed me that the 'textured backgrounds were a feature of dot painting and part of what made them sing and sell'.[15] He was certain that Namarari mixed the colours himself and that the Pintupi name for 'Possum is wayuta, whereas Mingatjara is literally "little black ants having"', and he surmised 'I wonder if the note-taker was a bit hurried'. He made a telling comment in response to my question: 'Could the large corner [spherical] objects be bandicoot homes?' adding, 'If Mick wasn't asked at the time we've no way of knowing'. [16] This is a reminder to be wary of speculation concerning a painting's subject matter or iconography unless the artist has been consulted.

Fortunately, Fannin's original documentation for the painting was located by Dick Kimber (a PTA staff member from the mid-1970s).[17] Fannin's 1973 annotation can now guide a fuller description of the image.[18] The elements include the caves where people camped, the flowing water and the indicative ceremonial ornamentation (perhaps body paint). It may or may not represent a ground painting. The *tjukurrpa* reference in the painting is to the *mingatjara*, a small ant-eating animal, and the site is either Marnpi (Namarari's birthplace) or to its east. The lack of information from Namarari thwarts any attempt to interpret the painting further.

The main lesson learned is that it is sometimes individuals who hold particular records that you seek, beyond the confines of the formal physical archive itself. An aspect of the researcher's role is to help bring such items into the archive for future reference. Again, several sources have been relied upon: the collecting institution's record, the painted design itself, two art advisers, and original documentation to capture the artist's description. Also, the best time to annotate paintings is at the time of their production, with the artist, preferably in their own language.

Case 3

Figure 5.3: Mick Namarari Tjapaltjarri, Rain Dreaming at Nyunman, *MN940293, 1994, acrylic on Belgian linen, 183 cm × 152 cm. © Estate of the artist licensed by Aboriginal Artists Agency Ltd.*

This linear composition in shades of pink and yellow was painted by Namarari at Kintore in early 1994 (Fig. 5.3). It remained in one private collection[19] after Namarari's 1994 solo exhibition at Utopia Art Sydney until auctioned in 2013 and acquired by the National Gallery of Australia. The published PTA certificate states 'Nyunman' as the site. However, the original PTA field note recorded at the time of its production reveals an error of transcription, as it states 'Rain Dreaming other side of Nyunman (Tjiterangu) sandhills on either side also spinifex and water in centre'.[20] The correct site is therefore Tjiterangu. Namarari's reference to 'other side of Nyunman' suggests that the site is to the south or east of Nyunman, given the notation was recorded at Kintore. The impact (if any) of that discrepancy is impossible to decipher without the artist's assistance.

This example points to areas where original field notes serve multiple ends. Firstly, they state the subject matter – the Dreaming or *tjukurrpa* origin and/or the site affiliated with the story that the artist is painting. The field notes in the archive can then be searched to locate other Rain Dreaming, or Tjiterangu, paintings. Secondly, the artist might describe aspects of the painted image and how it relates to the *tjukurrpa* or site or its local topography, although in this instance the information is minimal – not even the rain is mentioned (though it is inferred: 'water in centre'). The lesson here is simply that it is useful to check the 'title' or other descriptions of a painting against its original documentation; on occasion small corrections can be noted.

Case 4

Figure 5.4: Mick Namarari Tjapaltjarri, Tjunginpa, *MN980774, 1998, acrylic on Belgian linen, 153 cm × 122 cm. © Estate of the artist licensed by Aboriginal Artists Agency Ltd.*

An objective of an art historian, curator, critic or biographer may be the study of a series of related works by an artist. Two questions arise, the first being conceptual and the second pragmatic: which works constitute a series; and can sufficient examples be located for study? The artist's *catalogue raisonné* helps satisfy these questions, demonstrating its use as a tool for various objectives.

In the case of Namarari's renowned late-career Tjunginpa or Small Mouse paintings, such as the one illustrated here (Fig. 5.4),[21] the quantity is exceptional: he completed fifty-five Tjunginpa paintings from 1990 to 1998.[22] The majority (forty-three) were painted between February 1996 and August 1998 – nearly 50 per cent of his output for that limited period. They ranged in size from PTA's smallest canvases (46 cm x 38 cm) to its near largest (183 cm x 152 cm). During the mid to late 1990s all completed paintings were photographed by PTA's staff, thus for those original field notes there is fortunately an attaching colour image. This is very helpful in identifying possible paintings to study. However, the formal analysis of a painting must be made of the object itself; a photograph on its own does not suffice.

The visual similarity within Tjunginpa imagery suggests its suitability to be taken as a series on the basis of subject, style and palette. Analysis can attend to topics such as the nature of the design or composition, colour, the application of paint, and similarities or variations between paintings. While the curator might focus more on how the paintings are understood as Tjunginpa representations and their aesthetic appeal, the biographer utilises them as a window to the artist's character.

According to Namarari (in PTA field notes), his dots were no more than the mouse's footprints or its food (*kampurrarpa* flowers and berries). In these paintings the dots rarely if ever touch, there are distinct small zones of translucent and opaque dots with patches of densely packed and looser fillings. There is no foreground and background distinction and (virtually) no inadvertent drips. The seeming lack of 'traditional' Western Desert iconography attests to Namarari's inventiveness. However, Namarari had experimented with this imagery of the all-over dotted field as far back as 1982, in his 'Wallaby Dreaming' painting (MN821102), now in the Art Gallery of South Australia collection.

Following his study of Balgo art, John Carty recently summarised the features of abstraction in Western Desert painting as 'outlining, dotting and concentricity', where dotting was an infilling technique.[23] However, Namarari's Tjunginpa dotting is not 'infill'; rather it is the whole painting, where the negative space and the basecoat colour also play a part in achieving the image's visual effect. By comparison, his earlier Kangaroo Sleeping and Mingatjara works (cases 1 & 2, above), do exemplify Carty's deduction:

> The key to understanding the cultural coherence of abstraction in Balgo art (and perhaps in desert art more broadly) is, therefore, to situate the role of iconography, and its declining prominence, within an art historical consciousness of contemporary painting as an emergent and ultimately independent cultural practice, one that is no longer directly or necessarily referential to ritual or ceremonial forms. Within this changing system, the specific aspects of the Dreaming ancestors' activities have become less directly relevant to the discursive production of contemporary art.[24]

There are several lessons in this case. Though the critical source here is the artworks themselves – the painted surface – the art centre records are the essential resource in assembling the artist's *catalogue raisonné*. It is pivotal in identifying related paintings or identifying exceptional paintings for detailed analysis. Related paintings from a given time period can indicate how the artist went about his business day to day. The biographer wants to know: why did Namarari paint so many Tjunginpa works late in his career? It seems to me that he enjoyed himself when painting slowly and without interruption at PTA's premises in Kintore, and he allowed the image to unfold organically as he gradually worked his way around and across the canvas. The Tjunginpa paintings were popular and sold quickly, sustaining Namarari's income for his family and reinforcing his status as a capable provider, even in old age.

Conclusion

The task of assembling a *catalogue raisonné* brings biographical and art historical enquiry into the archive. In turn, research potentially adds new materials to the archive, highlighting the researcher's role in re-ordering extant data into new or different forms. Ideally, future researchers and the art centre's artists and staff will benefit from the legacy of each project that has utilised their archive. The PTA archive is the most significant source of information for the compilation of Namarari's *catalogue raisonné* and for a study of his art practice and career. The *catalogue raisonné* of his PTA art is the first such compilation for any PTA artist utilising its records and may serve as a model for similar projects, especially Namarari's contemporaries. It has provided the basis for a preliminary listing of Namarari's Dreamings or *tjukurrpa* affiliations and related sites. The study of individual paintings is a stimulating activity that pushes the researcher deep and wide – into the official archive and beyond it. Our understanding of Namarari's art practice will be enriched as more of his work is located and becomes available for analysis by curators and art historians, collectors and critics, and of course, biographers.

Through studying the archive over time the researcher learns how to read the records more adeptly, taking into account different recorders' handwriting, or the use of language, or diagrams, or indeed scraps of paper. Though time-consuming, a close study of various materials reveals information or insights that may improve the quality of the public record, little by little. PTA and other art centres or Aboriginal-owned art organisations can determine protocols for the proper usage of their cultural and intellectual property, including archival access guidelines and perhaps fees.

An art centre could consider maintaining a *catalogue raisonné* for each of its artists, for it represents a valuable form of intellectual property and is a pivotal resource for a range of interdisciplinary research interests. A *catalogue raisonné* serves, for example, as an aid in identifying numbers of paintings in given time periods such as output per annum, the number and style of paintings for a given subject, dimensions and use of materials, sales records, exhibition history and so on. It can also serve as a reference for the authentication of particular works. On a larger scale, a coordinated effort to produce a *catalogue raisonné* for several artists within a region could add another dimension to cultural and art historical research across that area.

Paintings from different times in the artist's career can illuminate broader art historical trends. Overall we can now see that the four selected paintings illustrate a broader trajectory within Namarari's practice: a shift in the representation of his chosen subject matter from a ceremonial or ritual affiliation to topographical or nature-inspired associations. What did not change was his meticulous brushwork, attention to detail and dedication to his craft. He was that kind of man.

Notes

1 Peter Fannin was employed by PTA and began in earnest in early 1973. PTA enjoyed the financial backing and moral support of the Aboriginal Arts Board, established in 1973 in Canberra.

2 G. Bardon & J. Bardon, *Papunya, A Place Made after the Story: the beginnings of the Western Desert painting movement,* Miegunyah Press, Melbourne, 2004.

3 See in particular V. Johnson, *Once Upon a Time in Papunya*, University of New South Wales Press, Sydney, 2010; H. Perkins and H. Fink (eds), *Papunya Tula Genesis and Genius,* Art Gallery of New South Wales, Sydney, 2000.

4 'Lot 216', *Aboriginal Art Sydney 20 October 2008*, auction catalogue, Sotheby's, Melbourne, 2009. This painting was subsequently included in the Origins of Western Desert Art: Tjukurrtjanu exhibition at the National Gallery of Victoria and illustrated in J. Ryan and P. Batty, *Origins of Western Desert Art Tjukurrtjanu*, National Gallery of Victoria, Melbourne, 2011, p. 171.

5 Personal communication with P. Fannin, 2008. Fannin's original spelling is kept intact throughout his extracts here.

6 ibid.

7 Personal communication with P. Fannin, 2009.

8 Personal communication with P. Fannin, 2008.

9 Papunya Tula Artists records, Folder 1, 28/28, AGNSW.

10 It was stored in a locked cupboard and brought to my attention by the manager, Paul Sweeney.

11 Stock Book 1-4-74, Papunya Tula Artists, Alice Springs.

12 These are to the south and southeast of Kintore.

13 The artist identification system is not exclusive: for example, Michael Nelson Jagamara and Makinti Napanangka also appear as 'MN' in PTA certificates.

14 Australian Museum Card, provided to author by K. Khan at the Australian Museum, May 2008.

15 Personal communication with P. Fannin, 2011.

16 ibid.

17 I viewed the documents on 26 October 2012 in Alice Springs, and made an audio recording of the written text on each diagram and photographed

(poor quality) each document. Kimber invited me to view the relevant Namarari annotations.

18 In the Dreamtime four families were camped in the cave's rockhole. They dug in and around themselves with bushes evidence of which can still be seen. The corroboree took place as it still does in the area around. [centre] Camp in centre water flowing in from higher holes, [top right] camp at cave in rocks, [middle right] corroboree decoration, [bottom right] people camped in cave, [below diagram] east of Manpi Mingatjara possibly southeast from Sandy Blight.

19 Illustrated in C. and E. Laverty (eds), *Beyond Sacred: Recent paintings from Australia's remote Aboriginal communities*, Hardie Grant Books, Melbourne, 2008, pp. 80–1.

20 PTA archive, original field note for MN940293.

21 Illustrated in H. Perkins and H. Fink (eds), *Papunya Tula Genesis and Genius*, p. 150.

22 Annual output figures identified through my *catalogue raisonné* research.

23 J. Carty, 'Rethinking Western Desert Abstraction', in N. Nadeau (ed), *Crossing Cultures*, exhibition catalogue, Hood Museum of Art, New Hampshire, 2012, pp. 105–18.

24 ibid., p. 108.

PART 2: HISTORIES FROM ARCHIVES

6

JOHNNY WARANGULA TJUPURRULA: HISTORY, LANDSCAPE AND LA NIÑA 1974

John Kean

Johnny Warangula Tjupurrula is a painter's painter.[1] He is exceptional among the twenty or so artists who assembled to create a new form of artistic expression at Papunya in 1971. Geoffrey Bardon worked closely with Warangula, praising the 'special brilliance and enthusiasm [that] make him unique', while noting Warangula's 'intensely personal style of tremulous illusion, and… great visual power'.[2] Curator Judith Ryan counts him 'among the first of the Papunya painters to forge an immersive poetic form of painting that exists on an aesthetic plane'.[3] Warangula's work is highly valued in auction houses and in art museums; though it must be said, the value of his works has not yet returned to the stratospheric heights that saw *Water Dreaming at Kalipinypa* sell for $486,500 to an American collector in late June of 2000.[4]

The Papunya Tula Artists archive provides a rich record of the geographic and mythic representation of this individual artist's *oeuvre*. I will demonstrate, through the examination of the life and early work of Johnny Warangula Tjupurrula, that the utility of art centre records can be enhanced if interpreted in conjunction with broader historic and environmental accounts, as much first-hand information as can be gathered. I will adopt an imaginative approach that attempts to walk in the footsteps of the artist and does not shy away from making intuitive leaps. The art centre archive or indeed any archive is not enough. We need to go where the archive cannot.

This account of the life and early work of Johnny Warangula Tjupurrula has its foundation in the author's experience of working and travelling with the artist.[5] It will also be supported with original annotations, based on interviews with the artist at the point of sale.[6] This documentation will be complemented with a reading of the historical context in which the artist emerged. Moreover, I will argue that an appreciation of the historical moment, when works were created, can enhance the assessment of the artist's intent and provide a basis for comparison with comparable works produced by non-Indigenous artists during the same period.

Myers has examined how Warangula's peer, Uta Uta Tjangala, drew on a profound bond with his totemic landscape for inspiration and expression of self.[7] Although Warangula was a contemporary of Uta Uta, and their country was close (in Western Desert terms), their lived experience was distinctly different. Uta Uta grew into manhood with minimal contact with other cultures.[8] In contrast, Warangula left his country as a child and grew up in Haasts Bluff, where Aboriginal people from three distinct cultural groups interacted with German speaking Lutherans and Arrarnta evangelists.[9]

Warangula's vision was shaped by 'classical' iconography learned in ceremonial settings; however 'Western' media, including Biblical posters of Palestine, cartoons and cowboy culture were also pervasive in mid-twentieth-century Central Australia.[10] As a young man, Warangula was familiar with Albert Namatjira, his work and that of his followers. It will be argued that the framing of the landscape, by the painters of Hermannsburg School, provided an important foundation upon which the Papunya painters would build.

The intercultural environment at Haasts Bluff provided a range of experiences and influences that were absent for men of comparable age, who came into manhood in relative cultural isolation of the Western Desert. Uta Uta Tjangala matured in an environment in which the Dreaming was regarded as a 'Total Social Fact'.[11] In contrast Warangula's formative experiences were defined by intercultural negotiation. So rather than assuming that Warangula's knowledge of country grew solely from the fact of his indigeneity, I will examine aspects of the artist's life, in the context of the broader historic, cultural and environmental influences he experienced.

To begin, I will set the scene by introducing the collective who, in 1972, became shareholders of Papunya Tula Artists Pty. Ltd (PTA). It was Peter Fannin, the first formally employed PTA Art Advisor, who instituted the systematic record keeping system that persists into the present. Fannin's annotations (1973–4) are a primary source for the interpretation for Warangula's paintings from the period.

I will then set out several key events of Warangula's life before he commenced painting at Papunya in 1971. Warangula learned the songs, dances and designs associated with his country at ceremonial camps around Hermannsburg and Haasts Bluff, far to the east of his ancestral homelands. Despite the regard with which he is held as an artist, little has been written about formative experiences that may have affected Warangula's development as an artist. I will trace his movement from the relative isolation of childhood, spent on his ancestral country, to his years as a young adult within the intercultural environment at Haasts Bluff.[12]

The next section will examine the effect that Albert Namatjira and his followers had on Warangula and his peers at Haasts Bluff.

Namatjira created an ideal art for his time – successfully encoding indigenous interests while creating a product that found a ready market with non-Indigenous Australians.[13] His vision also affected the men who founded contemporary Aboriginal art at Papunya. Johnson has recently documented the influence of Namatjira, while resident at Papunya, from 1959.[14] I will argue that such influence is more profound than Johnson recognised, for it commenced at Haasts Bluff in the mid to late 1930s and continued up to, and beyond, Namatjira's incarceration at Papunya.[15]

Having established key elements of the intercultural context in which Warangula became an artist, I will turn to a discussion of a particular series to reveal how his *individual* experience shaped his artist vision. It will be shown that the Dingo Dreamings series (1973) sheds light on Warangula's occupation as a 'dogger'.[16] The historical circumstances in which Warangula came to know country, as travelled in search of dingoes, will be discussed to more precisely identify a source for his inspiration. It will be argued that the Dingo Dreamings series, while set in a 'totemic landscape', can also be read as autobiographical narrative.[17]

Warangula is most renowned for his depiction of the Water/Storm Dreaming.[18] I will examine two sets of the Storm Dreaming country around Kalipinypa. The first series was created as Warangula found his singular painterly voice during the torrential late summer rains of 1972. The second series was painted in November 1974. Significantly, annotations pertaining to these works indicate that they too were created in response to a specific weather event – La Niña of 1974.[19] Accordingly both series will be considered in tandem with rainfall records to investigate the correlation between the sacred subject of Warangula's Storm Dreaming paintings and the actual seasonal conditions experienced as the works were created.

In conclusion, I will establish that Warangula was not alone in drawing inspiration from La Niña, 1974. Acclaimed landscapists John Olsen and Fred Williams were also affected by the dramatic climatic events of the year. While the specific impact on each of these artists is distinct, the abnormally wet conditions that prevailed across the continent provide a serviceable lens through which works by several of Australia's most significant landscape artists can be compared.

Papunya Tula Artists

Warangula was one of the men who commenced painting at Papunya in 1971. He was an original shareholder of PTA, the incorporated company that has been attributed with pioneering contemporary Aboriginal art.[20] Bardon took up the position as art teacher at Papunya in February 1971, and within months had embarked on a number of projects,[21] including facilitating the painting of murals at the local primary school. The Honey Ant Dreaming was selected as the principal subject for the murals. Papunya is a major Dreaming site and the nucleus around which a complex of interrelated Honey Ant songlines converged.[22] Like the spokes in a great wheel, Honey Ant songlines radiated for hundreds of kilometres to and from Papunya, linking the disparate home country of many of the community's residents.[23]

Warangula's paternal uncle, Parta Nananana (or 'Old Bert' as he was known to the authorities), was the senior custodian of a major Honey Ant centre called Tatata, near Ilpili, and his support was instrumental for the creation of the mural.[24] The ceremonies over which Parta presided reveal the actions of the ancestral Honey Ant sire who carried the ceremony from Tatata to Papunya, thence through Anmatyerr land and beyond to Ngkwarlarlanem (where the honey is) in distant Alyawarr country.[25] More significantly, Parta's authority as a Honey Ant boss provided the foundation upon which Warangula and his family could establish themselves within the inner circle of the new intercultural community at Papunya.[26]

On returning to Papunya from holidays in February 1972, Bardon established a painting room at the northern end of the 'old town hall', a Nissen hut in the administrative hub of the community.[27] The formidable edifice continues to symbolise the assimilation policy with an attendant increase in control of Indigenous lives by government, in the post-WWII period. The policy led to the establishment of Papunya and comparable settlements across remote Australia. Paradoxically, the works produced in the old town hall point outwards, towards an ancient and intricate network of sacred sites and songlines that span the continent. Although the artists initially worked without a formalised organisational structure, the old Papunya town hall can be regarded as a precedent for many Aboriginal art centres that have subsequently sprung up across arid Australia.

The winter of 1972 was the apotheosis of the men's painting room. The pressure of servicing up to fifty artists, eager to paint and insistent in their demand for cash, became too much for Bardon, who left the community in August 1972.[28] Despite tensions over payment to artists and the antipathy that he perceived from other European staff, Bardon managed to set in motion a plan for the formalisation of the loose cooperative that he had nurtured.[29] Accordingly, Papunya Tula Artists Pty. Ltd was incorporated in November and the first master of the movement, Kaapa Tjampitjinpa, was elected as its inaugural chairman. Peter Fannin, Bardon's flatmate, had come to know the artists and was coopted as the movement's first paid administrator/art advisor.[30]

Fannin's appointment in December 1972 coincided with the election of a Labor government under the leadership of Gough Whitlam, and the trajectory of Papunya Tula art during the last three decades of the twentieth century mirrored the change of government policy from 'assimilation' to 'self determination'.[31]

Fannin was a botanist and teacher of science at Papunya who brought academic rigour to the position.[32] Importantly, Fannin instituted a cataloguing regime that is still in use. In contrast to Bardon's subjective assessments, Fannin's catalogue entries can be approached with confidence. As a consequence of Fannin's cataloguing regime, paintings produced under the PTA umbrella can (usually) be assigned to a maker, dated to the month and therefore sequenced within that period; attributes that enable the construction of an orderly art history.[33]

The annotations that Fannin developed are foundational texts upon which subsequent PTA documentation has been built.[34] His botanical interest and love of nature informed his communication with artists. Moreover Fannin's scientific training provided a basis upon which he could interpret Indigenous taxonomy, a system that overlays and intersects with the cosmological realm described in the men's paintings.[35] Fannin understood that the artists were painting specific totemic ancestors, whose exploits shaped the contemporary landscape, and whose form is reflected in the plants, animals and natural phenomena of the visible world. Citations dotted throughout Fannin's annotations refer to anthropological texts, and on reading these, one can sense that he is learning on the job, systematically checking accounts offered by artists with evidence in the literature.

Johnny Warangula Tjupurrula

Johnny Warangula Tjupurrula was a passionate and dedicated songman. Documentation of his paintings indicate he held responsibility for a swathe of country, from Kampurarrapa (Mt Russell near Ilpili) to Yipa (near Lake Mackay).[36] He is acclaimed for his depictions of the Water/Storm Dreaming at Kalipinypa. Warangula was a rainmaker and thereby intimately connected with climatic oscillations, from drought to deluge. While the events at Kalipinypa occurred in the distant past, they are, in an ontological sense, connected to the present. Ryan has noted that the 'cycle of masterworks, competed in 1972, coincided with an unusual season of flooding rains and its ensuing regeneration of life'.[37] Warangula drew inspiration for his representation of 'mythological' events from the explosion of growth that followed drenching desert rain. I have also written that the attenuated space and desiccated motifs of his first large work on canvas, *Kampurrarpa* (1975, National Gallery of Victoria), conveys the long, dry interval between rain as 'a more typical experience of the desert – exposed and hot'.[38] Warangula's paintings can therefore be read as indexical of the 'boom and bust' ecology of the Australian heartlands – ostensibly unproductive ecosystems when dry but ready to explode into life when the storm ancestors are triggered.[39] Warangula's great achievement is to animate the union of the Dreaming with the dynamism of contemporary environmental systems to produce landscapes of great vigour.

Warangula's interest in the mosaic patterns of vegetation, growing in response to changing conditions, speaks directly to the work of the finest of Australia's landscape artists, from Eugene von Guerard to John Wolseley. Despite the absence of a horizon, Warangula's paintings can be understood as landscapes. Indeed, his works have previously been compared to his contemporaries, Fred

Williams and John Olsen.[40] Warangula's focus on the ephemeral qualities of vegetation make him exceptional among the founding Papunya Tula artists. But what factors shaped Warangula's imagination and artistic agency?

Contact

Warangula was born at Mitjilpirri at the commencement of a prolonged drought.[41] Western Desert people traditionally relied on a handful of permanent waters in such conditions. Warangula's family depended heavily on Kalipinypa, a 'native well' in sandhill country, and Ilpili, a bountiful spring in the Eherenberg Ranges.[42] Towards the end of the drought, when Warangula and members of his extended family were camped at Ilpili, they were surprised by a caravan of huge, unfamiliar animals. Led by Bob Buck and Ali Mohamet and Mohamet Bux, the camel train formed the advance party of the Mackay Expedition.[43]

After making camp and establishing contact with the resident Pintupi families, Bob Buck's party set about clearing a landing strip to be used as a base for the reconnaissance of an 'unchartered' area through Warangula's country to the north and west of the Eherenberg Ranges.[44] Thus 1930 marked Warangula's contact with non-Aboriginal people and the end of his family's isolation from the globalising forces of the twentieth century.

Having become familiar with the ways of camels, and their attendants, the Ilpili clan where shocked by the appearance of a silver *Walawurru* (Eaglehawk) in the sky directly above their home.[45] According to Warangula, the older men, including his father Ngalpilala Purukulu, attempted to use their power as sorcerers to shoot the aircraft out of the blue. Events became even more discombobulating when the roaring *Walawurru* landed in a cloud of dust, trundled to a halt and an aviator emerged from the belly of the monstrous shining beast. Warangula's family had came face to face with the mechanical miracles of the twentieth century. Soon after, Warangula was among seven 'nikiti' (naked), who were photographed kneeling on a low rise, hands folded shyly in their laps.[46]

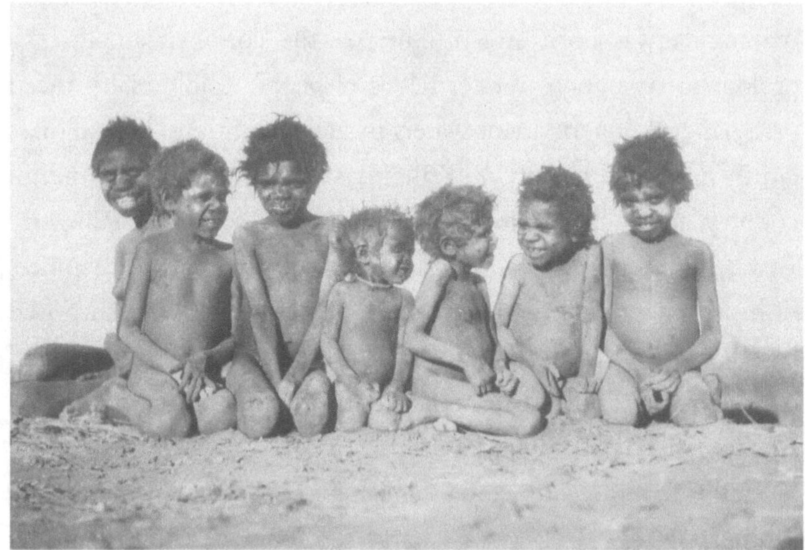

Figure 6.1: Argus *(Melbourne, Victoria), Seven children of the Pinto and Eumo (Pintupi and Yumu) tribes, Warangula far right, c. 1931,* Series 11 – Philip Crosbie Morrison Collection, *MS 13358. State Library of Victoria.*

The Mackay expedition was the first of a series of episodes in a pattern of increased European incursion into the Western Desert, and not all encounters were as benign as had been the case at Ilpili. Cumulatively, these forays had the effect of destabilising the Indigenous population, with many families abandoning their ancestral land.[47] Having tasted flour and sugar, and the promise of a constant supply of sweet food, Warangula's family commenced their exodus from the desert, following a chain of waterplaces, to the Hermannsburg, 270 kilometres to the east. Having seen the mission and becoming habituated to a diet supplemented by 'whitefella' rations, the family was then encouraged to move back west where they would become participants in an ambitious anthropological experiment.

Documenting the 'World's Last Prehistoric Race'[48]

A team from the University of Adelaide was planning an expedition to document what could be learnt of Western Desert people, 'before it was too late'. On hearing of his expertise, the university engaged the lay preacher, Ernest Kramer, to act as 'go between' tasked with collecting a hundred Pintupi, Kukatja, Ngaliya and Lurtija people at Mt Liebig (the westernmost peak of the Western MacDonnell Ranges).[49] While the exact itinerary is difficult to ascertain, the 'Illbilla Mob' joined an increasingly agitated group gathered at the foot of Mt Liebig (Yamunturrngu) in August 1932, where they encountered a research team led by pathologist J. B. Cleland, and a well-provisioned field laboratory.[50]

Characterised in the popular press as the 'World's Last Prehistoric Race', the assembled clans were scrutinised in what was one of the most intensive and intrusive anthropological exercises conducted on the Australian continent. The name, sex, age and 'tribe' of subjects were logged, biometrics collected, bloods taken, senses tested, life-casts made and a series of cognitive tests run. The language, songs and dances of subjects were recorded on audio and film. Still photographs taken at Yamunturrngu capture a bizarrely asymmetrical encounter between earnest scientists and quizzical First Australians.[51] The details of each of the participants have been preserved in the archives of the South Australian Museum (SAM); Warangula's card reads 'No: H 17, Native name Waralngola, Sex ♂, Age: c. 10, Tribe: Pintupi'. [52]

The youngest of the scientists, entomologist Norman B. Tindale, sought to extend the experimental scope of the expedition by encouraging subjects to make drawings. Unaware that he was creating art history, Ngaliplala (estimated to be fifty-five years of age) was one of several senior men who produced drawings with coloured crayons on brown paper; these are the first known inscriptions by Pintupi artists on introduced media.[53] Similarly, older male relatives of Mick Namarari Tjapaltjarri and Charlie Tarawa (Wartuma) Tjungurrayi (who, like Warangula, were assembled at Yamunturrngu), produced drawings for a set of works that now provides an important prelude to the work of the next generation who would go on to become founding artists at Papunya. The 'Illbilla Mob' apparently returned to Hermannsburg via a well-established track through the Western MacDonnell Ranges.

The period of Warangula family's residence at Hermannsburg coincided with the return of T. G. H. Strehlow, an eager young scholar who had grown up at the mission before completing a degree in classics and English literature at the University of Adelaide. Fortuitously for the art historical record, Strehlow documented an incised spearthrower made by Warangula's father. The signs and motifs used by Ngalpilala to depict the passage of the Storm Dreaming from Kalipinypa prefigure the iconography that his son would employ in his celebrated paintings of the same site. Strehlow's detailed interpretation of the meaning of each of the signs, in black ink on the back of the spearthrower, confirms the expression of an environmental narrative, poetically developed in his son's paintings, and has its source in 'classical' iconography. Intriguingly Strehlow's documentation also predicts similar annotations produced by art advisors at Papunya.[54]

Warangula was to pass through initiation into manhood at Hermannsburg. Significantly, Warangula had left his country before participating in *Maliyarra* (post-initiatory ceremonies) that dramatise the creation of the land. These ceremonies are performed to transmit the knowledge upon which the majority of early Papunya Tula paintings are based.[55] The following account of Warangula's life as a young man is intended to fill biographical blanks, during a critical phase, as he learned the songs, iconography and ceremonial sequences upon which he would rely as an artist.

Haasts Bluff

By the winter of 1935, the Ilpili clan had regrouped at Alyalpi, a soakage near the Haasts Bluff. While subsisting as traditional hunter-gatherers, the group also received some support from the nearby Haasts Bluff ration station that had been established as an evangelical outstation of Hermannsburg mission.[56] Gradually the population around the station swelled as further Pintupi, Kukatja, Luritja and Pitjantjatjara groups arrived from the south and west. These groups spoke mutually intelligible dialects of the Western Desert language and shared a common culture. They were joined by Ngaliya and Anmatyerr people, who spoke two distinctly different languages. These groups sought sanctuary at Haasts Bluff, having been forced from customary water places by pastoralists or having fled their homelands fearing the continuation of violence associated with the Coniston Massacre(s).[57] Despite the unfamiliar regimen of manual work, obligatory church attendance and supervision by Arranrnta evangelists, new alliances formed at Haasts Bluff grew.[58]

Namatjira and Warangula

Albert Namatjira, who is normally associated with Hermannsburg, was a regular visitor and occasional resident at Haasts Bluff.[59] Johnny Warangula, who is publically associated with Papunya, lived at Haasts Bluff for a quarter of a century, during the period when Namatjira used the community as a base for his painting expeditions. There is compelling evidence to suggest that Namatjira and Warangula had more in common than has previously been recorded.

The link between Warangula and Namatjira is particularly intriguing, for their paths crossed within months of Warangula leaving his desert homelands. Indeed it was 'Albert' who, as an aspiring evangelist, [60] recognised Warangula's youthful footprint near Mt Liebig. The date of their meeting is of particular significance as it occurred four years before Namatjira learned the principles of watercolour painting from Rex Battarbee. Warangula, who was then only ten years of age, would therefore have been aware of Namatjira and his career throughout his adult life.

Namatjira was a devout Christian, who, having grown up at Hermannsburg Mission, aspired to bring the gospel to 'bush people', such as the 'Illpilla Mob'. In 1932, 'Albert' joined an evangelical party, led by the accomplished bushman and lay preacher Ernst Kramer. [61] On 29 May, when travelling west from Winparku towards Yamunturrngu, Kramer's party became aware of the presence of a group of women and children; an occurrence that Kramer duly recorded 'we eventually pull up in Wotutitara Creek. Albert sees more tracks of natives – this Evening we have a Musical Concert after Reading 14 John glorious Cool still night…' The next morning Kramer directed two of his Arrernte assistants to make contact with the party.[62]

> I send two Boys down to the Creek to follow up the Native Tracks – they came back in 1 hours time & had seen 4 women and 7 children of Illbilla Mob…Hearing this we decided to Visit these natives for the evening & we arrived at the Camping Ground about 5. One track

> the Boys deducted as that of a Boy Called Yaragulla [Warangula] who had been to the Mission, they positively knew it by his peculiar shaped feet. [63]

It is apparent from Kramer's account that the Western Arrarnta evangelists were already aware of Warangula. Perhaps his inquisitive and exuberant personality was already evident, even amongst a group who were coming to terms with their first experience of 'settled' life at the mission.[64]

Namatjira suffered from the privations of Kramer's expedition, losing three kilograms; as a consequence he abandoned his evangelical ambitions. Instead, 'Albert' turned his hand to carving and decorating curios for an emerging tourist market, establishing a reputation as the most committed and ingenious of the Hermannsburg craftsmen.[65]

Painting the Landscape

It was in 1936, when Battarbee returned to Hermannsburg, that Namatjira offered his services as a 'camel-boy', guiding the visiting watercolourist to scenic locations in the Western MacDonnell Ranges, and receiving tuition in the technically demanding medium of watercolour on paper.[66] As a Western Arranrnta man, with strong associations with country to the west of Hermannsburg,[67] Namatjira ensured that Haasts Bluff was on the itinerary.[68]

In the early forties Battarbee returned to Haasts Bluff where he presented an informal exhibition of his paintings, including several portraits of recent migrants from the west. Photographs show Pintupi men, slightly older than Warangula, 'absorbed' in an exhibition in which they, or at least some of their close relatives featured as subjects.[69] Meanwhile Namatjira visited Haasts Bluff regularly, calling on relatives while capturing the familiar majesty of the Belt Range of which Haasts Bluff forms the eastern promontory.[70] Despite having origins in the 'picturesque' tradition, the intellectual property embodied in Namatjira's works would have been subjected to Indigenous patterns of rights and reciprocity. Initially at least, Namatjira only taught his closest relatives to paint.[71] Others would have respected Namatjira's proprietorial rights to his perspectival representation of the landscape, and would not have emulated his approach without permission.

Despite these limitations, Namatjira's framing of scenic locations within the landscape would have a significant impact on how country was perceived by others, especially those, like Warangula, who had not grown up with a familiarity of perspectival representation. Seeing the landscape as painted by Namatjira and his followers must have exerted a profound impact on the young men of Haasts Bluff, for it enabled them to see the landscape through the eyes of the painter, as well as being a manifestation of the action of ancestral heroes from the Dreaming.

Namatjira was a charismatic figure at Haasts Bluff, sought out by Lutheran missionaries and privileged Western visitors alike.[72] Inquisitive young men like Warangula, Wartuma and Namarari would have observed his every move, especially when arriving in a swirl of dust in his impressive American pick-up with, 'ALBERT NAMATJIRA, ARTIST, HERMANNSBURG' emblazoned on the door.[73] The success of the watercolour artists encouraged the 'western tribes', and sensing their interest Battarbee foresaw that 'some of these men may show us *a new form of art*' [author's emphasis].[74] Battarbee's prescient observation, together with considerable circumstantial evidence, can give us confidence that the young men of Haasts Bluff, who would later go on to found contemporary desert art at Papunya, stood over Namatjira's shoulder while he painted at favourite locations near their camps.

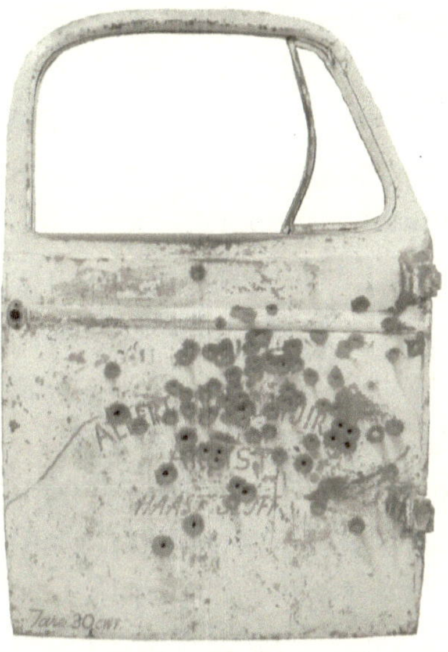

Figure 6.2: Albert Namatjira, Artist, Haasts Bluff, (truck door c. 1955), *Hermannsburg Historical Precinct. The author.*

Moreover, Namatjira and his followers proved that it was possible to earn cash by painting sites of personal significance.[75] Indeed, the life of an independent artist must have appeared a particularly desirable alternative to the backbreaking labour of road building, erecting fences, collecting firewood and gardening, the stock and trade for young men at Haasts Bluff. The influence that the Hermannsburg watercolourists had on the imaginations of the young men of Haasts Bluff is difficult to quantify, and its impact must finally rely on the weight of disparate evidence assembled from a variety of sources.[76]

Johnson has argued that several PTA artists, most notably Kaapa Tjampitjinpa, painted in the Hermannsburg style before 1971.[77] Relationships between watercolour artists, and those of

Papunya Tula, have been eclipsed by the histories of Papunya Tula that emphasise the rise of movement from the wreckage of the assimilationist policies.[78] Yet geographical and historical links between Hermannsburg, Haasts Bluff and Papunya suggest powerful points of contact and continuity linking the landscape tradition with the emergence of 'contemporary art' at Papunya. Gradually, as links between the Hermannsburg School and Papunya Tula emerge, the primacy of Geoffrey Bardon's interventions at Papunya (1971–2) are challenged and a more substantial history of central Australian art, which recognises the extent of Indigenous agency, is beginning to emerge.[79]

A formal analysis of works by Albert's third son, Ewald Namatjira, can, for example, be used to suggest stylistic similarities with Warangula's treatment of vegetation developed a quarter of a century later. The foreground of Ewald Namatjira's *Untitled,* (c. 1947, watercolour on paper, 19 cm x 21 cm, Araluen Arts Centre) is held taut with broad brushstrokes representing sparse shrubs, while the resulting flattened 'field' is animated with dots, before being terminated by a ridge, above which a mountain range is cast in a style more typical of his father. While I am not suggesting that Warangula's style is directly derived from Ewald's percussive landscapes, a comparison of the work of both artists reveals their convergence on a remarkably similar approach to the use of dots to represent desert vegetation.

Because 'Western Desert art' is superficially very different to 'landscape painting', the influence of the Hermannsburg painters is not immediately obvious. Yet, when questioned about landscape painting, Warangula painted *Untitled, (landscape with hills, around Papunya)* (1983, National Gallery of Australia) to demonstrate that he possessed the skills required to produce a passable landscape painting in the style of the Hermannsburg School, albeit with opaque acrylic paint on canvas board.[80] Although not celebrated as such in the literature, Haasts Bluff was the crucible in which vital components for the formation of the contemporary desert art movement were originally mixed, heated and incrementally fused.[81]

Dogging in the Totemic Landscape

It has been shown that the presence of Namatjira and his sons had a powerful formative influence on the aspirations of Warangula and his peers; this section will assess how other aspects of Warangula's lived experience in the 'Haasts Bluff years' informed his later artistic expression. While Warangula may have dreamed of becoming an artist, much of his working life was spent sweating on the major infrastructure projects that determined the course of his people's history. His powerful body was evidence of a lifetime of labour, clearing airstrips, making roads and fences as well as working on construction sites.[82] In 1940, Warangula joined a gang blazing the road from Hermannsburg to Haasts Bluff. Warangula's uncle Parta Nananana was a senior member of the gang.[83] Parta had previously guided Strehlow and Pastor F.W. Albrecht on an exploratory expedition into the Western Desert in the early 1930s, earning a reputation as a vital 'go between' for white authorities and his people.[84] Parta became a resourceful mentor for young Pintupi men, including Warangula, imparting on them the strategic benefits of assisting Europeans while forging a new identity in the cash economy.[85] When I met him in 1977, Parta was a 'pensioner' living at Warangula's camp at Papunya. The men were especially close, a bond likely to have been strengthened out bush when Parta introduced Warangula to sites celebrated in the artist's best-known works.[86]

Commencing with the Dingo Destruction Ordinance of 1924, a government bounty was introduced for dingo 'scalps'.[87] By the mid-1940s, the bounty had risen to £1 per 'scalp', and in an economy based on the exchange of labour for rations, the promise of cash provided the incentive for men to leave their families at Haasts Bluff and go 'dogging' out west.[88] Extended journeys, while notionally in search of dingoes, provided men with the opportunity to visit ancestral sites they had forsaken in previous decades.[89] Although most of what transpired has been lost with the passing of individuals who made these heroic journeys, rare insight into the agency of Aboriginal men, away from the gaze of colonial authorities, can be gleaned by occasional references to 'dogging' in the literature.[90] Food tins discarded by Warangula at Kalipinypa on one of his journeys provide tangible evidence of his presence at the site featured in many of his greatest works.[91] Knowledge of the country, embodied in men of Parta's generation (born in the first decade of the twentieth century), would have been essential to Warangula and his peers' capacity to navigate their ancestral land safely, while observing appropriate protocols at key sites.[92]

Mike Warangula Tjakamarra remembers stories of 'War Time' (WWII) when his father borrowed horses and camels from a friend in Hermannsburg to travel, with his mother, father and uncles, to Ilpili, where they re-established a semi-permanent camp. Tjakamarra's account of his father's frequent travels paints a picture of fluidity, as the people who camped around Haasts Bluff grasped every opportunity to return to their country.[93] Journeys of return to homelands provided an opportunity to visit, maintain and celebrate sites of significance. It was on these visits that senior Lawmen, such as Parta, could pass on their detailed knowledge of the 'totemic landscape' to younger custodians. These were critical experiences for Warangula, Namarari and Wartuma, who had left their country as uninitiated boys before the metaphysical dimension of land was revealed to them in ceremony. Without such journeys, the trajectory of contemporary desert art would have been very different, for the firsthand experience of particular ancestral sites provided the wellspring from which creativity emerged. At a more nuanced level, the experience of traversing country on foot, in a variety of seasons, informed Warangula's treatment of the landscape. Warangula's intimacy with the oscillating conditions of his country is of particular relevance to the discussion of works he created in 1974.

In the late spring and early summer of 1973, Warangula painted a series of six boards that featured sites associated with a Dingo Dreaming songline.[94] Collectively these works tell of the activities of a family of ancestral dingoes across a swathe of country west of the Yamunturrngu (Mt Liebig) to Walungurru (Kintore Range) near the Northern Territory/Western Australian border. The series is of note for several reasons: firstly the paintings focus on Dingo Dreaming sites along a songline rarely encountered in Warangula's *oeuvre*. Secondly, several of the paintings represent land to the south and east of the country for which the artist had ritual responsibility.[95] Why then did Warangula choose this subject at this particular point in time? A clue to the puzzle may be found in Fannin's documentation of *Dingo Dreaming at Talitjarayi* (1973, whereabouts unknown) in which he postulates that it 'is not surprising, then that the dingo pupping season gives us a series of dingo stories'.[96] Fannin was alert to the environmental and ecological nuances of the paintings documented, and his sensitivity directs us to the particular significance of the series.

Myers has written of the intersection of autobiographical and geographic levels in certain paintings by Shorty Lungkarta Tjungurrayi.[97] Whereas Myers focused on the 'revelatory regime' associated with ceremonial knowledge, I argue that the Dingo

Dreaming series is significant as a recollection of Warangula's everyday experience, working in the post-contact cash economy. If interpreted autobiographically, the Dingo Dreamings can be taken as an account of the artist searching for dens during 'the dingo pupping season' to the south of his ancestral country, way out west from Haasts Bluff. The sinuous lines (representing limestone ridges) and paw prints, in works such as *Dingo Camp at Tinki* (1973, private collection), recall his concentration, tracking adult dingoes along a rocky outcrop to pups waiting in the cool of their dens. Warangula's knowledge of dingo procreation and rearing was essential to his work as a 'dogger'. I contend therefore, that while the series was set in Dingo Dreaming country, Warangula was using paint to evoke his *personal experience* within the *totemic landscape* he visited as a 'dogger' in the 1940s and 1950s.

Warangula and the 'Totemic Landscape'

Warangula was the first of the Papunya artists to grasp the potential of using the medium of painting to describe the 'totemic landscape' in pictorial terms that approximate a Western conception of landscape. Prior to Warangula's innovations, the focus of Papunya painting had been on the representation of the ceremonial ground. In 1971, Kaapa had pioneered an approach that called on rudimentary perspective and a variety of Western 'ways of seeing', to frame a ceremonial scene, similar to an ethnographic photographer.[98] This approach was gradually refined and modified to conform to a fixed, bird's-eye view, favoured by the Anmatyerr painters. Alternately, Pintupi artists, including Uta Uta Tjangala, elaborated on 'classical' representations of ancestors and the land they created. Sutton refers to such paintings as 'icons, in the sense that they are typically conventional religious images that emphasise pattern rather than figurative faithfulness to the thing represented'. Seeking to distinguish 'icons' from 'maps' Sutton continues, 'while they embody spatial and other knowledge, [icons] are better described as being constituted by knowledgeable and emotionally rich *performance* rather than simply by a certain kind of [topographical] knowledge per se'.[99] The analysis of early works by the Papunya painters is made more problematic as they are typically multivalent, and resist hermetic classification into convenient Western taxonomies, for as Gell has suggested 'images and maps flow one into the other in mutually related ways'.[100]

Warangula's genius resides in his capacity to intertwine levels of meaning available to senior desert artists, and in so doing create an integrated, embodied and highly animate representation of 'country'. While Warangula's paintings share symbolic elements employed by both Pintupi and Anmatyerr peers, he improvises upon 'classical' iconography to emphasise phenomena perceptible to the uninitiated – swaying fields of desert flowers, burnt ground, even the squishiness of moist land underfoot. Whereas Namatjira uses 'Renaissance' perspective to lead one's eye from the foreground to the horizon, Warangula brings elements forward to the viewer, as painted marks on a flattened picture plane. Although they are representations of specific landscapes, the painterly surfaces of his work resemble the multi-levelled splattering of Jackson Pollock, more than they do the rugged ranges of Hans Heysen.

Kapi pulka, Big Rain

From the beginning of 1972, men whose country was located at all points of the compass shared their songs and stories in the hothouse-conditions of the men's painting room. Their works possess a special energy, derived from the excitement of experimentation, discovery and collaboration. Images by the photojournalist Michael Jensen capture crowded scenes inside the room. Men sit cross-legged painting. Completed boards lean against every surface. The stylistic variety of paintings under production at a single moment is astounding.[101] Roger Benjamin, who used these images to introduce the atelier for *Icons of the Desert* (2009) observed that Jensen's visit coincided with 'a period of very wet weather' in which the 'preponderance of paintings with storms as their theme' could be linked to 'the concurrent rains and storms', suggesting, in parenthesis, that 'it could be argued that the paintings were working to *bring about* the wet'.[102]

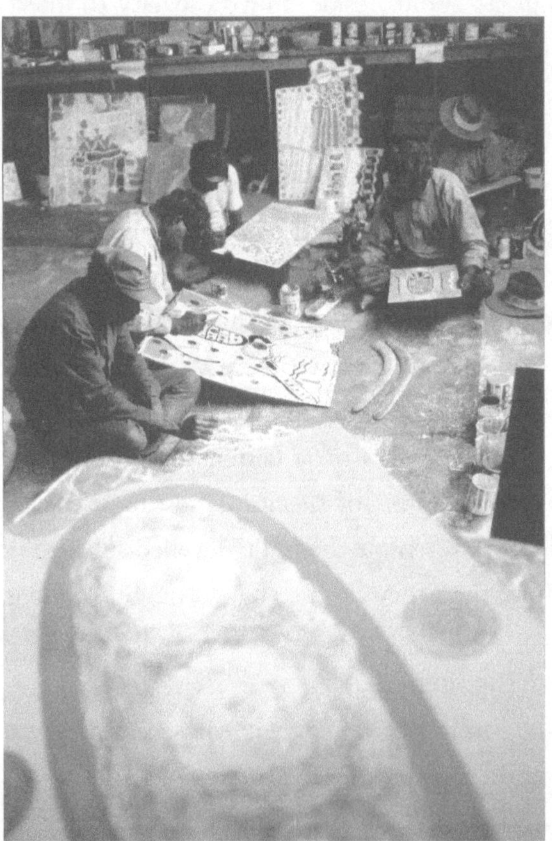

Figure 6.3: Michael Jensen, Untitled, *Indigenous artists Charlie Tarawa (Wartuma) Tjungurrayi, Johnny Warangkula Tjupurrula, Timmy Payungka Tjapangati and Kaapa Mbitjana Tjampitjinpa working at the artist's studio, Papunya, 1972. National Library of Australia (nla.pic-vn3210252).*

One of Jensen's most telling images reveals Warangula sitting adjacent to Kaapa and next to Wartuma and Timmy Tjapangati; the complex, imbricated florets of Clifford Possum Tjapaltjarri's *Honey Ant Ceremony* (1972, Art Gallery of South Australia) fill the foreground. Warangula is painting the *Water Dreaming at Kalipinypa* (1972, John and Barbara Wilkerson Collection).[103] Ever the songman, Warangula has a pair of boomerangs laid out, ready to be clapped in accompaniment to verses from the Water Dreaming – stanzas that are integral to the process of painting.[104]

Jensen's image conveys the physical proximity of the artists and the sense that singing shared songlines drove artistic performance. It also calls to mind Kaapa Tjampitjinpa's account of rainmakers singing up the elements of a storm, a responsibility that he shared with his friend Johnny Warangula Tjupurrula:

> They are making rain, Tjampitjinpa, Tjangala.
> They're singing Tjakamarra, Tjupurrula too.
> After one week you'll see 'im cloud, [from] no cloud you'll see 'im cloud.
> Every way lightning; then big wind from song.
> Start 'im raining now, rain 'e'll come.[105]

Kaapa expresses how men of the Tjampitjinpa, Tjangala, Tjakamarra, Tjupurrula kinship subsections, with custodial rights to sites along the Storm Dreaming songline, share a strong bond, forged as they worked together, in a ceremonial context, to make rain.

Jensen's photographs were taken in July 1972, a few months after Papunya had received the record-breaking 282 millimetres of rain in March.[106] Soil moisture persisted through winter resulting in an excellent season for plants and animals. The deluge bolstered Warangula, and the exuberant paintings he produced in

1972 evoke conditions he visualised far to the west, at Kalipinypa. Arcs, dots and dashes conceal sinuous lines to represent Winpa the lightning ancestor, massing clouds, pelting rain and subsequent floodwaters. The inscribed surface of *Water Dreaming at Kalipinpypa* also reprises the signs and gestures of Ngalpilala's spearthrower depicting the same site. Warangula's masterpiece was just one of a series of highly energised paintings he created as he found his unique lyrical voice. A powerful muse had called on Warangula in the form of the late summer rains. [107]

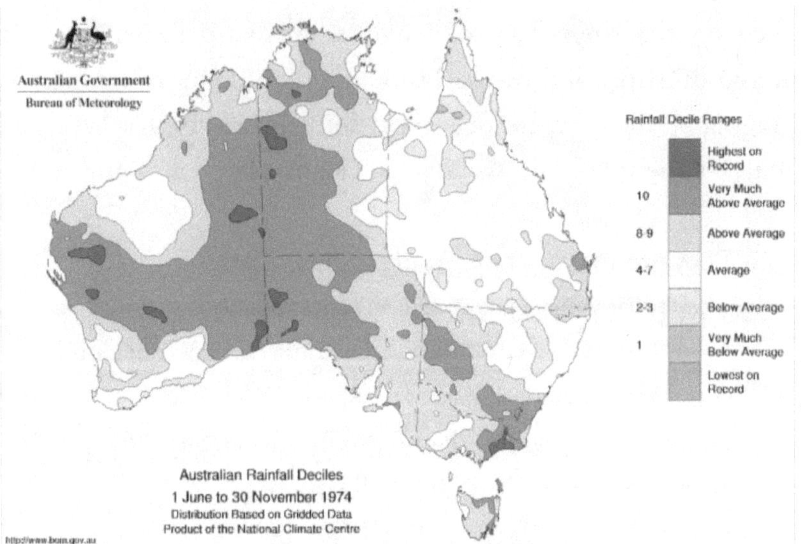

Figure 6.4: National Climate Centre, Rainfall Deciles 1 June to 30 November 1974, *Bureau of Meteorology, (http://www.bom.gov.au).*

The prevailing bars and dashes on the surface of *Water Dreaming at Kalipinypa*, (and their similitude to the incised surface of Ngalipilala's spearthrower) suggests that 'dot painting' was not an inevitable outcome of the invention of contemporary Aboriginal art at Papunya. Rather it was a contingent response, arrived at through a process of consensus that enabled lesser artists to produce marketable work in a recognisable style.

Storm Dreaming Country

I will now turn to a series Warangula painted in November 1974, during the wettest year on record, a period when rainmakers of the Tjampitjinpa, Tjangala, Tjakamarra and Tjupurrula kinship groups would have been well satisfied.[108] Importantly, this series was undertaken as the major stylistic parameters of Papunya Tula painting had coalesced into a familiar form.

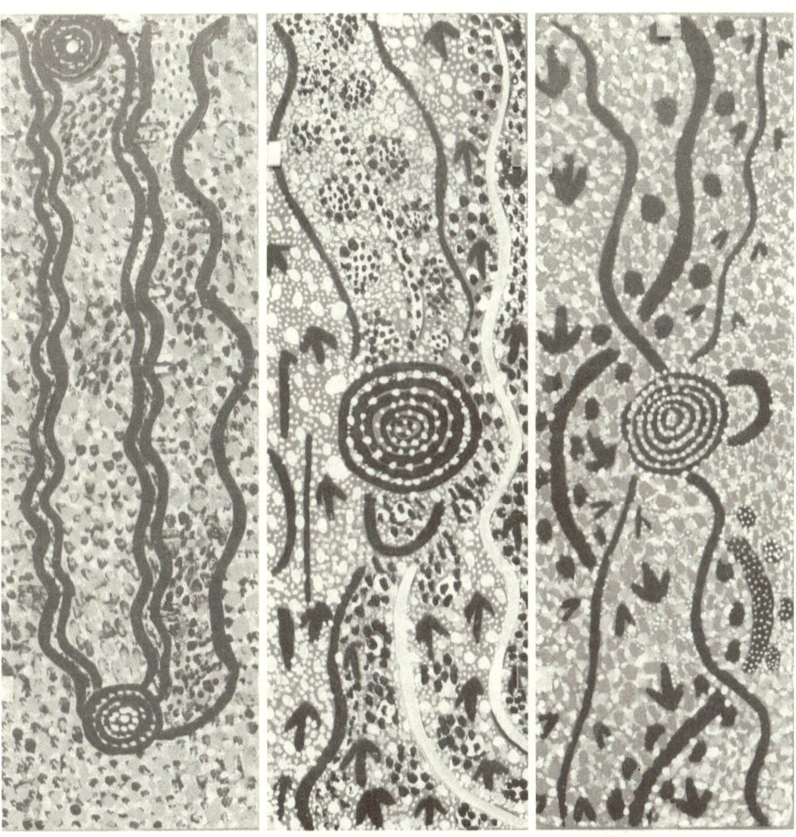

Figure 6.5: Johnny Warangula Tjupurrula, Lightning, Ibis, *JW74004, 1974, acrylic on composition board, 60 cm × 20 cm. South Australian Museum.*

Figure 6.6: Johnny Warangula Tjupurrula, Warrpanji (Kangaroo-rat), *JW74005, 1974, acrylic on composition board, 60 cm × 20 cm. South Australian Museum.*

Figure 6.7: Johnny Warangula Tjupurrula, Lightning, Ibis, *JW74001, 1974, acrylic on composition board, 60 cm × 20 cm. South Australian Museum.*

A powerful La Niña event precipitated a period of extraordinary creativity as Warangula applied the signs associated with the passage of an ancestral storm with unprecedented gusto. Icons that had hummed under dotted veils in 1972 were recast, with calligraphic self-confidence in the foreground of a pulsating visual field, as rain pelted down across the continent. The rains of 1974 had coincided, once again, with a critical juncture in Warangula's artistic development.

During mid to late November 1974, Warangula produced a series of ten small boards; each board was painted with similar materials on roughly the same format (60 cm x 20 cm). The sequence was created swiftly during a period of extremely high rain, even within the terms of this record-breaking year.[109] The paintings trace the development and impact of the storm. Despite their modest scale, they are among the artist's most assured works. The series was later gifted to the South Australian Museum (SAM); however the original documentation was mislaid in the transfer. Now, as a result of search of the PTA archive, the boards and their original documentation can be examined in parallel.

While focused around the effects of the storm, Fannin's documentation reveals that the passage of several associated 'stories' are also envisioned in Storm Dreaming country. In addition to the Storm Dreaming ancestors, Warangula also painted *Lungkata* (Blue Tongue Lizard), *Warrpanji* (Brush-tailed Bettong), Little Green Bird (Budgerigar?), *Nananana* (malevolent human-like ancestors), *Mala* (Rufus Hare Wallaby), *Martinpilangu* (giant dingo-like creature), *Tjakipirri* (Emu), Kalawa (Great Egret),[110] and *Walamilamila* (a water bird with webbed feet). Fannin's documentation notes that several of these ancestral characters were 'frightened' by the dramatic appearance of Winpa (the lightning man) at Kalipinypa.

Seen as a whole, and in association with Fannin's documentation, the series reveals how separate ancestral trails are conceived as being linked through metanarrative – the passage of storm ancestors through Warangula's country.

Fannin's searching annotations, written while the earth was still moist, enable the episodes of this ancestral epic to be (tentatively) viewed in sequence:

> When the lightning ancestor made his first appearance, he frightened many people. Here we see the ibis (?) armed with spear and boomerang [JW74004]. He was frightened. Warrpanji the kangaroo rat (?) was surrounded by friends. He was frightened too [JW74005].
>
> As the Dreaming progressed more water people were created...The design is more typical of lightning than running water. While the two groups of ancestors are separate, they are clearly regarded as related [JW74006].
>
> This is one of a series in which the artist describes the people frightened by lightning when it first appeared. Lightning arose at Kalipinypa. The emu place Wauwuwu is almost a day's walk away. [The painting JW74023 includes a representation of] Walamilamila is a short bird, probably with webbed feet.
>
> This is a typical pair of paintings. The year has been very wet. In the first painting [JW74032] the storm is gathering. In the second [JW74033] there is water flowing everywhere – a very familiar scene over the last year![111]

Warangula's paintings trace the development of the storm, as its individual elements are unleashed. Clouds, rain, hail, flood-waters and rainbows are 'sung up' and multiplied by Winpa, the Lightning Man and 'boss' of the storm. Winpa's ferocity 'frightens' other ancestors, whose journeys have placed them in the vicinity of Kalipinypa. Other ancestors are attracted to the proliferation of foods that emerge from the barren ground after the scouring effects of the flood. Winpa's influence is expansive and profound; it extends well beyond the direct line of travel of the Storm Dreaming ancestors from Kalipinypa through Karrku to Impalu and beyond.[112]

The Storm Dreaming narrative at Kalipinypa is comparable to the destructive force of the Biblical Flood unleashed by a wrathful God. Warangula's paintings describe the environmental succession that follows an actual flood in the Australian desert, without the weight of sin, which premeditated God to create the Great Flood of *The Book of Genesis*.

Warangula's 1974 Storm Dreaming series is particularly compelling for it reveals the artist's conception of his country as an integrated, ecologically complex whole, rather than as a series of discreet landmarks created by distinct ancestral heroes. The worldview, implicit in Warangula's Storm Dreaming series, finds a more pedagogical form in David Corby Tjapaltjarri, *Landscape with figures* (1979, Flinders University Art Museum). The youngest of the founding Papunya Tula artists, Corby was Warangula's son-in-law and countryman. He was an excellent cross-cultural communicator with a powerful grasp of both European and Indigenous visual conventions. While artist in residence at Flinders University, Corby produced a series of seven drawings, one of which deftly communicates a synoptic understanding of country, a mind map in four dimensions. Megaw explains:

> European conventions are used to help explain a particular story. The artist's ancestors travelled though emu and wallaby country camping at waterholes. Above them flew budgerigars and in the distance was the waterhole located in witchetty grub country.[113]

Corby uses an oblique perspective to communicate the interrelatedness of songlines, through time, over the land, below its surface and through the sky above. His diagrammatic image, intended for the instruction of a university professor, is a succinct representation of the spatial realm that underpins much desert art. It is also worth noting how Corby seamlessly integrates perspectival projection, characteristic of the landscape tradition, with planar representation of tracks and traces inherent to 'classical' desert idioms.

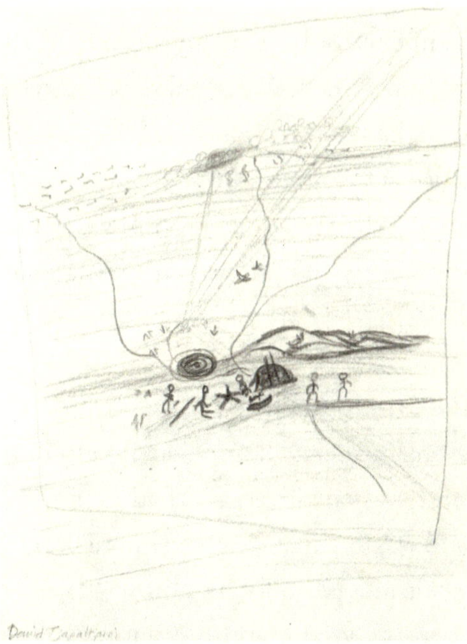

Figure 6.8: David Corby Tjapaltjarri, Untitled, *1979, pencil on paper, 37.5 cm × 28.1 cm, gift of the artist, FUAM collection (Flinders University). © estate of the artist licensed by Aboriginal Artists Agency Ltd.*

Our understanding of the intent of Indigenous artists can narrow when documentation, completed at a pace by highly pressured field officers, is taken as literal interpretation. The poetic nuance and spatial scope of an artist's intent was rarely recorded by PTA field officers, including myself, who typically focused on the meaning of particular 'signs' and 'icons' of the painting at hand. Such signs often refer to the actions of a particular ancestor or the topographical features of a site, but as we have seen in Warangula's Storm Dreaming series they are not inscribed upon a *tabula rasa*.

It has been shown that Warangula's dotted fields infer *country* through which multiple ancestors have traversed – ancestors such as Winpa who sung-up the rain, or Warrpanji, whose travels were affected by the fear of Winpa, as well as Tjakapirri (Emu) who came to find fruits that emerged after the deluge. We are fortunate that Fannin documented paintings with an awareness of their ecological intent, for his gleanings can be used to interrogate the various levels at which Warangula's paintings operate. It has been shown that the examination of a series of related works, in this case the Storm Dreamings, in association with Fannin's documentation, enables otherwise opaque links between paintings to be understood as subtly interwoven, at thematic, geographic and temporal levels.[114]

Landscape and Fruitfulness

Warangula was an inveterate storyteller in addition to his gifts as a lyrical painter. I was employed as art advisor and coordinator for PTA, 1977–9 and was fortunate to get to know Warangula as an artist and mentor, albeit in a period when his style was well established and relatively consistent, as compared with the first three years of experimentation.[115] Documenting Warangula's painting was a joy, for he would deliver an extended story, in a well-rehearsed form.

I watched entranced, as Warangula 'performed', scribbled notes, while attempting to follow his extravagant gestures and the signs on the canvas to which he referred. Warangula would routinely list food plants, declaiming 'kampurrarpa, wanki, wilkalpa, ipalu, namapurru',[116] then conclude with a wave of his arm towards his homeland and the exclamation 'Wampa!', by which he meant 'It is such good country, I can't tell you how many different types of fruits there are!'

It is worth recalling that Warangula's most lasting invention was the use of dots, to represent vegetation.[117] Subtle variation in the viscosity and colour of his dots, in combination with the direction of attack of his brush, result in inflected fields that call to mind the impressionism of Monet or Pissarro. Although there is no straightforward one-to-one relationship between particular coloured dots and a specific species of plant (Warangula was more spontaneous than that), the extent to which he put emphasis on the diversity of vegetation at a particular locale is exceptional among founding Papunya Tula artists.

Documentation, prepared by Fannin, maps the development of Warangula's work through a period of experimentation and consolidation. Their shared interest in plants, and the stories behind their distribution, resulted in a rich ethnobotanical archive that can only be partially examined within the context of the current essay. Significantly, most of Fannin's annotations include extensive lists of food plants, prompting questions of causation: 'Was it Fannin's botanical interest that made him attentive to Warangula's representation of plants?' or 'Did Fannin's interest incite Warangula to place more emphasis on plants?'

While the nature of their collaboration is difficult to determine, an examination of the PTA records confirms that the record-breaking rainfall of 1974 corresponds with a period of intense activity for Warangula. There can be no doubt that Fannin facilitated his output in the face of the competing demands of other artists, all of whom were clamouring for resources in the habitually cash-strapped organisation.[118] Once again it is difficult to attribute causation. 'Was it Warangula's overwhelming urge to paint that fuelled his comparatively prodigious output?' Or, 'Was it Fannin's appreciation that compelled him to provide a continuous flow of materials to Warangula in preference to other artists?'

These questions are not raised to interrogate the vexed relationship between artist and art advisor, for that has been discussed elsewhere,[119] rather to explore Warangula's artistic intention, and, in the process, argue for his recognition as a landscape artist, over and above his status as a consummate exemplar of Western Desert art.

The collaboration between the artist and botanist, Warangula and Fannin, is a telling example of the complementary skills that science and art can bring to a holistic understanding of the landscape. Rather than seeing the relationship of Warangula and Fannin as an encounter between the incommensurate desires of an art advisor and an artist, their relationship, at least in the case of the La Niña paintings, can be viewed as a prescient collaboration, resulting in an evocation of climatic variability in the driest of all continents – a poetic expression of 'deep time'.

La Niña 1974 – Painting a Continent in Flood

The phenomenon of scientists collaborating with artists in the 'bush' has grown incrementally since the mid-1970s.[120] Wondrously, while Warangula envisioned the flood and its aftermath at Kalipinypa, the naturalist Vincent Serventy asked John Olsen to accompany him to visit Lake Eyre in flood.[121] The experience was an epiphany for Olsen:

> Vin Serventy has asked me to form a party to go with him to Lake Eyre, the largest lake in Australia, which lies in remote and desolate country, 550 kilometres north of Adelaide. Extraordinary things are happening there. What is usually an empty, salt-encrusted basin has now filled with water, for only the second time since white settlement (the previous occasion being 1951–52). The present floods are the heaviest in 500 years, the scientists say, they have filled Lake Eyre for a distance of 175 kilometres, or three times the size of Sydney Harbour. Life is burgeoning everywhere around this. The Void has put forth. I feel there are great possibilities for my work there.[122]

Olsen continues with a word picture of Lake Eyre that could just as well be used to describe Warangula's Water Dreaming series:

> The lake is boiling with animal, bird and fish life, whose existence is precariously balanced on the rising and falling of the water. For Vin it is a naturalist's paradise – a copious microcosm, the whole cycle of life and death. On and around the lake there are thousands of silver gulls, black kites, cormorants, pink-eared ducks, chats and black swans, emus, dingoes and big red kangaroos. In the rivers and creeks there are further thousands upon thousands of living things: frogs, dragonflies, fish, water beetles – it goes on. And then there are the wildflowers in bloom…[123]

Olsen's overview of the event was enhanced during a series of aerial surveys in a light plane, from where he observed parallel patterns of vegetation, white dots of nesting water birds and the sinuous, sweeping forms of channels and lines left by receding water.[124] Warangula also conceived of the land in aerial terms, for he came from a culture in which one's location is continually monitored and reinforced in relation to visible topography, as well as by the position of known landforms beyond the visible horizon.[125]

The sketches and etchings Olsen created of Lake Eyre in flood and Warangula's *Water Dreaming* series of November 1974 were produced in response to the same climatic event, albeit in different Australian deserts. Not since Namatjira and Battarbee sat side-by-side, painting the same landscape, had there been an instance when the work of a 'black' and a 'white' painter could be so fruitfully compared.

Both Warangula and Olsen are intuitive artists, whose brush-strokes come from the core of their bodies to produce a generous supple line that infers subtle topographic variation. Generous of spirit, neither artist was persuaded by minimalism; rather their surfaces are full of incident and visual intrigue. Both are impressed by abundance, whether expressed by Olsen in 'paella' paintings or by Warangula in his joyful evocation of bush tucker growing profusely after rain. Despite their work being propelled by undisguised *joie de vivre*, both artists are alert to the deeper significance of food as essential for the 'whole cycle of life and death'.[126]

> I draw studies of insects, animals and birds, that will eventually be realised as prints and watercolours. My devotion to Chinese art and philosophy finds fulfilment in this experience. Nothing too small or too strange should escape my attention – an insect's wing, the leap of a frog, the flight patterns of dragonflies. They all induce poetic rapture. [127]

Olsen was profoundly affected by the scale of the flood at Lake Eyre, the energy evident in the microcosm of a frog's leap becoming a metaphor for an expression of wild joy that would continue to inform his painted gesture and symbolic vocabulary.

In contrast to Olsen's exuberance, Fred Williams epitomises restraint. While enjoying wine and cheese as much as his Sydney colleague, he embodied the more sedate side of post WWII Melbourne, aligning himself with the aesthetic rigours of the Western academic tradition. Williams painted slowly, patiently assembling a lexicon of painted marks, testing compositions, and refining his technique, serious efforts that culminated in major works painted with oil on canvas. A reluctant traveller, Williams was nevertheless affected by those places he visited. In 1967, he was profoundly impressed by the landscape around Tibooburra in western New South Wales, for it fulfilled his quest for an essential Australian landscape, as his work edged incrementally towards minimalism:

> The trip has been fascinating – it rather convinces me that there is something very similar running through the Aust. Landscape (any landscape) so much so that I may drop the regional titles from all paintings.[128]

The Australian Landscape series (1969) was painted in response to Williams' Tibooburra experience. These are among the most reductive of his works; dots and dashes act to stretch space laterally, while subtle parallel lines propose the continent as an infinite, cryptically marked plain. A horizon is implicit however, for despite their abstraction, Williams' Australian Landscape paintings have a top and a bottom. Intriguingly, Williams' dots prefigure similar marks that Warangula used to create his aerial images of 'country' in the next decade.[129] In contrast to Williams, however, there is no horizon implied in Warangula's paintings, just the country of other clans, linked by songlines and reciprocal relationships.[130] Does the abstract beauty of Williams' Australian Landscape series suggest an uninhabited land, emptied of meaning when compared with Western Desert art as Darren Jorgensen has suggested? [131]

The scale of the Australian landscape intrigued Williams, particularly when viewed 'from 1 mile up in the air'. The land's essential flatness caused Williams to muse, 'I suppose the most "universal" picture is a map? – it's worth thinking about'.[132] The taut, parchment-like surfaces of Williams' Australian Landscape series were created in the studio where environmental conditions could be controlled, as if in the laboratory, and appeared lifeless in comparison to his earlier works that emerged from more intimate observation. Nevertheless the encrypted cartographic marks that sit on the surface of Williams' Australian Landscape series bring to mind Gell's dictum: 'images and maps flow one into the other in mutually related ways'.[133]

Once achieved, the austere reductive surfaces of the Australian Landscape series did not satisfy Williams. For what distinguishes his work from that of lesser Australian landscapists is the subtle modulation of the paint (to signify topography and vegetation) within self-proscribed parameters. Williams would therefore continue to draw inspiration from direct observation of actual places.

While Warangula painted in the men's shed at Papunya, drenching rains compelled Williams to leave the studio and head into the field to paint *en plein air* at the Kew Billabong, and similar un-presupposing sites in suburban Melbourne. Williams' La Niña paintings were stimulated by the luxuriant growth he witnessed close to home. As one reviewer of his exhibition at the Rudy Komon Gallery in Sydney wrote:

> There seems to have been a lot of rain down south in Williams' country. The scrubby, sparsely-timbered landscapes for which he is noted are now awash with streams and bursting with wattle blooms. He uses flat areas of muddy water to introduce a new note of substantiality and to offset the bejewelled colour in the painting fringing the forest.[134]

Hart regards the works created as a result the artist's *en plein air* excursions as 'important additions to Williams' repertoire of water paintings', noting that 'Williams found sustenance in seemingly nondescript areas and, in this instance, the Kew Billabong paintings emerged like brilliant lotus flowers from the muddy swamp'.[135] Despite the familiarity of a degraded suburban wetland to which Hart alludes, the climatic conditions, during which Williams chose to paint, were exceptional, hence 'bursting with wattle blooms'. While Warangula was more exuberant, Williams also expressed his love for country with emotional intensity heightened by the season.

Conclusion

The remarkable weather conditions of 1974 had a profound effect on a number of artists sensitive to the surge of energy released by persistent heavy rain. Olsen and Williams strove to achieve a flattened picture plane, as did comparable mid-twentieth-century painters, working at artistic hubs such New York, Paris, Sydney and London. On return from stints in Europe, both artists took to the sky, and in so doing acquired deeper understanding of the essential flatness of the Australian continent – the planar perspective suited their artistic aspirations.

Serendipitously, the Papunya Tula movement emerged at this juncture, and flatness came naturally to desert artists, schooled in the tracks left by animals and the songlines that mapped the country. Paintings by the Papunya artists suggest compelling similarities to those produced by contemporary artists of the Western tradition, and when the scale and refinement of their paintings coincided with the prevailing visual sensibility, they found recognition, in white cube galleries, beyond the confines of the ethnographic museum.[136]

The translation of prescribed desert motifs, learned in ceremony, to the rectangular format had not been a seamless development. It required the work of an inspired collective, and the assimilation of idioms from a range of 'Western' visual media. Warangula stood out as exceptional among a cohort of talented artists, seizing the expressive potential of the new media to represent the abundance of his country, experienced while tracking dingoes for their scalps. Warangula's association with Namatjira (and the artists of Hermannsburg School) may have provided insight into certain Western pictorial conventions that, in turn, informed his singular vision. Crucially, this enriched context has enabled me to consider Warangula as a landscape painter of note, in addition to his standing as an exemplar of the Western Desert art movement.

As a rainmaker, the fecund conditions experienced in the early 1970s had special significance for Warangula. While aspects of the artist's ritual and cosmological realm are incommensurate with conventional art historical approaches, the series he produced in response to the La Niña event of 1974 can be isolated to enable sensible comparison with other artists, especially John Olsen and Fred Williams, who painted corresponding subjects from different cultural perspectives.

While the term 'landscape' does not encompass the ontological depth of Warangula's expression of 'country', insights gleaned from the original documentation of the Water Dreaming series can enhance our understanding of the artist's conception of his land as enmeshed in the process of renewal through the evocation of ancestral spirits – environmental cycles of 'boom and bust' are embraced. Despite its brevity, Fannin's incisive documentation affords depth to our understanding of Warangula's holistic intent.

Both Olsen and Williams produced important series in response to the La Niña event of 1974 and each artist possessed a repertoire of techniques and motifs suited to the expression of the tumultuous outpouring of life they witnessed. They too were alert to the phenomenological effects experienced at the high point of a ceaseless oscillation between phases of drought and flood that characterise life on the Australian continent.[137] Whether the work of these 'White' Australian artists can be regarded as signifying 'a desire to resolve the distance between Aboriginal and non-Aboriginal artists' remains contested.[138] The question is made all the more compelling through the uncanny convergence of perspective and mark making that exists between these masters of Australian modernism and the paintings of desert artists in general, and Warangula in particular. Such convergence exposes fertile ground for the formal comparison of artists operating within distinct visual traditions. Should we anticipate that the convergence of means infers a comparable convergence of intent? Or is it enough to enjoy the coexistence of two complementary artistic traditions operating in parallel? I suggest that the ongoing tension surrounding the interpretation of Indigenous art signifies a stubborn schism as Australia struggles to reconcile its colonial legacy. Warangula's paintings play at the very edge of the divide, their sensuous surfaces encouraging affinity.

This contextual analysis of Warangula's work is intended to establish a basis for his appreciation alongside the best of his non-indigenous peers. Like Olsen and Williams, Warangula speaks eloquently of the great environmental cycles that govern life across the Australian continent in paintings that communicate a yearning love for land and country from which he was separated by history.

Acknowledgements

Johnny Warangula and his wife Yawintji (Gladys) Napanunka opened their camp to me, as they would their own son; their zest for life and good humour remains an inspiration. I would also like to thank Matthew Tjapangati and Paul Sweeney of Papunya Tula Artists for providing access to the company archive. I am indebted to the noted historian and diarist Dick Kimber, who, in 1978, alerted me to the correlation between Fannin's interest in botany and Warangula's joyous representation of the growth of particular plants in response to rain; this essay is the belated result of Dick's insight. Particular thanks to Mike Warangula Tjakamarra, whose lucid recollection of his father's stories has enriched my understanding of Warangula's youthful experiences, before he became an artist. I am very grateful to Jackie Kerin, Darren Jorgensen, Ian McLean and Susan Lowish who have patiently guided me in the preparation of this essay.

Notes

1 I have chosen to use 'Warangula' in preference to the more commonly used spelling of 'Warangkula', as it more accurately represents the sounding in Pintupi, as well as reflecting the preference of the artist's oldest son, Mike *Warangula* Tjakamarra.

2 G. Bardon & J. Bardon, *Papunya, A Place Made After the Story: the Beginnings of the Western Desert Painting Movement*, Miegunyah Press, Melbourne, 2004, p. 28.

3 J. Ryan, 'Aesthetic Splendour, Cultural Power and Wisdom: early Papunya painting', in J. Ryan and P. Batty, *Tjukurrtjanu: Origins of Western Desert Art*, National Gallery of Victoria, Melbourne, 2011, pp. 11–27 at 26.

4 V. Johnson, *Once Upon a Time in Papunya*, University of New South Wales Press, Sydney, 2010, pp. 169–71.

5 The author worked as Art Adviser with PTA, 1977–9, commissioning the artist, documenting works and travelling with him to sites of personal and mythic association.

6 The selected works were painted from 1972 to 1975 and were, for the most part, documented by Peter Fannin, the first Art Advisor at PTA.

7 Fred Myers spells the artist's name 'Wuta Wuta' to better reflect its phonetic sounding. F. Myers, *Painting Culture – The Making of an Aboriginal High Art*, Duke University Press, Durham, 2002, pp. 39–53.

8 Unless otherwise stated biographical details are drawn from respective entries in V. Johnson, *Lives of the Papunya Tula Artists,* IAD Press, Alice Springs, 2008.

9 The area around Haasts Bluff has strong associations for both Western Arrarnta and Luritja people. The Western Arrarnta speak a dialect of the Arrarndic language while Luritja is a dialect of the Western Desert language. Ngaliya/Warlpiri people, speaking a dialect of the Ngarrkic language group, also settled at Haasts Bluff, making it a melting pot of the three major cultural traditions. The orthographies of language names is used according to R. Hoogenraad & B. Thornley, *Aboriginal languages of Central Australia and the places where they are spoken*, Jukurrpa Books, Alice Springs, 2010.

10 G. Bardon, *Aboriginal Art of the Western Desert*, Rigby, Adelaide, 1979, p. 26; Bardon & Bardon, *Papunya*, p. 20; J. Hardy, 'Visitors to Hermannsburg: An essay in cross-cultural learning', in J. Hardy, V. S. Megaw & M. R. Megaw (eds), *The Heritage of Namatjira: The Watercolourists of Central Australia*, William Heinemann Australia, Melbourne, 1992, pp. 137–75 at 157–8; P. Jones, *Ochre and Rust: Artefacts and Encounters on Australian Frontiers*, Wakefield Press, Adelaide, 2007, pp. 311–13; W. Rubuntja and J. Green, *The Town Grew Up Dancing: The Life and Art of Wenten Rubuntja*, Jukurrpa Books, Alice Springs, 2002, pp. 51–4.

11 Mauss cited in Myers, *Painting Culture*, pp. 50–1.

12 J. Kean, 'Lot 50', *Sotheby's Australia, Important Australian art, Sydney 13 May 2014,* Second East Auction Holdings, Melbourne, 2014, p. 92.

13 A. French, *Seeing the Centre: The Art of Albert Namatjira 1902–1959*, National Gallery of Australia, Canberra, 2002, pp. 23–35.

14 V. Johnson, *Streets of Papunya: the re-invention of Papunya painting,* New

South Publishing, Sydney, 2015, pp. 40–51.

15 ibid., p. 26.

16 'Dogger' is a colloquial term for one who hunts dingoes on which there is a bounty.

17 The term 'totemic landscape' was coined by T. G. H. Strehlow and is derived from an extended discussion of land geography, ceremonial authority and totemism. See T. G. H. Strehlow, 'Geography and the Totemic Landscape in Central Australia: A Functional Study', in R. Berndt (ed), *Australian Aboriginal Anthropology: Modern Studies in the Social Anthropology of the Australian Aborigines*, published for the Australian Institute of Aboriginal Studies by the University of Western Australia Press, Nedlands, 1970, pp. 90–140.

18 The terms 'Water Dreaming' and 'Storm Dreaming' have been used interchangeably to refer to Warangula's paintings of Kalipinypa. I have chosen to use the term 'Storm Dreaming' as it most accurately describes the violence of these events. Pelting rain, hail and a great flood followed the original storm.

19 The Bureau of Meteorology defines La Niña as 'the positive phase of the El Niño Southern Oscillation'. More specifically 'La Niña refers to the extensive cooling of the central and eastern tropical Pacific Ocean, often accompanied by warmer than normal sea surface temperatures…in the western Pacific, and to the north of Australia. La Niña events are associated with increased probability of wetter conditions over much of Australia, particularly over eastern and northern areas'. Australian Government Bureau of Meteorology website, viewed 30 July 2015, <http://www.bom.gov.au/climate/about/index.shtml?bookmark=enso>.

20 PTA was incorporated on 16 November 1972. Warangula's significance as a founding artist is discussed by I. McLean, 'The Gift that Time Gave: Myth and History in the Western Desert Painting Movement', in Jaynie Anderson (ed), *The Cambridge Companion to Australian Art*, Cambridge University Press, Cambridge, 2011, pp. 180–92 at 187–9.

21 Bardon & Bardon, *Papunya*, pp. 140–53.

22 J. Kean, 'Papunya, Place and Time', in *Papunya Painting; out of the desert*, National Museum of Australia, National Museum of Australia Press, Canberra, 2007, pp. 5–15 at 7.

23 The trails of the Honey Ant ancestors travelling to and from Papunya is are graphically represented in paintings such as Tim Leura Tjapaltjarri *Honey Ant Hunt* (1975), held by the National Museum of Australia.

24 G. Bardon, *Aboriginal Art of the Western Desert*, pp. 13–14; R. Kimber, 'Papunya – the dialogue of the country', in N. Amadio and R. Kimber

(eds), *Wildbird Dreaming: Aboriginal Art from the Central Deserts of Australia*, Greenhouse, Melbourne, 1988, pp. 73–6; V. Johnson, *Once Upon a Time in Papunya*, pp. 60–1.

25 T. G. H. Strehlow, 'Culture, Social Structure and Environment in Aboriginal Central Australia', R. Berndt (ed), *Aboriginal Man in Australia*, Angus & Robertson, Sydney, 1965, pp. 121–45 at 129.

26 Parta's son Reggie Tjupurrula demonstrated his agency by painting Warumpi, the major Honey Ant centre adjacent to the Papunya community. See V. Johnson, *Lives of the Papunya Tula Artists*, p. 265.

27 V. Johnson, *Once Upon a Time in Papunya*, pp. 11–43.

28 By his own account, Bardon was 'very ill' when he left Papunya, suffering a 'nervous breakdown'. He was hospitalised on his return to Sydney in August 1972. See G. Bardon & J. Bardon, *Papunya, A Place Made After the Story*, p. 39.

29 G. Bardon & J. Bardon, *Papunya, A Place Made After the Story*, pp. 37–9.

30 V. Johnson, *Once Upon a Time in Papunya*, p. 48.

31 F. Myers, *Painting Culture*, pp. 120–46.

32 Fannin's documentation of paintings from the period 1973–74 cites anthropological sources such as Spencer and Gillen, Mountford and Munn, indicating that he was supplementing what he learned from the artists with information gleaned from the literature.

33 The PTA catalogue number is composed from the initials of the maker, the last two numerals of the year, the month and the sequential number of the work for that month (includes works by all artists). Thus JW731068 is painted by Johnny Warangula (JW) in the year (1973) in the month of October (10) and it is the 68th work to be documented during that month (68).

34 The documentation of paintings produced by Fannin during 1973 remains in a privately held archive. PTA has retained Fannin's records from 1974, until his departure in mid-1975.

35 T. G. H. Strehlow, 'Culture, Social Structure and Environment', pp. 139–41.

36 See a map of the artist's country drawn by Warangula for the anthropologist Norman Tindale at Haasts Bluff in 1956, (South Australian Museum [SAM], AA346/23/18).

37 J. Ryan, 'Aesthetic splendour, cultural power and wisdom', p. 25.

38 J. Kean, 'Johnny Warangula Tjupurrula: painting in a changing landscape', *Art Bulletin of Victoria*, no. 41, 2001, pp. 47–54 at 51.

39 The term is derived from the title of L. Robin, R. Heinsohn & L. Joseph (eds), *Boom and Bust, bird stories for a dry country*, CSIRO Publishing, Collingwood, 2009.

40 J. Kean, 'Johnny Warangula Tjupurrula', pp. 51–3.

41 Mitjilpirri is near Ilpili (Ehrenberg Ranges) on the south-eastern perimeter of the land for which Warangula had responsibility.

42 T. G. H. Strehlow, 'Culture, Social Structure and Environment', pp. 122–4; R. Kimber, 'Papunya – the dialogue of the country', pp. 61–2.

43 R. G. Kimber, 'Walawurru, the Giant Eaglehawk: Aboriginal Reminiscences of Aircraft in Central Australia 1921–1931', *Aboriginal History*, vol. 6, 1982, pp. 49–60 at 50.

44 D. Corke, 'Aviation: The adventures of Love Bird and Diamond Bird', viewed 14 July 2012, http://www.australiangeographic.com.au/topics/history-culture/2010/02/aviation-the-adventures-of-love-bird-and-diamond-bird/.

45 R.G. Kimber, 'Walawurru, the Giant Eaglehawk', pp. 53–4.

46 P. Naparrula & J. Nakamarra, *Mamulama Ngalyananyi,* Papunya Literature Production Centre, Papunya, 1987, p. 12; see P. Batty (ed), *Colliding Worlds: First Contact in the Western Desert 1932–1984*, Museum Victoria Publishing, Melbourne, 2006, p. 42.

47 R. G. Kimber, 'Papunya – the dialogue of the country', pp. 39–77 at 59–63; M. Smith, *Peopling the Cleland Hills: Aboriginal History in Western Central Australia, 1850–1980*, Aboriginal History Inc., Canberra, 2005, pp. 51–68.

48 M. Lampshed, 'Expedition Leaves to Study World's Last Prehistoric Race', *The News*, Thursday, 4 August 1932, p. 12.

49 P. Batty, '"Primitive Blacks Face White Man's Laws": The 1932 Anthropological Expedition to Mt. Liebig, Central Australia', in A. Bell, A. K. Brown & R. J. Gordon (eds), *Recreating First Contact: Expeditions, Anthropology, and Popular Culture*, Smithsonian Institution Scholarly Press, Washington D. C., 2013, pp. 197–214 at 201.

50 A reconstruction of available evidence suggests that the family first travelled beyond Yamunturrngu to Hermannsburg, where they were scrutinised as the newest of a steady stream of emigrants.

51 P. Batty, '"Primitive Blacks Face White Man's Laws"', pp. 207–10.

52 P. Batty, '"When we first met white people: Five Biographies"', in P. Batty (ed), *Colliding Worlds: First Contact in the Western Desert 1932–1984*, Museum Victoria Publishing, 2006, p. 42.

53 Ngalpilala Purukulu, *Untitled*, crayon on brown paper, showing the tracks of Emu, Snake, Porcupine, Wildcat, Dog and Children's Python, SAM, AA346/12/6, Drawing No 10, South Australian Museum. For a detailed discussion of the crayon drawings made by Indigenous 'informants' for Australian anthropologists see P. Sutton, 'Aboriginal Maps and Plans', in D. Woodward & G. Malcolm Lewis (eds), *Cartography in the Traditional*

African, American, Arctic, Australian, and Pacific Societies, University of Chicago Press, Chicago, 1998, pp. 387–416 especially at 387–9. Ngalpilala's crayon drawing AA346/12/6 was reproduced in J. Kean, *East to West: Land in Papunya Tula Painting*, [Tandanya] Aboriginal Cultural Institute, Adelaide, 1990, loose leaf, unpaginated.

54 Ngalpilala's spearthrower, (SAM, A21292) was collected and documented by Strehlow at Hermannsburg in late 1933 and accessioned by the South Australian Museum collection in 1934. The signs on the concave surface of the spearthrower are interpreted as 'Storm clouds–rain drops falling–Flood beginning to flow underneath the lifting leaves and driftwood–Flood emerges from leaves & driftwood & rushes along clear of obstacles–Big barrier of leaves & dead twigs momentarily halting progress of flood'. An excited line of the concave surface of the spearthrower is interpreted as 'lightning from cloud'. Strehlow's sketch of the spearthower was first published in T. G. H. Strehlow, 'The Art of Circle, Line and Square', in R. Berndt (ed.), *Australian Aboriginal Art*, Ure Smith, Sydney, 1964, pp. 44–59 at 59, and in R. Benjamin & A. C. Weislogel (eds), *Icons of the Desert: Early Aboriginal Paintings from Papunya*, Herbert F. Johnson Museum of Art Cornell University, Ithaca, 2009, p. 38.

55 Documentation of Papunya paintings routinely refer to 'Maliyarra' or 'Punyunyu' ceremonies conducted for the education of post-initiates. Each evening over a period of weeks or months, episodes from the songline of totemic ancestors are re-enacted on a ground, prepared by older men during the day. The spatial organisation – iconographic elements from 'Maliyarra' or 'Punyunyu' ceremonies – inform the composition and treatment of many early Papunya paintings.

56 Henson notes that Pastor Albrecht visited the 'new camp' at Alalbi (Alyalpi) in July 1935, where 'Ngalibilala' (Ngalpilala) and the Ilipli people had settled. B. Henson, *A Straight-out Man: Pastor F. W. Albrecht and Central Australian Aborigines*, Melbourne University Publishing, Carlton, 1995, p. 91. In 1941, T. G. H. Strehlow made a census of people living at nearby Ngankeritara. Once again Ngalpilala was present. A twelve-year-old boy called Warangula is listed, but he is unlikely to have been our subject for in 1941 he was a young man of about twenty years of age. This in T. G. H. Strehlow, 'From 1941 Diary, Haasts Bluff Population Census, Taken Patrol Officer, T. G. H. Strehlow, 1941', Strehlow Research Centre, Alice Springs, p. 6.

57 The Coniston Massacre was in truth a series of murderous retributions led by Mounted Constable George Murray following the spearing of the white dogger Fred Brooks in 1928. Scores of Anmatyerr and Warlpiri

people were murdered. Those who were not killed were 'dispersed', seeking refuge at Haasts Bluff, Napperby and other stations where they could anticipate protection. There are several published accounts of the 'Killing Times', including a journalistic monograph by J. Cribbin, *The Killing Times: the Coniston Massacre 1928*, Fontana/Collins, Sydney, 1984.

58 Henson, *A Straight-out Man*, pp. 91–2, records that initially Ngalpilala resented the encroachment of the native evangelists, throwing a spear at the evangelist Titus. By 1935 Ngalpilala and his family were settled at Alyalpi, where they received rations and protection. For descriptions of Haasts Bluff see F.W. Albrecht, 'Hermannsburg from 1926 to 1962', in E. Leske (ed.), *Hermannsburg: A Vision and a Mission*, Lutheran Publishing House, Adelaide, 1977, pp. 54–9; W. Nakambala Tjungurrayi, 'Big Trouble came to Papunya' and M. Nelson Tjakamarra, 'Every Friday was ration day' in M. Bowman (ed.), *Every hill got a story: we grew up in country / men and women of Central Australia and the Central Land Council,* Hardie Grant Books, Richmond, Victoria, 2015, pp. 108–10; T. Rowse, *White Flour, White Power: From Rations to Citizenship in Central Australia*, Cambridge University Press, Melbourne, 2002, pp. 96–9; M. Strocchi, *Ikuntji: Paintings from Haasts Bluff, 1992–1994*, IAD Press, Alice Springs, 1995, p. 2.

59 M. Edmond, *Battarbee and Namatjira*, Giramondo Publishing Company, Artamon, 2014, pp. 159–272.

60 The man who we have come to know as Namatjira was referred to as Albert at Hermannsburg Mission. The first recorded use of his father's name 'Namatjira' came in 1938, at which time he started signing his pictures 'Albert Namatjira'. Edmond, *Battarbee and Namatjira*, p. 165.

61 Kramer proselytised on the fringes of the desert, contacting small groups at isolated waterholes and introducing them to elements of Western material culture and captivating them with a gramophone, miraculous magic lantern shows and posters of the Holy Land. See P. Jones, *Ochre and Rust,* p. 312. Intriguingly, Kramer's report (see below) is interspersed with strongly drawn elevations of the adjacent landforms, sketches that would have fascinated Namatjira. Could Kramer's elevations have exercised a significant formative influence on the young Namatjira at a phase of his life as he was searching for a deeper purpose?

62 E. Kramer, *Report on the Western Tour 1932,* PRG–1322 Series 1–11 Kramer Family, Mortlock Library, Adelaide. A card prepared by Norman Tindale estimating that Warangula was ten years of age at the time of the encounter. See P. Batty (ed), *Colliding Worlds*, p. 42.

63 E. Kramer, *Report on the Western Tour 1932,* pp. 12–13.

64 From my experience working with Anmatyerr, Luritja and Pintupi people,

individuals are readily recognised by subtle diagnostic differences in footprints.

65 P. Jones, *Ochre and Rust*, pp. 313–7.

66 J. Hardy, 'Visitors', pp. 154–5.

67 J. Morton, 'Country, People, Art: The Western Aranda 1870–1990', in *The Heritage of Namatjira*, pp. 23–62 at 39–40. According to the founding PTA artist Walter Tjampitjinpa, Jonathan Namatjira (Albert Namatjira's father) had been born at Blackwater, now an outstation on the northern slope of Ulunparru in the Belt Range between Papunya and the Haasts Bluff community. D. Kimber interview with the author, 30 June 2015.

68 Hardy, 'Visitors', pp. 154–5.

69 Jones, *Ochre and Rust*, p. 322.

70 Edmond, *Battarbee and Namatjira*, pp. 159–272. It is apparent from the viewpoint that several of Namatjira's best-known works were painted near Haasts Bluff, including the first of the artist's works to be acquired by a state institution, including Albert Namatjira, *Illum-Baura* (Haasts Bluff) (1939) in the Art Gallery of South Australia.

71 R. Battarbee, *Modern Australian Aboriginal Art*, Angus & Robertson, Sydney, 1951, p. 33.

72 The lay preacher Sam Gross took several photographs of Namatjira including *Communion at Haasts Bluff* (1941), an image that shows Namatjira dressed immaculately in white, standing in the second row of the Arrarnta congregation in front of the church at Haasts Bluff, Gross collection, number 1867, Strehlow Research Centre, Alice Springs.

73 Namatjira owned a succession of light trucks throughout the 1940s and 1950s, and the signwriting on the doors of the vehicles can be used to trace his principal base and his artistic trajectory from mission-based artist, *Albert Namatjira–Artist–Hermannsburg*, to independent traveller, *Albert Namatjira–Artist–Haasts Bluff*, and finally to Australian citizen, *Albert Namatjira–Artist–Alice Springs.* The door emblazoned with *Albert Namatjira–Artist–Haasts Bluff* is now exhibited at the Art Gallery in the Hermannsburg Historic Precinct.

74 Battarbee, *Modern Australian Aboriginal Art*, p. 54.

75 Haasts Bluff (the geographic feature) and the Mereenie Range were popular subjects for a number of Hermannsburg painters over many years.

76 This relationship will be explored in detail in the author's PhD thesis, 'To Reveal and Conceal', currently in preparation.

77 V. Johnson, *Streets of Papunya*, pp. 47–50.

78 H. Perkins & H. Fink (eds), *Papunya Tula: Genesis and Genius*, Art Gallery of New South Wales in association with Papunya Tula Artists, Sydney, 2000;

Bardon & Bardon, *Papunya: a place made after the story*, pp. xxiii and 39; I. McLean, 'The Gift that Time Gave', pp. 180–92.

79 Johnson, for instance, has written of the significance of Namatjira's presence at Papunya, particularly in the months preceding his death in 1959. See Johnson, *Streets of Papunya*, pp. 40–51. 'Hermannsburg' landscapists, Keith Namatjira and Joshua Ebatarintja were active as artists at Papunya as 'contemporary art' first emerged. See J. Morton, 'Country, People, Art', p. 39; V. Johnson, *Once Upon a Time*, pp. 29–30; G. Bardon & J. Bardon, *Papunya: a place made after the story*, pp. 22–3; V. Johnson, *Streets of Papunya*, pp. 41–2.

80 V. Johnson, *Streets of Papunya*, p. 50.

81 S. Kleinert, 'The Critical Reaction to the Hermannsburg School', in J. Hardy, J.V. S. Megaw and M. R. Megaw (eds), *The Heritage of Namatjira*, pp. 217–47 at 243.

82 J. Kean, 'Johnny Warangkula Tjupurrula', in J. Ryan & P. Batty (eds), *Tjukurrtjanu*, pp. 258–60 at 259.

83 B. Henson, *A Straight-out Man*, p. 142.

84 ibid.; M. Smith, *Peopling the Cleland Hills*, pp. 66–8.

85 According to Mike Warangula Tjakamarra, Parta wanted to marry Kamutu's daughter, and 'chased' her around Ilpili. However, she had been 'promised' to Ngalpilala, and the two men (who were classificatory brothers) fought over her for years. Despite their animosity, Warangula was close to Parta, especially after Ngalpilala's death at Haasts Bluff in the 1940s. M. Tjakamarra, interview with the author, 24 December 2014.

86 It is very likely that Parta introduced Warangula to the cave of the Nananana men at Tjikarri, a site celebrated in several of the artist's best-known works. Parta's critical role in the post-contact destiny of his people was recently memorialised when Nananana Street, Papunya, was renamed in his honour.

87 Parks and Wildlife Service, Northern Territory, *A Management Program for the Dingo (Canis lupus dingo) in the Northern Territory of Australia, 2006–2011,* Parks and Wildlife Service Department of Natural Resources, Environment and the Arts, Darwin, 2006, p. 8.

88 D. Young, 'Dingo Scalping and the Frontier Economy in North-West of South Australia', in I. Keen (ed.), *Indigenous Participation in Australian Economies: Historical and Anthropological Perspectives*, ANU ePress, Canberra, 2010, pp. 91–107 at 98.

89 Charlie Tarawa (Wartuma) Tjungurrayi interviewed on various occasions by the author, Kintore, 1984–5.

90 Warangula's age mates and fellow artists including C. Tjungurrayi, Nosepeg

Tjungkata Tjupurrula, George Tjangala and Ray Inkamala Tjampitjinpa also went on 'dogging expeditions'.

91 Kimber, 'Papunya – the dialogue of the country', p. 69.

92 Warangula's country is dominated by numerous parallel sand dunes, plains and salt lakes. In normal conditions, free water can only be found at a few cryptic soaks, rockholes and springs. Strict protocols govern the approach to such sites; other sites are perceived as being 'dangerous' unless approached by individuals of authority in a prescribed fashion.

93 M. Tjakamarra, interview with the author, 24 November 2014.

94 The Dingo Dreaming paintings created by Warangula in from late October to early December 1973 are: *Dingo Dreaming at Talitjarayi* (JW731068), *Mala, Matiplangu, Carpet Snake and Dingo* (JW731107), *Piruwata*, (JW731111), *Dingo Camp at Tinki* (JW731152), *Women with dingoes at Ngutlulnga*, (JW731167), *Walungurru and Tinki* (JW731201).

95 J. Kean, 'Lot 50', p. 92.

96 Peter Fannin, documentation for JW731068, October 1973 (private archive).

97 F. Myers, 'Emplacement and Displacement: Perceiving the Landscape through Aboriginal Australian Acrylic Painting', *Ethnos*, vol. 78, no. 4, 2013, pp. 435–63.

98 J. Gibson and J. Kean, "'New Possum Found!' Photographic Influences on Anmatyerr Art", *emaj*, Issue 9, May 2016.

99 P. Sutton, 'Icons of Country: Topographic Representations in Classical Aboriginal Traditions', in D. Woodward & G. Malcolm Lewis (eds), *Cartography in the Traditional African, American, Arctic, Australian, and Pacific Societies*, University of Chicago Press, Chicago, 1998, pp. 353–86 at 362–3.

100 Gell cited in P. Sutton, 'Icons of Country', p. 363.

101 See M. Jensen, *Photographs of Indigenous artists, Papunya, 1972*. Digital Pictures Collection, National Library of Australia website, viewed 9 November 2015, <http://nla.gov.au/nla.pic-vn3301193>.

102 R. Benjamin & A. C. Weislogel (eds), *Icons of the Desert*, pp. 14–19.

103 M. Jensen, *Untitled* (Indigenous artists Charlie Tarawa (Tjaruru) Tjungurrayi, Johnny Warangkula Tjupurrula, Timmy Payungka Tjapangati and Kaapa Mbitjana Tjampitjinpa working at the artist's studio, Papunya, 1972). Digital Pictures Collection, National Library of Australia website, viewed 9 November 2015, <http://www.nla.gov.au/apps/cdview/?pi=nla.pic-vn3210252>. The remarkable trajectory of *Water Dreaming at Kalipinpypa* from the men's painting room via Sotheby's to the John and Barbara Wilkerson Collection is discussed at length by Johnson, *Once Upon a Time in Papunya*, pp. 156–71, 180, 200.

104 For a vivid account of the progress of *Winpa* the Lightning Boss and the development of the storm at Kalipinypa see Kimber, 'Papunya – the dialogue of the country', pp. 45–6.

105 Kaapa Tjampitjinpa, interviewed by the author at Papunya, 1984.

106 Monthly rainfall for Papunya, Bureau of Meteorology website, viewed 11 August 2015, <http://www.bom.gov.au/jsp/ncc/cdio/weatherData/av?p_nccObsCode=139&p_display_type=dataFile&p_stn_num=015612>.

107 The development of Warangula's singular style can be traced through fifteen works held in the collection of Museum and Art Gallery of the Northern Territory (MAGNT). Several of these works were among the first consignments sent from Papunya in 1971. Early works employ relatively simple signs on unadorned backgrounds. Works produced in early 1972, demonstrate the freedom of line and complex multi-layered surfaces associated with Warangula's most acclaimed paintings. The first work in which his signature style is apparent is *Rain, Lightning and Stars at Night*, WAL-0039, delivered to MAGNT on 13 March 1972. *Rain, Lightning and Stars at Night* is likely to have been created in January or February 1972, before the onset of the torrential rain experienced in March.

108 Based on records from the Bureau of Meteorology (BOM) for Yuendumu, 80 kilometres north of Papunya (records were not taken for Papunya during much of 1974). Monthly rainfall for Yeundumu, Bureau of Meteorology website, viewed 11 August 2015, <http://www.bom.gov.au/jsp/ncc/cdio/weatherData/av?p_nccObsCode=139&p_display_type=dataFile&p_stn_num=015528>.

109 PTA records show that Warangula painted at least seven additional works on various formats during November 1974, most of which featured Tjikarri, the site of his father and grandfather's birth.

110 Fannin identifies the bird as an ibis, however it is almost certainly *Kalawa* (Great Egret), an ancestral that figures in many of Warangula's later versions of the storm and its aftermath at Kalipinypa.

111 The series comprises of *Lightning, Blue-tongue Lizard*, JW74001, *Little Green Bird*, JW74002, *Lightning, Ibis* (probably egret), JW74004, *Warrpanji the Kangaroo Rat*, JW74005, *Lightning and Water*, JW74012, *Lightning frightens the Emu*, JW74023, *Lightning and Water*, JW74028, *Storm Clouds*, JW74032, *Deluge*, JW74033, *Common water pattern*, JW74087. The PTA catalogue numbers for this series are anomalous for they omit numerals to indicate the month of production (11). Original annotations confirm they were painted/documented in November.

112 While the series is thematically expansive in scope, it was not exhaustive. Later works by the artist tell of the arrival of Kalawa to hunt for frogs

and other creatures of the flood, and a horde of Tjakapirri who travelled to the area to feast on the bush fruits that erupted from the earth as the floodwaters receded. Other works evoke the expansion, from Kalipinypa, of *Yala* (Bush potato).

113 J. Maughan et al., *Dot and Circle: A Retrospective Survey of the Aboriginal Acrylic Paintings of Central Australia*, Communications Service Unit, Royal Melbourne Institute of Technology, Melbourne, 1986, pp. 104–5.

114 For a discussion of the process of interpreting Western Desert painting in series see, F. Myers, 'Intrigue of the archive, enigma of the object', in J. Ryan and P. Batty, *Tjukurrtjanu*, pp. 29–40 at 39–40.

115 Warangula assumed the role as my classificatory father and as a consequence I camped with his family, particularly when visiting his outstation at Ilpili. Warangula, his countrymen Philip Batty and I made an extended bush trip to sites including Tjikarri and Karrku in 1978.

116 This list of plants is extracted from Fannin's documentation for JW780357.

117 J. Kean, 'Johnny Warangula Tjupurrula: painting in a changing landscape', p. 48.

118 Fannin provides a rare and telling insight into the philosophy that underscored his management of PTA during the period under question. See V. Johnson, *Lives of the Papunya Tula Artists*, p. xii.

119 F. Myers, *Painting Culture*, pp. 147–83.

120 During the 1980s, the same pair collaborated on an extensive expedition of northern Western Australia. More recently, multidisciplinary surveys have attracted continued support, as is evident in the cross-cultural investigations at Paruku (Lake Gregory) that saw the collaboration of Martu artists with ecologist Steve Morton, landscape artist Mandy Martin, geologist/archaeologist Jim Bowler and anthropologist John Carty. See S. Steve et al., *Desert Lake: Art, Science and Stories from Paruku*, CSIRO Publishing, Collingwood, 2013.

121 V. Serventy, *The Desert Sea: The Miracle of Lake Eyre in Flood*, Macmillan, South Melbourne, 1985, pp. 6–12 and 92.

122 J. Olsen, *Drawn from Life*, Duffy & Snellgrove, Sydney, 1997, p. 114.

123 J. Olsen, *Drawn from Life*, p. 115.

124 V. Serventy, *The Desert Sea*, p. 33.

125 D. Lewis, 'Observations on Route Finding and Spatial Orientation among the Aboriginal Peoples of the Western Desert Region of Central Australia,' *Oceania*, vol. 46, no. 4, 1976, pp. 262–71.

126 J. Olsen, *Drawn from Life*, p. 115.

127 ibid., p. 116.

128 F. Williams, January 24, 1967, cited in J. Mollison, *A Singular Vision: the Art*

of Fred Williams, Australian National Gallery, Canberra, 1989, p. 133.

129 I use the term 'country' to encompass the mythic, topographic, environmental and historic associations that concur to constitute an Indigenous understanding of land.

130 P. Sutton, 'Icons of Country', pp. 381–3.

131 D. Jorgensen, 'Nowhere Man: The Countryside of Fred Williams after Western Desert Painting', *EMAJ: Electronic Melbourne Art Journal*, issue 6, pp. 1–15 at 12.

132 F. Williams, January 24, 1967, cited in J. Mollison, *A Singular Vision*, pp. 133.

133 Gell cited in P. Sutton, 'Icons of Country', p. 363.

134 W. E. Pidgeon, 'New look at old scenes', *The Sunday Telegraph*, Sydney, 20 April 1975.

135 D. Hart, *Fred Williams: Infinite Horizons*, National Gallery of Australia, Canberra, 2011, p. 129.

136 A. Brody, *The Face of the Centre: Papunya Tula Paintings, 1971–84,* National Gallery of Victoria, Melbourne, 1985, p. 8; I. McLean, 'Aboriginal Cosmopolitans: A Prehistory of Western Desert Painting', in J. Harris (ed.), *Globalization and Contemporary Art*, Wiley-Blackwell, West Sussex, 2011, pp. 147–160 at 151–2; R. Radford, 'Director's Foreword: Fred Williams: Infinite Horizons', in D. Hart, *Fred Williams,* pp. 9–11 at 9; Jorgensen, 'Nowhere Man', p. 12.

137 Warangula, Olsen and Williams worked with a greater degree of ecological appreciation than earlier artists, Drysdale and Nolan, who appear to explore drought as a metaphor for existential angst and social dislocation.

138 Jorgensen, 'Nowhere Man', p. 12.

7

BETWEEN ROCKS AND HARD PLACES: MARY PUNTJI CLEMENT AND THE KALUMBURU ART PROJECT

Philippa Jahn

Close to Napier Broome Bay on the central north Kimberley coast of Western Australia nestles an artefact of the early twentieth century's civilising mission to the original inhabitants of the region: the isolated Kalumburu community, first established as a Spanish Benedictine Mission outpost in 1908. Once known as Drysdale River Mission, the settlement occupies a picturesque floodplain adjacent to a deep, cajuput-fringed pool on the King Edward River. At one end of town sandstone Mission buildings occupy an ordered garden precinct. Opposite the church is the most recent construction: a museum housing a frontier *wunderkammer* including, amongst a collection of curiosities from around the world, an array of secular and sacred historic local material curated according to the idiosyncratic preferences of the last Benedictine priest posted there. Rampant bougainvillea defines the border between the Mission precinct and the rest of the community where a grid of streets has been imposed on the river flat. To the west is the gravel airstrip, where stringybark trees shoot through the rusting remains of World War II aircraft crashed or abandoned in the bush to one side. A short walk from here leads to crystalline streams and low sandstone formations featuring the enigmatic mulberry-coloured shadows of Kiro Kiro rock art figures. The awe-inspiring landscape harbours a complex settlement history, and the development of Kalumburu art is closely linked to its trajectory. Extreme isolation has meant that Kalumburu has constituted little more than a footnote to studies of Kimberley art generally, overshadowed by the achievements of communities further south such as Fitzroy Crossing and Warmun. This essay intends to shed a little light on art from this region and on one artist in particular: Mary Puntji Clement. It utilises records of her work kept by the Waringarri Art Centre. Although based at Kununurra, Waringarri has been running an art project at Kalumburu since 2009. This essay also turns to records of an earlier period of art production in the community, when Wanjina were painted on bark and canvas by such luminaries as the Karedada family, Alec Minjelmanganu, and Ignatia and Waigan Djangara.

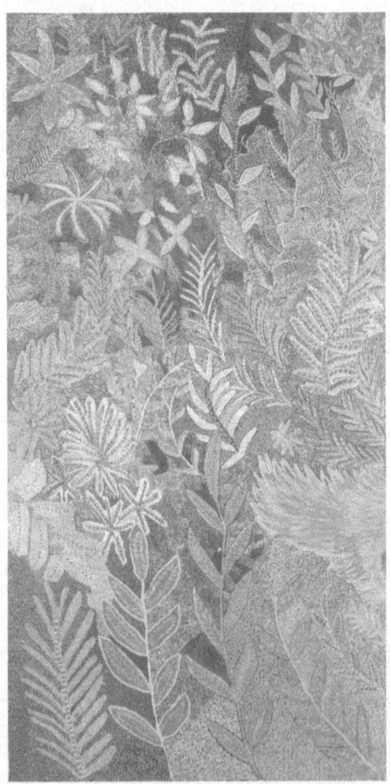

Figure 7.1: Mary Puntji Clement, Bush Tucker, *2011, ochre pigment on canvas, 240 cm × 120 cm. © Kiro Kiro Art Centre, image courtesy of Waringarri Art Centre.*

Historical Context

Every weekday Clement makes the slow walk from her house to the dilapidated shed which serves as a studio. She settles herself in her customary place, sweeps the previous day's detritus to the other end of the table and waits patiently for a cup of tea from whichever younger artist is willing to oblige. Yesterday's paints are retrieved and checked for usefulness before she embarks on the day's work. By mid-morning the old box air-conditioner has an incongruous chunk of ice hanging off the front grille as it struggles with the futile task of keeping the shed at a comfortable temperature, but Clement is too engrossed in her work to do more than crack a passing joke about it. The dilapidated assortment of chairs is soon occupied by other regular painters and perhaps a few younger women whose family commitments don't allow daily attendance. The atmosphere is collaborative and calm, punctuated by lively discussions of community incidents and cackling laughter about the merits or failings of each other's work. Paintings are propped on every available surface, awaiting the occasional curious visitor or eventual air transport to Kununurra for sale.

Clement was born at the Drysdale River Mission in 1948. Her mother Ignatia, of the Worora and Ngarinyin language groups, was brought to the Mission early in 1940 by police who had been scouring the area for children, as well as people showing symptoms of leprosy. Kimberley people felt justifiable fear of being captured, chained and removed from their own country.[1] As Clement recounts, all the men ran away when the police found their small family group, leaving her mother and elder sister to be taken alone. Ignatia subsequently met her second husband (and Clement's father), Kwini man Gregory Puntji at Kalumburu.[2]

Clement's childhood was deeply impacted by Mission policy dedicated to educating and 'civilising' the young they saw as needing rescue from the corrupting influence of traditional life and predatory frontier settlers.[3] To this end, nuns were permanently stationed at the Mission from 1931, and segregated dormitories were established in 1937. From a young age Mary lived in the girl's dormitory, with her daily care needs met by the sisters. Contact with family was not discouraged however and, after obtaining permission, children had access to relatives outside hours spent dedicated to schooling and Mission labour. Certain traditional activities were not entirely frowned upon by the missionaries, provided they did not overtly clash with Christian values. To the extent that they fitted in with the obligations entailed in daily life at the Mission, secular dance and song performance were not forbidden and were a regular event for special visitors. Ritual sorcery, and secret ceremonies such as the travelling cults believed to have originated in the desert area to the south, were rigorously opposed however.[4]

It is difficult to ascertain from the historical record the extent to which traditional cultural practices were maintained away from Mission scrutiny as the twentieth century progressed. It appears the missionaries, and the Aboriginal people forced to accommodate their presence, forged a rapprochement designed, to an extent, to fill the needs of both groups. Certainly people chose to wander from the Mission and resume traditional life as they pleased in the early days, much to the chagrin of the missionaries who were caught between their desire for a permanent Aboriginal settlement and the impossibility of implementing this prior to achieving full self-sufficiency. Later, Mission diaries speak of forbidden rituals being conducted in secret. Mention is also made of sacred objects being wilfully destroyed by missionaries in the presence of senior men.[5] It is likely that much of this material was kept well hidden from the prying eyes of white settlers, as reports from later decades confirm.[6] Whilst the community was still under Mission control it would not have been advisable for local people to be open to outsiders about their degree of engagement with traditional practices. However, this secrecy also led to hasty assumptions that local culture was fast disappearing. Equally the missionaries were keen to downplay evidence of activity incompatible with Christian values, as this did not quite accord with their carefully constructed narrative of Mission success. Another picture can be gleaned from the work of several male researchers from the 1960s and 1970s, who discovered many customary practices had continued unabated, if in somewhat altered form according to the dictates of changing social circumstances.[7] Until the 1960s older residents continued to live a relatively traditional life constrained (or perhaps abetted) only by the fact that many of them occupied two camps at the periphery of the Mission compound. The camp across the river, outside the reach of formal missionary control, was a particular focus for activities banned on the Mission proper.[8]

As elsewhere in the Kimberley the impact of disease, dispossession, linguistic disruption and indiscriminate 'dispersal' resulting from white settlement generally,[9] combined with the steadfast imposition of Christian morality and materialist European values, heavily impacted on aspects of pre-contact cultural practices for people now resident at Kalumburu. Rather than a cultural genocide, cultural praxis was transformed. There is evidence that colonising processes even intensified some traditional practices, particularly in the second half of the twentieth century. Modernised transport and the impact of disparate groups being thrown together in new settlements enhanced opportunities for exchange of material culture, ceremony and ritual.[10] Some investigators have linked nascent political awareness and dissatisfaction with entrenched inequality with the spread of certain cults which, whilst observing traditional protocols and forms, nevertheless incorporated some European symbolism and powerful emergent themes of anti-white sentiment.[11] Later, Native Title claim processes emphasised demonstrations of unbroken traditional culture and links to land. Of particular importance was the rapidly growing interest in the rock art of the region which engendered disputes over origins and cultural relevance, and thence to efforts by traditional owners to reclaim it via contemporary art production. Casual observers sometimes declare Kalumburu has 'no culture left', yet paradoxically seek the art that must arise from it.

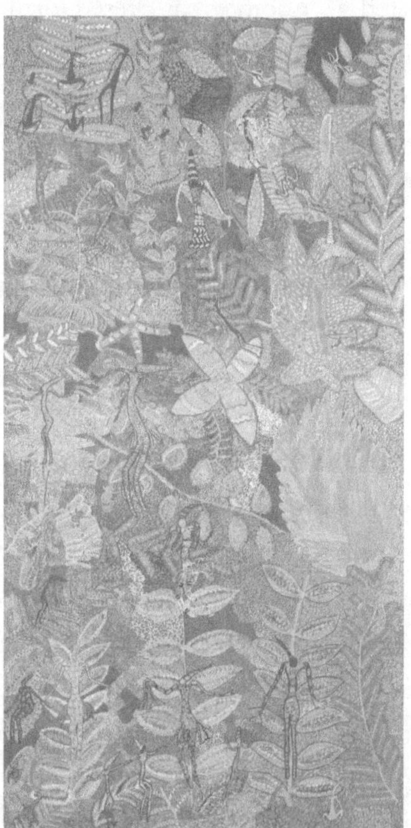

Figure 7.2: Mary Puntji Clement, Kira Kiro, Jirlinya and Bush Tucker 2, *2011, ochre pigment on canvas, 240 cm × 120 cm, © Kiro Kiro Art Centre, image courtesy of Waringarri Art Centre.*

The Mission venture at Kalumburu holds the particular distinction of simultaneously being responsible for the disappearance of some aspects of local culture and the continuing expression of others through art. It does not bear this distinction alone however; post-settlement Aboriginal art developments across the continent were enmeshed in this nexus of two religious systems and two economies embodied by the Christian mission.[12] The list of missions which became centres of art production for outsiders is extensive. Ernabella, Hermannsburg, Port Keats and Yirrkala are but four at which the history of cross-cultural engagement has been written into a procession of evolving art forms.[13]

In the first decades of the Drysdale River Mission several individual missionaries expressed interest in the language and culture of those they had presumed themselves upon, not always because an understanding of these was essential to the Christianising endeavour. In 1910 Father Nicholas Emo, a Trappist monk who helped establish the Benedictine Mission, undertook the first intensive exploration of rock art in that area and recorded his finds in a journal of ninety small watercolours. The missionaries had a camera with them from the first and were able to include portraits in the photographic documentation of their work. The monks remark on local people gifting 'products of their own artistry' after being shown such novelties. They also supplied 'easel and canvas to those who...were interested and proficient'.[14] No painted canvas has been found from this time; it is likely the author was referring to a collection of thirteen pencil drawings from 1914–15, executed on the back of sundry scrap documents and attributed to named individuals.[15] Father Theodore Hernandez, stationed in the Mission during the 1940s, left anthropological studies of some historical value,[16] as well as a small collection of paintings by local men. Another engaged in linguistic study in order to translate Biblical tracts.[17]

From the beginning, items of material culture were collected from people around the Mission.[18] Initially these were valued for their significance as emblematic of 'stone age culture' rather than their aesthetic appeal; their decorative charm was generally described as novel but crude. Amongst the first items to be sent away were a suite of paintings on slate, displayed at the Vatican in 1925 in a monumental exhibition exalting international Catholic missionary efforts. In 2010 these were retrieved from storage for an exhibition at the Vatican Ethnographic Museum, where they were rehabilitated as contemporary artworks at an event associated with the canonisation of Mary McKillop.[19] Mary Puntji's father has subsequently been identified as one of the creators of these slates, thereby establishing a link between two exhibited artists spanning just two generations and almost a century. The region has a rich history of art production and performance, from the multiple styles of rock art to secular and sacred ceremony with associated body adornments and ritual paraphernalia. Visual manifestations of esoteric themes expressed through human agency were an integral feature of Aboriginal life prior to European incursion. Exchange of artistic expression between groups was essential to the maintenance of religious belief, country and identity. In the crucible of engineered settlement, the transition from localised classical expressions to mainstream contemporary art has had a long and steady gestation.

Gradually the forms of some objects were altered by the new tools, materials and inspiration offered by a changing cross-cultural milieu. Many early Kalumburu artists and craftspeople who later achieved renown as artists in the mainstream art world found that visitors to the Mission constituted a ready market for crafted items. The establishment of an air base near the Mission during World War II provided particular stimulus in this regard. For the first time, local men found themselves working alongside a large group of newcomers with a somewhat more egalitarian style of interaction compared to the missionaries, and, since they were often labouring away from Mission surveillance, experienced greater autonomy in how they conducted these relationships.[20] Two military artists were also stationed at the base for a period, and both the military artists and local artists were known to have drawn portraits at the Mission. This must have been a reciprocal activity to some extent as one even offered to pay the costs of art tuition for a local man he thought particularly talented.[21]

An important catalyst for art produced for outsiders were partnerships with anthropologists who found the Mission to be a convenient base for their research activities. The Frobenius Expedition of 1938–39,[22] and Peter Lucich, Ian Crawford and Kim Akerman's close involvement with their informants in more recent decades, were all linked to the production of bark paintings and drawings. They were closely followed by the first of the dealers and entrepreneurs to venture to the Kimberley in the late 1970s, brought by the swelling interest in indigenous art as a contemporary fine art phenomenon rather than as strictly ethnographic or tourism-related. Mary Macha was the most prominent in Kalumburu, forging long-standing relationships with people whose artistic development she nurtured over many years.[23] As manager of Aboriginal Traditional Arts in Perth, she was one of the first to develop the role of marketing and cross-cultural liaison later filled by remote community art centre managers. She was exceptionally proactive in initiating and promoting Aboriginal art production from the state's north in the 1970s and 1980s and was integral to the national recognition given to the progenitors of contemporary art from Kalumburu. The powerful Wanjina paintings of the Karedada family, Alec Minjelmanganu, and Ignatia and Waigan Djangara amongst others demonstrated to a community struggling with fledgling self-determination the potential of art to enliven traditional culture, strengthen identity and assist with economic independence. How this actually manifested in terms of art and social consequences in the community is a vexed question which bears some scrutiny, as will be seen.

Art Centres and the Politics of Self-Definition

An art centre came relatively late to Kalumburu, commencing operation as the Kalumburu Art Project in 2009. Despite community advocacy for the establishment of an art centre, fortified by evidence that art programs support community wellbeing on multiple fronts,[24] the necessary government support was not forthcoming until Waringarri Arts in Kununurra received basic funding to auspice the project. For several decades prior to the establishment of the art centre, material choices available to painters here had been limited to the poor quality acrylics and canvases available at high cost through the community store. Few were able to avail themselves of the ochre to be found in country locally, the traditionally used yellows, reds and whites. Non-manufactured supports such as bark and slate were also difficult to obtain and labour intensive to prepare. It was hoped that a dedicated art centre would help to overcome some of these difficulties. Whilst two families had managed to liaise with external dealers with some success, much art production was occurring informally at home and sold independently to tourists and transient community employees. Whilst there is an argument that this was at least an engagement unmediated by white control, it was also true that such transactions frequently entailed the potential for exploitation. Furthermore, people painting this way had little opportunity or incentive to develop their art work beyond the limiting expectations of outsiders seeking traditional, somewhat formulaic, reproductions of local rock art and artefacts.

Narrow perceptions of 'traditional' Aboriginal art held by buyers are largely responsible for certain art styles becoming entrenched amongst artists painting from home or exclusively for the tourist market in the Kimberley. For people from Kalumburu this is now closely (although not exclusively) linked to the figures known as Kiro Kiro, a local word for the rock art style previously referred to as Bradshaw art and now more widely known as Gwion Gwion.[25] Certainly they are prominent in the corpus of rock art to be found in the north Kimberley, and are also relatively free of cultural constraints regarding rights to replicate them in artwork.[26] Debates regarding the relevance of these figures to local groups have occupied rock art specialists for some decades. Wider public attention was directed to this art style in the 1990s by researcher Grahame Walsh's controversial assessment that they could not have been the work of the ancestors of people now living in this region.[27] The timing of this assertion was particularly unfortunate as it proved useful for competing interest groups wanting to undermine local Native Title claims.[28] As a consequence, Kalumburu residents can be understandably sensitive about opinions regarding its provenance. The people in whose country this rock art is found now experience great difficulty in maintaining regular connection with it; most have neither vehicles nor expensive fuel to access sites. Whilst protocols regarding consultation and permissions are increasingly observed by many investigators, it is still easy for non-Aboriginal people with amateur or proprietorial interest to control access, site mapping, knowledge production and use of photographic imagery of Kiro Kiro.[29] It could be argued that the people who historically hold responsibility for the country in which these sites are found are claiming ownership in the one way left to them, via the iterative process of replicating this singular art style in their contemporary paintings.

The political dimension of this late post-settlement use of the Kiro Kiro figures as a marker of Kalumburu contemporary art to the wider world extends beyond the field of rock art to circumstances within the community itself. It appears to date from the late 1970s, in the critical period before the withdrawal of Mission administrative control and subsequent independence in 1982. Prior to these changes there is not yet evidence that these elegant, highly stylised figures were used in artwork for outsiders. In terms of figuration, it was almost exclusively depictions of Wanjina with their animal familiars and mythically linked items of material culture, the Rainbow Serpent Ungud and characters from the suite of spirit beings both benevolent and malevolent. However a survey of the Kalumburu Art Project image database reveals a curious decline in the use of Wanjina iconography and representations of Ungud as primary subject matter since the art project began. Possibly this is because Wanjina and Ungud are linked epistemologically and sometimes painted together, but this is unlikely to be the sole explanation. They constitute primary source material for many painters of the North Kimberley, are perceived cross-culturally as 'belonging' to many people now living in this area, and are intrinsically linked to historical and contemporary social identity. Why then might their use be waning at the art centre?

The answer to the decline in the painting of Wanjina and Ungud is possibly lodged in the changing politics of regional self-definition in the north-west Kimberley. The Kalumburu community is composed of several discrete cultural groups, historically distinct but forced into close proximity at the Mission as a consequence of white intrusion into the Kimberley. Residents hold much in common, yet the history and art of the people reflect the ruptures caused by imposed unification and distance from country. Primary allegiances to one or another persist, despite complex affinal relationships which often extend in both directions. Today the principal social distinction is between the Kwini (those 'from the east') and the Kulari (those from the 'stony country' to the west, the Wunambal/Gambere, Worora and Ngarinyin people). The community was founded at the western periphery of Kwini territory, something of a cultural transition zone marking, as far as is currently known, the diminishing cosmological significance of the Wandjina mythologies. The further east one travels the less significant the Wanjina is, despite the fact that Wandjina-type images continue to feature in the rock art. A number of Kulari painters were responsible for a collection of highly collectible barks executed in Kalumburu in the 1970s and 1980s. Wandjina imagery was used almost exclusively in these works but since this time, the Wanjina has become the principal motif used by artists at Mowanjum Art Centre at Derby in the west, rather than at Kalumburu. Originally another mission settlement, Mowanjum is comprised of artists drawn from three language groups with a degree of cultural homogeneity expressed in the Wanjina cosmology: the Wunambal, Worora and Ngarinyin peoples, described on the art centre website as the 'Wandjina Tribes'.[30] The Wanjina's fame, and with it that of Mowanjum, was given particular impetus by the opening ceremony for the Sydney 2000 Olympics. Wanjina mythologies and their relationship to specific clan estates have also been important to formalising Native Title claims for these groups.[31] More recently, in a novel attempt to prevent the frequent use of Wanjina imagery by those not culturally authorised to do so, they have successfully applied for trademark protection[32].

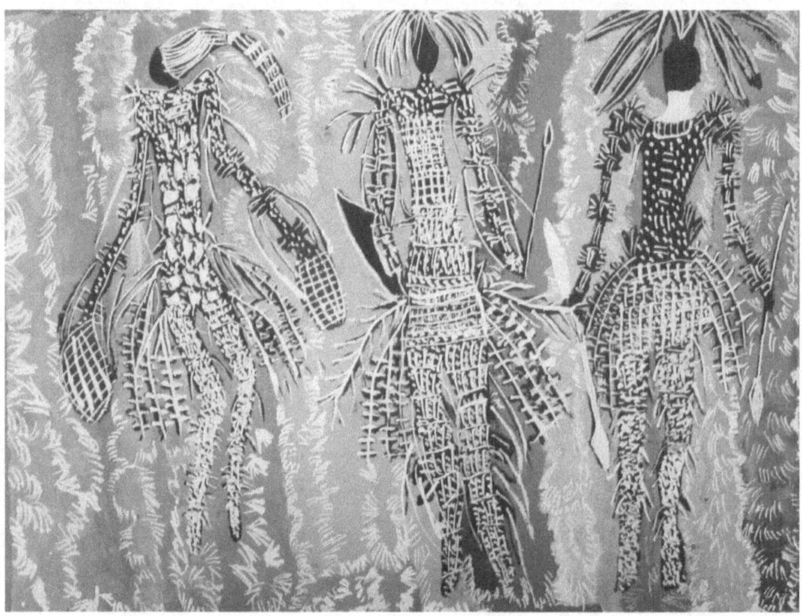

Figure 7.3: Mary Puntji Clement, Dancers, *2011, ochre pigment on paper, 28 cm × 38 cm, © Kiro Kiro Art Centre, image courtesy of Waringarri Art Centre.*

At Kalumburu, it is now the Kiro Kiro which constitutes their difference from Mowanjum and other art centres in the Kimberley. Indeed, the centre has been named after them: the Kiro Kiro Art Centre. Image analysis of art centre works shows that the choice of subject matter overall is also reflective of intra-cultural political sensitivities. Paintings of animals, plants and semi-naturalistic landscapes, for example, can be grounded in an Aboriginal world view without tending to overt didacticism. Such subjects are also freely available to families who are no longer able to maintain intimate association with defined tracts of country as they once would, or whose primary affiliations have been complicated in the present.[33] It is also significant that many of the people currently painting at the art centre identify primarily as Kwini. It is possible that as the art centre is located on Kwini country, some who believe their roots belong in Wandjina country to the west resist involvement. Contemporary art and social processes intersect here, as reifying aspects of Western culture come to define the visual identity of different groups. This was a conclusion also reached by Katie Glaskin, who described the objectification of elements of culture in Native Title processes. Legal processes that want to translate these elements into a Western legal system mean that internal group relationships are prioritised over intergroup relations 'with important consequences for the descendants of the current generations and for the ongoing reproduction of their culture and property relations over time'.[34]

Kalumburu Art Centre and Mary Puntji

The earliest paintings produced at the art centre in 2009 were small works on canvas or bark, all reproductions of the various forms of rock art imagery particular to the north Kimberley, executed solely in black, white and the unmixed earth colours of this traditional art form. They are somewhat tentative as one might expect, given these were some of the artists' first attempts at painting, but hold a particular charm nonetheless. Initially most were various sprite-like figures as well as Wanjina and totemic animals. Some were generic representations, reflective perhaps of the historical fact of the diaspora from traditional country over the last century and the logistical difficulties associated with return. Others were clearly representations of specific Wanjina found in particular tracts of country linked by family association to the artist. Clement, too, followed these conventions, depicting the subject matter most important to her mother. However she gradually shifted focus to the cultural priorities of her paternal

Kwini inheritance: Kiro Kiro, spirit figures and animals, as well as saltwater and botanical themes of her own interest.

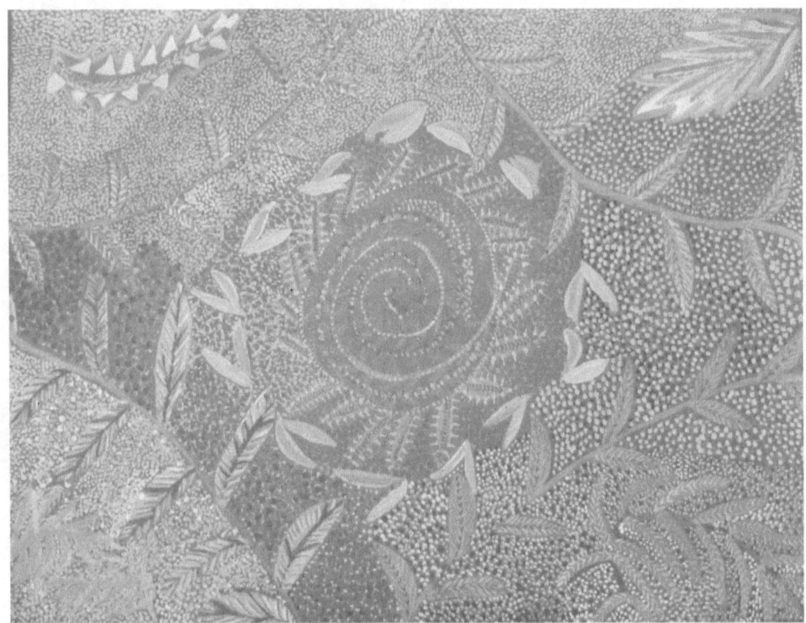

Figure 7.4: Mary Puntji Clement, Honey Season Time, *2011, ochre pigment on paper, 76 cm × 56 cm, © Kiro Kiro Art Centre, image courtesy of Waringarri Art Centre.*

A closer examination of Clement's work is illustrative of the divergence between art centre paintings and the work of the previous generation. Remarkably, she had never painted prior to the first days of the art centre. Despite being surrounded by older relatives who actively engaged in painting and artefact production when she was younger, she was reluctant to do so herself. She recounts sitting with Louis Karedada or her mother Ignatia as they crafted pieces and painted in the 1970s and 1980s. Ignatia preferred to work in silence, but Karedada loved to talk as he painted, describing country and story to anyone who would listen. Clement allows that the old ways held little interest for her until she was older. This might well have been a result of the assimilationist influence of her Mission education and childhood, but she was also fully occupied by the daily obligations of caring for a large family. In elder-hood however, pressing social concerns led to an acknowledgement that certain traditional values and practices were important for community well-being.

Clement's work itself is highly idiosyncratic. It is easily identified amongst other Kalumburu work and has developed to the point where stylistic links to work first produced for the contemporary market in the 1970s are almost non-existent. Her first paintings share the gentle, imprecise brushwork of her mother Ignatia, but they have not directly referenced the formal changes so successfully developed by her older relatives as they adapted rock art imagery to the constraints of canvas and the new milieu of a contemporary art marketplace. The most noticeable difference in this respect is in the use of the demarcated painting surface offered by bark, canvas and paper. The previous generation showed a preference for extending the principal subject of a painting right to the edge of the work. Masterful illustration of this can be found in the large barks and canvases of Alec Minjelmanganu, in which close framing serves to reinforce the enigmatic authority of his Wanjina depictions. Thirty years later the opposite can be seen occurring in Mary's paintings, where multiple subjects drift across a canvas, secreted in the background to reappear as the viewer gaze sweeps across the picture plane.

The other most obvious departure is the move away from the classical palette of unmixed white, red and yellow ochre and charcoal found in the paintings of the previous generation, to the commercially processed ochre (iron oxide) pigments provided by Waringarri. The rules for colour mixing with these are not always self-evident however and some hues are not available at all. To be a technically adept colourist with oxide pigments requires sensitivity to the interplay between different shades and tints within a work. The medium's expressive range is exploited quite differently by each of the principal artists at Kalumburu, but reaches a particular sophistication in Clement's work. Her earliest paintings utilised a limited palette, and dotted marks were sparse and large. She was quick to realise the potential of colour mixing however, partly as a result of using denser dotting which inevitably produced the effect of combining hues. Mixing colour to depict solid figures was soon followed by the use of variegation in the foundation coat as well as multi-coloured fine dotting and dashing. These techniques were established in the space of just a few months, and were progressively refined and established as the signature appearance of her work to date.

Clement enjoys experimenting with pattern infills in her figures. During the first year of painting her work became dense with delicate dashes and arabesques, the background dotting increasingly fine. The distinction between the ground and figure became ambiguous and the relative scale distorted. In much of her work, the subject matter – Kiro Kiro, spirit figures, flora and fauna, fire and earth – melts into a background of complex colour and texture creating dazzling optical effects and a strong sense of interconnection between the two. This radiant aesthetic can be read as a visual representation of her intuitive understanding of the interplay between country, the living beings which occupy it and the occulted ones who enliven it. They are not simply imagined effusions however, but the result of painting as an immersive experience; as she paints she enters the world of her canvas, her brushstrokes light and measured as breath.

Much of the subject matter which Clement favours is found in the rock art of the north Kimberley and their use neatly illustrates the use of recursive practices related to rock art raised by Howard Morphy.[35] Rock art imagery of this region is not simply a static relic of an unknowable past but a still-relevant visual assemblage of accumulated codified knowledge; an illustrated key for interpreting the interplay of classical culture and the material world which exists on a continuum from the distant past up to the present. More importantly, it continues to play a more personal esoteric function as a spiritual mnemonic device, as well as an inalienable statement of connection to country in the face of ongoing struggles to maintain this. It is easy to see why the rock art becomes the most significant and fecund source of inspiration for contemporary art and craft practices: it can be, 'in effect, curated...The meaning in the present may thus be created through the modifications of earlier representations, as well as by incorporating earlier images in contemporary compositions'.[36]

The majority of Clement's paintings feature Kiro Kiro. Unlike the iterative use of these figures by those who paint from home however, whose work consciously replicates the rock images with little or no stylistic experimentation, her figures are placed in entirely new contexts, the significance of which is quite personal to her. No longer anchored to a rock face, they instead assert their presence in the bush, by the sea, amongst ceremonial, hunting and wildfire scenes. She has taken the traditional use of dynamic dotting and dashing in the rock art, believed to have its own symbolic significance, and uses the technique to animate her own work. In a striking parallel to processes of the past where imagery was interpreted and re-interpreted according to the dictates of transforming socio-cultural requirements, in reclaiming these figures as a personal motif she is simultaneously restoring them to a symbolic politico-cultural prominence in the present.

The recursive use of rock art imagery is by nature a selective process. There are other figures which Clement also replicates, as well as some she omits. The local rock art corpus includes a panoply of mischievous spirits and sorcery figures dated from the distant to the more recent past. As a result perhaps of her Mission upbringing and Catholic faith, there are no 'devil-devil' figures or overtly sexualised anthropomorphic sorcery motifs in her paintings. She does however make liberal use of the Jilinya, described by Clement as a benevolent female mangrove sprite, as well as Jarnba and Jimi figures, again interpreted as benevolent, if prone to mischief. Her interpretations are revealing in this context. Jarnba figures are associated with a travelling cult rigorously opposed by the missionaries, who perceived elements of its practice as deeply antagonistic to the moral standards they had tried so hard to establish. She has rehabilitated them according her own religious beliefs. As painted subjects she relieves them of their original omniscient power to harm.[37] An additional explanation presents itself in some anthropological interpretations of Jarnba figures, which described them as powerful agents of resistance against white dominance.[38] It is possible their revived use in contemporary art for Clement and others serves similar symbolic intent, in the post-colonial context of disempowerment and social upheaval.

As Clement has made this traditional subject matter her own, it can be seen that her expression has grown in confidence and rapidly become experimental. Her frequent use of smaller boards and papers, necessitated by difficulties with transporting large works, has rendered innovation less risky. The supportive atmosphere of the art centre space itself also encourages originality, especially amongst the senior artists. It is interesting to note that while she remains fond of highly decorated figurative painting, from 2011 her work shows a developing interest in abstraction and simplification of motifs, where the densely marked surface remains but the subject is highly stylised. For Clement, this development is a natural consequence of her abiding interest in pattern and texture rather than a response to market demand for such paintings. The motivation for painting is not primarily economic. Given her material responsibilities towards her large family the economic reward is only ever short-lived, welcome as it is. Clement is not unaware of buyer preference for certain works over others. Neither is she exempt from buyer criticism – occasionally visitors to the art centre will declare that the use of dotting in her work more properly belongs to the desert for example, but she graciously ignores such ill-informed feedback and quietly continues to paint exactly as she pleases. The pleasure of creativity for its own sake, for re-enforcing identity as an example for the next generation, for carving a peaceful zone out of chaos – the act of painting is all these things and while its foundation might be cultural, the driver is the satisfaction of achieving a degree of personal autonomy and communal independence.

Watching Clement paint, it is hard to escape the impression that turning to the rock art for inspiration is a kind of solace as well as a pleasure. She acknowledges that coming to the art centre each day is an escape from the tumult of daily life, but more than that, the interior world she accesses when painting is a holistic domain where the borderline between the material and the intangible is not clearly defined – no less, it would appear, than was so for her forebears. Previous generations painted on rock as a component of symbolic acts of regeneration and identification with country. It is possible to view Clement's work as an echo of their intent; putting brush to paper creates her world anew. She paints a life as people once painted a place.

Acknowledgements

With thanks to Mary Puntji, without whose inspiration and generous contribution this essay would not have been written.

Notes

1 E. Perez, *Kalumburu War Diary*, R. Pratt & J. Millington (eds), Artlook Books, Perth, 1981, pp. 199, 201; H. Petri, *The Dying World in Northwest Australia*, Hesperion Press 2011 facsimile edition, Perth, 1954, p. 138; S. Saunders, 'Isolation: the development of leprosy prophylaxis in Australia', *Aboriginal History*, vol. 14, no. 2, 1990, pp. 168–81 at 171.

2 *Kwini* currently refers to several language groups traditionally from the east of Kalumburu. For further discussion of north Kimberley languages see W. McGregor, *Languages of the Kimberley, Western Australia*, Routledge Curzon, London, 2004.

3 C. Choo, *Mission Girls: Aboriginal women on Catholic missions in the Kimberley, Western Australia, 1900–1950*, University of Western Australia Press, Perth, 2001.

4 E. Perez, *The Benedictine Mission and the Aborigines, 1908–1975*, Kalumburu Benedictine Mission, via Wyndham Western Australia, 1977, pp. 122–3; H. Petri, *The Dying World in Northwest Australia*, p. 179.

5 H. Deakin, 'The Unan Cycle: a study of social change in an Aboriginal community', PhD thesis, Monash University, 1978, p. 52; T. Hernández, 'Myths and Symbols of the Drysdale River Aborigines', *Oceania*, vol. 32, no. 2, 1961, p. 121; E. Perez, *The Benedictine Mission and the Aborigines*, pp. 121–3.

6 H. Deakin, 'The Unan Cycle', pp. 225, 267–8.

7 I. Crawford, 'Late Pre-historic Changes in Aboriginal Cultures in Kimberley, Western Australia', PhD thesis, University of London, 1969, p. 61; H. Deakin, 'The Unan Cycle'; P. Lucich, 'Ethnographic Survey of the North-West of Australia Part I: the Northern Kimberley', held at AIATSIS, Canberra, 1963; P. Lucich, *Dance-Time Kalumburu* (film), 7.5 mins, produced and distributed by AIATSIS, Canberra, 1965.

8 H. Deakin, 'The Unan Cycle', p. 267; Personal communication with Kalumburu informant.

9 M. A. Jebb, *Blood, Sweat and Welfare: A history of white bosses and Aboriginal workers*, UWA Press, Perth, 2002; P. Smith, 'Station Camps: legislation, labour relations and rations on pastoral leases in the Kimberley region, Western Australia', *Aboriginal History*, no. 24, 2000, pp. 75–97.

10 K. Akerman, 'The Renascence of Aboriginal Law in the Kimberleys', in R. & C. Berndt (eds), *Aborigines of the West; their past and present*, University

of Western Australia Press, Perth, 1979, pp. 234–42.

11 H. Deakin, 'Some Thoughts on Transcendence in Tribal Societies', in E. Dowdy (ed.), *Ways of Transcendence: insights from major religions and modern thought,* Australian Association for the Study of Religions, Adelaide, 1982, pp. 95–109 at 106; E. Kolig, 'A Sense of History and the Reconstitution of Cosmology in Australian Aboriginal Society: the case of myth versus history', *Anthropos,* vol. 1, no. 3, 1995, pp. 49–67 at 60; A. Lommel, *Die Unambal: A tribe in Northwest Australia,* Takarakka Nowan Kas Publications, Brisbane, 1997, pp. 96–7; Petri, 1954, pp. 178–87; T. Swain, *A Place for Strangers,* Cambridge University Press, Melbourne, 1993, pp. 212–64; E. A. Worms & H. Petri, *Australian Aboriginal Religions,* Nelen Yubu Missiological Series no. 5, Spectrum Publications/Nelen Yubu Missiological Unit, Sydney, 1998, p. 156.

12 M. Langton, 'Religion and Art from Colonial Conquest to Post-Colonial Resistance', *The Oxford Companion to Aboriginal Art and Culture,* in S. Kleinert & M. Neale (eds), Oxford University Press, Melbourne, 2000, pp. 16–24 at 16.

13 U. Eickelcamp, *Don't Ask for Stories: the women from Ernabella and their art,* Aboriginal Studies Press, Canberra, 1999; J. Hardy, J. V. S. Megaw & R. Megaw (eds), *The Heritage of Namatjira,* William Heinemann, Melbourne, 1992; H. Morphy, *Ancestral Connections,* University of Chicago Press, Chicago, 1991; G. Ward & M. Crocombe, 'Port Keats Painting: revolution and continuity', *Australian Aboriginal Studies,* no. 1, 2008, pp. 35–55.

14 E. Perez, *The Benedictine Mission and the Aborigines*, p. 23.

15 Now held at a private archive in Western Australia.

16 T. Hernández, 'Social Organization of the Drysdale River Tribes, North-west Australia', *Oceania,* vol. 11, no. 3, 1941, pp. 211–32; T. Hernández, 'Children among the Drysdale River Tribes', *Oceania*, vol. 12, no. 2, 1942, pp. 122–33; Hernandez, 'Myths and Symbols of the Drysdale River Aborigines', pp. 113–27.

17 T. Gil, 'A Dictionary of the Pela Language used by the Natives of the Coastal Regions of East Kimberley in W.A', held at AIATSIS, Canberra, 1934; T. Gil, 'Concise Catechism of Christian Doctrine Written in the Pela Language (Drysdale River Mission)', held at AIATSIS, Canberra, 1934; T. Gil, 'Translation into Pela of Short Life of Our Lord', held at AIATSIS, Canberra, 1934.

18 This was a reciprocal endeavour; local people appropriated useful items from the missionaries (particularly metal) just as the newcomers acquired 'local arts and manufactures'.

19 M. Neale, 'God Lives in the Dreaming; Aboriginal treasures in the Vatican', *Artlink,* vol. 31, no. 2, 2011, pp. 114–17.
20 Perez's *War Diary* notes Mission disapproval of these encounters, which they saw as socially destabilising and potentially undermining of their own authority. See Perez, 1981, pp. 103, 66.
21 ibid., pp. 166, 179, 205. There is no evidence that this offer was taken up, however the descendants of the man concerned are now a prominent painting family in Kalumburu.
22 H. Petri, *The Dying World in Northwest Australia*, p. 141.
23 J. Ryan & K. Akerman, 'Shadows of Wandjina: Figurative Art of the North-west and Central Kimberley', in J. Ryan with K. Akerman (eds), *Images of Power: Aboriginal Art of the Kimberley*, National Gallery of Victoria, Melbourne, 1993, pp. 10–19 at 16–17.
24 V. Ware, *Supporting Healthy Communities Through Arts Programs,* Closing the Gap Clearinghouse, Resource sheet no. 28, Australian Institute of Health and Welfare, 2014.
25 *Kiro Kiro* is a Kalumburu *Kwini* (possibly *Miwa* subgroup) word, with several spelling variations. *Gwion,* (also *Kuyon*), is from *Ngarinyin*, spoken further south.
26 M. Donaldson, 'The *Gwion* or Bradshaw art style of Australia's Kimberley region is undoubtedly among the earliest rock art in the country – but is it Pleistocene?', *IFRAO Congress, Symposium: Pleistocene art of Australia (Pre-Acts)*, 2010; Ngarnjo, Ungudman, Banggal, Nyawarra, in J. Doring (ed.) *Gwion Gwion: secret and sacred pathways of the Ngarinyin Aboriginal people of Australia*, Konemann, Cologne, 2000; G. L. Walsh, *Bradshaws: ancient rock paintings of north-west Australia*, Édition Limitée, Geneva, 1994.
27 G. L. Walsh, *Bradshaws,* p. 60.
28 I. McNiven & L. Russell, '"Strange Paintings" and "Mystery Races"; Kimberley rock art, diffusionism and colonialist constructions of Australia's Aboriginal past', *Antiquity,* vol. 71, 1997, pp. 801–9 at 807.
29 A. Redmond, '"Alien Abductions", Kimberley Aboriginal rock paintings, and the speculation about human origins: on some investments in cultural tourism in the northern Kimberley', *Australian Aboriginal Studies* no. 2, 2002, pp. 54–64 at 55.
30 Mowanjum, accessed 1 March 2014.
31 C. Graber, 'Aboriginal Self-determination vs the Propertisation of Traditional culture: the case of the sacred Wanjina sites', *Australian Indigenous Law Review,* vol. 13, no. 2, 2009, pp. 18–34.
32 Arts Law Centre, accessed 30 August 2015.
33 This is not to suggest that Wanjina imagery does not appear at all, either

at the art centre or in the work of people painting from home. Some Kalumburu artists with connections to Wanjina country continue to draw inspiration from this religious schema. Similarly, some painters at Mowanjum include Gwion/Kiro Kiro figures in their work. The difference between usage at the two centres is clear however.

34 K. Glaskin, 'Claim, Culture and Effect; property relations and the Native Title process', in B. Smith & F. Morphy (eds), *The Social Effects of Native Title; recognition, translation, coexistence,* Research Monograph no. 7, Centre for Aboriginal Economic Policy Research, ANU, ANU EPress, Canberra, 2007, pp. 59–77 at 73.

35 H. Morphy, 'Recursive and Iterative Processes in Australian Rock Art: an anthropological perspective', in J. McDonald & P. Veth (eds), *A Companion to Rock Art,* Wiley-Blackwell, Hoboken, 2012, pp. 294–305.

36 ibid., p. 295.

37 H. Petri, *The Dying World in Northwest Australia*, pp. 180–1; T. Swain, *A Place for Strangers*, p. 36; Worms & Petri, *Australian Aboriginal Religions*, pp. 154–5.

38 H. Deakin, 'Some Thoughts on Transcendence in Tribal Societies', p. 161.

8

WILD STYLES AT THE OUTSTATION: JACKIE GILES AND NGIPI WARD AT PATJARR

Darren Jorgensen

Long before the establishment of an outstation at Patjarr in 1992, and Kayili Artists in 2004, this region of the Western Desert was known as a place where 'wild Aborigines' lived. The 'Patjarr Mob' lived here until the late 1960s, hunting and gathering despite the attractions of Warburton Mission to the south. For the people of the Mission the Patjarr Mob were embarrassing relics of the recent past.[1] This may have been why Ian Dunlop set his film *People of the Australian Western Desert* (1966–70) there. Filmed in Patjarr Creek, *People of the Australian Western Desert* remains stock footage for documentary makers wanting to show the hunter-gatherer lifestyle.[2] However, these scenes of hunting and gathering are as much a performance as they are an archive.[3] Nancy Carnegie stars in the film as a girl, but at the time she met Dunlop she was living at the Mission, and was taken back to Patjarr Creek to re-enact the lifestyle of the hunter-gatherer. Some forty years later, Carnegie was again a part of a wild performance at Patjarr, as she joined Kayili Artists, known for their 'bold abstractions' and 'audacious' and 'exuberant' paintings.[4]

In 2007, three years after Kayili's beginnings, and at the peak of a market boom in desert abstractions, several artists exhibited paintings on salvaged car bonnets at the Gallery of Modern Art in Brisbane. The first use of car parts as a support for Australian desert painting was probably a commission by Rodney Gooch at Utopia around 1990.[5] The styles of the Kayili doors are more abstract than the Utopia car doors, conflating loose styles of painting with the ubiquitous wrecks that appear on desert roads, as if Western Desert painting had met the *Mad Max* film series (1979–2015). More recent exhibitions of Kayili's paintings have carried on this conflation of the radical with the remote, as in *Way Out West* (2012) and *Boards from the Edge* (2013) at Raft Artplace in Alice Springs.

Two artists quickly came to prominence amidst this group. Kurltjunyintja Jackie Giles was one of them, his confident use of the interlocking key design, classically engraved on pearl shells and shields, marking his paintings out from other Western Desert artists. Ngipi Ward was the other, her idiosyncratic style capturing something of the colour and energy of the remote desert. Their first known paintings were not for Kayili, but for the Warburton Arts Project some fifteen years earlier. The Project specialised in large canvases, with a view to documenting the Dreamings of the Ngaanyatjarra Lands. In *Karrkurrutjintja* (1989), Giles paints an intense network of sites and paths, roundels and parallel lines tying it all together. Ward's *Wanampi Talup Talpu (Tjarlpu Tjarlpu) at Karilywarra* (1991) is an experimental patchwork of colours. Both paintings have great *wanapi* (snake) figures crossing their compositions, as these Dreaming figures cross the desert itself. The detail of these canvases betrays the visionary ideals of the Warburton Arts Project, while paintings from Patjarr, made much later, are looser, more audacious and less precise.

Such differences can be explained historically, as they reflect what the nineteenth century French critic Hippolyte Taine called an ensemble, a 'school or family of artists of the time and country to which he belongs'.[6] For Taine, the point of studying art is to diagnose the state of a society, and in the differences of paintings from Warburton and Kayili it is possible to see the differences between one kind of remote Aboriginal Australian centre and another. While Warburton is a major remote settlement, the administrative and population capital of the Ngaanyatjarra Lands, Patjarr is a homeland settlement or outstation, established amidst the flush of policies of self-determination that supported small groups returning to country in the 1980s and 1990s. There are institutional differences too between the Warburton Arts Project and Kayili Artists. The first is a community arts project, driven to document the details of the artist's country. The second is a commercially driven art centre, run amidst a boom in sales of Western Desert painting, that found a place at the high end of the Australian art market.

Giles and Ward register this changed situation with a looseness in their Kayili work, adapted to the heady boom in sales of desert painting. Yet this freedom to make their own way in painting was also doubled by the historical uncertainty of the outstation itself. For in the ongoing politics of national Aboriginal affairs, the outstation's future has never been assured, and remains all too dependent on supportive infrastructure from the larger settlements. So it was that while in 2005 *The Australian*'s Nicolas Rothwell was able to write, 'Some of the most distinctive art on view at Desert Mob comes from Kayili Artists, barely a year into its productive life',[7] only two years later he turned Patjarr into a symbol of the outstation's end: 'Only a diehard optimist would assume that tiny desert places such as Wingellina and Patjarr, the homes, respectively, of the ultra-successful Irrunytju and Kayili art centres, will still exist in a few years'.[8]

At Patjarr politics was taking place on several fronts, from the excision of the Gibson Desert Nature Reserve, where Patjarr is located, from Native Title claims, to the closure of the Patjarr school in 2009, followed by the big rain of 2010 that flooded the road, and the subsequent, steady erosion of finance for the overall maintenance of the road and community. After the closure of the school and the exodus of young families, life at Patjarr became even more isolated than it was, its population and services reduced to the bare minimum. Giles and Ward register this uncertain historical situation, the fluidity of modernity, with their wild, fluid styles of painting. All the while the content of their work remains bound to the deep time that Patjarr has been inhabited, depicting the rockholes around the outstation that sustained life for the Patjarr mob and their ancestors.

In the first year of making paintings at Patjarr, Ward names these places: Tjantiwarra (two large rockholes), Patantja (large clay pan with *wanampi* or water snake), Wandandarri (big rockhole), Tjanginya (two deep rockholes), Kurrutjiti (a creek bed with four rock pools, including two deep ones with a *wanampi*), Pirrin (a deep hole that people had to get inside to get water) and Yarrapan (another site with a *wanampi*). This essay charts the ways that Giles and Ward registered their new historical situation at the outstation through their wild styles, and through an examination of the archives of their paintings held by Kayili Artsts, Papunya Tula Artists and the Warburton Arts Project.

Jackie Giles

The wildness of Giles's painting at Kayili comes from his use of the interlocking key design, such as in *Tingari* (2007), that puts parallel single or double colour lines into a maze-like pattern, and produces optical afterimages in the eye. In the art world, such optical effects were made famous by the English painter

Bridget Riley, but unlike Giles she relies on measuring tape, rulers and compasses to create them. Giles had no such prostheses, but painted directly out of his mind.

The interlocking key probably came from classical Aboriginal designs on engraved shields. The gallerist Gabriella Roy remembers Giles visiting her at Aboriginal and Pacific Art in Sydney in 2009. From a collection of wooden items, he picked up two boomerangs and a woomera and told her they were his. Despite her protests, Giles went back to the desert with them.[9] The woomera was carved with an interlocking key design. The other source of this design in the desert are the incised pearl shells that were traded from the far north-western coast for magical purposes.[10] Yet it may be that the interlocking key design is not tied to an actual classical, Aboriginal origin than it is to a quality of Giles's personality, that is born of a particular historical conjunction. David Brooks describes Giles as having a 'psychic capacity', one that was born of his particular place in the colonial history of the Western Desert.[11] He is one of the 'great travelling men' of the era, who rose to power after the arrival of white people, and after the Warburton Mission was established in the Gibson Desert.[12] Such men used the changing historical situation to roam across tracts of country much more vast than they would have in pre-colonial times, making connections and accumulating power as they went. This culminated in Giles playing a central role in founding Patjarr itself, isolated and deep in country that he knew intimately.

As Giles is a rare figure in this time and place, so the interlocking key is hardly used in the contemporary desert painting movement. Its scarcity is a compelling argument for its power. Walmajarri artists Jimmy Pike and Peter Skipper brought the design to the river country of Fitzroy Crossing from the deserts to the south. In the Western Desert itself, Papunya Tula artist

Timothy Payungka Tjapangati employed it as late as the 1990s. Giles's ties to the artists like Payungka and other Papunya Tula painters may constitute a second explanation for his use of the interlocking key.[13]

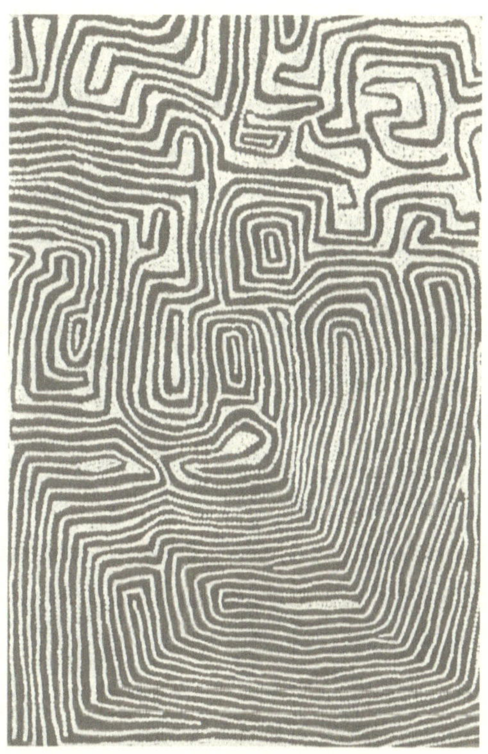

Figure 8.1: Kurltjunyintja Jackie Giles-Manyjilyjarra, Travels of two Tingarri men to the site of Jupiter Well, *2002, synthetic polymer paint on canvas, 91.2 cm × 61.3 cm irregular, National Gallery of Victoria, Melbourne. Gift of an anonymous donor through the Australian Government's Cultural Gifts Program, 2009. © Jackie Kurltjunyintja Giles/Licensed by VISCOPY.*

In the documentary *Art and Soul* (2010), Giles comes across a painting by Ronnie Tjampitjinpa at the Art Gallery of New South Wales in Sydney, and sings to it, knowing its Dreaming. While painting for Papunya Tula Artists in Kiwirrkurra, however, a place where Ronnie has authority, Giles does not reveal the full power of his own artistic voice, as if not wanting to distinguish himself too much from the other artists working there. He only painted the interlocking key in the corner of one 2002 painting, *Travels of two Tingarri men to the site of Jupiter Well*, but quickly abandons it in the rest of the canvas, instead creating an L shape redolent of the *tingarri* square. This may have been his first use of the interlocking key in contemporary painting, but he quickly abandoned it. Subsequent works made while visiting Kiwirrkurra, even after the opening of Kayili, consist of *tingarri* squares, but these are slightly different to those of his fellow artists, consisting of a single spiralling line rather than concentric parallel lines. It is as if Giles is coding his own personality into the most optically powerful male designs of the Papunya Tula artists, passing as a *tingarri* painter but without the *tingarri*'s typical rectilinear sensibility. Meanwhile at Kayili, Giles flourishes in his full power as a painter, employing the dazzling optics of the interlocking key.

The anthropologist Fred Myers has long puzzled over the *tingarri* square designs of the Papunya Tula painters. In 2002, he describes the way that this distinct motif is a development from classical site-path designs, the famous dot and circle paintings of the 1980s. Writing of Anatjarri Tjakamarra's paintings, Myers argues that the development of the rectilinear *tingarri* style from the site-path arrangement visualises the relationship of desert places to each other, rather than the places themselves:

> Resorting in a striking fashion to rectilinear imagery, this painting emphasizes some of the relationships *among* the places created in the Tingarri movements as the native cat brought the Tingarri men toward Lake Macdonald. This narrative emphasis is a common strategy by painters

> who wish to indicate the *coinvolvement* of geographically distinguishable features in a larger story.[14]

In a later, 2009 study Myers describes these compositions of double and multiple squares as 'op-art innovations', the lingering afterimage of parallel lines in the eye appearing to create a virtual, second level of the composition. Here Myers is no longer insisting upon reading these works with a relational sensibility, instead emphasising the way that their precise relationship with the country is more indexical than iconographic.[15]

Whether indexical or relational, Myers reflects the interpretive uncertainty that accompanies the reception of these optically powerful desert paintings, the way that their interpretation wavers in the mind as much as in the eye. Giles's interlocking key produces this very uncertainty, as the formal drama of this design is to a great extent its own puzzle, its relationship with the country it represents shrouded in mystery. What is more clear is the way that Giles establishes a relation of commonality and difference with his fellow artists to the north, as he shares with them the interest in optically exciting designs, while also marking his difference from them in using his own distinct visual idea. In this, Giles asserts his place in this part of the country, amongst other powerful desert painters and men with their own claims to the *tjukurrpa* and the land.

Ngipi Ward

Fellow Kayili artist Ngipi Ward creates a very different kind of wildness at Patjarr. For while Giles was able to repeat his interlocking key design without peer, Ward's innovations come from her ability to mimic and morph the styles of her fellow artists, combining them into her own idiosyncratic, colourful and tangled arrangements. From Pulpurru Davies, Ward borrows the overlapping half-circular style of doing *tali* (sandhills), in a style that resembles the 'hair-string' paintings of Katjarra Butler, Nyarapayi Giles and Makinti Napanganga. She also borrows Davies's colourful patchwork designs, and the thick dotting of Coiley Campbell and Nola Campbell.[16] In 2008 and 2009, she used trees in her paintings after being influenced by visiting artist Jonathan Kimberley. Always, she is painting in several styles, and combining these styles with each other. Rather than a master of her own individual vision, Giles is a master of all visions, all modes of painting that surround her in the Patjarr studio.

It is with this inclusive sensibility that Giles began calling her paintings Kapitu-Kapitu, that the Kayili database describes as 'a series of water sites that belong to the artists husband, which he and Ngipi used to travel between, kapitu-kapitu, water to water'. Ward had not lost this movement from waterhole to waterhole at the time she was painting these works, as she spent many afternoons hunting goannas between the rockholes around Patjarr. In her paintings, such waterholes are marked by roundels, and sit amidst whatever style of painting Ward has adopted.[17] Her paintings all convey a sensibility of mobility, one grounded in an intimate knowledge of the country, and of the hunter-gatherer lifestyle. Her appropriations of many different styles of painting are a metaphor for the nomadic life itself, expressing a shifting between sandhills, of movement from water to water.

The most dramatic of Ward's appropriations is the introduction of trees into her paintings, trees that were inspired by Jonathan Kimberley, who in turn had been inspired by trees while on a residency in Italy. Ward first painted trees in collaborative paintings with Kimberley and other Kayili artists in

2008 and 2009, before using the tree as a motif in her solo work. Kimberley's influence is most visible in *Punu (wood or tree)* (2009), the first work she made after the collaborations, and in which two trees stand as tall as the painting itself. Here Ward is painting with materials introduced by Kimberley, a 'thinned down acrylic', and stretches the trees across the entire composition as he does.[18] In subsequent paintings, Ward's trees become smaller icons, typical of desert paintings, sitting amidst dotting, paths and roundels. In many of these compositions, the trees sit around a rockhole, such as in *Talala* (2009), a rockhole near Patjarr.

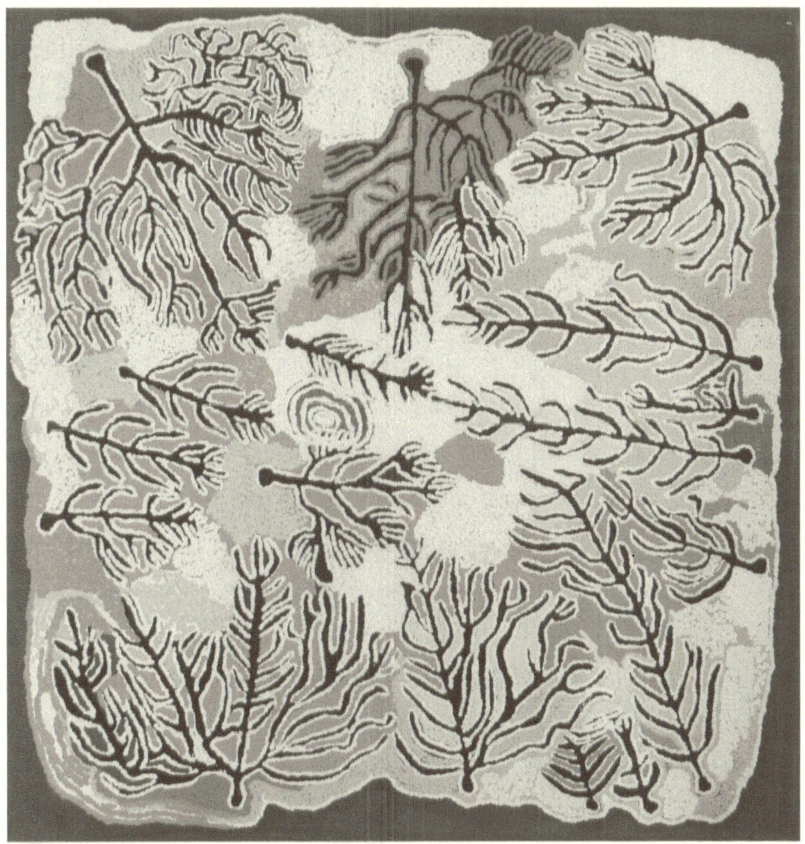

Figure 8.2: Ngipi Ward, Talala, *2009, acrylic on canvas, 102 cm × 102 cm.*

Ward's interest in trees takes place within a broader desert context, one in which trees are part of a culture of underground water and *purnu* making. It is worth turning to two other artists from this region to explain this context. Simon Hogan, who lives on the northern edge of the Nullarbor Plain, explains the trees in his paintings, the *purnu*, as representing several things: the water that they draw from rock holes; the shade that they cast onto the ground; and the wood that desert artists craft into all kinds of things.[19] The Pitjantjatjara term *purnu* means as 'tree' or 'wood', but is often used to describe the practice of making wooden items such as carved lizards and boomerangs for an Aboriginal art market.[20] Kayili artist Nola Campbell explains her painting in terms of a history of *purnu* making. 'I never had a job', she says, 'I have just done *purnu*, a bit of *tjanpi* and painting, this has been my jobs'.[21] *Purnu* is not originally a Ngaanyatjarra term, but came into use in this part of the desert with the arrival of the *purnu*-man, Peter Yates, who came to buy wooden craft from communities and outstations in the mid-1980s through the newly created Maruku Arts and Crafts.[22] Yates began his fieldwork among Pitjantjatjara speakers, and on the country south of Uluru, where craft projects had a long and intermittent history. When Maruku spread its operations to Ngaanyatjarra people, *purnu* became a part of the regional discourse on wooden craft. The use of the Pitjantjatjara term *purnu* rather than the Ngaanyatjarra word *warta* is one example of the way in which desert cultures undergo persistent change – what Ian McLean calls indigenous cosmopolitanism, or simply modernism.[23] So it is that the *purnu* tree describes a doubled modernism in Ward's painting, as it stands both for the appropriation of a motif from a non-indigenous context, and the modern art movement driven by Maruku Arts.

Styles of the Outstation

The wildness of the styles in the paintings of Giles and Ward appear as individual responses to life at the outstation Patjarr. As Giles asserts his place at the outstation distinct from his fellow artists to the north, Ward expresses the modernity of desert life through a transforming series of painting styles. Their wildness pushes the genres of Western Desert painting, from the optical double square of the *tingarri* to the hair-string or *tali* style of women painters, into more distinct visual identities. This edginess can be read as an expression not only of the isolation of this outstation from other desert centres, but as a political expression that has to do with the circumstances of the outstation itself. Jon Altman has written of the way in which the development of outstations in Arnhem Land empowered John Mawurndjul's styles to shift from strength to strength, to resolve themselves over and over again in the materials and ideas of his country.[24] Here the reverse is the case, as the history of Kayili Artists coincided with a period of political uncertainty at Patjarr. So that while Patjarr is on the one hand immersed in a long history of walking between rockholes, of hunting lizards and of the Patjarr Mob persisting well into the twentieth century, the history of Kayili Artists coincides with historical uncertainty about its future as an outstation. Their work more generally stands for the political valence of an art movement that has arisen in a post-mission era and that is concerned with cultural recognition, Native Title and return to country marked by contingency, by the way that history plays itself out amidst the *tali*, the rockholes and paths between them.

Acknowledgements

Thanks to Tim Acker, David Brooks and Tim Pearn; Paul Sweeney of Papunya Tula Artists; Edwina Circuitt and Emilia

Galatis, former managers of Warakurna Artists; Kathryn Davey and Rohan Robinson, both formerly of Kayili Artists; and Jane Menzies, who is at the time of writing the manager of Kayili Artists and Warakurna Artists.

Notes

1 D. Brooks, 'An Emerging Present: A Short History of the Ngaanyatjarra Lands', in T. Acker & J. Carty (eds), *Ngaanyatjarra: Art of the Lands*, University of Western Australia Publishing, Perth, 2012, pp. 1–11 at 6.

2 See for example *Contact*, directed Martin Butler & Bentley Dean, Screen Australia and Contact Films, 2009.

3 H. Morphy, 'The Aesthetics of Communication and the Communication of Cultural Aesthetics: A Perspective on Ian Dunlop's Films of Aboriginal Australia', *Visual Anthropology Review*, vol. 21, nos 1–2, pp. 63–79.

4 J. Carty, 'Bold Abstractions' in T. Acker & J. Carty (eds), *Ngaanyatjarra: Art of the Lands*, pp. 15–33; C. Bullen, 'Ngipi Ward', in *Western Australian Indigenous Art Awards 2013*, exhibition catalogue, Art Gallery of Western Australia, Perth, 2013, pp. 46–7 at 47.

5 A. Brody, 'Reflections on the Rodney Gooch Files', essay this volume.

6 Cited in N. Hadjinicolaou, *Art History and Class Struggle*, trans. L. Asmal, Pluto Press, London, 1978, p. 31.

7 N. Rothwell, 'Lines Shimmer into Shape: Desert Mob 2005', *The Australian*, 13 September 2005.

8 N. Rothwell, 'Colour Fades into Shadow', *The Australian*, 22 June 2007.

9 Personal communication with G. Roy, 2015.

10 On the interlocking key, see K. Akerman with J. Stanton, *Riji and Jakoli: Kimberley Pearlshell in Aboriginal Australia*, Northern Territory Museum of the Arts and Sciences, Darwin, 1993, pp. 36–7 and Akerman, untitled catalogue entry for 'Lot 42' and 'Lot 43', *Mossgreen Auction Catalogue: The Marc and Elena Pinto Collection, Melbourne 20 May 2015*, Mossgreen, Melbourne, 2015, p. 31.

11 D. Brooks cited in N. Rothwell, *Another Country*, Black Inc, Melbourne, 2007, pp. 20–9 at 26.

12 Personal communication with D. Brooks, 2015.

13 *Art and Soul*, documentary, directed by Warwick Thornton, Screen Australia and Hibiscus Films, 2010.

14 F. Myers, *Painting Culture: The Making of an Aboriginal High Art*, Duke University Press, Durham, 2002, p. 98.

15 F. Myers, 'Graceful Transfigurations of Person, Place, and Story: The Stylistic Evolution of Shorty Lungkarta Tjungurrayi', in R. Benjamin & A.C. Weislogel (eds), *Icons of the Desert: Early Aboriginal Paintings from Papunya*, Herbert F. Johnson Museum of Art, Cornell University, Ithica, 2009, pp. 51–63 at 62.

16 The Kayili archives show the first thickly dotted Nola Campbell painting catalogued as 04-323, and her husband Coiley Campbell using the style at 04-234. Presumably, then, this was originally Coiley's style, one Nola borrowed some hundred Kayili paintings after he first invented it. However, such a history cannot be certain. For while such visual borrowings can be precisely dated, they cannot so simply put into a lineage of influence in the desert. For it may be that, although 04-234 is attributed entirely to Coiley, Nola collaborated with him on this large, long canvas. Indeed, it turns out that this painting, called *Tjitju Tjukurrpa* (2004), is accompanied by a story that Nola told the art manager of the time, who transcribed it onto a certificate of authenticity for the painting. So this *Tjitju Tjukurrpa* was a shared story, and possibly a shared style.

17 If there is a distinct style that Ward could call her own, it is a series of paintings of small, cascading dots in many colours, running parallel to each other down the canvas. These shimmering dots are loose and fluid, echoing each other in their parallel movement, and amidst them roundels appear and disappear, as if among dunes.

18 This is written on the Kayili Artists certificate of authenticity for this painting, 09-059.

19 S. Hogan, artist's talk, Art Gallery of Western Australia, 4 July 2015.

20 J. Isaacs, *Desert Crafts: Anangu Maruku Punu*, Doubleday, Sydney, 1992, p. 15.

21 N. Campbell, 'Nola Campbell', in T. Acker & J. Carty (eds), *Ngaanyatjarra: Art of the Lands*, University of Western Australia Publishing, Perth, 2012, p. 229.

22 J. Carty, 'Maruku Arts and Crafts', in T. Acker & J. Carty (eds), *Ngaanyatjarra: Art of the Lands*, pp. 127–37; J. Isaacs, *Desert Crafts: Anangu Maruku Punu*, pp. 44–55.

23 I. McLean, 'Aboriginal Cosmopolitanism: Modernism's Means of Production', in J. Harris (ed.), *Globalization and Contemporary Art*, Wiley-Blackwell, London, 2011, pp. 14–160; I. McLean, 'Aboriginal Modernism in Australia', in K. Mercer (ed.), *Exiles, Diasporas and Strangers*, INIVA and MIT Press, Cambridge, Mass., 2008, pp. 72–95.

24 J. Altman, 'John Mawurndjul: Art and Impact', *Art Monthly Australia*, no. 225, pp. 22–5.

PART 3:
INDIGENISING ARCHIVES

9

MEMORY, HISTORY, ARCHIVE: NGAANYATJARRA HISTORY PAINTINGS

Emilia Galatis

Aboriginal art centres in remote Australia are social and business enterprises in which every art work is catalogued, photographed and given a monetary value. The art centre archive is thus a hybrid product born from the needs of commerce, of having transparency with money, while documenting artist career development amidst the archival impulse of modernity more generally. Creating a sound art centre archive is a full-time job, plagued by time pressures, lack of resources and language barriers between the archivist and the artists. This essay is based on one such archive, at Warakurna Artists, of a group of history paintings that are themselves an archive of a particular exhibition about the beginnings of Christianity in the Ngaanyatjarra lands.

The Ngaanyatjarra lands are in the far east of Western Australia at the junction of the Great Victoria and Gibson Desert regions. Spanning over 160,000 square kilometres, they support a population of more than 2,000 people. The *yarnangu* (Indigenous people of this region) have had an unbroken connection to land and 'country': 'this is the boon that the people of this area take with them into their future – that as a group they have never left their country, nor has their country ever been annexed by outsiders'.[1] It is one of the few regions of Australia where Indigenous people are the numerical majority and exercise a degree of control over their lives at a local level.[2]

As its manager since Warakurna Artists opened in 2005, Edwina Circuitt established the centre's archive and was its main archivist until she left in 2014. As the succeeding art centre manager, I am in a privileged position to write this article. I became particularly interested in how this complicated commercial record also documents a history of remote desert regions in Western Australia. This information is not readily accessible outside of the archive, but if you asked any living *yarnangu* in any community, the stories documented in the archive are common knowledge; they form the collective consciousness of contact and colonisation.

The main limitation of the archive for research is due to it being compiled using the standard art centre database software program, SAM (Stories, Money and Art), which doesn't have the facility to search by subject or content. Fortunately I was in a position to ask artists directly about their work to draw more information into the archive and for this particular essay. The Ngaanyatjarra lands in Western Australia have a reputation for occasionally creating 'history' or 'early days' paintings, in addition to the abstract Dreaming stories that characterise most Western Desert art. These history paintings can be broadly described as figurative works that articulate everything from first contact events to contemporary community life. The Warburton Arts Project curated the first significant exhibitions of this style of work: *Mission Time In Warburton: An exhibition Exploring Aspects Of The Warburton Mission History, 1933–1973*, in 2002, and *Trust* (exploring the history of mining in the region), in 2003. Both were held within the Ngaanyatjarra lands at the Tjulyuru Regional Gallery in Warburton.

Both exhibitions encouraged artists to explore specific contact themes surrounding life at the Warburton Mission at its inception in the 1930s that were still in public memory. The *Mission Time* catalogue claims that 'artists had been freed from the tyranny of dots, expressing their own visualisations and memories of cultivation, religion, mobility and literacy that form a living collective social history in the Ngaanyatjarra lands.[3] Warburton Mission was established by the United Aboriginal Missionaries (UAM) in 1933 and formally closed in 1973. The original priority of the Mission was to evangelise the natives and phase out traditional ceremonial and cultural practices. While this aspect of the Mission was largely unsuccessful, the modernisation it brought to the region was embraced, including increased levels of both settlement and mobility. Camels, cars, letters, telephones and English literacy changed the way *yarnangu* accessed the world and each other.[4]

Warakurna artists have been painting 'history paintings' since the art centre opened in 2005, with artists such as Judith Chambers and Eunice Porter instrumental in initiating these projects. At Warakurna, the term 'history' is an accepted term that refers to the post-contact period – what might be called the time of history, or history-time. This effectively began at the turn of the twentieth century with the intermittent intrusion of prospectors, doggers and ethnographers. The main legacy of this period are many unidentified photographs in anthropological archives that until recently assumed 'indisputable ownership of the past they reflect'.[5] The history paintings reclaim this gaze upon *yarnangu*. In 1955, when a large team of men created the cut line that forms the main road through the region, it was a momentous occurrence for the local people. The main purpose of building this road was to create the Giles Weather Station in connection with a weapons testing program at Maralinga. The locals watched the new structures being built over the next two years without any consultation. This was also a period of severe drought in the region, further restricting people's movements and attracting them to the permanent white settlement. These developments are particularly salient in the early history paintings at Warakurna, reclaiming a past that is shared by all Ngaanyatjarra people, asserting *yarnangu* perspective into the wider world.

Warakurna artists have been creating 'history paintings' at exhibition level since their first history painting exhibition, *All the Stories Got Into Our Minds and Eyes* at Outstation Gallery in Darwin in 2011. While their subject matter pre-dates some of the artists' lives, they are fresh in contemporary oral histories. As memories of memories, they retell stories, recording and reconfiguring oral information much in the same way that *tjukurrpa* (Dreaming) paintings are retold or modified to provide a worldview for contemporary events. In this respect the history paintings are part of the way in which the region has long operated as a highly structured system of social relations that govern and define most aspects of people's day-to-day lives from commerce to residence.[6] As Fred Myers explains, *yarnangu* 'do not simply "experience" the world; they are taught – indeed, disciplined – to signify their experiences in distinctive ways',[7] and the history paintings fall into this long-practiced epistemology. As Myers writes, 'Subjects acquire knowledge of the environment only partly through direct perception or engagement: this environment is actively produced as meaning, is objectified and revealed, through the signifying practices of various commentators and instructors...'[8]

Applying these same principles to the history painting movement, we find that place making and identity construction are reconfigured through first contact memories of the Ngaanyatjarra people. Thus the history paintings affirm Myers's claim that contemporary Aboriginal self-making and place-making can be seen as continuous with earlier practices, rather than abruptly disjointed or somehow a departure from traditional ways of making meaning.[9] The early history paintings employed *tjukurrpa*-style dots and figuration, as artists negotiated and explored an appropriate way in which to represent history time and capture the curiosity of first contact.[10] Viewed as a sort of imaginative geographical mapping of history in a place that is infinitely connected through proximity and cultural practice, the early history paintings trace a 'rich and vibrant social landscape of the Ngaanyatjarra lands'.[11] As David Brooks explains, in the Ngaanyatjarra lands culture and social systems have remained alive and intact. Dreaming is kept alive and vital by bringing elements of *tjukurrpa* law into new circumstances, allowing *yarnangu* to confront the challenges of the contemporary world within their own worldview.[12] The paintings in *All the Stories Got Into Our Minds and Eyes* testify to the social value of art within remote communities.[13] Sometimes filled with elements of humour, darkness and honesty, these stories and histories speak of shared histories and a collective identity that has been persistent throughout the Ngaanyatjarra lands despite the disruptions of first contact. The traumas of many of the events retold or directly experienced are remembered with both bravado and humour.[14]

Despite the initial interest in the history paintings, artists only paint them sporadically, perhaps testament to the pain or intellectual anxiety caused by retelling these stories. Even when a project or exhibition is imminent, one or two figurative works will often be followed by a small series of *tjukurrpa*-style paintings. This may be because of the established cultural protocol and boundaries surrounding *tjukurrpa* form and content; in other words, a certainty and deep knowledge of what can be presented and by whom. As the Ngaanyatjarra linguist Lizzie Giles explains, in Ngaanyatjarra culture there is 'no licence to look where ever you want', too many eyes or a direct engagement can produce negative physical effects.[15] This protocol is evident in history paintings where personal memories or reflections may or may not be available for public display. For example, some artists will paint clothes on the naked bush people after they have already been painted. Some artists will paint the story after someone else has painted the same narrative, perhaps because there is more security in presenting information that is already public. Time is also a factor, as the ease with which artists paint *tjukurrpa* works is juxtaposed to the intellectual strain of comprising a history piece. Some artists are also competitive; they will wait to see what everybody else has done and take the time to think of something new or different.

Artists have also been experimenting with new mediums to keep these stories alive. In 2013 at *Desert Mob*, an annual exhibition curated by art centres and held at the Araluen Galleries in Alice Springs, Warakurna Artists presented a body of new work in a series of handcrafted light boxes by artists including Eunice Porter, Polly Jackson, Diane Golding and Judith Chambers. The wooden boxes were first painted and then drilled with fine holes. LED lights were then fitted inside the box so that light could penetrate through to the front painting, thus illuminating individual aspects of each work as intended by the artist. This new medium revised artistic expression, moving cultural comment in new ways. Warakurna artist Polly Jackson states: 'new technologies have helped us to think differently about stories and what we are doing. They help us talk about life and the early days'.[16] Most recently, the artists have also begun using recycled elements within the works, sculpting or building with found objects.

Contemporary history paintings capture the intangible speed at which new information is amalgamated into Ngaanyatjarra world-views. Seeing bulldozers for the first time when the road was cut for the weather station more than forty years ago or the building of the mobile-phone tower just last year are memorable experiences in people's lives. What initially seem ironic or quaint scenes become pictures that document the unwritten importance of collective consciousness in the Lands. Making sense of these moments, placing them onto canvas, is part of *yarnangu's* long-standing desire to share information with a wider audience; 'cataloguing cross-cultural encounters on the colonial frontier'.[17]

Trauma and Humour in the Work of Judith Chambers

Judith Yinika Chambers is one of the founding members of Warakurna Artists. A varied and prolific artist, she is a tireless perfectionist, often changing her work many times to achieve the desired result, painting over elements she feels don't work or that are not physically accurate enough. When viewing her seemingly 'pretty' projections of life and nuanced moments in time, a much deeper message is always subterranean. This is the impressive paradox of Chambers' work; the dainty flowers, the delicate camels, the perfect *wiltja*s (shelters) gloss over the impossible meeting of incongruous worlds colliding within the remote desert. According to Terry Smith, contemporary art consists of situations that are incapable of mutual resolution (such as bush life and missionary life), but remain true to themselves, absolutes: 'every situation that is truly contemporary is an outcome of the friction between them'.[18] The most exemplary contemporary art projects are those 'that discern the antinomies of the world as it is, that display the workings of globality and locality, and that imagine ways of living ethically within them…'[19] Past and present narratives as well as simultaneous ways of life unfold comfortably within her work without a hint of disjunction or displacement.

Chamber's fascination with making things 'pretty' is not limited to her art; it stems from all aspects of her life. Having a desire to do things properly and efficiently, with order and integrity, is a key aspect of her personality. This is why her history paintings are so powerful; they only ever reveal what she wants to reveal, they are in no way accidental, everything is placed within the format and context of the specific event. However, when speaking to Chambers about her work, and asking why there are flowers here and different trees there, she asserts that this is historically accurate: different plants and flowers were cultivated at mission times, things were 'prettied up' in a way that must have been foreign to a nomadic culture. Judith will always make you stop to pick flowers, is always tending to her garden, suggesting that her ordered and gentle aesthetic is part of her worldview rather than a tool used to sublimate traumatic events. Or perhaps the two are intrinsically linked; the fact that life goes on and that many people out here have survived some truly impossible life events means that memory, trauma and survival become linked to day-to-day ways of operating. In this way, the 'prettying up' in Chambers' work becomes an example of her resilience, her total control over her disposition, portraying the facts as part of a continuous life and culture that has witnessed and remembers massacres, nuclear testing and cultural disintegration.

Ron Eyerman describes cultural trauma as a process in which old collective practices and beliefs can be reaffirmed and new ones created, so while disrupting space and groups, it can draw them back at the same time.[20] The history paintings suggest that an accumulation of individual memories taps a collective unconsciousness, as if, as it is for many *yarnangu*, everything is in a cycle of infinite connection, past and present, place and identity. This is far too simple a definition of Yarnangu epistemology but the matter-of-fact elements in Chambers' work hint at such connections, whereby drawing upon them these recent memories somehow connects the events with a deeper *yarnangu* worldview.

Eyerman argues that cultural trauma is 'not things, but processes of meaning making and attribution, a contentious contest in which various individuals and groups struggle to define a situation and to manage and to control it'.[21] The history paintings are emotionally difficult works to create for many artists because, for whatever reason, they mobilise opinions and occurrences that have been left dormant or not given a prominent place in people's psyches. The matter-of-fact way that Chambers interprets and explains her work – 'this is how it is, this is how it was' – suggests that these histories, while long part of the oral culture, are being told for the first time to a new audience (not each other). Chambers finds it incredibly important to include details that may seem to the outside viewer unimportant in the larger narrative; for example, the exact number of fence posts around the church, the way the camels are strung together, the shadow on each side of the mountains, the windmill's placement and what side the water tank was on. Her zealous and controlled effort to retell the events in a precise fashion hints at her ability as an artist to work through these moments with intense accuracy. They also show the affection with which many embraced mission life, even if it did seem strange and foreign at the beginning. Speculatively, the attention to detail in Chambers' work could also be seen as an annotated distraction from the serious and challenging issues on which they touch. Her light box from 2013's *Desert Mob* exhibition, *Circus Waters Massacre* (2013), delicately depicts an event that many artists recall their father or mother telling them about. An intense sorrow or loss is associated with this site. Typical of Chambers' narrative strategy, she chooses to present this tragic story for presentation on a light box, making the tragedy more poignant through light and colour, as Quentin Tarantino uses technicolour violence to address very disturbing issues in America's past in his comic-tragic film *Django Unchained* (2012). A careful balance between tragedy and playfulness is maintained in most of Chambers' work.

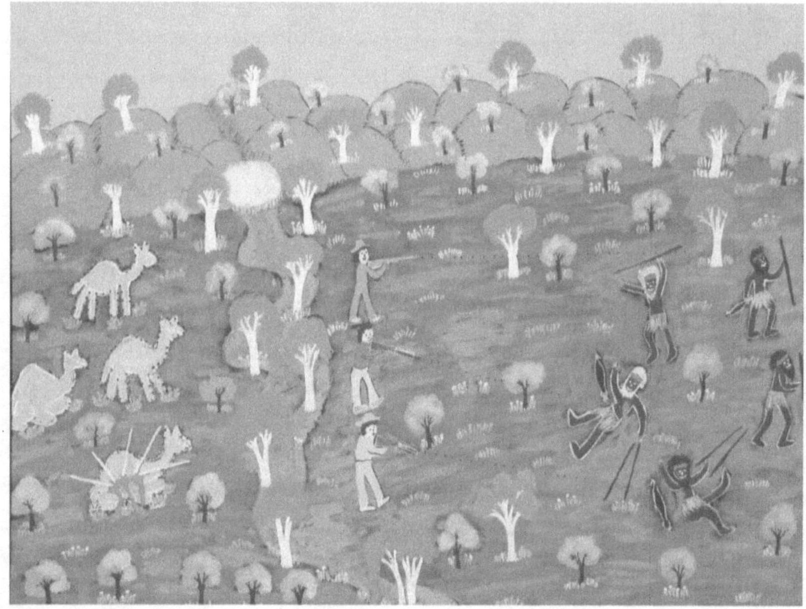

Figure 9.1: Judith Chambers, Circus Waters Massacre, *2014, acrylic on plywood light box, 30 cm × 40 cm.*

The Last Bush People to Warburton

Even though there is a joy and happiness commonly associated with mission life and early days narratives, the total readjustment would have been culturally traumatic. The 'last bush people to Warburton Mission' is a popular topic. Part memory and part mythology, it is a story about the groups of nomadic *yarnangu* that arrived at the Mission a long time after everybody else had been settled there. David Brooks explains that there were groups of nomadic people who came to the Warburton Mission some thirty years after its inception.[22] Whether they were forced to do so or came on their own accord is not clear. The nomadic groups confronted the settled mission *yarnangu* with 'what amounted to a vision of one's own past', and what Brooks says was an uncanny confrontation with a positive universal vision of the traditional past that had become a lost origin.[23] When artists like Jackson and Chambers painted these last bush people to arrive at the Mission, they remarked excitedly, 'they were all *nikiti* (naked), they didn't know clothes, this is a true story!'.[24] At the time I was unaware of the significance: the idea of a past where nomadic people had been naked and living in the desert is not foreign to most, least of all Jackson and Chambers. But to a group of originally nomadic people that had been sedentary for almost thirty years at the Mission, going to school and living a very different life, these naked nomads must have been almost mythical, marking a monumental occasion especially for the children at the Mission, many of whom are now current artists.

Wobbly History and the Work of Nora Holland

Nora Holland had been living in Warburton for many years prior to moving to Warakurna a few years ago. Originally from near Mantamaru (Jameson), she also spent many years of her youth in the Ernabella Mission with a foster family. Being a generation or two older than the other ladies, her mission paintings fuse *tjukurrpa* aesthetic and historical figuration in fantastically bizarre ways. Even though the other ladies tease her and sometimes joke that what she says she is painting often doesn't look like what she says she is painting, Holland is undeterred. Spurred on by the other ladies' representations, she painted a three-dimensional light box, also entitled the *Last Bush People to Warburton Mission* (2014), that became a finalist piece in the 2014 Telstra Aboriginal and Torres Strait Islander Art Awards. In her early eighties now, she has an artistic freedom in her history paintings not evident in the younger ladies' work. In *Last Bush People to Warburton Mission*, a young couple feature, very large in size, their nudity the main element in the overall composition. The other ladies got excited, 'yeah, all *nikiti*, true story!' Where they had almost hidden their naked figures or tried to paint clothes on them, Nora had nudity featured in large-scale, marvellously wonky figures. There was a unanimous excitement in the art centre as she had told the story with the greatest gusto.

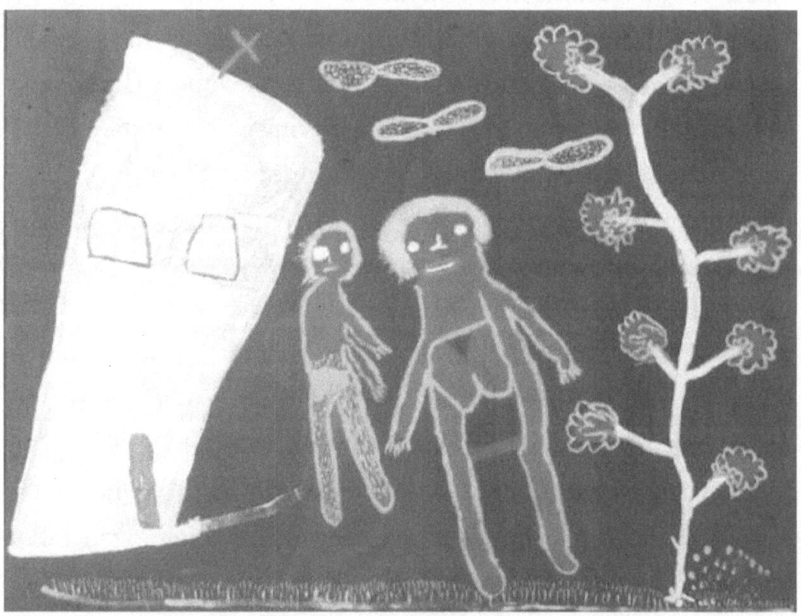

Figure 9.2: Nora Holland, The Last Bush People to Warburton Mission, *2013, acrylic on plywood light box, 80 cm × 60 cm. Highly commended, Telstra art awards 2014.*

Another example of Holland's unconventional view on history can be seen in *Christmas Father and all the Kids* (2013). This was part of a series of works that were exhibited at Christmas in the Ngaanyatjarra lands at Outstation in 2013. The dominant themes in the show were Bible stories, but Holland painted a female figure with two children in the rain. She explains 'it's Christmas and they had no *wiltja* and anyway, they got wet'.[25] In other words, Christmas time for Nora represents the time of the year when it rains, a seasonal depiction of what life would have been like in the early days at that time of the year; it's simply the time of the year when it rains. In another work, *Olivia the Pig* (2014), Holland documents a recent occurrence when police arrested Olivia, her pet pig, taking it away in the back of a paddy wagon after community complaints about it breaking into their yards and eating everything. The pig is portrayed in the back of the paddy wagon with the policeman taking her away. The criss-cross of connecting fuzzy lines at the bottom is her *wiltja*, as Holland sleeps outside most of the year round. The large bright yellow and blue shape is her house, shown in aerial perspective. When she tells this story

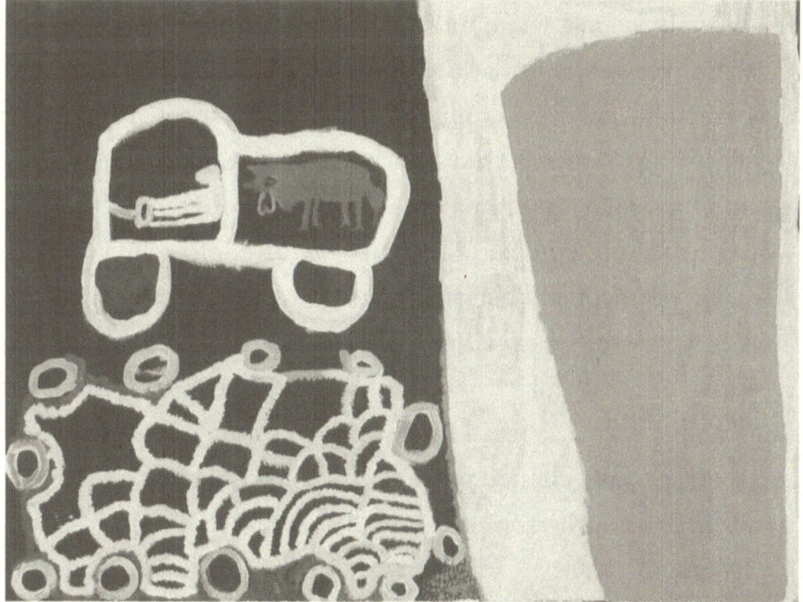

Figure 9.3: Nora Holland, Pig in the Paddy Wagon, *2014, acrylic on plywood, 80 cm × 60 cm.*

she gets upset: '*Pulkana* (big) money – they took that pig and sold it for big money!'[26] This particular painting, one could argue, is so random, so out of line with other work, that it perhaps should hide in the back of the art centre. However, it is moments and paintings like this that make the idea of documentation incredibly interesting. While events like this one are specific, other paintings are more generic. *Funeral at Warakurna Hall* (2014) depicts a large community funeral service at Warakurna in the hall, the coffin prominently placed in front of the building. However, whose funeral it was and when it took place is irrelevant. Here Nora is relying less on specific memories and specific events to convey the overall myriad possibilities of history on the Lands.

Towards Global Art: History Paintings in Context

As the world is increasingly looking towards movements outside traditional Western art spheres, remote Aboriginal artists may be finally included in contemporary discourse previously not reserved for them. However, the lack of commercial viability for paintings that are not explicitly about the *tjukurrpa* makes it difficult for artists to pursue genres such as the history paintings. As many remote artists rely on the income generated from the sale of their work, they are often deterred when artworks don't sell. The intellectual investment and personal offerings within history paintings are often painful or exhausting for many artists, and when they are not rewarded for their efforts it seems that the emotional outpouring was in vain. History paintings at Warakurna have relied on specially curated projects rather than the market, but the sponsorship of such projects is sporadic at best.

While Aboriginal art is beginning to be included in contemporary art university courses globally,[27] because of their geographical location remote Aboriginal artists face almost insurmountable challenges in developing cohesive conversations with the wider art world. The art centre archive is an invaluable tool to help artists and the art world alike overcome these challenges in the future. If there were ways to make these archives more accessible to academics at a global level, and if there were ways for remote Aboriginal artists to access international biennales through well curated projects, the future would start to change for many remote artists. If contemporary art is simply art that is contemporaneous and deals with issues of national identification, new internationalism and new media,[28] what does that mean for remote artists? If curators are trying to establish global networks through biennale-scale exhibitions, where and when will these networks be meaningful to remote art centre life? One of the greatest challenging aspects of contemporaneity is the 'world (dis) order' in which these networks are being formed and operated.[29]

If 'recent biennales were created to celebrate new trends in the contemporary art world as well as to examine other issues in relation to art: postcolonialism, displacement, migration, transnationalism, race, urbanization, the environment and other pressing global issues',[30] then surely remote Aboriginal artists have a place within this framework. If, as a group of remote organisations, we could offer international curators access to art centre archives, there would be a greater pool of information we could draw upon to enter global arenas. As a bunch of basically small businesses that need to make money in order to survive, there is a competitive nature, but that is true of any artist in the world. Working collaboratively, especially in terms of cohesive bodies of information and accessible archives, will produce much better results for everyone. In the Ngaanyatjarra lands, an alliance of art centres called Western Desert Mob has sought to tie the region together through collaborative projects, seeking strength as a group, pooling information with limited budgets and presenting the outside world with projects that capture the desert's fluidity and interconnectedness, rather than emphasising our commercial differences. Our archives, even though incredibly diverse, often offer work by the same artists, who paint shared histories, part of the collective consciousness of this region as a whole.

The crux of the problem here is that art centres have been set up as small businesses, places that need to sell work in order to survive and for their artists to survive. If artists are to produce new and exciting work outside the pressures of the market, there must be avenues to create in this way. Like any artist in the world, cracking the market, doing new things takes an incredibly long time. But unlike urban areas where artists have access to support systems and other jobs, remote artists have the additional pressure of simply surviving on a day-to-day basis with extremely limited access to outside information in terms of the market, contemporary art and exhibitions. They rely mostly on the information from just one person – the art manager – and if the new work doesn't sell, it's hard to provide reasons for why people should continue to create it.

At Warakurna artists feel comfortable doing *tjukurrpa*-style works three times in a row and will only then tackle a history painting again. There is something important about creating these works, however they do require additional intellectual direction to create. People are sometimes very self-conscious of their work and incredibly aware of what they are revealing or offering to outside audiences but eager to learn their reactions. However, due to locality, logistics and funding, many remote artists miss representing their work across Australia, and these conversations about the importance of their work are not being had. As much as everybody hates money story, it is an unavoidable and integral part of remote art centre geography. To pretend that any artist alive in the world is not motivated by success (monetary or through institutional legitimacy) is a farce. For remote artists, most of the time success is only seen in the form of money. Tangible results are thus measured as such, simply because the availability of other tools for success is scarce. Yes, there is always more an art centre manager can be doing; yes, there are always more competitions, more grants, more exhibitions to chase. However, if somehow in the future we can present the art centre archive to wider audiences through more interesting alliances, we can build a history for our artists that is more coherent, more legitimate than everybody standing alone, fighting for the same wall space and slice of the pie.

Even if managers have to be sales driven, these databases in the most remote regions of Australia archive some of the most important and comprehensive accounts of remote life and mythology in existence. In many ways, the art centre archive documents not only cultural information and contemporary information, but also the career of individual artists. These databases exist really only within the framework of selling art and returning money to artists, but, if managed correctly, they could also become invaluable tools for future research.

Notes

1 D. Brooks, 'What Impact the Mission?', in V. Plant & A. Viegas (eds), *Mission Time in Warburton: An Exhibition Exploring Aspects of Warburton Mission History 1933–1973*, Warburton Arts Project, Warburton, 2002, pp. 76–80 at 78.

2 P. McGrath, 'Hard Looking: A historical ethnography of photographic encounters with Aboriginal families in the Ngaanyatjarra lands, Western Australia', PhD thesis 2010, Australian National University, p. 5.

3 V. Plant & A. Viegas, 'Re-membering the Past', in V. Plant & A. Viegas (eds), *Mission Time in Warburton*, Tjulyuru Regional Arts Gallery, Warburton, 2001, pp. 1–9 at 3.

4 ibid., p. 4.
5 ibid., p. 2.
6 P. McGrath, 'Hard Looking', p 8.
7 F. Myers, 'Ways of Place Making', *La Ricerca Folklorica*, no. 45, 2002, pp. 101–19 at 103.
8 ibid., p. 114.
9 ibid., p. 115.
10 P. McGrath, 'Hard Looking', p. 210.
11 ibid., p. 212.
12 D. Brooks, 'An Emerging present: a short history of the Ngaanyatjarra Lands', in T. Acker & J. Carty (eds), *Ngaanyatjarra Art of the Lands*, University of Western Australia Publishing, Perth, 2012, pp. 1–14 at 11.
13 J. Carty with E. Circuitt, 'Warakurna Artists', in T. Acker & J. Carty (eds), *Ngaanyatjarra Art of the Lands*, University of Western Australia Publishing, Perth, 2012, pp. 191–203 at 199.
14 V. Plant & A. Viegas, 'Re-membering the Past', p. 4.
15 Cited in P. McGrath, 'Hard Looking', p. 52.
16 Cited in E. Galatis, 'Yuwa Walkumunu Telephonepa – lampatju (Hello, I've got a mobile phone)', *Artlink*, vol. 34, no. 2, 2014, pp. 75–6 at 76.
17 P. McGrath, 'The Past is Everywhere: Ngaanyatjarra History Paintings' in T. Acker & J. Carty (eds), *Ngaanyatjarra Art of the Lands*, pp. 209–19 at p. 209.
18 T. Smith, 'Contemporary art and Contemporaneity', *Critical Inquiry*, vol. 32, no. 4, 2006, pp. 681–707 at 698.
19 ibid., p. 698.
20 R. Eyerman, 'Social theory and trauma', *Acta Sociologica*, vol. 56, no. 1, 2013, pp. 41–53 at 43.
21 ibid., p. 43.
22 D. Brooks, 'What Impact the Mission?', p. 77.
23 ibid., p. 77.
24 Personal communication with the artists, 2014.
25 Interview with E. Circuitt, 2013.
26 Personal communication with the artists, 2014.
27 R.A. Lockard, 'Outside Boundaries: Contemporary Art and Global Biennales', *Art Documentation: Journal of the Art Libraries Society of North America*, vol. 32, no. 1, 2013, pp. 102–11 at p. 102.
28 T. Smith, 'Contemporary art and Contemporaneity', p. 683.
29 ibid., p. 707.
30 R.A. Lockhard, 'Outside Boundaries', p. 103.

10

WUKUN WANAMBI'S NHINA, NHÄMA, GA NGÄMA (SIT, LOOK, AND LISTEN)

Robert Lazarus Lane

Introduction

All the infrastructure involved in circulating Wukun Wanambi's archival art – the warehouses of servers, the bulbs of electronic displays, the vaults of museums, the media of recording devices – become mechanisms for generating the trajectories of ceremony's archival project. When discussing this publication with Wukun I asked him what was driving his archival art. He answered: 'using the archive in my art is a way for people to understand Yolngu cultural practices'. 'Which cultural practices specifically?' I enquired; he replied 'archiving…on the ceremonial ground'.[1]

Wukun[2] is a contemporary artist and ceremonial leader producing archival art by reconstructing ceremonial archives from deconstructed documentary archives. Working with documentary archives as cultural materials using post-production is not a means by which to stage recordings of intangible heritage, or hide cultural loss in romanticised antiquity; instead his work is visualising the ceremonial archive.

Archives made up of artistic media underlie every ceremonial performance. During ceremony the archive is used to sequence songlines, images and choreography within a clan's domain-specific collection. Archiving using an ensemble of media relies on information being carried in a range of containers, including performer's bodies. Dancers perpetuating archives follow the steps of what they believe others, or themselves, have performed on previous occasions as instances of ancestral action.[3] In this sense, Yolngu from Arnhem Land on the northern coast of Australia have developed practices in which artistic media produces an actual network composed of archivists who document a ceremonial system. Indeed, any choreography that appears to originate fully from the dancer, and not from the archive, is not ceremonial, because it's outside the archival process.

All the affiliations between people, place, and all the associations fostering growth and exchange circulate through archiving on ceremonial grounds. And it is the capacity of ceremonial archives to integrate activities passed down from generation to generation and actualise new mechanisms to enrich that inheritance as a process of succession which enables archival art of ceremonial documentation. My analysis of Wukun's time-based media will picture archiving networks of different durations and dynamics both present in the work, and circulating around it, as part of an archival chain. This layered engagement is an attempt to link with the artist's scholarly practice of connecting multiple archiving processes.

Today art centres such as Buku-Larrnggay Mulka, who host audiovisual media archives featuring ceremonial documentaries made by, or with, its members, are key sites for inventive procedures that are directly impacting on continuous cultural processes. By supporting ceremony, art production and audiovisual archives as part of art centre business, senior artists can make and maintain their connections between cultural practices. In this respect Indigenous owned and operated art centres can be considered local examples of the archival turn seen in contemporary art practices since the 1990s. A key work in this field is Wukun's *Nhina, Nhäma, Ga Ngäma (Sit, Look, And Listen)* (2014),[4] a media installation using audiovisual archives, editing software and multichannel displays to document a succession of acts linking ceremonial trajectories with archival turns.

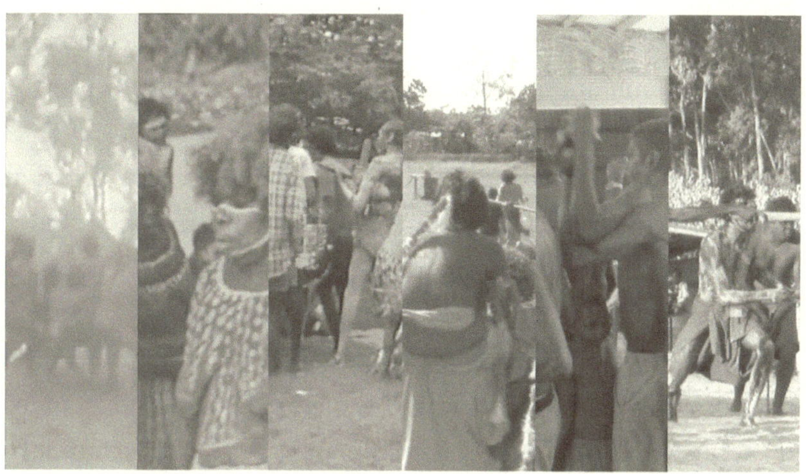

Figure 10.1: Wukun Wanambi, Nhina, Nhäma, Ga Ngäma *(Sit, Look, And, Listen), video still, 2014, 10 mins 21 sec.*

In *Nhina, Nhäma, Ga Ngäma,* Wukun's production process starts and ends with the archive. First, he captures dance scenes from the network of ceremonial grounds onto his editing timeline. The central motivation is to index rather than cut, to loop instead of narrate, creating six scenes from the archive referencing different repertoire and variable velocities simultaneously. Wukun presents multiple events at the same time, not to synchronise, but to bring together documents into a bounded screen space. He is applying normal rules of ceremony, whereby clan groups perform sequences of song and dance alongside one another generating autonomous arrangements on shared ground.

Wukun's postproduction is displayed as a six-channel ceremonial media installation, which divides, shifts and multiplies in a variety of dancers, generating archival art that extends a performance network across generations. In split screening images and layering song using archival film of six performances between the 1920s to the 2010s, Wukun creates his own multiplication of archival events – the graphical interface as magnification of the network in action.

In our convergent world, artists increasingly move between diverse communities, discerning and respecting multiple perspectives. Using archival art, Wukun is operating between regional contexts and wider settings, dealing with the qualities of duration, place, affiliation and affect arising out of contemporary conditions, and exhibiting networks, interfaces, performances and transmissions within the documentary material itself. He conveys today's local and non-local processes by declaring: 'Now I have been recognised by the old people and the art galleries as a ceremony man'.[5] How Wukun moves between art galleries and ceremonial grounds will be developed by the following assumptions: ceremonies use artistic media as documentation, which produces an archive; documentary of ceremony's artistic media produces an archive of an archive; a ceremonial leader using documentary as artistic media produces archival art; archival art retrieves the ceremonial archive inscribed in the documentation.[6]

Ceremonies Use Artistic Media as Documentation, which Produces an Archive

Wukun began painting to fulfil a complete geographic catalogue of the exhibition Saltwater Yirrkala Bark Paintings of Sea Country (1997). His first work won best bark at the Fifteenth National Aboriginal and Torres Strait Islander Art Awards in 1995. Paintings of underwater scenes depict swarms of tightly painted mullet circulating through changing currents and turbulent tides, creating swirling patterns. In the Saltwater project his barks adjoined paintings by forty-seven artists from neighbouring sites. As the landowner of Gurka'wuy, a coastal estate, his painting of Trial Bay's physical and intellectual properties was envisaged as an index of coastal country, documenting defining features rather than mapping borders. Taken together the artist's works in Saltwater articulated Yolngu sea rights. The funds raised from selling the collection to the Australian Maritime Museum were used to extend Buku-Larrnggay Mulka into an audiovisual archive and video production house, under the title of The Mulka Project.[7]

In Yirrkala, a former missionary town where the art centre's archive is housed, repatriated archival records bring together the struggles of the surrounding homeland estates. A century of documentary work by ethnographers, missionaries and government has produced an extensive archive of the region and the fifteen clan groups. This archive has become embedded in – or is mutually constitutive of – the places and identities bound together by the network of ceremonial grounds that comprise the overarching Yolngu identity of the clans. Like the development of the word 'Yolngu',[8] the Mulka archive performs network-oriented strategies of localisation. The desire to create such a network was manifested in 1998 when artists from competing clans collectively invested their individual artist fees towards the establishment of The Mulka Project. According to Wukun, the will behind the artists' investment is 'To show people how Yolngu law is connected to our art practice. The Mulka Project can bring together all our stories in a public ceremony'.[9]

The application of culturally relevant protocols and workflows over local documents composes archival functions according to Yolngu law. The Board governing procedures and policies of the art centre comprises ceremonial archivists, artists and leaders acting in concert. Applying rules governing the shared ground between clans to the archive means 'bringing together all our stories' because connectivity produces powerful programs that execute specific and successive Yolngu legal frameworks between landowners. The capacity to circulate documents between clans is derived from linkages within the file structure. Governing the archive is not organising discrete media objects, rather all archival procedures explicitly support a Yolngu network across three sites communicating shared ground – Northeast Arnhem Land, its art centre, and its archive. This is not simply about the Western European ideologies Jacques Derrida applies when he writes about how 'effective democratisation can always be measured by this essential criterion: the participation in and the access to the archive, its constitution, and its interpretation'.[10] Before participation comes the site to gather participants. Yolngu use Mulka as residence for the archive. Controlling relational datasets, which are already predicated on existing social structures, holds and protects documents that bind and bound participation. Creating archives to exist within an art centre that represents a region and its landowners has produced expressions of Yolngu law as archival evidence in legal proceedings and archival art for gallery events.

The Mulka Project of establishing an audiovisual archive of work originating in and located on Northeast Arnhem Land was envisaged as a vital step in resisting the marginalisation of people and place in the larger politics of the nation state, and asserting a political intent to maintain control over one's image and intellectual property. The archive – such as the ethnographic films featured in Wukun's archival art – is a means of applying not just ceremonial language from the past but a sense of historical development that connected past, present and future Yolngu cultural practices. The ethnographers of Western modernity catalogued documentation systems of song, sculpture, dance and painting using the static one-dimensional methodology of object-based archives, which had descended from library catalogues. Here recordings become buried spreadsheets like rows of file names in cemeteries. However, the repatriated recordings imported into the Mulka Project are a means of accumulating cultural capital upon which contemporary Yolngu ceremonial leaders can draw, breathing new life into Yolngu cultural practices. At the centre of the Mulka Project's conception is a belief that the archivist is an artist – a notion that goes well beyond Hal Foster's diagnosis of an archival turn in contemporary art.[11]

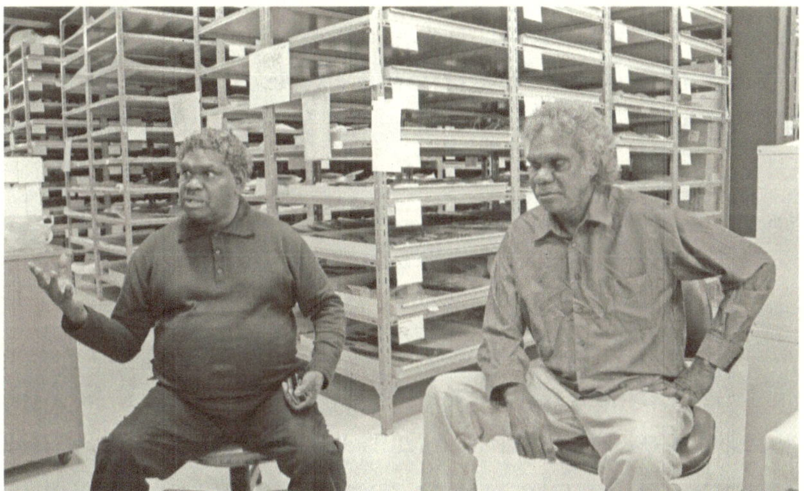

Figure 10.2: Wukun Wanambi (left) and Yumutjin Wunungmurra in the Australian Museum storage collection area, 2010. Photo: Robert Lazarus Lane.

Using the analogy of painting, Wukun states: 'the first layer is recording in camera. The second layer is art in gallery'.[12] The pursuit of a gallery interface for the artwork suggests the task for *Nhina, Nhäma, Ga Ngäma* is not a nostalgic journey into a cultural memory damaged by massive social upheavals, but excavates cultural history previously made invisible by endless bureaucratic glitches and ongoing political acts of exclusion in delocalised archival systems. Archival art turns restoration into something more than simply retrieving the past; it applies programmatic procedures to the material, producing a successive process.

Media archives attending to local users dismantle the abstract coordinates of time and space in centralised archives.[13] The reassertion of local authorship using the archive as a network of connected people and places bypasses centralised castles dictating what deserves a place, and what should be cut from the cultural record. Wukun restores some measure of symmetry, determining what is to be properly filed, what is to be muted, and what is to be amplified from existing archives in the sound design of *Nhina, Nhäma, Ga Ngäma*. Reconfiguring operations occur with the inclusion of virtual waves that rise and fall as oppositional rhythms nest beneath muted song. Ceremonial dance, underscored by white noise, recalls the changing tides of twentieth-century encounters.

This move to switch between 'excavation sites' and 'construction sites' shifts the emphasis away from a culture of loss to one of orchestrating archives for future remix.[14] Reparticipation in local documentation systems requires interventions into the material itself. The archive contains random edits of performance traditions for the sake of distant analysis, artefacts of cinematic confusion and evidence of colonial propaganda. Reconstruction must find a way to reframe documentary conventions, which not only assumed a dramatic loss of cultural diversity due to the encroachment of modernity but also assured it by using the assassin's knife of voiceovers and cutaways – and that is before the archival cataloguing of ethnographic museums further eroded Yolngu epistemology.

Documentary of Ceremony's Artistic Media Produces an Archive of an Archive

Ceremony has been captured on recording devices for nearly a century in Northeast Arnhem Land. Western ethnographers introduced these archival technologies without understanding that the Indigenous ceremonial events of their recordings were themselves archiving processes using artistic media. The desire to document using the fidelity of the new photographic documentary technologies drew anthropologists to the visual aspects of ceremony that otherwise were difficult to render. Ceremonial leaders were drawn to these new technologies of visual documentation, now able to combine duration with mobility.

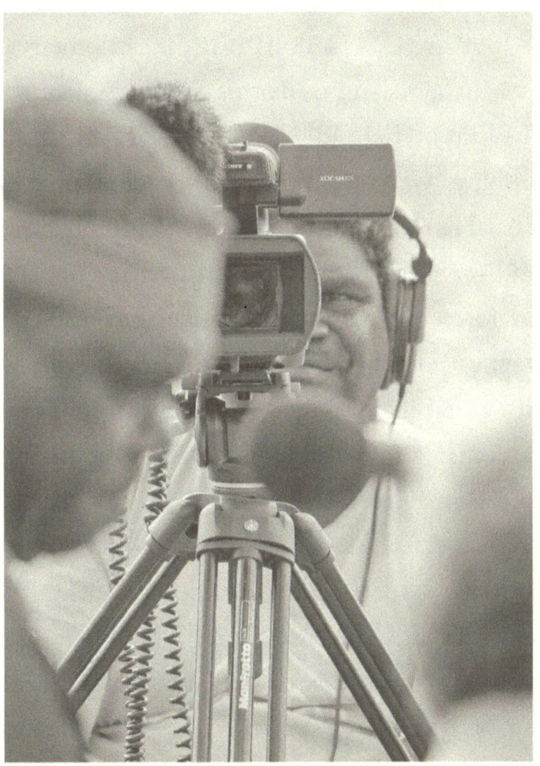

Figure 10.3: Wukun Wanambi filming ceremonial performance at Garma Festival, 2010. Photo: Robert Lazarus Lane.

This is not to say that ceremony needed cameras whirling for it to occur. Rather, new photographic and sonic recording devices were absorbed into the porous logic of ceremony, as another activity within its documentation system. Ceremonial orchestrations produce a resistance to documentation approaches not operating as part of its matrix of mediums. Consequently, anthropologists who could film were of use to Indigenous ceremonial leaders because they provided another means to archive the specific expressions inherent in ceremonial activity. As an exchange process, ceremony's documentary modes and documentary's ceremonial modes served dual interests.

The Western desire to reconstitute ceremony's enduring qualities was insatiable from the moment the cine-camera was invented in 1895. In 1898 A. C. Haddons was 600 kilometres away from Yirrkala, on Murray Island in Torres Strait, recording ceremonial dance.[15] The intent behind Haddon's early cinema, according to A. Grimshaw, was to produce 'documentation of a "dying" culture'. What Haddon did not entirely comprehend from within his nineteenth-century paradigm, but perhaps his Murray Island actors could foresee, was that the moving film of the Lumiere cinematographe did much more than trace gestural traces from the past – its visual technologies made evident a coherent performance of a continuous cultural process.[16] Documentation made to move enters a network to be mobilised not stilled, becoming progressively subjected to variable material states as it migrates between formats, which in turn exposes cultural processes to different velocities as it enters new archives.

In a time of memory cards and cloud storage, the complex scenography of Indigenous performance still creates a 'certain cognitive indecipherability'[17] in the minds of dehydrated and sunburnt film makers, who pass through places like Torres Strait and

Arnhem Land with an ever-increasing frequency. Interestingly, the archive of contemporary recordings still demonstrates how long-duration performances, with intense physical acts and multiple scenes occurring simultaneously, remain too advanced for most recording apparatuses. However, when Wukun archives, ethnography captures ceremony's complex uniting of gestures, images, props and sounds as more of a database cinema, as opposed to a documentary film approach.

> Through our journey Yolngu law was passed on to outsiders with their cameras and microphones who wanted to understand the way we live and survived. Now we're still passing on our law through cameras and microphones, but instead we got the facilities on our country, to share our law with our people and the world.[18]

Using documentation alongside performance, art centre leaders, who are experienced choreographers, composers, archivists and performers, reject claims that the artistic media of ceremonial production is being cannibalised by new media recordings. The idea that new media documentation replaces the thing itself is premised on media being tools for memory, as if it destroys the memorised procedures of dancers, songmen and others. What in fact is happening, of course, is quite the opposite: the world of new media is now just one part of ceremonial production in general.[19]

Wukun is best known as a painter and sculptor, but has been working as a video artist since 2008. He has tethered his media and painting studio practice, which sees him moving between editing software and earth pigments, sometimes on a daily basis. It's commonplace to discuss assembling video files in multi-track timelines while he patiently layers detailed patterns across memorial poles.[20]

Perhaps it is due to growing up around film crews recording his family members or perhaps it is due to the Yolngu notion of temporality, but Wukun is not burdened by Western perceptions of difference between traditional and new media. Instead of a binary trap, leaders of Wukun's Marrakulu clan in Gurrkawuy showed him how cinema can be thought about alongside ceremony as a cultural transmission if you 'open your mind for the future, and don't be trapped, because culture has always been flowing'.[21]

Ceremonial Leader Using Documentary Material as Artistic Media Produces Archival Art

Wukun's artworks are not about archiving film history but projecting Yolngu relational databases of agency and personhood. There is no opening scene, nor centre, and no particular image that grounds the artist's position. As a site of exchange, records are evenly drawn from a database, and arranged as a picture of ceremonial worlds.

Making archival films on the ceremonial ground continues a political agenda to develop affiliations between traditional and new media, between past and present, and between cultures. Howard Morphy, a long time anthropologist and collaborator with Yolngu artists, notes how global forces, 'are not restricted to any one context but move back and forward across contexts creating a dialogical relationship between Yolngu society and the encompassing world'.[22]

Ceremonial media is not a tool for memory, but another way in which Yolngu 'recognises and develops a mass of documentation with which it is inextricably linked'.[23] Rather than block ethnographers or denigrate film's capacities, ceremonial leaders recognise and exploit documentary power in creative and progressive ways.

In *Nhina, Nhäma, Ga Ngäma,* Wukun strips back 100 years of documentary filmmaking using post-production to retain that to which his senses have, through ceremony, been attuned. In this way archival film becomes a means of extending 'the work expended on material documentation' by predecessors to reconstruct 'within the documentary material itself unities, totalities, series, relations'.[24] Deconstructing documentary to reconstruct ceremony produces exchanges between generations of performers. Archival art becomes part of a ceremonial continuum to bind local networks in the face of counterforces, through the installation of multiple streams, channels and screens in the gallery space.

The moves made by Wukun are neither static readings of past events drawn from archives, nor improvised chants trying to infill bare remains. His work is a passage through ceremonies that is orchestrated by interlocking mediums, a montaging of methods and spectrums of channels. The postproduction processes used by Wukun, a ceremonial leader who places emphasis on being always connected to mobile networks and contactable via an array of media, reveals an artist as facilitator of multiple modes of transmission.[25] Multiple in his functions, he performs as a clan member, an artist, an archivist, a recorder, a diver, a counsellor, a translator, an editor. Generating multiple identities, supporting connectivity is a way of being: in the medium of the ceremonial ground; present in multi-sited social networks; neo-traditional in the art world.[26]

Standing in front of *Nhina, Nhäma, Ga Ngäma,* one can sense Dziga Vertov's celebration of photographic and urban mechanisms in Wukun's ambition to intensify movement using framing devices. Unlike many works coming from art centres, the clans, locations, authors and narratives featured within the work are not framing its display. Wukun's archival art is not using ceremonial recordings to provide evidence of authenticity. Rather, he is using the archive to make evident innovative ceremonial practices. Using cinematic apparatus to celebrate dynamism embraces how ceremonial practice channels adaptation, alteration, malleability, diversity, versatility, variability and development.

The calibration of new media into existing documentation systems – of which digitisation is now but one – situates the performances archived in Wukun's film as the grounding events from which documentary development is then determined by or through. The transformations in *Nhina, Nhäma, Ga Ngäma* of ceremonial ground becoming film becoming newsreel becoming ethnography becoming file becoming installation is an indexical series of appropriations in which the reiterations remain grounded. But the digitisation of appropriations frees ceremonial documents from devices and objects to what counts on the ceremonial ground: exchanging currencies, connecting channels, overlapping currents. This all points to the mediating role of ceremonial grounds as 'spaces of contemporaneity' in the literal sense of being places where connections between different temporalities are facets or perhaps nodal points linking production, circulation and use in a meshing of multiple temporalities. In this sense *Nhina, Nhäma, Ga Ngäma* is a documentation platform, that in '*transforming simultaneously* past, present, and future' is 'a system for recreating a whole economy of the temporal'.[27]

Archival Art Retrieves the Ceremonial Archive Inscribed in the Documentation

The key idea behind redocumentation, in regards to how Wukun uses archives today, is the reversibility of archival processes without changing its fundamental properties. On entering the installation one views a frame symmetrically arranged into six vertical panels. Each pole-shaped panel is filled with one continuous dance scene.

The arrangement of archival films is not linear either spatially or temporally. Further, then dancing is not interrupted and remains on screen throughout the work: Wukun is thinking through movement and space, not words and dates.[28] Using Gilles Deleuze's intellectual suite of tools from movement-image, a viewer can see how Wukun is not using postproduction to intercut various scenes of dance to produce a montage, but is showing recordings as they occurred because 'movement is indivisible, or cannot be divided without changing qualitatively each time it is divided'.[29] Retaining the flows of dance and the choreographed moves of ceremony as a system in itself serves the interests of performance, rather than interpreting the literary arcs of Western teleology.

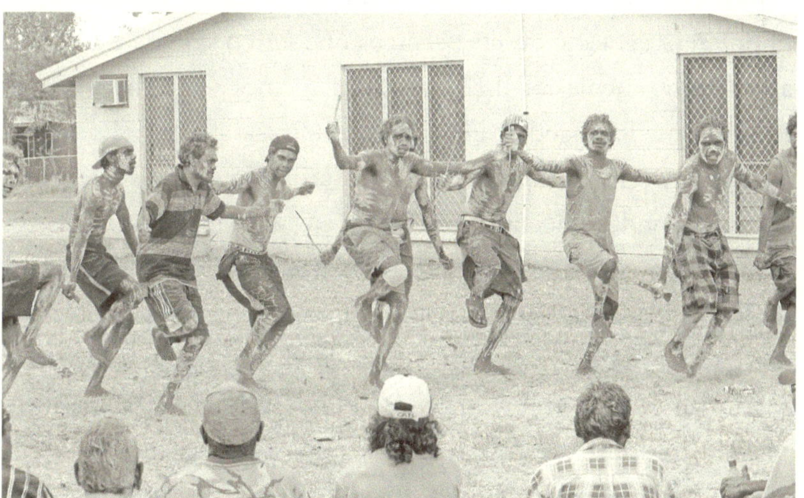

Figure 10.4: Djapu performance in Yirrkala during Wamut Dhapi, 2010. Photo: Robert Lazarus Lane.

Local networks visualised in Wukun's *Nhina, Nhäma, Ga Ngäma* produce a program of dance. Having grown up as a performer, then a choreographer, now an editor of dance, Wukun is redoubling imagery, retrieving historical performances and producing a different way of setting up and passing on history.

It recalls Lepecki's idea of porousness within the dance archive, in which 'the body as archive re-places and diverts notions of archive away from a documental deposit or a bureaucratic agency dedicated to the (mis)management of "the past"'.[30] The dancers' bodies do not depict history, they perform cultural lineage as media carriers. As a choreographer of movement and editor of timelines, Wukun splices together dancing media carrier bodies into a 'lineage machine'.[31]

Redocumenting the archive reorganises events previously separated by independent and private space into an affective fabric of interconnected acts. The ten-minute arrangement of overlapping percussion clashes events that have been previously synchronised autonomously. Off-screen voices and the overwhelming build-up of different acoustic events becomes one stereo sound. This is less about using media for the retrieval of memory and more a push to bring media together into one soundtrack as layered seams of a database. The complexity of cross-affiliation, as opposed to a managed model of identity, produces interwoven forces that merge dates, sites and bodies into a ceremonial assemblage, documenting networks of affect. Wukun's archival art is a network in form by using reframing and reiterating procedures on content designed to capture and document connections between linked performances. The artwork becomes not merely a way to document something but is itself another iteration of that which it is documenting.[32]

Nhina, Nhäma, Ga Ngäma is a six-channel video installation in which the artist has stacked, rather than sequenced, archival records, and movement is used to establish lineage as a dynamic procession of dance dynasties. This approach to real dance movements and abstract split screens produces two effects: looping dance clips as they happened invites viewers to find succession; arranging events into six cells crops and divides space into one whole choreographic pattern. Wukun's affectual composition is not archiving 'the body' but endeavouring to reconfigure a body's archive.[33]

Wukun's project becomes a library and museum of ceremony, because its media is produced in the self-conscious relationship to earlier media,[34] archiving how every dance finds synchronisation and each song cycle becomes harmonised when no longer separated by individual histories and archived as autonomous movements. Thus the different historical scenes are made to 'belong to a single, identical, homogeneous space, while the movements are heterogeneous, irreducible among themselves'.[35]

By redocumenting a performance legacy on Northeast Arnhem Land's network of ceremonial grounds, Wukun projects a genealogy of dynamic mechanisms for aggregating documentation. The filmmaker's intent is not privileged as the archival nature of the art traces the genealogies of moving image work in ceremonial performance. His strategy is to build on the role of the dancer as director. By not being interviewed and not being organised by narrative arcs that exist outside of ceremony itself, the dancer is in control. Wukun's editing emphasises the dance film as mutually constituted.[36]

What matters is the system, the choreography regulated by a formula, the archiving of a move or a step. Applying Deleuze, one can suggest *Nhina, Nhäma, Ga Ngäma* is the editing of affect more than representation, projecting a system of choreographed actions and impacting forces rather than a system naming images to archive in a regime of signs.[37] While Wukun's approach to affect may appear like he is documenting archival fragmentations and degradations, this is not the case if one's modes of inquiry begin with networked movement rather than static states, with a focus on translation processes rather than what position to take.[38]

Approaches to works made from performance and media can oversimplify analysis by mapping the relations of subjects and objects in a historical period, or collecting narrative statements to reveal artist intent. This mental analysis can overlook how editing dance is primarily a musical effort to generate intensity.

So despite symmetry-breaking events via different recording devices, changing media carriers and destructive editing techniques, the ceremonial dance documented over decades in *Nhina, Nhäma, Ga Ngäma* fully coexist with one another, revealing how components interface and can be exported out of one event, inserted into another, and produce a rhythmic coherence as a virtual archive functioning as parts of a whole. The resuscitation of archival materials through the mobilising effect of reconnecting generations through a shared dance enables the genesis of small differences to be tracked, traced and used in their own right. Here Wukun indexes movements through calculating factors such as stability, growth and adjustments. Documenting gradual variation and slippages, he exhibits video streams as a collective wave, showing succession, where 'imitation is the propagation of a flow'.[39]

Conclusion

Nhina, Nhäma, Ga Ngäma is an intensive audiovisual retrospective ruminating on the multiple incarnations of ceremonial dance archived on film in Northeast Arnhem Land, its vital intersections with twentieth-century ceremonies when recording devices documented dancers, and with twenty-first century events when dancers redocumented recordings. Repeating and multiplying a historical idea is predicated on a drive to produce documentation. My proposition is that this drive in Wukun's work is fuelled by performing ceremony – a document-generating machine. Access to new media technologies make it possible for Wukun to modify and recirculate media content in powerful new ways, but the image of an Indigenous person holding a camera is not the recognition this essay seeks. Beyond filming, archiving and editing tools, we need to recognise that the origin of Wukun's archival art is in its subject: the skills and knowledge coming from ceremonial practice, driving him to deploy media apparatus toward production processes.

After half a century of film projects, Yolngu leader Roy Dadaynga Marika, in 1970, declared an ongoing Yolngu drive to produce documentation: 'This is our chance to record our history for our children, for our children and our grandchildren'. With cameras and dancers looking on he continued: 'We should do this while we are still alive. Before we die we should make a true picture...our own Yolngu picture, that will teach our children our dances and law and everything – our singing, our own Yolngu culture'.[40]

The production of ceremony enables recording acts, induces documentation actions, inscribes the actor's memory and ultimately reproduces itself by unfurling these durational spools of tape conserving past events until the recorders from which they flow cover the ground, awaiting to be rewound differently.[41] By inscribing new combinations onto existing components, archives reinvent the present in the past by reperforming the new upon the substrate of the old and vice versa. Yet, as Henri Bergson says, 'no two moments are identical in a conscious being'.[42] Rewinding the tape implies a replaying the past but does not imply that the viewers watching Wukun's archival art experience the same past in the modern moment. Different montages from Wukun's past are not interpreted; rather a newer scene is combined with an older one, and thus, when another scene occurs, it is added onto all the other old ones plus new ones from before. The filters and variations, qualities and relations compose worlds Bergson calls the mobility of temporal progress.[43] Never motionless, Wukun's archival activity is a creative relay process produced by persistent pasts and enduring connections. In many respects the circulation is what matters, not the particular forms that it causes to emerge. The event is not the thing, nor is the recording process, but amid the continuity of progress what is passed on – what is redocumented in real time. Mario Perniola argues the recognition of reality 'is not what appears at any moment, but what is conserved'.[44]

To think about Wukun's multi-screen realisation of ceremony's virtual archives, one can quote Vertov's brother and director of photography, Mikhail Kaufman. He is discussing Vertov's editing method as a way of world-picturing that is 'infused with the particular thought that he is actually seeing the world for other people'. 'Like a kind of scholar', says Kaufman, 'he is able to gather empirical observations in one place and then in another. And that is actually the way in which the world has come to be understood'.[45]

Wukun's scholarship captures the archive as the nodal point of intellectual property and its performance, through a postproduction process reframing dance to capture ceremonial documents on digital interfaces. Artists using the archive to retrieve documentary recordings of performance histories, and reiterating events in the gallery, connect legacy and progress. This marks the media connections occurring in his body of work and presents a ceremonial leader developing practices in which artistic media and virtual archives network to expand Yolngu intellectual mobility. Wukun's scholarly reframing of audiovisual archives through a postproduction process continues ceremonial intellectual practices using ensembles of cultural techniques and transmission formats.

In effect, ceremonial leaders making archival art like Wukun document how ceremony works, or perhaps, more accurately, how ceremony archives itself.

Notes

1 Private communication with Wukun Wanambi, 2015.

2 I refer to the artist by his first name because there are many Wanambi artists generating artwork in northeast Arnhem Land.

3 H. Morphy, 'Art as a Mode of Action: Some Problems with Gell's Art and Agency', *Journal of Material Culture*, vol. 14, no. 1, March 2009, pp. 5–27.

4 Exhibited in 135th Meridian-East 2014, The Australian Experimental Art Foundation and Unsettled, National Museum Australia 2015.

5 Artist Statement, viewed 20 October 2015, <http://www.waterfront.nt.gov.au/darwin-waterfront-precinct/parklands/public-art/>.

6 These ideas are expanded in my forthcoming thesis.

7 Investment in multiple manifestations of ceremony's manifold forms continues at Buku-Larrnggay Mulka, with the recent extension of The Mulka Project with the addition of a sound studio and performance space.

8 Word meaning 'person' now used for inhabitants of Eastern Arnhem Land to affiliate members from different clans under an umbrella term. It's rare for people from Northeast Arnhem Land to refer to themselves as Indigenous or Aboriginal. Most people refer to themselves as Yolngu when talking to non-Yolngu and continue to refer to themselves by clan when talking to other clan members.

9 R. Lane, 'To Hold and Protect: Mulka at Yirrkala', *Artlink*, vol. 31, no. 2, 2011, pp. 82–3 at 82.

10 J. Derrida, *Archive Fever: A Freudian Impression*, trans. Eric Prenowitz, University of Chicago Press, Chicago, 1995, p. 4.

11 H. Foster, 'The Artist as Ethnographer', in J. Fisher (ed.), Global Visions: Towards a new internationalism in the visual arts, Kala Press in association with The Institute of International Visual Arts, London, 1994, pp. 12–17.

12 Private communication with Wukun Wanambi, 2015.

13 J. Jacobs, *Edge of Empire: Postcolonialism and the city*, Routledge, London, 1996, p. 158.

14 Thomas Hirschhorn quoted in H. Foster, 'An Archival Impulse', *October*, no. 110, Fall 2004, pp. 3–22 at 22.

15 Viewed 20 October 2015, < http://aso.gov.au/titles/historical/torres-strait-islanders/clip1/>.

16 A. Grimshaw, *The Ethnographer's Eye: Ways of Seeing in Anthropology*,

Cambridge University Press, Cambridge, 2001, p. 24.

17 A. Gell, *Art and Agency: An Anthropological Theory*, Clarendon Press, Oxford, 1998, p. 96.

18 R. Lane, 'To Hold and Protect', p. 83

19 Suppose a writer who does not play soccer tells the richest football club – Real Madrid – that media coverage will impact their players' memory. All the techniques developed in their bodies and the tactics built up across generations of performances will be dismantled once they start watching tape of games. What has occurred in sport is the inverse scenario: everything on the pitch is recorded and analysed down to the smallest pixel of interaction, yet crucially, practice on the training ground still means everything.

20 In the same period, Wukun produced a Larrakitj installation showing the processual layering of six ceremonial poles, and his six-panel, vertically cropped video work – *Nhina, Nhäma, Ga Ngäma.*

21 Private communication with Wukun Wanambi, 2015.

22 H. Morphy, 'Art as a Mode of Action', p. 20.

23 M. Foucault, *Archaeology of Knowledge*, trans. S. Smith, Pantheon Books, New York, 1972, p. 7.

24 ibid., p. 7.

25 N. Bourriaud, *Relational Aesthetics*, Les Presses du réel, Paris, 2002.

26 T. Spear, 2003, 'Neo-Traditionalism and the Limits of Invention in British Colonial Africa', *The Journal of African History*, vol. 44, no. 1, pp. 3–17 at 4.

27 M. Foucault, *Archaeology of Knowledge*, quoted in A. Lepecki, 'The Body as Archive: Will to Reenact and the Lives of Dances', *Dance Research Journal*, vol. 42, no. 2, 2010, pp. 28–48 at 30.

28 H. Lefebvre, *The Production of Space*, trans. D. Nicholson-Smith, Blackwell Publishing, Cambridge, Mass., 1991, p. 406.

29 G. Deleuze, *Cinema 1: the movement-image*, trans. H. Tomlinson and B. Habberjam, University of Minnesota Press, Minneapolis, 1986, p. 1.

30 A. Lepecki, 'The Body as Archive', p. 34.

31 R. Schneider, quoted in J. Blocker, 'Repetition: A Skill which Unravels', in A. Jones & A. Heathfield (eds), *Perform, Repeat, Record: Live Art in History*, Intellect, Bristol, 2012, ebook.

32 R. Rappaport, 'The Obvious Aspects of Ritual', *Ecology, Meaning, and Religion,* North Atlantic Books, Berkeley, California. 1979, pp. 173–221 at 177.

33 Spinoza quoted in M. Gregg & G. J. Seigworth, 'An Inventory of Shimmers', in M. Gregg & S. J. Seigworth (eds), *The Affect Theory Reader*, Duke University Press, Durham, 2010, pp. 1–25 at 3.

34 M. Foucault, 'Fantasia on the Library', *Language, Counter-Memory, Practice*, D. F. Bouchard (ed.), trans. D. F. Bouchard & S. Simon, Cornell University Press, Ithica, 1967, pp. 78–110 at 92–3.

35 G. Deleuze, *Cinema* 1, p. 1.

36 A. Escobar, 'Culture sits in Places: Reflections on Globalism and Subaltern Strategies of Localization', *Political Geography*, no. 20, 2001, pp. 139–74 at 146.

37 G. Deleuze, *The Logic of Sense*, trans. Charles Stivale, Columbia University Press, New York, 1990.

38 B. Massumi, *Parables for the Virtual: Movement, Affect, Sensation*, Duke University Press, Durham, 2002.

39 G. Deleuze & F. Guattari, *A Thousand Plateaus: Capitalism and Schizophrenia*, trans. B. Massumi, University of Minnesota Press, Minneapolis, 1987, p. 219.

40 This sequence was included in a film called *Pain for this Land* (1995) which serves as a general introduction to the *Yirrkala Film Project*, a collection of twenty-two documentary films made over a period of thirty years by Ian Dunlop, from which one panel in Wukun's work originates: *Marrakulu funeral – Yirrkala 1974*.

41 Hardwired for musical inscriptions, brains keep 'singing' long after a song has ended. Haunted, we repeat the song over and over in our mind. The more you repeat, the more you inscribe; eventually you're stuck in an unending song cycle. The memory system recording song is called the phonological loop; ceremonial song cycles use this 'short loop of recording tape that continuously stores a small amount of auditory information' to structure musical scores.

42 H. Bergson, *The Creative Mind*, trans. M. L. Andison, The Citadel Press, New York, 1992, p. 164.

43 L. Lawlor & V. M. Leonard, 'Henri Bergson', in E. N. Zalta (ed.), *The Stanford Encyclopedia of Philosophy*, viewed 20 November 2015, <http://plato.stanford.edu/archives/win2013/entries/bergson/>.

44 M. Perniola, *Enigmas*, trans. C. Woodall, Verso, London, 1995, pp. 65–6.

45 M. Kaufman quoted in L. Manovich, *The Language of New Media*, MIT Press, Boston, 2001, p. 240.

11

OUR ART, OUR WAY: TOWARDS AN AṈANGU ART HISTORY WITH AṞA IRITITJA[1]

John Dallwitz, Janet Inyika, Susan Lowish and Linda Rive

We are here to have a conversation about art and people. How information about them gets saved, who benefits from it in the future, how it grows and how peoples' memories can be collected are very important issues for Pitjantjatjara people (Aṉangu). It is the reason Aṟa Irititja was started – too many nameless people in photographs going unacknowledged. Aṉangu are very keen to make sure the records are straight, and they know who's who in many of the photos. Aṟa Irititja is all about responding to Aṉangu; holding digitised archival material alongside born digital recordings in culturally appropriate relationships, accessed through a sensible interface, easily searchable, and with results that hold meaning for Aṉangu.

'The Aṟa Irititja project works to accommodate Aṉangu wishes for the delivery of regularly updated, high quality interactive multi-media databases, in Ngaanyatjarra, Pitjantjatjara, Yankunytjatjara language and English, onto their communities. The project is dedicated to maintain regular Aṉangu access to these databases and is accountable to Aṉangu in its management and delivery of this historical material'.[2] In accordance with the United Nations *Declaration on the Rights of Indigenous Peoples* (2007), Aṟa Irititja has always operated from the understanding that Aṉangu have the right to be informed about collections that exist relating to them, their culture, language and heritage. We also believe that they have the right to determine use and access provisions for their heritage materials.

As of November 2015, the Ara Irititja digital archive held 147,600 photographs, 5,166 documents, 491 movies, 523 sound clips and 5,196 objects (almost all art and craft works) – a total of 158,976 items.[3] It is the greatest digital archive of Anangu life anywhere in the world, and it was recently recognised as an outstanding project with an award from the Association of Tribal Archives, Libraries, and Museums (ATALM) in a ceremony held at the Smithsonian in Washington, D.C. It has always been thought that the project should never finish and that it needs to be more inclusive, not more exclusive. In particular, 'we wish many more of the schools would send photos to us for inclusion in the archive. We would also love it if more of the art centres across the Lands shared their collections with Ara Irititja so that all Anangu can see the great work they do'.[4]

Our presentation today will demonstrate the important role that art already plays in the archive, how it has the potential to feature more prominently in the database, and the benefits this would bring to both Anangu and the field of Australian Aboriginal art history. We also give a glimpse of some aspects of Anangu art history from Anangu perspectives and recommend that a much richer and more multifaceted Aboriginal art history would come from a more equitable engagement with Indigenous peoples through museums, galleries and individuals engaging with and supporting an existing community resource such as Ara Irititja.

Due to the size and diversity of materials in the Ara Irititja archive, there are a number of things that are of great interest to Anangu, and hold significance to them but not necessarily to anyone else. There are many items in the archive that bring back memories and ideas, often from long ago. These memories are still alive for Aṉangu and are triggered by viewing or listening to items that they can access when they want, how they want and without outside help or permission.

We are talking here today about the history of Aṉangu art, and a specific history that starts about ten to fifteen years before most remote Aboriginal art centres' archives began. In this instance, we are also focusing our discussion and being guided in its content by a very important person – Janet Inyika, long-serving member and Director of the Ngaanyatjarra Pitjantjatjara Yankunytjatjara Women's Council; regional representative of Desart – the non-profit, peak industry body that represents over forty Central Australian Aboriginal art centres; and former member of Amata Community Council.[5] She is a great supporter of Aṟa Irititja.

Janet is an Elder and leader in her community and has played a major role in addressing problems of petrol-sniffing deaths on the Aṉangu, Pitjantjatjara, Yankunytjatjara (APY) Lands. In early 2005 she launched the then new Opal low-octane 'unsniffable' petrol at the BP terminal in Largs Bay, SA, with the former Federal Minister for Health, Tony Abbott. In 2008, she gave evidence to the Senate inquiry into petrol sniffing in Central Australia. She is tireless in her efforts to give back to her community.[6]

Janet has also performed in the stage play *Ngapartji Ngapartji* that toured nationally between 2005 and 2008 and was one of 330 Aboriginal women who took part in the Sydney 2000 Olympic Games Opening Ceremony. She has been an artist for most of her life. At the beginning of her career she painted with Tjurma Arts in Amata in the APY Lands; today she is an artist with Maṟuku Arts and Walkatjara Art Centre and a weaver with Tjanpi Desert Weavers. She has also produced batik works, with one being purchased by the National Gallery of Australia.[7]

In this presentation, we are really linking things together. We might be talking about the art centre of today, in the end, but we are able to put it in a context that goes back long before today's art centres. For example, one of the earliest pictures we have of Janet that relates to art is an image of her as a very young girl lying in the sand making drawings. If you look at the sand near the girls, you can see the remnants of many drawings.

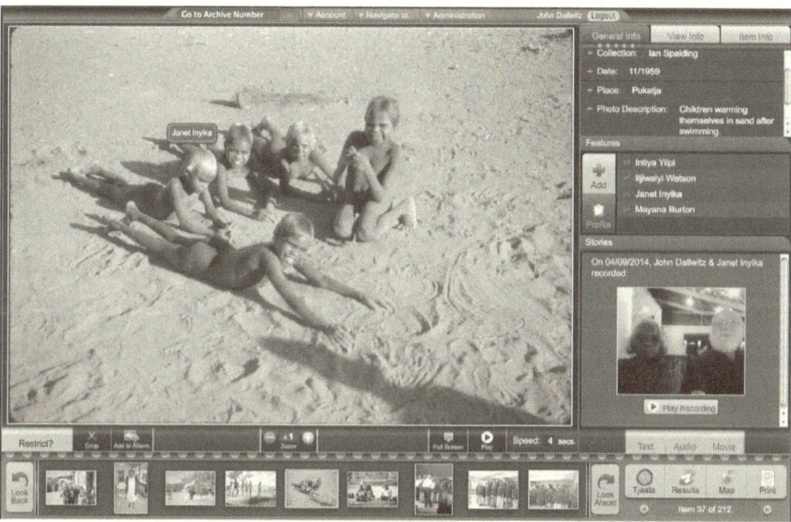

Figure 11.1. Screenshot of the A̱ra Irititja archive in use during the 2014 Art Centres Art Histories symposium in Alice Springs showing Janet Inyika and friends as young children making sand drawings (centre), metadata fields and live recording (bottom right) of Janet Inyika and John Dallwitz annotating the 1959 photograph. Photo A̱ra Irititja 26290. Photographer Ian Spalding.

We are demonstrating the live facility of A̱ra Irititja to record stories for these images, and Janet has chosen a special image of herself as a young girl with some dear friends no longer with us. It is sad, but also an important example that makes clear the continuity of drawing to painting, and the connection between social history and art. We can provide extra information about this photograph just by adding our names and turning the camera and sound on to record directly onto this computer, because we have the opportunity to address this topic of children's drawings, and the way 'art' started, and the way the people started using art in Ernabella back in the 1940s and 1950s. We know it has been the subject of a lot of discussion and people have written a great deal about it, but this is a story just for today.

We have the opportunity now of recording a person, who was there, who was a kid at the time, whose mother was a great artist, dancer, singer, whose auntie was a great artist, whose whole family were great artists. What we are calling 'art' today is integral to the environment she grew up in, so it is only natural that the kids should be on the ground making drawings. Janet can give us a little bit of background about this photo if she wants to, and Linda can translate. [A live movie annotation now takes place, filming Janet via the in-built camera on the computer and recording it directly onto Ara Irititja. Janet starts speaking in Pitjantjatjara and Linda interprets into English.] 'We'd just been swimming, because we had a swimming pool there at Pukatja and afterwards we had been running around in the sunshine to get dry and roll in the sand and draw pictures. So that's what we'd been doing'.

We have now saved this live recording on our server in Sydney, it is now part of Ara Irititja, and the recording is forever attached to the photograph, a permanent part of the metadata for that photograph. The recording is locked to that photograph and it will stay there, but the translation is not there. Linda did not interpret Janet's movie annotation for inclusion in Ara Irititja, because that story is for the archive and the archive is for Anangu. Janet does not need to have her story interpreted for herself, but a text annotation of the translation could be included for future researchers. We have kept the interpretation for the purposes of this exercise – to demonstrate to outsiders the integral connection between people and art practice, but also how old photographs, documents, movies and sound recordings trigger memories and how easily these memories can be recorded and shared through Aṟa Irititja.

We want to share some more items from the archive and demonstrate how, through the active re-engagement with this material, A<u>n</u>angu people in central, southern and western Australia affirm, enliven and consolidate their own history. What we today recognise as 'art' is very much a part of history in a much broader sense, and is much more strongly connected to places, people, song, dance, (what we might call 'ceremony'), law and country from A<u>n</u>angu perspectives than is usually communicated by viewing an object in a museum vitrine or on a gallery wall. It is a great strength of Aṟa Irititja that it re-establishes, maintains and makes clear these connections.

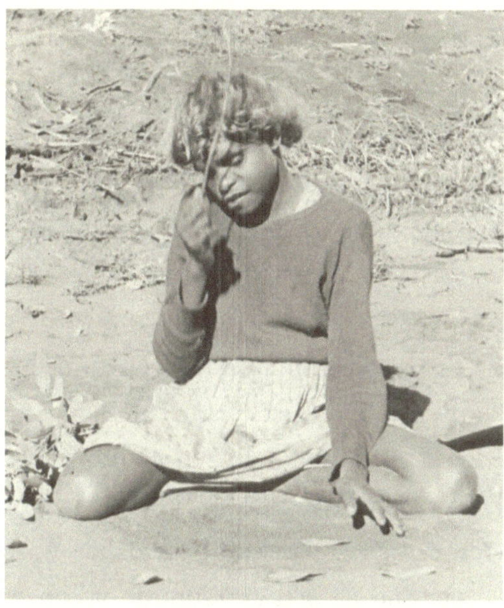

Figure 11.2: Janet Inyika at Amata in 1966 storytelling in the sand with a stick and gumleaves (milpatjunanyi). *Janet utilised similar materials in her presentation at the symposium. Photo Aṟa Irititja 51921. Photographer Bill Nicol.*

[Janet begins speaking about another item she has chosen to show us from the Ara Irititja archive. This time it is an old photograph in black and white of just her, a little bit older than last time. She is drawing in the sand, this time with something that looks like a piece of wire commonly used to make the scorched marks on carved wooden objects or *punu*.] Janet tells us 'It is a stick, not a piece of wire, and that's how we do the *milpatjunanyi* – storytelling. And I am making the story up in my own mind, and it is a family story. So I am using these three leaves – the dad, mum and a little kid. These are Anangu mob'.

[Janet switches from referring to the old film image of herself, as a young child playing in the sand and telling stories with leaves, to addressing the audience in the room. She has brought leaves and sticks collected from the ground just outside the conference centre and begins to re-enact the story in the archive, but with a distinctly modern twist].

'And also these white coloured leaves are *piranpa* [white people] that are living in Amata, different colour, Dad, Mum and the kid. So I am using those leaves to tell a made up story as I am going along in the sand to myself'. As was noted shortly after the presentation, 'Janet selected the photographs of herself as a child drawing as the pedagogical tool for the conference audience. The photograph activated a precise visual memory, animating the past and making it meaningful in the present…The photograph is the visual record of an action, which allows repeating of the action in the proper way'.[8] Janet's performance was also effective in imbricating her and us in a continuum of engagement that is reflective of the situation then and now.

When we were planning this talk, seeing the earliest drawings in the Ara Irititja archive inspired Janet. Her family members made these early drawings. Linda took the opportunity to record Janet's history of art in a short film. The film is also in the archive. Here is the interpretation of Janet's Anangu words provided by Linda, with stills from the film added to illustrate the points Janet makes about the different designs.

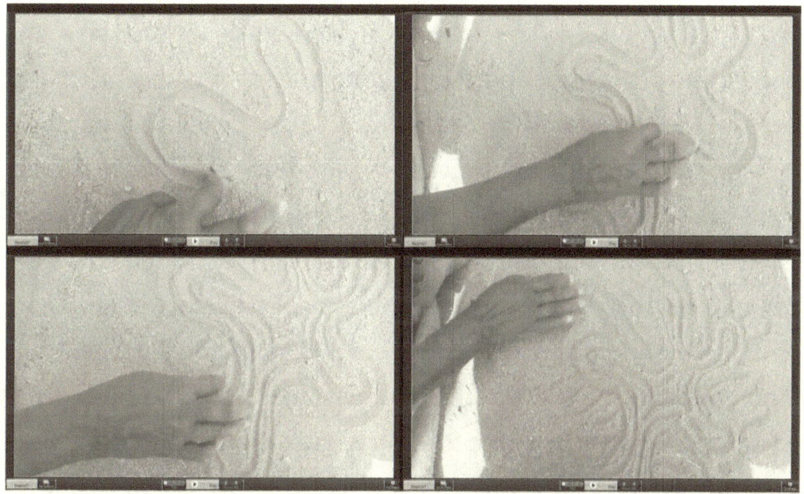

Figure 11.3: Screenshots from the Ara Irititja movie made by Linda Rive and Janet Inyika to show at the symposium. Janet demonstrates the progression of the linework in the drawings made at Ernabella when she was a child. Movie Ara Irititja 152294. Film Linda Rive and Janet Inyika.

We are quoting the English subtitles on a film Linda has made of Janet to accompany our presentation here today. It is an account of Anangu art history, as Janet tells us: 'The first drawings we ever did – a very, very long time ago – in the days when Ron Trudinger was living at Pukatja – were patterns like this [Janet draws the first Ernabella-style pattern in the sand]. These were the first ever of the drawings on paper, which were later developed and turned into paintings. This design was the first ever recorded, so it dates back a long way, but is still in use today. I remember seeing these designs when I was a schoolgirl. The second pattern was a development on the first one [Janet draws pattern number two, which included dozens of fringe-like lines emanating from the outside of the first style drawing]. After that, dot painting started'.[9]

'Back in the very early days of Ernabella, the old people were wood carvers. They made snakes, lizards, spear throwers and spears out of wood – and they still do today, of course. But back then they soon started to branch out. They started making birds, smaller tjati lizards, tiny souvenir-style spear throwers, and small perentie lizards. This is when they first started producing woodcarvings for the souvenir industry. Batik started around about the same time that the second [number two fringed] design came in. The early designs were incorporated into hooked floor rugs. The young women made those. They used hooks to hook short lengths of dyed wool into the base, and created beautiful floor rugs. Everyone had a particular skill. Some were good painters. Others were wonderful batik artists.[10]

'When I started going to school, I learnt how to draw on paper. We learnt how to make lines and do drawings and we learnt how to read and write. We had teachers who taught us how to write. [Janet writes in the sand] I went to Pukatja School. Our teachers taught us how to sew as well. We used to make little bags and sew these designs into them. We did not use a sewing machine. All our sewing was hand stitching. Our designs developed further, and we began using design number three. We did not stop using the first two designs though. We just had a bigger repertoire'.[11] Janet reveals a sequencing of styles that demonstrate a shared knowledge of innovation and experimentation with design and subject. 'We painted with watercolours I think and also crayons. I remember painting, but I do not think it was acrylic back then, I think it was watercolour. I was younger than the earlier artists. Tjikalyi, Tjalara and Tjunkara and all those ladies were older than me, and they were the first artists'.[12]

This lineage and association of different media with different time periods has helped to establish a history of An̲angu art. It is important to note that it is not a linear history, with clearly delineated styles and motifs. As Janet makes clear, the use of the earliest designs did not stop. Instead, they were adapted and changed, reinvented and renewed in a continuum that both acknowledges the past and looks to the future.

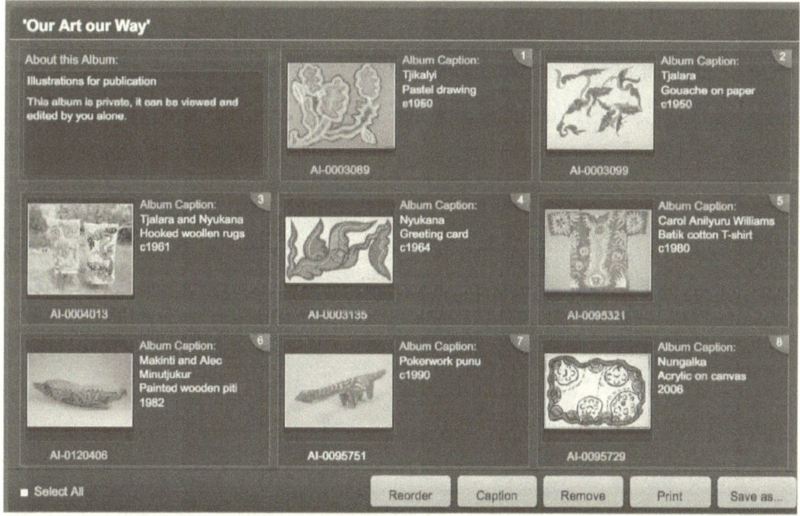

Figure 11.4: Screenshot of an 'Album' in Ar̲a Irititja. A selection of images from the archive collections illustrates the diversity of art and craft works from Ernabella.

'Pictures of all these works are on Ar̲a Irititja, old and new, from a long time ago and up until the present. On Ar̲a Irititja there must be hundreds of images of works that An̲angu have made over the years. *It is our own art history archive.* All the first dot paintings are on there. All our first drawings are there. Even some of my own first drawings are on Aṟa Irititja'.[13]

There is a wealth of knowledge and information on the archive and much to be shared with younger generations. As Janet states: 'Aṟa Irititja has everything! All our first early patterns are on our archive. There are great examples of work that we did when I was at school. Aṟa Irititja is simple and easy to use. It is a good educational tool'.[14] We all feel very strongly that Aṟa Irititja could be used a lot more in the schools and that a lot of student projects could be centred on the archive. Students can show Aṟa Irititja to their relatives and ask them to tell stories about the old days. This would be good for the students and valuable for adding to the archive. Students know a lot about plants and animals. They could be adding this information to the archive if they were given time, encouragement and opportunity at school. There is much talk about school attendance and literacy and numeracy levels of Aboriginal children. Students might be more interested in attending school if it meant engaging with content that was more relevant to their local environment. Interacting with Aṟa Irititja on a daily basis could help with these things.[15]

Aṟa Irititja is a positive, community-focused and multi-purpose entity. Janet echoes the sentiments of several Aṉangu Elders and Leaders when she states: 'When I saw those beautiful old early pastel drawings on Aṟa Irititja I was so excited...Every time I have anything to do with Aṟa Irititja I always feel really inspired, and I just want to keep doing more and more on it. For instance, right now, I am planning to record a longer, more detailed autobiography. I want to start from my babyhood, and include my growing up and my school days, and go up until today. I want to put down my own story. I also want to record stories of my family, because there is always a risk that I might forget who

I am or forget some of my own history – my own story, my own history. Stories might be forgotten. It is now or never. Time is of the essence. So we are going to be starting that now.[16]

'I really love Aṟa Irititja – as do a lot of people, it is very inspiring and I love all the old records on Aṟa Irititja. It is great to see images of me when I was just little, to be reminded of those happy days, and to see pictures of my extended family. I find them a source of inspiration. I continue to be inspired when I look back at our early history. Furthermore, I want to draw on them to do a series of new paintings – because I am a painter – I want to do a series of autobiographical paintings'.[17]

As a result of making the movie for this symposium presentation, and of Linda showing the movie to a handful of people, specifically the directors of the NPY Women's Council – to clear it with the directors, as we do, because it is a nice thing to do, proper etiquette – Rene Kulitja, also an important artist, community leader, Pitjantjatjara Elder and Director of the NPY Women's Council, expressed her desire to engage more directly with the archival material.

Born in 1958, in Ernabella, South Australia, Rene became involved in arts and crafts at the women's centre early in life and went on to become founding director of Walkatjara Art Centre. In 2002, Rene worked with Balarinji Studio in Sydney to design the exterior of a Qantas Boeing 737 fuselage and, in 2006, she became the chairperson of Maṟuku Arts. Rene works with a range of media, including paint, glass, ceramics and *tjanpi* (desert grass) and is also known for making traditional-style jewellery using modern techniques and media. Rene's work has been exhibited across Australia, Europe and Asia. Examples of her artworks are held in the National Gallery of Australia and the National Museum of Ethnology in Osaka. Most recently, Rene took part in *Kuka Irititja* (Animals from Another Time), a collaborative work between Fiona Hall and Tjanpi Desert Weavers included in Hall's exhibition, *Wrong Way Time*, at the 56th International Art Exhibition at the Venice Biennale 2015. Rene also travelled to the opening of the Biennale.[18]

Rene has held important positions within the Pitjantjatjara–Yankunytjatjara community for several years. She has been a member of both the Mu<u>t</u>itjulu Community Council and the Board of Management of Ulu<u>r</u>u-Kata Tju<u>t</u>a National Park. She is a long-serving member and Director of the Ngaanyatjarra Pitjantjatjara Yankunytjatjara Women's Council. As a community advocate, Rene has also campaigned to address the issues of petrol sniffing in Aboriginal communities in central Australia.[19]

Janet had been telling everyone about the film she'd made and it sparked everybody's interest. Linda had a steady stream of artists coming to her office to see the film, and everybody was talking about their thoughts on how art on paper first started, and the first time they had drawn on paper and how the first designs had originated. It was unanimous that they had originated from *milpatjunanyi*. Rene came into Linda's office to see Janet's film, and again the next day, and then she told Linda: 'I have been thinking all night about those early pastel drawings from 1954, because my aunties did them. Because my aunties did those drawings I think I have got copyright over them. I am going to replicate them. I am going to do dot paintings, or dot versions of those early pastel drawings. My father's sisters did some of those drawings, so they are on the family line'.[20] There are thousands of artworks in the A<u>r</u>a Irititja archive, from the earliest pastel drawings, and even little tiny watercolours produced in the Ernabella School by the children using those old watercolour blocks of hard colour requiring much skill and patience. A<u>n</u>angu are really only just finding out what is in the archive. Who knows what could happen from here?

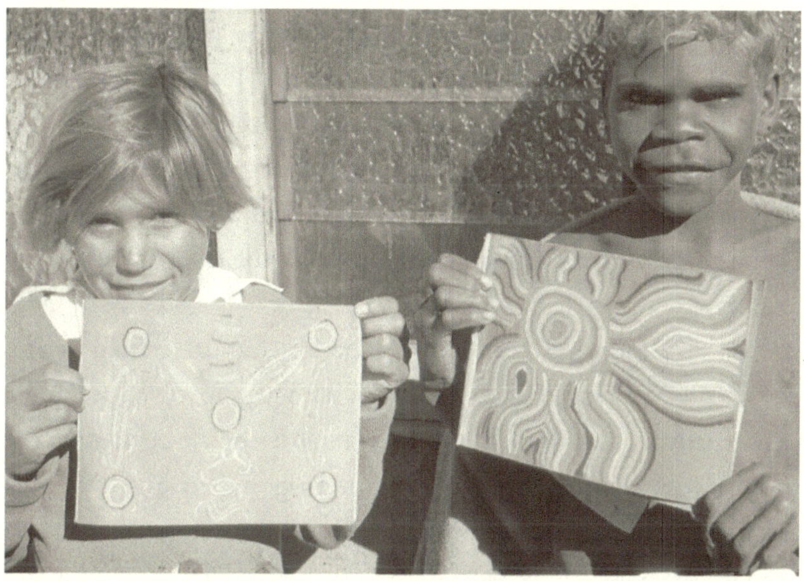

Figure 11.5: Schoolchildren Lucy Turner and Douglas Baker with pastel drawings at Ernabella in 1953. In 2002 Lucy annotated this photo in A̲ra Irititja: 'We are holding drawing books. The books had white protector pages to separate the drawings and keep them clean. We each had our own book. The teacher used to ask us to hold our drawings up when we had finished'. Photo A̲ra Irititja 24264. Photographer Ron Trudinger.

All A̲n̲angu have access to A̲ra Irititja. Once you have the URL, there is a login screen. There are password-protected accounts, and A̲n̲angu can login using their own password and view their own profiles. There is also a guest login account, by which outsiders and non-A̲n̲angu people can access material on the archive, except for that which has for any reason become restricted. This can be due to sensitivities surrounding nudity in really unpleasant old anthropological photographs, or because of sorrow, or due to contemporary cultural concerns; anything can become restricted at anytime. It is very fluid and very responsive to individual and community wants and needs. It is an A̲n̲angu project, an Aṉangu archive and an Aṉangu collection. It is not on Google and it is not a public research resource. However, if there are other people who want to access the archive and have a good reason for it, they will be allowed to do so – for example: PhD students doing research with clear benefits for Aṉangu; school principals and art centre managers out on the APY Lands who are going to be regularly asked by Aṉangu to access Aṟa Irititja. It is set up very carefully so that the amount and type of content you can access is very much determined by the level of permission you have.

The relationship between Aṟa Irititja and art centres is also very fluid. We would love to see the art centres involved and there is certainly a great deal of enthusiasm inside the art centres on the Lands. For example, knowing we were going to give this presentation, Dora Dallwitz, Digital Archive Officer for Aṟa Irititja, imported items from a hard drive we received some months ago from Mimili Maku Arts with some beautiful material on it. There were at least 1,500 photographs of artists, over 2,000 photographs of artworks, and other things – some 5,500 items in total. We were hesitant to put so much material into the database without having much information to accompany it, but the art centre coordinator told us to go ahead saying that the artists would love to see their work on Aṟa Irititja, and that somehow they will find a way to document it. We do not presently have much information to accompany them, but they are there on the archive, and we are hoping that the art centre coordinators can find time and resources to add more documentation into the archive.

This situation is roughly equivalent to when Hilary Furlong left the Ernabella art centre many years ago. She realised that the physical archive was in peril – the rats were into the back room and there were many boxes of material in there, so she sent four or five pallets all in one go to Ara Irititja – all sorts of things: little exercise books that the school kids used in the 1950s and 1960s, payments made to artists, costs of paints and paper, business records, accounts, invoices, even the names of some of the people who bought some of the paintings – important material from an art historical point of view. Due to Ara Irititja being so inclusive, we have ended up with this extraordinary collection of Ernabella material; including lots of artwork, with the main criteria for us to get it was that it had no commercial value at the time. But we've actually ended up with some really unique material, and that's fantastic. There are things that there might actually only be three of, things that they didn't actually want to exhibit, experimental works, things that did not fit, for whatever reason.

It would be great to get some process going in these overworked, understaffed art centres, in a way that is facilitated possibly by linkages between the Ara Irititja software (Keeping Culture KMS) and the art centre software – a new version of which is currently being rolled out in the APY Lands. Because it is still being developed, we are hoping the developer will say 'well, it would be nice if this bit of information out of our database could fit into the Ara Irititja archive'. We would like to know if the story for the artwork could be shared, if the artist's biography could be placed in the archives, not the taxation records perhaps, but you never know. If there are any art centre managers, any art centre committees, or any national committees about art centres who can come up with a way that their material can be shared, or even just some of the information could be shared for the benefit of the people who originally made the work and their families, it would be a step in the right direction. As previously stated, we believe that Anangu have the right to be informed about collections that exist relating to them, their culture, language and heritage.

We also believe that they have the right to determine use and access provisions for their heritage materials. Aṟa Irititja makes that a reality.

Although the Aṟa Irititja project is not just about archives and is much more than the technical stuff, the computer program that forms the core of the project has been carefully developed in consultation with Aṉangu from the very start. It reflects their cultural and linguistic social conventions. For example, the program enables files to be sorted into Open Access, Sensitive and Sorrow – this last category indicating that persons seen, heard or named in the files are recently deceased. There are also divisions between men's and women's materials, sacred and secular, and so on. This has resulted in a living archive that is responsive to the needs and concerns of present-day Aṉangu, frequently used, much loved and admired.[21]

The software program is being used by the Northern Territory Library (NTL) for installation in regional libraries, community centres and computer rooms. First renamed 'Our Stories' and most recently 'Community Stories', this same software is aimed at helping Aboriginal people gain computer literacy and record their local history. There are other projects that focus on supporting Indigenous people to engage with communications technology, like the Indigenous Remote Communications Association (IRCA), and others that seek to provide resources for researchers to work collaboratively on collections in a closed environment and then choose to either publish the data or export the data to an archive such as Online Cultural Collections Analysis and Management System (OCCAMS).

Aṟa Irititja is unique in the service it provides to Aṉangu, but clearly there is scope to apply this program to the recording of the history of Aboriginal art. As we have demonstrated, Aṟa

Irititja has already begun this history for Anangu. Working collaboratively on a social history of Aboriginal art opens up part of an industry that is currently dominated by non-Indigenous people. It gives a much-needed historical and contextual dimension to the contemporary Aboriginal art world. With more meaningful and valuable art records returning to and being documented by Indigenous people, it will become more and more difficult to say, 'Aboriginal art, it's a white thing'. Additionally, this historical context can provide the foundation for the much-requested critical reception of the genre, as it has become increasingly evident that Aboriginal art criticism is not possible without a strong sense of history in which to ground it.

While it is clear that focusing on history is not a cure-all, it is certainly one way of aiding the contemporary culture of Aboriginal art. Moving away from the money story toward a more equitable, educational context for one of the planet's most vibrant, diverse and dynamic cultures will surely be an improvement.

Notes

1 This chapter is based on a voice recording originally made on Thursday 4 September 2014 at the Chifley Alice Springs Convention Centre. The main speakers at the event were John Dallwitz, Janet Inyika and Linda Rive. Susan Lowish gave a brief introduction on the day, but is mostly responsible for ensuring that members of the Ara Irititja project team were included in the event. With assistance from John and Linda, Susan also wrote up the chapter using John's guiding narrative, and Janet's words with Linda's interpretations. Other sources drawn upon are acknowledged in endnotes throughout the text. We thank the event organisers Ian McLean and Darren Jorgensen and the NPY Women's Council for making Janet's participation possible on the day.

2 'Who are we?', viewed 26 October 2014, <http://www.irititja.com/about_ara_irititja/who_are_we.html>.

3 Ara Irititja, '*Nganampa warka*: Annual Report to Pitjantjatjara Council, APY and all Anangu', December 2015, p. 3.

4 Ar̲a Irititja, '*Nganampa warka*', 2015, p. 3.

5 Ngaanyatjarra, Pitjantjatjara and Yankunytjatjara (NPY) Women's Council, 'Janet Inyika, NPY Women's Council Director 2011–2013', viewed 26 October 2014, <http://www.npywc.org.au/about-npywc/directorate/janetinyika/>.

6 ibid.

7 ibid.

8 S. Thorner & J. Dallwitz, 'Storytelling Photographs, Animating Anangu', in J. Decker (ed.), *Technologies and Digital Initiatives*, Roman and Littlefield, New York, 2015, pp. 53–60 at 58.

9 Janet Inyika speaking in Pitjantjatjara on a film made and translated by Linda Rive for Art Centres Art Histories Symposium Alice Springs 2014.

10 ibid.

11 ibid.

12 ibid.

13 ibid. (Emphasis added later.)

14 ibid.

15 Ar̲a Irititja, '*Nganampa warka*', p. 6.

16 Janet Inyika, speaking.

17 Janet Inyika, speaking.

18 Ngaanyatjarra, Pitjantjatjara and Yankunytjatjara (NPY) Women's Council, '2010–11 Director's Report', p. 17; 'Tjanpi at the 2015 Venice Biennale', viewed 26 October 2014, <http://www.npywc.org.au/2015/06/tjanpi-at-the-2015-venice-biennale/>.

19 Ngaanyatjarra, Pitjantjatjara and Yankunytjatjara (NPY) Women's Council, 'NPY Women's Council Directors' Biographies', viewed 26 October 2014, <http://www.npywc.org.au/>. Archived from the original.

20 R. Kulitja, personal communication with Linda Rive, September 2014.

21 S. Lowish, 'Ara Irititja: adding more value to Aboriginal art through education', *SangSaeng*, no. 20, 2008, pp. 8–11.

12

THE THIRD ARCHIVE AND ARTIST AS ARCHIVIST

Margo Neale

When I was asked to write about how artists use the archive, the words of two Indigenous elders immediately came to mind. The first was an Inuit man, Bob Dempsey, who said, 'the trouble with whitefellas is that they keep all their brains in books', and the other was the late Kimberley man Paddy Roe who made the profound observation that, '*You* people try and *dig* little bit more *deep* – *you* bin *digging only white soil*'.[1]

For Bob Dempsey the idea that one's knowledge would come primarily from humans rather than from the creator ancestors, and be deposited in something as disembodied and dislocated as books, is difficult to understand, if not unfathomable. Or as a Pintubi man put it to anthropologist Fred Myers, the law 'is not our idea'.[2] Rather, in the ur-archive humans are documents, archived according to kin and ancestral relations – which is what artist and writer Kim Mahood means when she says that the 'Martu don't need maps because they *are* the map, all of them custodians of the interlocking story that is Martu country'.[3]

Archives exist in places other than books, documents stored and other modern formats such as cloud computing and various electronic platforms. In remote Australia, for example, possibly the oldest human archive that exists is in good shape. This ur-archive takes radically different forms from the Western archive. It might have human archivists but the actual archive is embedded in the natural world, in the country, oceans and cosmos.

When British colonists arrived on the Australian continent thinking they had discovered a *terra nullius*, they began archiving – measuring and mapping, naming and writing, and all the other things from which they make their archives. They didn't realise that every inch of the continent was already archived. Many Aboriginal families, particularly those like mine who were deeply impacted by colonisation, have long consulted both the Western archive and what remains of their Indigenous ur-archive.

The Indigenous impetus to assimilate aspects of Western archival procedures into their own ur-archive is a natural part of the contemporary circumstances of Indigenous cultures in the wake of colonisation. A good early example is the Yuendumu Men's Museum, first opened in 1971.[4] This initiative grew from Darby Jampijinpa Ross's work at the South Australian Museum in the mid-1960s when Bob Edwards was a newly appointed curator. With the support of Director Peter Crowcroft and later his successor W. Grant Inglis, the Men's Museum eventuated. It is also an early example of an Indigenous-led, museum-facilitated project. The purpose of the museum was to centralise secret sacred material and stories dispersed in secret caves across Warlpiri territory in the new settlement of Yuendumu, where many Warlpiri were now settled and seeking to develop a Warlpiri type of modernity.

The interaction between the two archives has unlimited possibilities but only if each talks to the other. Recent projects designed to making this happen in a systematic way – the development of a third archive from that combines elements of the Indigenous ur-archive and the Western Enlightenment archive – are the subject of this essay. What is this archive held in country – and how is it distinguishable from the Western archive? How does it work?

How are the artists or cultural practitioners the archivists? What is the relationship between these two archival systems and how does the Indigenous artist figure in the space between?[5]

Songlines as Archive Held in Country

Songlines, a term coined by Bruce Chatwin in 1987, are knowledge systems archived in the land.[6] A complex set of arterial connections or Dreaming tracks, they comprise an organic network of lines criss-crossing the continent along distributed nodes of concentrated knowledge, often referred to as sites of significance or sacred sites. These sites, which are called 'country', are on one level open archives, their landforms telling the history of its making. A landslide of red rocks may tell of a bloody ancestral battle; the fissure in a rock face is associated with the Seven Sisters and their journey to escape a lustful pursuer. In this respect landforms are a type of writing – ancestral scripts – their signs serving as a mnemonic that are rearticulated in 'open' or popular songs, dance and painting. As the late Yirrkala elder and artist Wandjuk Marika once said, 'The land has no voice so we must speak for the land through our songs, stories, dancing and art'.[7] On another level, though, these sites are terminals to which only a few archivists have the password. This password gives them access to deeper more secret histories, the story behind the story, which are often told in a language considered to be ancient and not accessible to others. These stories, whether they be open or secret, are portable versions of the ur-archive embedded in country, with which one travels.

Indexing Country

The use of songs to call up country – 'singing up the land' – is, perhaps, the most ancient form of indexing.

> Story was patterned into songs that told the names of country, told when and where edible plants grew, where the marlu and kipara and parnajarrpa lived, told of the grasslands and sand dunes and salt lakes and the ancestral beings who inhabited them. And water, always water. Yinta and Jurna and Jila, the life force of the desert.[8]

Songs are learnt 'as people travelled to the places named in the song and the rhythm of walking took the song into the body. Through the body song became dance which in turn became ceremony'.[9] Painted with the signs of the ancestral beings being sung, the dancing body unlocks the knowledge of the ur-archive. The contemporary practice of painting on canvas is an extension of such archival practices, but geared to the enforced sedentary lifestyle and a capitalist economy of today. Thus to this day many Indigenous artists sing in a kind of chant as they paint. Indeed, many Western contemporary artists paint to music, as if fulfilling an ancient habit. As Anmatyerre artist Emily Kame Kngwarreye (c. 1910–1996) sung her brush across the canvas, she would raise her head and peer to a place beyond the canvas in the direction of Alhalkere, her homeland that was the source and subject of the song. At other times, in a gallery distant from country, she would touch different parts of the painting singing its particular verses.[10]

The power of song to access the Aboriginal archive underpins a project that Sue Davenport and Peter Johnson, founders of Kanyirninpa Jukurrpa, developed with the Martu people from the Pilbara region in Western Australia. Being familiar with both Western and Aboriginal ways of archiving country – that is, Western visual cartography and Aboriginal songs – the Martu provided a classic opportunity to text the third archive. Martu people would, through singing, locate inaccessible remote sites, that they had either never visited or not visited since they were children, on a Western map. Later when it was checked against a satellite map the degree of accuracy cartographically speaking was remarkable.[11] Singing country can locate places previously unknown by the singer. When Bruce Neale (husband of the author) was driving in the area of the Canning Stock route in August 2012 with two local Aboriginal people aged in their early to mid-fifties, every ten minutes or so a land feature would cue them into song. At one point one of the men excitedly asked Bruce to stop the car and indicated that over to the left side of the road there was a waterhole high up on the downside of the escarpment. On asking him how he knew this if he had not been there before, he said that it was in the song his Aunty had taught him. With some scepticism Bruce agreed to walk several hundred metres and scale the rubbly escarpment to find the waterhole located in the song. To his amazement it was exactly where the song stated, but this was no surprise to his informants. They would have been amazed if it wasn't there.

The Third Archive: The Songlines Project

How is the relationship between the Western and Aboriginal archives exploited by contemporary Aboriginal artists? What are the cultural, political and economic imperatives driving this archival turn? At a national (and indeed global) level, museums in the twenty-first century can no longer ignore Indigenous people's rights and responsibilities to their cultural material and heritage, which are intimately bound up in their archives. They are now under pressure to discharge their responsibilities to the First Peoples – to our histories, our knowledge systems (archives), our values and our voices – in ways that are beyond being politically correct and patronising. We are no longer captive to anthropological discourse and unequal power relations that define indigenous as 'lesser' and 'other', or as 'special in other instances – to be approached with caution'. Instead we engage in liberating strategies in diverse ways by negotiating new positions that release us from imposed narratives and passivity, to new positions of agency where we add voice and value to collections, to exhibitions and to museum culture generally. It no longer has to be only about how museums work with Aboriginal and Torres Strait Islander (TSI) peoples, but also about how Aboriginal and TSI people work with museums.[12] In other words, Indigenous agency has primacy in working relationships with museums and their archives. Underpinning this agency is not just the ur-archive from which indigenous people draw their power, but the Indigenous invention of a third archive.

It is this thinking that compelled me, as an Indigenous curator at a national museum, to be part of a pioneering collaborative research project, *Alive with the Dreaming! Songlines of the Western Desert* initiated by the A<u>n</u>angu people of the Western Desert cultural bloc. [13] An epic intercultural and interdisciplinary research project, it explores a radically new approach to the integration of Indigenous and Western knowledge systems in understanding and managing our shared cultural and natural environment. Tracking the Seven Sisters Songlines across three states and deserts in the A<u>n</u>angu, Pitjantjatjara and Yankunytjatjara (APY) Lands, Ngaanyatjarra and Martu lands, it explores archaeological, ecological, visual and performative aspects of the songlines in an integrated, not a compartmentalised, way – which is how these desert people know their country.[14] Most importantly, it departs from many past and present collaborative projects where the museum is the originator and communities are consulted (often in a transactional mode) to assist a project conceived wholly within a Western archival paradigm. Instead, Indigenous communities initiate the project and museums assist or facilitate the communities to extend their archival paradigms using Western models and new technologies. In this hybrid model Indigenous ways of knowing and being are integrated in a governance structure that is led by the elders according to the *tjukurrpa* (Dreaming). As the project develops, A<u>n</u>angu and major partners together continually seek approval and guidance through the APY Law and Culture Council and the Nyaanyatjarra, Pitjantjatjara and Yankunytjatjara (NPY) Women's Council to a degree rarely, if ever, seen in previous collaborations.

A large group of A<u>n</u>angu Traditional Owners initiated the songlines research project with a sense of urgency, expressed by A<u>n</u>angu elder Mr David Miller as Chair of A<u>n</u>anguku Arts and Culture Aboriginal Corporation, at a partners' meeting in Canberra: 'I believe you mob can help us...these songlines, they are all broken up now...you can help us put "them all back together again"'. [15] This was an entreaty heard many times over the preceding years by anthropologist Diana James and others who were working on the lands. It was a huge and complex undertaking and A<u>n</u>angu had approached various funding bodies, without success. Elders feared the loss of knowledge as a consequence of the younger generation being distracted by the technological wonders of the twenty-first century, 'they don't want to hang around with the Elders, they've got rap, hip hop and smart phones'. As Elder, Lizzie Ellis says, 'when the young people today are at that young stage, they don't realise the importance of their culture. It is only when they get to be older in the mid-year. We need to have it all there in the digitised world, in places like A<u>r</u>a Irititja for them, for when they are ready.'

A<u>r</u>a Irititja, the subject of a chapter in this volume, is an online Western-style archive overseen by an A<u>n</u>angu board.[16]

Similarly, Tapaya Edwards, revealingly the only young person actively engaged in the Songlines project over many years, also made a heartfelt plea at the first meeting of Elders and partners at Amata in 2012 when he said, 'many young people in my community of Mimili are *ngurpa tjukurrpa* (they don't know the Dreaming), people my age…when the Elders pass away, we're going to lose the story, the story is going to be gone. We need to boost this project; we need these things in the lands'.[17] As well as being made part of Ara Irititja, select research and documentation components including those accrued beyond the grant period, will also be housed at the National Museum of Australia (NMA), the Australian Institute of Aboriginal and Torres Strait Islander Studies and the Australian National University to maximise protection and access.

Collectively, Anangu and Western scholars, referred to as knowledge holders, combined their respective skills to track the songlines cartographically, archaeologically, ecologically, visually and performatively over some 7,000 kilometres and 600,000 square kilometres. Through Ara Irititja, the Songlines Project radicalises the Western idea of the archive by bringing the concept closer to the Aboriginal ur-archive. Ara Irititja effectively processes the Aboriginal archive through a Western archival system. The arts are a primary medium for this translation, as the idea that art itself is an archive is something that each archive shares.

The intention of this project, as it is for Ara Irititja and other Aboriginal community archives, is that future generations will perform similar translations as a kind of repatriation exercise.[18] Ara Irititja archive is culturally nuanced organisationally and operationally to accommodate this translational role. While anthropologists and other researchers have deposited knowledge of country and culture in the Western archive since colonisation, unlike A<u>r</u>a Irititja the typical Western archive is not geared to the repatriation of knowledge – though many such archives are now heading in this direction by incorporating Aboriginal agency in all directions and at multiple levels. This front-end process is enacted by Aboriginal people for Aboriginal people in an Aboriginal-managed archive, in contrast to the back-end variety of research motivated by fear of Aboriginal people dying out. Instead of the salvage mentality of old is a living processes of translation in which agency is embedded in Aboriginal knowledge holders.

The intent of the Western and Aboriginal archives is associated with the universal desire to maintain cultural integrity and transmit knowledge over the generations. The third archive aims to combine the additional preservation and other advantages of the Western archive with their own knowledge systems, while at the same time reaching beyond the limits of the objectifying systems that underpin the modern Western archive.

It was with this in mind that we – Western and Aboriginal researchers, Aboriginal Elders and others – set about re-archiving into a hybrid Indigenous-Western format – a third Seven Sisters archive. At Kuru Ala, some 200 kilometres from Blackstone or twelve hours by Toyota west of Alice Springs, is an area comprised of a collection of sites rich with the imprint of the Kungkarangalpa or the Seven Sisters. Their presence, and that of their relentless pursuer who brutally violated the elder sister, is so palpable at Kuru Ala where we camped in April 2014 (and again in August 2015), that A<u>n</u>angu spoke in hushed tones for fear of disturbing Wati Nyiru and for other reasons not disclosed.

This was a long awaited bush trip, initiated by the thirty or so A<u>n</u>angu custodians and others, undertaken to regenerate the archive, engage in knowledge transfer and document it for preservation in A<u>r</u>a Irititja. Over many days they walked the sites telling the stories, singing the songs and touching places as they reconnected. An authorised few painted their breasts with circles of ochre, replicating markings on the rocks and the smoke re-activating the healing process through dancing and singing, which climaxed in a performance danced across the land. The stage set was the knowledge-laden features of the land itself and the cueing device for the performance undertaken. Like a time lapse re-enactment staged in country, the seven Elders, painted up and wearing head pieces and black skirts, filed through the grass, forever vigilant of Wati Nyiru, who darted from rock to tree, hiding as he went or sitting atop a rock surveying the land for sight of them. Likewise, they too stopped en route to huddle with their backs to each other and with hands shielding their eyes as they peered into the distance scanning for their relentless pursuer. Eventually the Sisters descended into a gully with a waterhole where they disappeared from sight. Rising some twenty to thirty metres from the gully floor was the face of Wati Nyiru, deeply gouged into the craggy rock face with pronounced eye sockets squinting cat-like. There was no escape.

The tableau of dance across country was captured on film for the Seven Sisters' project and exhibition, as it had been a number of times before, while on canvas the story was painted into being, simultaneously strengthening it for re-absorption into the site; spiritually caring for country.[19] The painting as ceremony was ritually supervised by bosses and managers (known as Kurdu and Kuralangu in some parts of the desert), who oversaw the narrative event. The artist-archivists engaging in this painting ceremony had particular relationships to each other, to the story and to the site. With so many players involved – six female and one male – and with the complexity of A<u>n</u>angu kinship and familial relationships, I expected extensive and time consuming negotiations to occur, to determine who would sit where and who would paint what. Instead, everyone quietly and purposefully formed themselves around the canvas according to these relationships, and spatially orientated themselves to the particular sites they were recording and connected to.

Mrs Woods, recently deceased but then believed to be in her nineties, was the most senior custodian on the day. She was strong in this story, taking the lead role for the women's side. Her knowledge of *turlku*, *tjukurr(pa)*, the dance and the country was profound and apparently unrivalled, according to anthropologist Bryony Nicholson who described how in the past Mrs Woods danced the most potent parts of this *tjukurrpa* [sic] along with the late Mrs Miller, with drama and undisputed authority (particularly in the violation scenes). Facing Mrs Woods' back was the monumental craven face of Wati Nyiru, the lustful old man at whose hands the sisters were violated. Mrs Woods depicted Wati Nyiru on the canvas with large circles, like eyes, suggesting not only his watchfulness but also the acts which she used to so dramatically enact. Robert Woods, the son of one of Mrs Woods' husband's other wives, and her son by kinship, positioned himself on the adjacent corner of the canvas where he was boss of the men's part of the story, and he faced the site of the carpet snake which was one of Wati Nyiru's many guises (with obvious reference to his sexual intent). Between them and flanking Mrs Woods, were her daughters, half-sisters Anawari Mitchell and Angilyiya Mitchell, with the former telling the story of catching the 'carpet snake', the consumption of which would enable Wati Nyiru to enter them. The other sister painted the story of strengthening and healing the damaged and dying older sister by feeding her meat *(kuka)* and dancing up healing power.[20] Located beside Robert Woods was Jennifer Mitchell, Mrs Woods' other daughter and Robert

Woods' half-sister. In kinship terms Mrs Woods was mother of the three sisters and their brother Robert. Sitting separately on the remaining side of the canvas were Lala West and Lesley Laidlow, representatives from a different but related family who claim connection to the site through the fact that their mother Numitja Laidlaw was born at Kuru Ala, thus constituting one of the strongest claims to place. The Woods/Mitchell family who sat opposite were, on the other hand, not born there, but their rights were hereditary and their knowledge strong as a consequence of on-going engagement with the place, keeping the story alive.

For the painting to have cultural authority as a document of value, both sets of knowledge holders needed to be part of the telling. The selection of artists to paint that story at that time in that place was subject to a shifting hierarchy, encompassing cultural, spatial, temporal and genealogical factors that are always present and inform every work to some degree. For example, at this same site in 2011 an apparent disagreement between knowledge, experience and antecedence from family members born at Kuru Ala came to a head. There was an impasse between people who knew the story versus a particular family member of Numitja (who was born there), when consensus was needed on who should or could dance the story. It was finally resolved through what anthropologist Bryony Nicholson, who was present, described as 'ceremonial conflict resolution that resulted in a targeted, intensive knowledge transfer session for this person who now has the confidence to dance this story and is acknowledged by all the women as being able to do so'.[21]

The inclusion of Leslie Laidlaw as a painter on the canvas *Kuryala* in 2015 was an outcome of these negotiations four years earlier where Numitja's rights were thus re-confirmed.[22] Laidlaw appears not to have really taken on the *turlku* [sic] or the dancing for this place. Instead she seemed more comfortable acknowledging her mother's connection than in asserting her own. Based on precedence and inherited rights, her family must have a seat at the table to do the story 'proper way'. This example not only hints at the complexity of accessing, affirming and transmitting archival knowledge in multiple ways but more precisely how the bona fides of the 'archivist' for the Aboriginal archive are established through family lineage. In Western archival terms it could loosely be seen as a form of validation of the documentation through cross-referencing.

Artists can access the Aboriginal archive remotely, a facility that has been active for centuries prior to the new technologies of today – a kind of wi-fi of the cosmological variety, putting a new twist on cloud platforms. On another desert research trip with Aṉangu, the cueing device for the Seven Sisters' saga was the Orion constellation and Pleiades star cluster canopied above, rather than the surrounding topography as at Kuru Ala on the APY Lands. In an isolated riverbed in a remote region beyond Ernabella, in September 2012, some fifty Aṉangu people gathered to do *inma* (performance) for an episode of the Seven Sisters story far to the west of Kura Ala on the APY lands where the sisters travelled from Wallara Range toward Atila (Mt Connor). Week-long rehearsals were underway in preparation for a public performance at the NMA as part of Canberra's centennial year of celebrations, interrupted only by that other great celebration on the lands at that time of year, a footy grand final. After sundown, when full dress rehearsals took place, the inky nights were punctuated by tongues of flame from the crackling fires and the glistening bodies of the dancers. The rhythm of walking country as a way of remembering was emulated in the rhythm of dance movements, as the dancers took the song into their bodies, informing the dance and the vocalisations, unifying past, present and place with the human and the ancestral.

The collective bank of stories were sung out, day after day, night after night, recalling deeply imbedded places in the mind, until by the last night the performance took on an edge not seen before. A senior traditional owner of the episode being performed was quivering and shuddering on the ground as if in death throes after the ravishing by Wati Nyiru, with the younger sisters protectively circling in movements and gestures of mourning and healing. Endless negotiations on the deepening story occurred as different parts and snippets of knowledge were jigsawed back into place. In performances like these but usually at significant sites, places, edible plants and animals are often named from half-remembered songs as the songline travelled from water source to water source. Literally and metaphorically, the learning of ecology, geology, botany, medicine and husbandry were revealed, along with codes of behaviour and roles and responsibilities.[23] This is how A<u>n</u>angu 'know' their country. This is what they learn from the archive and this is what they read back into the archive through a process of curating painting, song and dance.

Mirrored in the night sky, with a degree of clarity only experienced in the desert, the saga of Wati Nyiru and the Seven Sisters continues – then as now, 'as above, so below'. Each night as Orion and Pleiades come into view the archive is revived. They are a constant reminder of the knowledge contained in this narrative replicated in the Pleiades star cluster seen as the Seven Sisters and in the view of some, Wati Nyiru by his phallus replicated as Orion's belt.

The Artist as Archivist: *Parnkupirti Men's Painting*

The ur-archive is an organic, living and breathing personage, often referred to as 'our mother' by Aboriginal people. Further access to deeper knowledge is not democratic but gendered, age-graded and continually negotiated. One's bona fides as an archivist are strictly based on family lineage where the traditional owner (TO), with custodial responsibilities to a site, becomes simultaneously the keeper, the archivist, the reader and the contributor. While the Western archivist has to also go through training, she need not have a familial relationship to the archive. Non-Aboriginal artist John Wolseley, who is a serial collaborator with Aboriginal artists, experienced this difference in a project at Blue Mud Bay when working with Yolngu artist Djambawa Marawilli.

> Since the early days of European settlement there has been a tradition of heavy footed artists drawing and documenting parts of the continent about which they know little. As for myself, when I arrived at Banyula I was just plainly discombobulated. Here I was with Yolngu artists…with such brilliant ways of expressing in paint their vast knowledge about the place. [24]

Wolseley felt he was starting from scratch and that in the etchings he produced he 'may have found a way of making ignorance a virtue'. 'There I was', he says, 'standing on the edge of the sea with a blank etching plate and an empty mind'. While Wolseley's interest was in its exquisite patterning, shape, hues and random placement of, for example, a mangrove leaf, for Djambawa standing beside him at the time the leaf was a prompt for ancestral stories related to Banyul.[25]

Experiencing the empty mind, a starting point and desired condition for many non-indigenous artists, is an impossibility for Aboriginal artists. As incarnations of ancestral beings their minds are brimming with associative information. Whilst country is an archive of ancestral actions, the full extent of the archive can only be accessed and worked by the custodians with the knowledge and authority to do so. As with all archives, the archivist doesn't just guard the archive, she interprets and adds to it, engaging creatively with it to keep it alive – or to keep its knowledge relevant and active in the present. For the Aboriginal 'archivist' it is more than a job or even a passion – as one might see with Western archivists – instead it is their *raison d'etre*. As archivists they are effectively present-day incarnations of their archive.

The anthropologist Alan Rumsey described Aboriginal archiving as 'an inscriptive and interpretive practice through which "country" becomes "story"'.[26] In other words the Aboriginal archivist – whom we know as the artist – activates the knowledge imbedded in the site by carrying some part of that knowledge to the site and carrying away an enhanced experience of that knowledge. A kind of mutual knowledge transfer occurs between place, person and history.

A good recent example of the active role of both Indigenous and Western archivists in the interpretation, ongoing maintenance and re-creation of an Indigenous ur-archive is *Parnkupirti Men's Painting* (2011), which hangs in pride of place in the rangers' office in Mulan.[27] However this is not the only 'original'. The other one hangs in the Nevada Museum of Art and Science, USA. One painting, two originals. How can this be?

In 2011, deep in the Kimberley by a desert lake called Paruku or Lake Gregory, some thirty people gathered to undertake an artistic collaboration between Indigenous and Western knowledge holders in relation to the complementarity of art and science. William L. Fox, Director for the Centre of Art and Environment at the Nevada Museum of Art and Science, performed the role of Western archivist, recording the cross-cultural transactions as they unfolded in typical Western fashion: with pen, paper, camera and audio recorder. Other members of the party comprised scientists, writers, photographers, Indigenous and non-Indigenous artists and young rangers from the area. The project was instigated by artist Mandy Martin, with the location and the Aboriginal participation coordinated by artist and writer Kim Mahood, who was instrumental in this project in a number of ways. Not only had she spent some of her childhood growing up at Mongrel Downs, now Tanami Downs, maintaining close contact with the locals, but she had worked for many years on cultural and environmental mapping projects with the Walmajarri custodians of Paruku, in particular with Walmajarri Elder Veronica Lulu with whom she has been collaborating for decades.

The *Parnkupirti Men's Painting* was just one part of a larger third archive combining Indigenous and Western knowledge systems. As a collaborative work involving Indigenous and Western artists and knowledge systems, it also is, on its own, an example of this third archive. However, the focus of this section is the role of the Indigenous archivist in the fabrication of the painting and his hermeneutic recasting of the ur-archive.

As part of the project Martin wanted a collaborative painting between the Indigenous and non-Indigenous artists, and asked Mahood to create a template based on satellite imagery – a practice she and Lulu had developed in their collaborations. After consulting with the custodians about an appropriate site and other relevant matters, Mahood painted a five panel template of Parnkupirti Creek, the site of an archaeological excavation and the resting place of two ancestral dingoes.

The custodians had decided that this collaboration between two white women artists and the senior Walmajarri artists, mostly women, was women's business. However, once on site, and despite extensive prior consultations, a concurrence of factors caused the women to emphatically declare that they couldn't work on this story. According to Mahood in her rendition of the story, 'there was no gainsaying'. The other white artist, Mandy Martin, who was very excited about this epic project but not as experienced as Mahood in these matters, would I imagine be gobsmacked when, in an instant, after months of expectations and preparation, things changed so dramatically. The women handed the panels over to the men to paint. According to Mahood the role of the senior Walmajarri women changed from 'artists to custodial sentinels'. They remained at the consultation site above the creek for the first day, while the men moved down near the creek to paint.

Nearby there were two hills which belonged to the Dreaming of Hanson Pye's father and uncle and which Hanson 'creatively' linked together in another telling of the story.

Serendipitously one of the rangers had a pamphlet with him which reproduced a painting by Hanson Pye's father done years earlier about his Dreaming at this site. It had triggered the renegotiation of the narrative and a shift in cultural authority from one gender to the other. It also meant a shift from artists to non-artists as none of the rangers were artists except for Hanson Pye.

The men's dilemma now was how to do a collaborative painting with only one artist and no idea of how to paint the story. The dilemma was resolved in a creative and culturally-based way: they used the image of the painting by Hanson's father as a guide and then relocated to a site further down the creek where there was shade and a sandy creek bed. However this did not solve the problem of how non-artists were to paint figurative images like dingo paws, which they clearly saw as a problem, judging from their attempts to solve it. They started by co-opting Hanson's dog into the collaboration by painting his paws and pressing them onto the canvases. This didn't work. Next they had a go at painting the dingo prints on the five boards themselves which resulted in five different renditions of dingo paws, making it look like multiple dingoes and not the same two. Disillusioned they blacked out the white creek bed, painted previously by Mahood as part of the original template, painted it white again, and one person painted all the dingo prints. This worked to their satisfaction.

Once the five panels were completed and the dog prints passed muster, the men decided that the works meant too much to them to part with. They could not send them off to Nevada for an exhibition as agreed, as the painting had acquired a 'sacred' value through the high degree of cultural engagement and revelation involved in its recreation. Instead they would do another 'original' to be sent to the exhibition. This decision entailed a further collaboration in which Mahood, as a white female artist, had the role of creating another set of five canvas panels using the satellite image and then passing over control to the men and withdrawing from sight, like a ritual of another kind. The second painting was completed by Hanson and the head ranger, and was not painted on site.

While the Walmajarri were engaged in their cultural translation exercise with the Aboriginal archive, William L. Fox was also engaged in a cultural interpretation exercise of his own. He is an international expert and writer on art and the environment, and art theory, who proffered the view that once the Walmajarri decided it was a men's story and not a women's story, the issue of the white woman's involvement as the template maker and the first hand on the canvas became problematic. In his view this would explain why the men blacked out her white-painted creek bed in order to re-inscribe the tracks of the sacred dingos upon a surface they painted black, then white again. It was feasible, given that the women were now eliminated from the story even to the extent that the two dingos, one male and one female, were now being re-interpreted by Hanson as two dingo brothers associated with the two hills that related to his father and his father's brother. However this does not account for the fact that the white female artist was later called upon to re-do the template on the canvases for the 'second original'. Not knowing Hanson's views on this matter, he may have been able to rationalise that the second painting was not the true one so that the involvement of a woman was not an issue and the fact that she was a white women rendered it even less controversial as she was outside the culture.

John Carty, an anthropologist known to the men and a friend of Mahood's, was at the men's painting site and dispelled Fox's assumption that the reason the white was painted out with black paint was not only to remove the dingo prints but more pertinently to erase the white woman. But why not paint out the dingo prints with white paint which would do the same job as the black overpainting, given that the black was then overlaid with white again? Why use black at all for this task if there was no other intent? Equally there is no evidence that both possibilities did not co-exist, as such articulations by Aboriginal people to non-Aboriginal people in such intense cultural situations are not an exact science. Sometimes omission is not agreement, or the views of one or two people are not necessarily the view of the group, or indeed the views expressed to an outsider do not necessarily reflect the actualities. Sometimes there is a reluctance to cause offence, especially to someone as closely connected to them as Mahood, who was so fundamental to the project. To tell a friend and countryman that Mahood's presence was to be erased, if indeed that was the motivation, is, in my experience, highly unlikely. We will never know.

Another profound negotiation took place when Hanson Pye, a natural storyteller renowned for his creative embellishments, was speaking to the painting at the exhibition, in front of an eager group of listeners.[28] He told the story of the painting as he did the story of the country, one standing for the other, including how the black male dingo and the white female morphed into two dingo brothers as mentioned earlier – the older one was said to be white due to the greying of age now to denote femaleness. In attendance was the old Aunty who was one of the 'custodial sentinels' at the creek bed, with significant cultural authority. She felt that Hanson's transformation was a step too far. Without regard to the audience and to the potential embarrassment of Hanson she pulled him up on the spot with, 'No! No! Not the right story!' Mahood's reading was that Hanson was 'so utterly transfixed by the symmetry of the two hills, the two brothers, the two dingos, and the site, and aided by his father's painting in the pamphlet, that in his mind that this version was the only one to tell'.[29] Though he retreated at the time of telling to the original version in response to Aunty's interjection and no doubt out of respect for her cultural authority, Mahood conjectures that the story is so lodged in him now after what was a transformative experience that the story of this place may never retreat from his preferred rendition.[30]

We can never know what constitutes a so-called 'true' or 'truer' story. It could be a new story or a reclaimed story, but whatever it is, it will take time with lots of retellings or renegotiations, or both, to gain sufficient authority to enter the archive fully or transcend older interpretations. But re-enter the archive it has, via the paintings that now exist as documented evidence, and the many more they will probably spawn. This story at Paruku reveals and reinforces a number of points about the apparent mutability and immutability of the Aboriginal archive. Hanson renewed and recreated the archive in the process of accessing it. The painting as an archival document will be read back into the country in its retelling in one or more ways. One may well ask how this accords with the view that the Dreaming is immutable and cannot be changed by man? The short answer is that it functions at many levels. At its deepest level it is not ambiguous and mutable. This deep meaning sets the boundaries within which there is some mobility of interpretation at the narrative or story-telling level. The story shifts in the hands of different storytellers, in different circumstances, at different times, with different groupings of people, at different sites, but the 'inside' essence or the metadata is unchangeable. This shifting and movement arising from a variety of cultural engagements keeps the Dreaming alive, keeps the archive active and relevant.

Conclusion

Much of the writing on the archival turn in contemporary times cannot see beyond the Western archive. However, the prominence of the archive in contemporary art brings a new perspective to knowledge held in country. Thinking of country as an archive endows a level of authority on Indigenous art not previously acknowledged beyond, perhaps, anthropology, and establishes new relationships with Western institutions such as museums, which think in archival terms. While Indigenous and Western knowledges are organised very differently, each is nevertheless an archive and thus shares some common ground.

Like the Western archive, country is a site of power and meaning, with active archivists and unsettled discourses despite the authority of its ancestral connections. Moreover, as I have outlined, a third archive, both Indigenous and Western, is in the making.

In Australia there has been a discernible escalation over the past decade in the overt and intentional public use by Aboriginal people of both Aboriginal and Western archives, as evidenced in the proliferation of epic intercultural, multidisciplinary projects like the Songlines Project, the Lake Paruku project, the Canning Stock Route project and the Martu project, *We Don't Need a Map*.[31] While each of these projects have art-making and exhibition objectives, they share a deeper cultural purpose focused on the preservation, and also active articulation and interpretation, of the Aboriginal ur-archive in a contemporary context. They also share a collectivist approach that acknowledges the multiple agencies of Indigenous and non-Indigenous knowledge holders, as if this is not just a feature of country in the modern world but also a model for the official archive of the Australian nation that resides in its museums and other institutions.

Acknowledgements

I would like to acknowledge the traditional owners of the Seven Sisters songlines who have shared their culture for preservation purposes and thus enlisted the support of the National Museum of Australia and a range of other partners to be part of that process. See http://archanth.anu.edu.au/heritage-museum-studies/songlines-western-desert. Also I acknowledge Kim Mahood, Ian McLean and Christiane Keller in the preparation of this paper.

Notes

1 Spoken by Bob Dempsey at the opening of the exhibition, *People of the Cedar: First Nations Art from the Northwest Coast of Canada* at the National Museum of Australia (NMA), Canberra, 2 March 2006; Paddy Roe in K. Benterrak, S. Muecke & P. Roe, *Reading the Country: Introduction to Nomadology*, Fremantle Arts Centre Press, Perth, 1984, p. 168.

2 F. Myers, *Pintupi country, Pintupi Self: Sentiment, place and politics among Western Desert Aborigines*, Smithsonian Institution Press and Australian Institute of Aboriginal Studies, Washington and Canberra, 1986, p. 53.

3 K. Mahood, 'Why the Martu Don't Need a Map', *We don't need a map: A Martu experience of the Western Desert*, exhibition catalogue, Fremantle Arts Centre, Perth, 2013, pp. 40–41 at 41.

4 Yuendumu Men's Museum re-opened on 6 September 2015, after years of abandonment.

5 While I acknowledge that the use of terms like archive and provenance have precise meanings in different contexts, my use of archive in the context of sites and stories on country allies more closely to the archaeological and museological use of the term in the Western context and not the academic definition.

6 B. Chatwin, *The Songlines*, Picador, London, 1987.

7 W. Marika, *Wandjuk Marika: Life story*, University of Queensland Press, Brisbane, 1995, p. 40.

8 ibid.

9 ibid.

10 Sydney Gallerist Christopher Hodges talks about this in the film, *Emily in Japan: The Making of an Exhibition*, director Andrew Pike, Ronin films, 2008.

11 Similarly collaborative paintings using songs and sites with cross-referencing to satellite maps is a process that Canberra-based artist Kim Mahood and Walmajarri artist Veronica Lulu from the Kimberley engage in.

12 The exhibition *Encounters: Revealing Stories of Aboriginal and Torres Strait Islander Objects from the British Museum* (2015–16) is an example of how a museum works with communities while the exhibition *Seven Sisters Songlines* (2017), also at the NMA is conversely an example of how communities work with museums. The former exhibition starts with objects followed by community engagement and the other starts with community followed by objects.

13 *Alive with the Dreaming! Songlines of the Western Desert* is a major ARC funded research project (2012–15) with multiple major partners including the NPY Women's Council, A͟nanguku Arts, the NMA and the Australian National University (ANU).

14 While the Songlines project as a whole tracked two significant songlines which included the Ngintaka (Perentie Lizard man) and the transcontinental Seven Sisters songline, the NMA was committed to the transcontinental Seven Sisters songline.

15 David Miller, Chairman Aṉanguku Arts and Cultural Aboriginal Corporation, Canberra meeting of Songlines Elders and Partners, ANU, Canberra, 2010. Nicholas Rothwell records a similar situation where he refers to Karilywara community members John Ward and Mr Giles, who needed a vehicle to care for their waterholes some distance away. Rothwell expressed it as, 'They had the desire: I had the Toyota Four-Wheel-Drive' in N. Rothwell, 'Quicksilver: Reflections', viewed 25 February 2016, <http://nicolasrothwell.com/quicksilver-reflections/ >.

16 Aṟa Irititja, an Aboriginal managed archive in Alice Springs, is a community-based, multimedia digital archive, designed at the request of Ngaanyatjarra, Pitjantjatjara and Yankunytjatjara (Aṉangu) communities. Through the Pitjantjatjara Council, the communities own Aṟa Irititja which has a brief to 'preserve and give us access to our cultural history'.

17 Amata meeting April 17 2012. See M. Neale & T. Keenan, 'Talking around Songlines: Kungkarangkalpa and Ngintaka', *Goree*, vol. 9, issue 2, November 2012, pp. 16–17.

18 Concepts of repatriation now extend beyond the return of physical returns, be they ancestral remains or cultural belongings, to returns that include digital repatriation, figurative repatriation (which academic Jennifer Kramer from the University of British Colombia refers to as exhibitions), or to spiritual repatriation (which is how Australian Aboriginal artist Christian Thompson describes photographs he creates in response to ethnographic collections).

19 There are at least two previous films of this performance at Kuru Ala: the original by CAAMA in the 1980s http://www.indigitube.com.au/video/item/694 and a later version by Ngaanyatjarra media, http://www.indigitube.com.au/video/item/356.

20 The story as told and approved by Anawari Mitchell and Angilyiya Mitchell for public use.

21 Bryony Nicholson, personal correspondence, 20 August 2015.

22 Adjoining country where the sisters flew from Kuru Ala to escape Wati Nyiru. It is a definable area on the side of the canvas that Lesley Laidlaw and Lala West painted.

23 Naming in this way was evidently not a feature of this particular rehearsal.

24 *Djalkiri: we are standing on their names, Blue Mud Bay*, Nomad Art Productions, Darwin, 2010.

25 ibid.

26 A. Rumsey, 'The dreaming, human agency and inscriptive practice', *Oceania,* vol. 65, no. 2, 1994, pp. 116–30.

27 A painting by Hansen Pye in collaboration with a group of young rangers Joshua Kungah, Jarvis Fernandez and Lloyd Mudgebell.

28 Personal communication with Kim Mahood, 2015.

29 The original story of the male and female dingoes is well-established and often told, as is the story of the two brothers who intersect with the dingoes before becoming the two hills, so this is an active re-interpretation by Hanson of two known stories.

30 Hanson only told his version, that the dingoes were the two brothers that became the two hills, and only acknowledged the original version when challenged by his Aunty.

31 See http://wedontneedamap.com.au/.

PART 4: DECOLONISING ARCHVIES

13

LOSING THE ARCHIVE: JULIE GOUGH AT THE MAA, CAMBRIDGE AND CHRISTIAN THOMPSON AT THE PITT RIVERS MUSEUM, OXFORD

Jessyca Hutchens

Archival art is often framed as a form of discovery: a process of searching, finding and revealing the 'lost object' in the archive. In his article, 'An Archival Impulse', Hal Foster describes how 'archival artists seek to make historical information, often lost or displaced, physically present'.[1] A frequent problem with this way of understanding archival art is that it foregrounds the archive as a readily searchable site for the lost and displaced, without also contending with it as a site that signifies more permanent and on-going forms of loss. For Indigenous peoples, an object of material culture held in a colonial archive or museum might represent not only historical dispossession and loss but also on-going violence towards immaterial aspects of culture that the object was, and remains, linked to.[2] To reconnect with what is lost may require creative and imaginative processes that resist aspects of the archive, or attempt to get out from under it, to symbolically lose the archive rather than to ask it to reveal something.

This chapter will examine two artist projects that developed in response to archives in anthropological museums: Christian Thompson's *We Bury Our Own* (2012), at the Pitt Rivers Museum in Oxford, and Julie Gough's *The Lost World (Part 2)* (2013), at the Museum of Archaeology and Anthropology (MAA) in Cambridge. Both works perform a kind of reconnection with the archive, while also symbolically allowing its objects to be released from it. They manage, in different ways, to decentre the archive as a primary site of knowledge, while still treating as significant the cultural objects it holds.

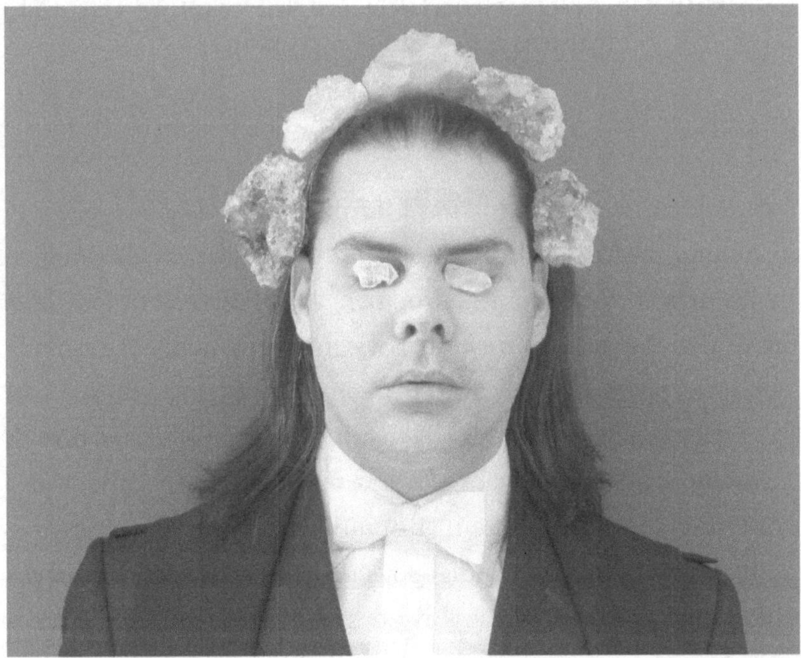

Figure 13.1: Christian Thompson, Down Under World, *100 cm × 100 cm, Fuji Pearl Metallic Paper, c-type print, 2012. Courtesy of the artist and Gallery Gabrielle Pizzi, Melbourne and Michael Reid Gallery, Sydney and Berlin.*

Working in response to the Australian photographic collection held at the Pitt Rivers Museum, Thompson created a series of eight photographic self-portraits and a video installation that drew inspiration from the archive, without using its images directly. In the catalogue for the project, Thompson describes how artworks can perform a 'spiritual repatriation'.[3] Thompson created the work while at the University of Oxford, where he was one of the first Australian Indigenous students ever to be accepted to study. The photographs show Thompson, dressed in traditional

Oxford subfusc (the academic dress required to be worn at formal University ceremonies and examinations), adorned with or holding a series of enigmatic objects that could be said to stand-in for the archival materials witnessed. While overtly performing the role of archival interpreter Thompson also subverts this role, turning away from the archival nature of the archive by encoding it into an idiosyncratic mix of signifiers.

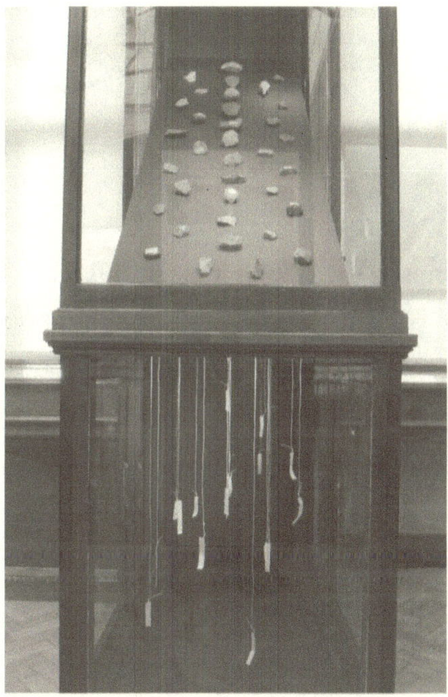

Figure 13.2: Julie Gough, The Lost World (Part 2), *partial installation view, Museum of Archaeology and Anthropology, University of Cambridge, 2013. Photograph by Mark Adams.*

In *The Lost World (Part 2)*, Julie Gough produced two simultaneous exhibitions – at the Museum of Archaeology and Anthropology (MAA), Cambridge, and at Contemporary Art Tasmania, Hobart – that centred around thirty-five stone tools from the MAA archive. The tools were put on display in Cambridge, and were relayed, via video feed, to Hobart. The project featured a video of Gough placing printed photographs of the tools, taken by Christoph Balzar, in different locations around Tasmania, roughly where the original artefacts were removed from, and a live web feed of one of the 'returned' photographic objects situated in the land. These gestures opened up a multiplicity of connections, allowing for both the archival objects to return to site of origin, and the site to be returned to the objects in the museum. But in rendering these connections as temporal, durational and contingent, the work functions both as a therapeutic ritual of returning and a meditation on permanent displacement and loss.

Reconnecting the Archive

Christian Thompson's work at the Pitt Rivers was initiated as part of a wider project: 'Globalization, Photography, and Race: the Circulation and Return of Aboriginal Photographs in Europe, 2011–2015'. The project, led by Dr Jane Lydon from the University of Western Australia, involved collaborations with four European collections, including the Pitt Rivers, which houses an important archive of nineteenth-century photographs of Aboriginal people. As part of the project, the museum's curator of photograph collections, Dr Christopher Morton, visited Indigenous communities in Australia, raising awareness of the digital archive, providing copies, and sharing knowledge. Thompson's work thus sits alongside a project aimed at connecting communities with archival materials significant to them. While his work doesn't explicitly share or reveal the content of the archive, it can be read as a complementary gesture of reconnection. His work creates links to the archive that cannot be achieved by sharing copies or uploading them online. In a catalogue essay for Thompson's exhibition at the Pitt Rivers, Christopher Morton writes:

> As Christian Thompson's new work shows us, Aboriginal artists and curators are moving into an exciting new phase of creative engagement with their visual history, one that moves the debate on from the politics of race and injustice, towards multiple, complex and hybrid identities in the present, and into the future.[4]

This move departs from the kinds of museum interventions that proliferated during the 1990s. Such interventions were generally site-specific, oftentimes into non-art museums, and sought to shed critical light on some aspect of the museum's collections, practices or politics, particularly their representational politics. In the Australian context in particular, museum interventions were often viewed as a form of post-colonial critique.[5]

With the rise in artistic research as a common rubric for understanding art practice, as well as a broader archival turn in contemporary art, archives have become less a site for intervention and more a source of inspiration for a broad range of artistic use and interpretation. Foster distinguished between art focused on the museum and archival art, the latter being 'not as concerned with critiques of representational totality and institutional integrity'.[6] Indeed, claims Foster, archival art often both draws from the historical archive and is productive of new archives. One of Foster's key examples is Tacita Dean's *Girl Stowaway* (1994). Beginning with a found archival image of an Australian girl who stowed away on a ship in 1928, Dean's work traces her personal journey researching and connecting with this story, so that the project becomes, in Foster's words, 'an allegory of archival work'.[7] But the shift Foster outlines, from overt political critique to more generative forms of archival interaction, should not be taken to imply that the latter does not also critically reflect back upon the archive. Artist archives, Foster writes, can be seen as 'perverse orders that aim to disrupt the symbolic order at large'.[8] In the broader discourse, these archival forms are often positioned as idealistic alternatives to the archive or counter-archives. Tom Holert goes as far as to claim: 'Most of these practices engage in revisionary, often imaginative, sometimes utopian projects'.[9]

Rather than directly intervening into the site of the archive, or performing a critique of institutional conventions, Thompson utilised the archive to inspire creative forms that move away from its primary content. He writes how he 'asked the photographs in the Pitt Rivers Museum to be catalysts and waited patiently to see what ideas and images would surface in the work'.[10] Thompson's work accords the archival materials he witnessed great significance, while also turning away from many of the things that code them as archives – historical information, modes of categorisation and display – replacing this information with his own unique chains of meaning. The content of his images appear to mix signifiers of cultural identity, colonial history, the natural world, spirituality, which all coalesce around the figure of Thompson himself. Thompson, as subject, becomes as unfixed as the archive he interprets. Yet, at the same time, his figure anchors these interpretations in the realm of personal identifications. It is not only in generating new creative forms from the archive that the artist might 'disrupt the symbolic order', as Foster describes.[11] It is in its very disconnection from the archive, its refusal to use it in archive like ways, that marks this work as disruptive. In performing a role of cultural reconnection in the archive, Thompson also attempts to disconnect from the archive itself.

In shifting from inviting interventions to opening up the archive for a variety of purposes and usages, is the museum instrumentalising the cultural identities of artists in new ways? Is there a particular danger for artists with cultural ties to the archive that their creative engagements will be performing a redemptive form of cultural reconnection? It is worth pointing out that even when museums invited in more explicit forms of critique, their aim has often been to establish better connections with groups they have long marginalised. One of the most seminal museum interventions of the 1990s, Fred Wilson's *Mining The Museum*, arose partly out of the Maryland Historical Society's desire to reach out to local communities.[12] Wilson, through his focus on highlighting marginalised histories, could be said to effectively critique the politics of the museum and assist it in connecting to a more diverse audience. Strategies have changed, but artists such as Gough and Thompson continue to navigate their relationship within the archive as one comprised of both aligning interests and a variety of tensions.

Touching the Archive

In an era where historical archives are becoming increasingly accessible via digital reproductions and online databases, many contemporary artists nevertheless strongly desire to be physically present within archives and collections. The archival turn in contemporary art has drawn artists to both the historical content and materiality of both archives and the things in them. In part this is because many of the objects are much more than visual images: often they were made to be held, worn or used in performances. Moreover, while visual artists might translate their experiences into visual images, invariably these experiences are phenomenological and multi-sensory. The ability to spend time in archives and collections, to interact with their materials, has been increasingly enabled by artist residencies in museums and archives.

The proliferation of museum residencies in recent years is perhaps concomitant with the museum's desire to allow greater access to those spaces traditionally exclusively the domain of museum curators and staff. In 1992 Eilean Hooper Greenhill wrote: 'Now, the closed and private space of the early public museums has begun to open, and the division between private and public has begun to close'.[13] Such boundaries have not been completely dissolved, but access to formerly private areas is conditionally extended to more people, more frequently, especially in the name of postcolonial redress. Moira Simpson describes museum objects held in the stores as being in a 'semi-restricted region' where they are 'less accessible but still available to members of the public who receive permission to access them, such as bona-fide researchers, students or others who are considered appropriate on cultural or academic grounds'.[14] Contemporary artists have become a group for whom access to museum archives is now routinely extended, even solicited. Claire Robins has even linked the use of contemporary artworks in certain museums with the museum's desire to re-invest in sensations, emotion and affect – forms of visitor experience that were curtailed in nineteenth and early-twentieth-century museums due to their concerns for care and preservation.[15] For Robins, 'Artwork in the museum can provide a site where visitors' sense modalities, cognitive and emotional faculties will be engaged and "activated"'.[16] Further, artist projects facilitated by museums provide a kind of compensatory access. Unable to extend access to all, the experiences of the artist in the archive, translated or represented via their work, can represent the museum's commitment to opening up their collections for broader and more direct public use.

When the archive holds cultural significance for the artist, this interaction has added weight; relevant communities may have rarely, if ever, had physical access to their cultural heritage in the museum, and an artist's interaction with materials in such cases is often seen to be on behalf of their communities. In Julie Gough's words: 'The artist, to achieve access to their cultural objects, becomes an accidental diplomat and uncomfortable interlocutor'.[17] Such access might be bittersweet, fulfilling an artist's desire to interact with and convey cultural objects but with the knowledge that they will likely remain physically inaccessible to others, and, moreover, that such interaction can unduly promote the museum's access credentials.

Both Thompson and Gough have emphasised how physical interactions with archival materials were significant to their work. Thompson has said he declined to be provided with digital copies of the images he was working with, but opted instead to make successive visits to the archive.[18] Gough too, felt the need to spend time with the objects in the archive:

> In the museum I took my time to choose the tools to be photographed. Holding them clarified if they felt right in the hand, cold or warm, what type of stone – some were familiar. Could I have made this, did an ancestor?[19]

In contrast to the often sterile and alienating experiences many Indigenous people face when confronting ancestral objects behind glass in the museum, art that addresses the archive has an opportunity to both reflect on the materiality of archives, the significance of communing directly and privately with them, and also on their continued inaccessibility. Instead of pulling something from the depths of the archive in order to make it accessible, these works seem to extend the archive's surfaces, in either partial or temporary ways. Thompson has written:

> I was drawn to elements of opulence, ritual, homage, fragility, melancholy, strength and even a sense of play operating in the photographs. The simplicity of a monochrome and sepia palette, the frayed delicate edges and the cracks on the surface like a dry desert floor that reminded me of the salt plains of my own traditional lands.[20]

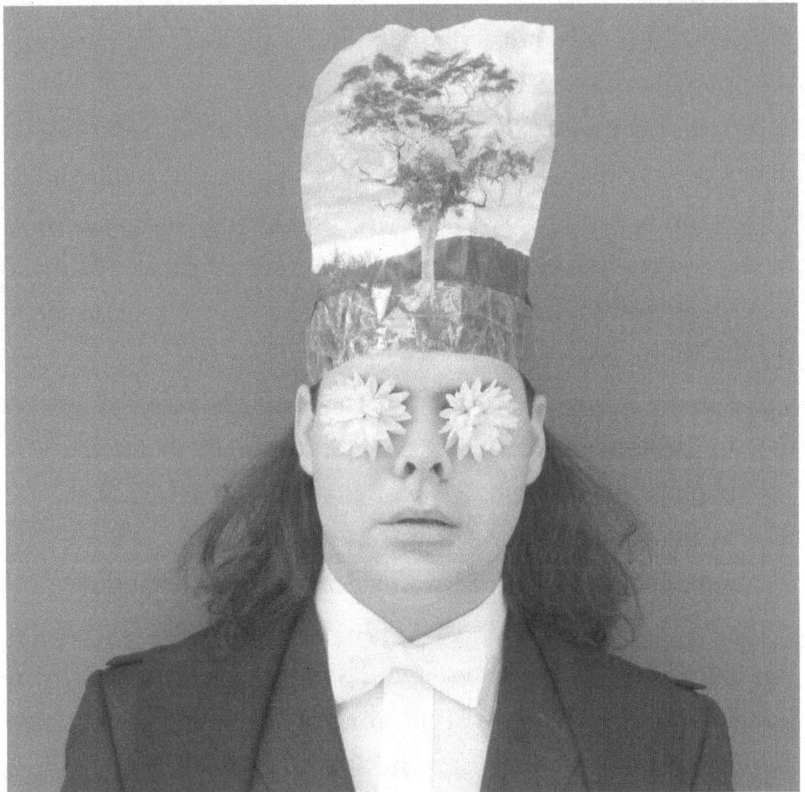

Figure 13.3: Christian Thompson, Desert Melon, *100 cm × 100 cm, Fuji Pearl Metallic Paper, c-type print, 2012. Courtesy the artist and Gallery Gabrielle Pizzi, Melbourne and Michael Reid Gallery, Sydney and Berlin.*

Many of the elements of which Thompson writes are precisely those that are erased in reproduction; not only the textured surfaces of a degrading vintage print, and the edges and frames that are usually cropped out, but also some of the more affective associations more likely to be elicited through an interaction with an original object. Photography historians Elizabeth Edwards and Janice Hart have described the photographic object as 'enmeshed with subjective, embodied and sensuous interactions'.[21] Instead of looking primarily to its image content, Thompson instead foregrounds a highly personal and physical interaction with the archive. Indeed, Thompson's photographs seem to directly bear the trace of tactile surfaces – from the patterning created by a pair of painted hands, to a delicate lace veil that traces the contours of Thompson's face, to the crinkled surface of a printed image of a ghost-gum tree – the phenomenological aspects of the original photographs seem to have been lifted into the image content of Thompson's work.

Gough's work also shows a strong a sense of wanting to convey the materiality of objects held in the archive, but instead of trying to remove the veils of mediation that usually distance the original archive from its audience, Gough proliferates these layers as if to draw attention to the ways in which archives distance us from the original meanings of things. *The Lost World (Part 2)* reproduces the original archive of thirty-five stone tools that Gough worked with via interconnected virtual mediations: the video of Gough placing the photographs around Tasmania, which was projected in the Andrews Gallery in Hobart and from MAA to the opposite building in Cambridge, along with the two live web feeds: one of the tools on display in Cambridge (shown in Tasmania), and the other of one of the 'returned' photographs in Tasmania (shown in Cambridge). Each element became a different kind of screen for the archive, assisting it in being relayed across time and space, while also flattening it out. Instead of a pretence towards accessibility and openness that usually accompanies the photographing, digitisation and uploading of an archive, Gough codes her reproductions as durational and contingent. Moreover, in activating the digital photographs that were taken of the stone tools, she also highlights precisely what these kinds of reproductions cannot convey when they attempt to transmit the physical archive. Rather than flat and mounted on a wall, Gough's prints become curved objects, nestled amongst grass and twigs. In thus simulating the process an archival object would undergo if placed back onto the land, Gough highlights what is lost in such ubiquitous archival technologies as photography.

Like Thompson, Gough represents the materiality of archival objects, but even more pointedly reveals our inability to reach out and touch, to have the kind of 'sensuous interaction' experienced by the artist and the original makers and users of them. In both artists' works, there is a sense of responsibility shown towards the materials viewed, handled and experienced in the archive, and a corresponding desire to convey them. But these representations of the physical archive, and the archival experience, are personal, partial, temporal and mediated. In accepting their role as archival mediator, Gough and Thompson also make plain the limitations and loss of experiencing on behalf of others.

Losing the Archive

> Some years ago, when I began to realize that the archive, in the more limited and technical sense of being a series of organized historical records, more often than not, and too easily, gave me what I was looking for, I decided that it was an interesting departure to make things up.[22]

Art historian Adrian Rifkin points to a curious form of frustration with the archive, not that the knowledge he seeks is difficult to find but that the archive too readily provides it. Rifkin goes on to say that some of his best archival discoveries he has chosen never to reveal, writing how 'in a research culture dominated by the commodity-notion of "output", their privacy is all the more treasured'.[23] Perhaps the ease of archival discovery, which makes Rifkin so uneasy, is borne of a certain equivocating of different desires between, for example, the archive's desire to reveal itself and the desire of marginalised groups to recover repressed histories. Rifkin's given example is of finding a dossier on gay sailors in Toulon, precisely the proof he needed to support a point that he already considered obvious.[24] The archive can and does offer proof after proof of its complicity with oppressive power, but how might we begin to detach ourselves from the powerful hold of the archive itself? Might the work of destabilising the power of the archive be performed both by revealing its recorded atrocities and suppressions, as well as by symbolically refusing to reveal?

In his article, 'Against The Archive', Ory Dessau points to instances where artists have withdrawn from, decontextualised or otherwise obscured archival sources in their work.[25] In Mirosław Bałka's work *Four Something* (2012), a wall text quotes an exchange in the film *Shoah* (1985), where the wife of a Nazi schoolteacher struggles to remember the number of Jewish victims killed at the Chełmno extermination camp, saying: 'Four something, four hundred thousand or forty thousand'. Dessau writes how Balka's work is a 'gesture of distancing the already distancing testimony, negating the already negating image'.[26] Instead of explicating the historical record, such works seem to shout back at it from a distance. Strategies of concealment and withdrawal are also at play in the works of Thompson and Gough. Through gestures that deliberately conceal archival content or let it slip away over time and space, the archive is shifted from its usual position of primacy. Rather than only asking the archive to reveal lost objects, these works also ask the objects to lose the archive.

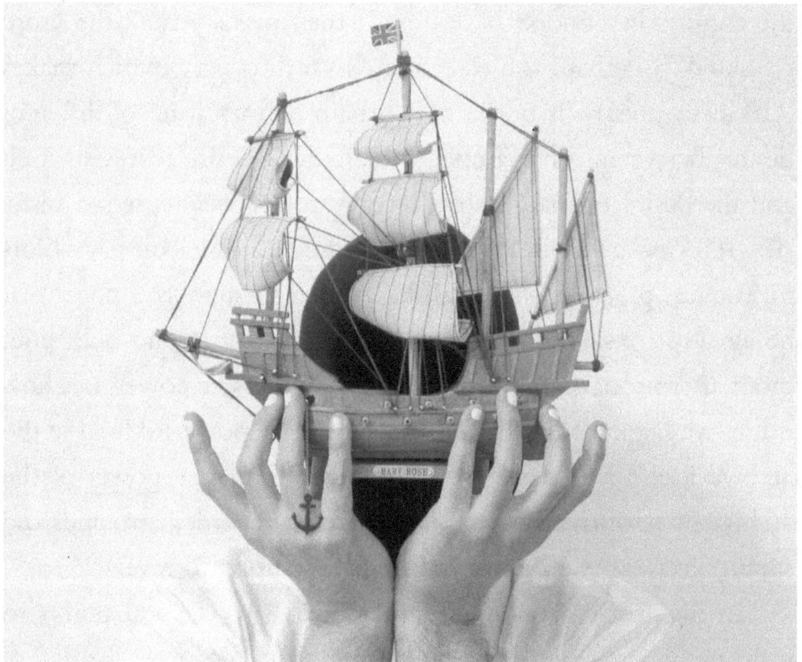

Figure 13.4: Christian Thompson, Invaded Dreams, *100 cm × 100 cm, Fuji Pearl Metallic Paper, c-type print, 2012. Courtesy the artist and Gallery Gabrielle Pizzi, Melbourne and Michael Reid Gallery, Sydney and Berlin.*

Thompson's work is notable for not directly quoting the archival sources that inspired the work. Through the act of taking self-portraits, which Thompson describes as a form of ceremony, he embodies, performs and responds to archival materials, while throwing off the archive *as* archive.[27] Thompson also avoids the tendency of much archive-based art to mimic and subvert archival processes. Instead of performing the work of researching, historicising and displaying, Thompson instrumentalises the archive for purposes uniquely his own. In an interview on the work, Thompson discusses how Indigenous votive objects were typically discarded following ceremonies.[28] An analogous gesture is being made by the work itself; having communed with the archive, Thompson is able to discard it, or at least to shed its recognisable content. In all of the photographs in the series *We Bury Our Own*, Thompson's eyes are shielded from view, covered by different objects: crystals, butterflies, flowers, his two adorned hands, a replica ship. As witness to the photographic archive, Thompson would have no doubt stared into the eyes of countless photographed subjects, and yet in representing this interaction, he denies us access to his own gaze, adding another layer of concealment. In performing his role as archival mediator, the figure of Thompson stands as a literal in-between – we see neither the archive nor the eyes that gazed upon it – but are drawn to look upon the enigmatic objects that Thompson offers up in their place.

The archive is by no means entirely absent from Thompson's work. Christopher Morton has suggested how Thompson's self-portraiture may be an inversion of 'the more scientific end of nineteenth-century *ethnographic* portraiture; head-and-shoulders, full-face, looking directly into the camera'.[29] The work also appears to contain more general references to the colonial context of the archive, the image of rippling water in *Danger Will Come* and the replica ship in *Invaded Dreams* seem archetypal references to the British invasion of the Indigenous nations of Australia. But noticeable on the ship is the label 'Mary Rose', denoting it as a Tudor warship, a fact that doesn't entirely undo it as symbol of colonialism, but is indicative of the way Thompson uses unstable combinations of signifiers; that flit between times and places and identities. Ultimately, the archival trace is buried amidst a plethora of sources from which Thompson draws, such that we can never be certain whether he is directly performing the archive or his role as archival interpreter.

Thompson's use of objects and costuming in his self-portraits resembles a kind of stagecraft; careful selections and arrangements have been made but there is also a sense of using things ready to hand. A cheap plastic boat, held to cover the entire face, or a crumpled paper printout fashioned into a crown, operate like stage props, coming alive through performance. As with the votive analogy, these objects feel destined for a particular and perhaps temporary usage. Indeed, many of them are commonly used votive offerings across many different cultural contexts, such as flowers and candles and crystals. Thompson has written:

> I wanted to generate an aura around this series, a meditative space that was focused on freeing oneself of hurt, employing crystals and other votive objects that emit frequencies that can heal, ward off negative energies, psychic attack, geopathic stress and electromagnetic fields, and, importantly, transmit ideas.[30]

The archival aura in Thompson's work accords both immense power to the archival materials witnessed, highlighting their ability to be hugely affective, even traumatic, for onlookers, while also turning away from the usual methods by which the archive itself attempts to give these materials meaning. This may also acknowledge that certain ways of giving these materials meaning constitutes an inappropriate appropriation of another person, family or community's material history. Thompson's responses to the archive acknowledge its colonial context, infusing it with personal identifications, but content likely to hold specific cultural and historical meanings is not re-worked or revealed. Instead,

Thompson's photographs record the final stage of a process of witnessing, performing and releasing the contents of the archive. It is in this sense that the original photographic objects can be said to lose the archive through Thompson's work.

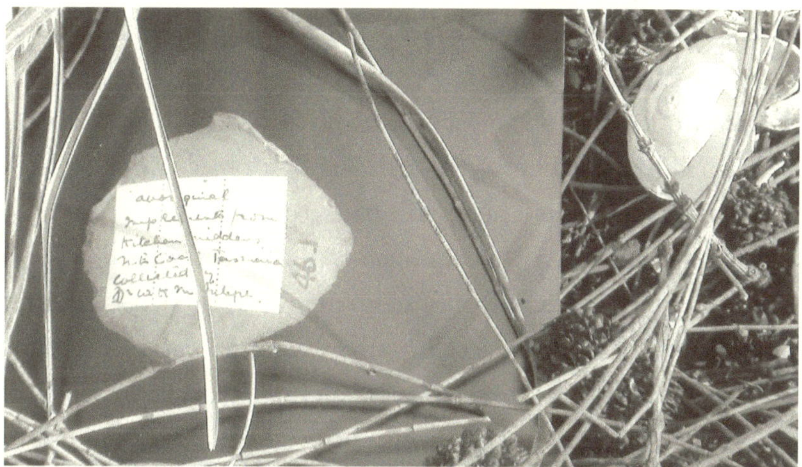

Figure 13.5: Julie Gough, The Lost World (part 2)*, 2013, film still, HDMI video, 1:15:32, edited by Jemma Rea, artefact photography by Christoph Balzar.*

Gough's work employs a very different strategy to Thompson's. Her work directly quotes its archival sources, proliferating a series of representations derived from them. But while Gough's work functions as a form of archival revelation; making visible a series of stone tools recovered from boxes in the MAA archive, it also interrogates the work of the archive – what it means across different contexts, to lose, find and reveal cultural objects. Gough's various iterations of the same set of archival objects as photographs, film and live feed puts these iterations (or representations) in constant flux. The video work for the project, also called *The Lost World (2)*, depicts Gough in a variety of different Tasmanian landscapes, placing photographs of the stone tools into natural settings – amongst reeds, held by a tree trunk, partially buried in sand dunes. Via these gestures, Gough symbolically finds the original locations for the tools and assists them to lose the archive site (its walls, and boxes, and temperature control) by returning them to the land. But these actions are also only approximations; digital prints stand-in for the stone tools, the notion of an 'original location' is necessarily imprecise, with the only available information being the Western place names that were, in many cases, written directly onto the tools themselves. Gough's work acts as a finding and revealing of the archive's 'lost objects', but is also a meditation on the permanent loss they represent.

Gough also seems to ruminate on a certain precariousness of the archive. By giving her new archive a fixed duration, in both having the video feeds lasting only as long as the exhibitions and exposing her photographs to elements which will quickly degrade them, Gough speeds up the archive's demise to a time span we might witness, thus marking its disappearance and making it visible. This loss is staged rather than actual – the stone tools remain safely stored away at the MAA, the project has itself been documented and archived, the photographs in the land will continue to degrade away from our watchful gaze – but the stability and permanency of the archive has been called into question. Derrida has famously linked the archive with the death drive, arguing that in 'what permits and conditions archivization' is nothing other than that which exposes it 'to destruction, and in truth what menaces with destruction'.[31] It is this very anxiety that Gough teases out. If an archival object really went back into the earth, would it be lost? Was it ever really found in the first place, if the finding meant displacing it from everything that originally gave it meaning: people, place, culture, language and land? The archive's very desire to care for and preserve is what creates the 'lost object' – those rarely seen items in dim corners of rooms lined with boxes. The land, as living archive for cultural heritage, can also carry our objects forward into the future, and they may be no less lost to us there.

Returning the Archive

> I maintain that the encounter with cultural difference cannot be done by representing a loss or an absence, but needs to come about by the museum acknowledging and enacting a loss on some part of itself.[32]

The anthropological museum, in seeking to redress the lack of Indigenous voices, perspectives, and agency within its walls, has invited Indigenous people to perform interventions, interact with its collections and undertake research. However, as Irit Rogoff argues, the museum's attempts to include multicultural perspectives often only serves to embellish what already exists without destabilising structures that have enacted and perpetuated exclusion in the first place.[33] Gough wrote on her experience in the archive:

> Effective communication is allied with being successfully cross-cultural, being able to 'work it' (in) the Western system, not being overtly threatening, angry, nor proprietorial about the objects. There is some kind of unspoken trade-off in the transaction; to be able to find something—something else feels lost.[34]

Here Gough points to the underlying logic of the archive, that it welcomes archival discoveries but not subtractions. Ultimately, revealing the lost object is very different from claiming it. If

Gough talks about a trade-off produced through interaction with the archive, then perhaps we need to ask: what part of itself is the archive willing to lose in this exchange? How to avoid merely representing loss and absence? Both Thompson and Gough's work might be read as confronting the archive on its inability to enact such loss.

Gough's work explores different forms of loss that complicate any notion of a simple returning and reconnecting of lost objects to their original places and peoples. The work attempts to expose and ameliorate the absence of certain information lost to the archive; for example, Gough used the original Aboriginal place names for the locations the objects were removed from, handwritten onto delicate paper, and displayed hanging below the stone tools. But such a gesture, in being inherently temporary and ephemeral, both reveals an absence and then incompletely remedies it, inserting a kind of loss back into the site of the archive.

The most unambiguous form of an archive enacting a loss on itself is via the physical repatriation of cultural objects. Gough's performed returning of lost objects, and Thompson's spiritual repatriation of witnessed materials, both enact a form of symbolic repatriation of cultural objects such that the artist and artworks become literal conduits of the archive's return or release. In their highly personal, performative and affective approaches, the works could be said to shift away from the anthropological, museological and legal discourses that usually dominate the discourse on repatriation. But while these gestures feel, in part, healing and restorative, they also explicitly point to the inability of the archival materials dealt with to physically return home. Gough is explicit in this regard:

> *The Lost World (Part 2)* was the response to my incapacity to return the actual stone artefacts or tools to their home country – across Tasmania – my maternal homeland. My driving force was the need to overcome, by whatever achievable means I could muster, the debilitating sense of powerlessness resulting from visiting overseas museum-held objects.[35]

The healing gestures performed by Thompson and Gough do not remedy the archive by returning it. However, in forming meaningful and creative connections with the archive, they assert some continuing if ambivalent agency over it from a distance. Their symbolic repatriations are not substitutions for physical ones but gestures of coming to terms with the archival objects' continued displacement and physical absence.

The title of Thompson's work at the Pitt Rivers, *We Bury Our Own*, is also poignant in this regard. Thompson has spoken of how this sentiment came from traditions of his people.[36] On the one hand, the title seems an explicit reference to the perceived role of the Indigenous person in a museum, the 'we' and 'our' linking Thompson's gesture to a broader Indigenous community. The title could also be read as asserting Indigenous agency over the archive, distancing the work from any notion of a cross-cultural exchange process. Finally, it could also reference one of the most contested and sought forms of physical repatriation, the return of human remains. In Thompson's project, to 'bury' the archive is to commune with it and then, in Thompson's words, 'it's about setting something free', his final works bearing the traces of this process.[37] This gesture highlights that it is not only the obviously stolen, displaced or unethically displayed that might have traumatic resonance for Indigenous peoples, and that the need to see can exist alongside a need to bury. Alongside the important work of communicating the content of the photographic archives, already being done by the larger project at the Pitt Rivers, Thompson's work notably does not perform a parallel strategy of what Irit Rogoff might term 'compensatory visibility'.[38] Instead it obfuscates and personalises, and, symbolically buries. Gough's work perhaps also attempts a symbolic burial for the archive. While never completely covered, many of the photographs that Gough places on the land have their edges obscured by sand and soil and plant matter, and we can assume by now that they have sunk deeper underground. The works of Gough and Thompson do not only represent absence in the archive, they also imagine processes by which objects may truly lose the archive.

Notes

1 H. Foster, 'An Archival Impulse', *October*, no. 110, Fall 2004, pp. 3–22 at 4.

2 M. G. Simpson writes that, 'The Western museum's emphasis on objects does not really accommodate the need for preserving "living" culture, an important limitation for those in societies in which less emphasis is placed on preserving the materiality and more on maintaining the intangible aspects of heritage, including the relationships, knowledge and activities that give objects meaning'. In 'Charting the Boundaries: Indigenous models and parallel practices in the development of the post-museum' in S. J. Knell, S. MacLeod & S. Watson (eds), *Museum Revolutions: How Museums Change and Are Changed*, Routledge, London & New York, 2007, pp. 235–49 at 235.

3 C. Thompson, 'Artist Statement', *We Bury Our Own*, 2012, exhibition website <https://www.prm.ox.ac.uk/christianthompson.html>.

4 C. Morton, 'Spiritual repatriation and the archive in Christian Thompson's *We Bury Our Own* (catalogue essay)', in *We Bury Our Own*, 2012, exhibition website <https://www.prm.ox.ac.uk/christianthompson.html>.

5 Jennifer Barrett and Jacqueline Millner are explicit in this regard, writing: 'In the 1990s post-colonial critique was as a significant practice for Australian artists'. In J. Barrett & J. Millner, *Australian Artists in the Contemporary Museum*, Ashgate, Farnham Surrey, UK, 2014, p. 39.

6 H. Foster, 'An Archival Impulse', p. 5.
7 ibid., p. 12.
8 ibid., p. 21.
9 T. Holert in B. Abbas & R. Abou-Rahme, 'The Archival Multitude: Basel Abbas and Ruanne Abou-Rahme (in Conversation with Tom Holert)', *Journal of Visual Culture*, vol. 12, no. 3, December 2013, pp. 345–63 at 345.
10 C. Thompson, 'Artist Statement'.
11 H. Foster, 'An Archival Impulse', p. 21.
12 C. Robins, *Curious Lessons in the Museum*, Ashgate, Farnham Surrey, UK, 2013, p. 176; L. G. Corrin (ed.), *Mining the Museum: An Installation by Fred Wilson*, The New Press, Baltimore & New York, 1994, p. 10.
13 E. Hooper Greenhill, *Museums and the Shaping of Knowledge*, Routledge, London & New York, 1992, p. 200.
14 M. G. Simpson, 'Charting the Boundaries', p. 245.
15 C. Robins, *Curious Lessons in the Museum*, pp. 155–76.
16 ibid., p. 174.
17 J. Gough, 'The Possessed Past. Museums: Infiltration and Outreach and *The Lost World (Part 2)*', in Khadija von Zinnenburg Carroll (ed), *The Importance of Being Anachronistic: Contemporary Aboriginal Art and Museum Reparations*, Discipline in collaboration with *Third Text* Publications, an affiliate of Third Text journal, Australia, 2016, pp. 65–66.
18 C. Thompson interviewed in *Christian Thompson – We Bury Our Own*, video recording, The Pitt Rivers Museum, Oxford, film by Michael Walter, A Two Dogs Caged Production for Troika Editions Video, 2012, viewed 9 July 2015, <http://www.prm.ox.ac.uk/christianthompson.html>.
19 J. Gough, 'The Possessed Past', p. 57.
20 C. Thompson, 'Artist Statement'.
21 E. Edwards & J. Hart, 'Introduction: Photographs as Objects', in E. Edwards & J. Hart (eds), *Photographs Objects Histories: On the Materiality of Images*, Routledge, London & New York, 2004, pp. 1–15 at 1.
22 A. Rifkin, 'Dancing Years, or Writing as a Way Out', *Art History*, vol. 32, no. 4, 2009, pp. 806–20, at 806.
23 ibid., p. 807.
24 ibid., p. 807.
25 Ory Dessau, 'Against the Archive', *Flash Art International*, vol. 46, no. 292, October 2013, pp. 102–6.
26 ibid., p. 103.
27 C. Thompson interviewed in *Christian Thompson – We Bury Our Own.*
28 ibid.
29 C. Morton, 'Spiritual Repatriation and the Archive in Christian

Thompson's *We Bury Our Own* (catalogue essay)', p. 14.

30 C. Thompson, 'Artist Statement'.

31 J. Derrida, 'Archive Fever: A Freudian Impression', trans. E. Prenowitz, *Diacritics*, vol. 25, no. 2, Summer, 1995, pp. 9–63 at 14.

32 I. Rogoff, 'Hit and Run—Museums and Cultural Difference', *Art Journal*, vol. 61, no. 3, 2002, pp. 63–74 at 64.

33 ibid., p. 64.

34 Gough, 'The Possessed Past', p. 62.

35 ibid.

36 C. Thompson interviewed in *Christian Thompson – We Bury Our Own.*

37 ibid.

38 I. Rogoff, 'Hit and Run', p. 66.

14

BLEEDING THE ARCHIVE, TRANSFORMING THE MYTHSCAPE

Genevieve Grieves and Odette Kelada

First Nations artists are forging dynamic spaces for political expression and reclamation. In particular, this chapter examines how artists are 'hijacking' official archives to carve strategic interventions into the body of the nation state and ideas of hegemonic 'truth' and 'history'. A growing body of global Indigenous art bleeds the archives for artistic affective and political currency. This chapter will examine the productive ways in which contemporary Australian Indigenous artists are reconceptualising and orchestrating artistic 'archival interventions'. Rather than simply adding another version/voice or story to a monolithic 'Australian history', these artists are producing creative works that are catalysts for revising the role and conception of archives, and ideas of how 'history' is retrieved and re-membered/dismembered. These artistic practices highlight how the idea of the 'archive' and redeployment of documentation, film and images are powerful sites for countering oppressive narratives and contemporary racism.

A memory retrieved from the personal vault [Kelada] – the Art Gallery of New South Wales 2009 exhibition *Half Light: Portraits from Black Australia*:

> Walking past a photo – a scene straight from the colonial archives, staged romanticised 'others' dressed to perform for the imperial eye – and it moves. A series of

> photographs on the wall begin to shift and morph. They are alive. These images are not photographs but film. I watch as bodies enter the frame. The frame is broken. It is permeable. A border invaded. A white man enters the scene. The colonial photographer is captured in his own creation. Shot literally in the act. The fantasy is detonated from within. Now time has moved and the story of what was bleeds into what is now until history as told by the white lens is corrupted and there is no longer a 'history' to speak of.

The work described above through an experiential encounter with the images is titled *Picturing the Old People* (2005). The series, by collaborator in this essay, artist, academic and filmmaker, Genevieve Grieves, references the legacies of colonial photographers such as J. W. Lindt, Charles Kerry and Fred Kruger. Here Grieves stages a intervention through her slow-moving images which are described as mimicking 'the long exposure times required historically yet also offer a pace open to memory and dialogue to bring the "Old People" to life'[1]. This installation, using video and sound, is an example of what we argue in this essay is part of multiple interventions by contemporary Aboriginal artists actively decolonising the archives. The archives are located here as both sites and entities of trauma.

A response to memory [Grieves']:

> I had been repatriating these images to communities across Victoria as part of my work at the Koorie Heritage Trust. We were digitising images from various institutions and connecting them with individuals and families as part of a wider process of strengthening culture and

> identity. There were a series of images, the colonial portraiture I explore in this work, that were nameless, placeless – dislocated, disembodied – clearly constructed images of Aboriginality. They haunted me. Particularly the images of women, laying under "humpies" whose eyes betrayed the images themselves; within their gaze you could sometimes see disdain but mostly mourning. The work came to me in a half-waking state, I could see an image of an Aboriginal woman being taken by a photographer, he holds her as they slowly waltz across a studio floor.

Historically, as Stephen Muecke states, 'The Aboriginal Other has long occupied a place of psychic denial in Australian national consciousness'.[2] Deborah Bird Rose points to the inherent violence of such a totalising monologue, resulting in a perpetual one-sided conversation. This violent act of absence universalises and normalises a singular narrative. Rose utilises the work of Emil Fakenheim who conceptualised *ethical dialogue* – a form of engagement that seeks relationships across otherness without seeking to erase difference – as a way of shifting monological power.[3]

While Indigenous voices, perspectives and knowledges are now increasingly acknowledged in wider local, regional and national narratives, they are often incorporated in ways that fail to shift dominant conceptions of history and archives. In a similar vein, Frances Peters-Little argues that while many historians have been preoccupied with redressing the 'silence' and fighting the rejection of Aboriginal histories in the 'History Wars', they failed to hear the 'racket' from Aboriginal artists, writers, film and theatre makers presenting, sharing and telling Aboriginal experiences of the past.[4]

This racket, we argue, constitutes contemporary acts of war on cultural frontiers. For example, Brenda Croft, then Indigenous curator at the National Gallery of Australia, used the term 'Culture Warriors' as the title and theme for the inaugural National Indigenous Art Triennial in 2007. In a similar vein, critical race theorist, Aileen Moreton-Robinson, describes Vernon Ah Kee as a 'sovereign warrior' at war in the 'white postcolonial borderzone' that is contemporary Aboriginal arts.[5] This chapter explores the connection between activism, art and archives with the focus on Aboriginal artists who emerge through resistance movements. We examine in particular how the artists Vernon Ah Kee and Yhonnie Scarce are creating art that decolonises the archives. This art constitutes contemporary acts of war on cultural frontiers morphing and emerging from geographic frontiers.

Linda Tuhuwai Smith, Maori author of *Decolonising Methodologies*, argues that the key to the decolonising project is '*re*writing and *re*righting our position in history'. It is driven, she says, by 'a very powerful need to give testimony to and restore a spirit, to bring back into existence a world fragmented and dying'.[6] Artists such as Ah Kee and Scarce are decolonising archives in ways that strategically foreground resistance to monological forms of history. They are undertaking a process of *representing*, bringing forth Indigenous voice, perspectives and understandings of colonialism from the point of view of the colonised.[7] They are *reframing* the experiences of Indigenous Peoples outside the colonial gaze and taking control of how Indigenous issues and peoples are framed.[8] A primary way in which they take control is through the genre of storytelling, unravelling past narratives, melding them to the present, and collapsing the temporality of white history to speak to ongoing colonisation. *Storytelling* is a key decolonising process identified by Tuhuwai Smith. Stories, she says, can be presented in various forms beyond the oral. It is vital to extend the 'concept of *story* to embrace the expressions of visual artists, film, and performance', drawing from deep traditions of sharing knowledge through oral forms in Indigenous ontologies. These stories connect the generations, sharing knowledge and values with a sense of hope that they will be held and continued: 'The story and the storyteller both serve to connect the past with the future, one generation with the other, the land with the people and the people with the story'.[9] Some theorists contend that this term, 'decolonisation', is often used as a metaphor when it requires the actual repatriation of Indigenous land and life. This is ultimately incommensurable with the dispossessing frameworks of settler-colonial societies and the ideology of the nation state. Decolonisation requires an 'unsettling' that does not exist as an end point, but is rather an 'elsewhere' outside of settler-colonialism.[10] Sarah Keenan applies this idea to an Australian context and argues that Indigenous activism, in resisting the settler-colonial project, has created an *elsewhere* to it.[11] Working within the framework of Australian law that has 'functioned to discursively historicise Indigenous Australia', she identifies 'moments of decolonisation' in which Indigenous Australia 'asserts a contemporary presence in opposition to and outside of colonial Australia'.[12] The artist-activists we explore here create such 'moments of decolonisation' in a Deleuzian sense: their works 'deterritorialise', moving and shifting colonial occupation and discourse, creating new 'lines of flight'.[13] Art in this form is harnessed to become a weapon, which through witnessing, testimony, humanising and evidence, can shift understandings of 'history' and legacies of archival containment.

In her detailed insight into the colonial archive and how the imperial gaze has historically constructed representations of the 'Native' integral to the making of supremacist European identities,

Anne Maxwell cites Franz Fanon's observation that in colonialist discourse 'native' people are not positioned within the psychoanalytic structures of self and other but are relegated to the universe of objects where they remain beyond the limits of cultural intelligibility.[14] The dehumanisation process in this imagery relies on the anonymity of the subjects, with the people in these photographs often unnamed. One photograph that Maxwell includes to demonstrate anthropometric practice is of an Indigenous woman holding a measuring ruler in front of her body, positioned side on to the camera. Maxwell describes how, in the method prescribed by scientist Henry Huxley, the subject remains both an anonymous specimen of the tribe and recipient of the colonisers' gaze: 'There is no attempt to solicit or record any information that might reveal her as a thinking, feeling human being other than to suppose that she and her people were expendable'.[15]

Akin to Grieves's sense of images that 'haunt' her, Christine Nicholls observes in her review of the exhibition *Re-Take*:

> It is little wonder that the subjects reconfigured through the lens as objects frequently look back to the camera without expression or alternatively return the camera's gaze with grim expressions inflected with tension, anxiety or fear.[16]

Nicholls makes the critical point that this legacy continues to impact contemporary colonisation, stating that:

> the tradition continues in some contemporary photographic journalism and the perpetuation of negative images and predatory image-making and image-taking.[17]

These are the traumatic archives that artists such as Grieves, Ah Kee and Scarce open up to memory and dialogue.

The Archives Brought to Life Through Art Intervention

In investigating methodologies of intervention in relation to archives and art, Suzi Tibbets argues that:

> The archive is a collection of the past, with the capacity to define our social and collective history and to give meaning to our understanding of the present. It is a powerful structure, with both a physical material presence and an abstract and authoritative entity. The dusty, stagnant view of the archive as monument to the past masks the reality of the archive's potential as a dynamic, discursive organism. The archive lies dormant until it is brought to life through an intervention or interrogation.[18]

Despite this definition making numerous problematic assumptions with the repetition of the collective possessive pronoun 'our' history/'our' understanding as well as positioning the archive as *able* to lie 'dormant', Tibbet's lively description of archives as discursive 'organisms' is useful when examining the power of art that draws on images, texts and collections born from the imperial drive for colonisation. Thomas Richards stresses the critical role of fantasy in the notion of 'imperial archives', which he defines as 'a utopian space of comprehensive knowledge…not a building, nor even a collection of texts, but the collectively imagined junction of all that was known or knowable', and seeks to demonstrate how 'the imperial archive was a fantasy of knowledge collected and united in the service of state and Empire'.[19] Richards notes that it is no coincidence that the word 'classification' changed its meaning in the late nineteenth century to encompass not only the ordering of information in taxonomies but 'knowledge placed under the special jurisdiction of the state. In the fantasy of the imperial archive, the state actually succeeds in superintending all knowledge'[20]. For this fantasy to gain power, it relies on obsessive repetition manifested in intensive classification and collection as generative actions of authoritative power. This repetition plays out the Derridean notion of 'archive fever'.[21] While described in the context of an unquenchable desire for seeking origin, in the imperial archive this feverish 'sickness' also has the momentum to embed racist ideologies indelibly and persistently into lived realities. Representations emerging from the imperial archives play out in scenes that demonstrate the extent of effective racialised socialisation. A classic example is Frantz Fanon's evocative encounter with a white child's terrified reaction to the sight of his black body: 'Mama, see the Negro! I'm frightened'[22]. As Stephanie Newell argues, Fanon here:

> experiences a form of terror as the effects of colonial history spread across his skin and mark him permanently. Centuries of 'ways of seeing' contribute to this moment of social recognition in the child. In an instant, Fanon is positioned inside an archive of colonialist images, and his plural self fills up with the 'realities' of others' beliefs and perceptions. Upon realizing this, 'Fanon' falls apart. His specificity as a human subject is replaced with a different type of specificity, a racial identity produced within a visual economy that dissects and classifies its objects.[23]

Fanon's body here exists in the site of trauma that is the colonial archive; centuries compacted and able to be triggered in a moment. There is no dormancy in this archive but a constant alienating imperative that keeps white bodies in places of structural and institutional dominance.

Vernon Ah Kee's work *He said...She said* (2007) commences with a replay of this kind of encounter. A series of photographs stretch around the walls with text beneath each shot. With the filmic resonance of a storyboard, the viewer sees a conversation between Ah Kee and Belinda Miller unfolding. To hear their conversation, one must walk around with each image and read the text below each photograph to listen in on what 'he said' and what 'she said'. The opening lines are: 'He says a child stared and pointed at him. Then the child's parents said "He's black" and then they walked away'. As opposed to Fanon's 'falling apart', Ah Kee's account continues opening into a compelling dialogue on racism. The scene of the child is the start of a conversation continuing along a street and to the beach, with commentary deconstructing the dynamics of race politics in Australia and skin as the 'colour barrier'. Ah Kee writes:

> The two characters share in the punching, in the delivering of the blows...It's meant to be like serve and response, volleys here and there. It's leading to the last text, where he says, 'We are in a war', and she says, 'I know'. Which is the way blackfellas feel; it's just that few get the opportunity to express it effectively.[24]

Bleeding the Archives as *Evidence*: Vernon Ah Kee

Ah Kee's work *The Tall Man* (2010) literally captures this war on film. Here the focus is the Palm Island riots in 2004. *The Tall Man* emphasises that the imperial archive is ongoing. A four channel video installation, the archives drawn upon are current technological reservoirs of memory obtained in part from anonymous sources: insider police recordings of the riot and their reactions, fragments of the riot caught on mobile phones, shaky hand-held cameras and news footage interspersed with tourist-like panning and aerial shots of Palm Island's tropical vistas.

Palm Island is a place steeped in the memories and continuing impacts of ongoing colonialism. It was established as essentially a 'penal settlement', a place to exile Aboriginal Peoples considered 'disruptive' or 'undesirable'. Queensland's 'Chief Protector of Aborigines' observed in 1916 that it was both 'the ideal place for a holiday' and a penitentiary for 'individuals we desire to punish'.[25] It is a place where today reports continue of violent abuses, neglect and authoritarian regulation. The Palm Island riots erupted in response to the release of a coroner's report concluding that Cameron Doomadgee, a young Indigenous man who died in police custody 45 minutes after arrest, had suffered from an 'accidental fall'. This finding came in the face of Doomadgee's massive internal injuries, broken ribs, ruptured spleen, torn portal vein, black eye and liver almost split in two. The injuries were described as 'akin to a high speed car or plane crash victim'.[26] The report did not speak to the evidence of police brutality and the view that Sergeant Chris Hurley murdered Doomadgee. On the day of the riots the police station and Hurley's house were torched.

The Tall Man includes footage of the rising anger and grief against the injustice of the coroner's report outside the police station. The footage chops to a view from a camera inside showing the officers loading their guns. Audio of an officer's voice can be heard: 'scare the shit out of these cunts'. Ah Kee's work, cutting sharply between scenes and perspectives, exposes the violence of police culture and explicit racism towards Indigenous Peoples.

The four channels of *The Tall Man* are intermittently broken up by SMPTE colour bars, the television test pattern designed to indicate how signals have been altered in transmission, enabling monitors to be set to receive information correctly. These are accompanied by the continuous mono audio sound technically termed a 1000 Hz tone, which identifies ownership of the transmission line. While unreadable by a lay person, these are tools to aid engineers in calibrating signal reception and communication. Ah Kee uses this test pattern and sound to interrupt the stream of juxtapositions and voices captured in the videos until all four channels are filled with the colour bars. At the end of the loop, the viewer sits in the dark with only these 'unreadable' codes glaring across the screens, deafened by the ear splitting Hz tone. The affective use of these bars/sound can read as provocative interventions cutting through space and 'jamming' transmission, a searing commentary on spectatorship and mass passivity in the face of deaths in custody. The strategic deployment of such physically discomforting barriers to hearing and seeing the 'news' and 'insider' footage confronts the audience with the in/ability to witness the 'truth' of violences which remain concealed. The interruption of the media works as a powerful reminder and indictment of the manipulation of communication, justice and law.

The video material Ah Kee utilizes in *The Tall Man* manifests also as a legal archive with the prosecution drawing on footage of the day as evidence to convict Doomadgee's relative, Lex Wotton. Wotton spoke out against the findings of 'accidental' death. He was found guilty of inciting the riot and imprisoned with a gag order. The police officers, including Hurley, received bravery awards from the government for the day of the riot. Hurley was promoted to the coveted post of the Gold Coast. He has since been implicated in further violent arrests. In a later 2010 coronial inquest into the death of Doomadgee, the Deputy Chief Magistrate, Brian Hine, found that he could not make a definitive ruling because of inconsistencies in evidence and testimonies. He found however that Hurley had lied consistently and that police conspired with each other and colluded and tainted the evidence.[27] Hurley remains at liberty.

Ah Kee's un-archiving of the police and state prosecution's archive reveals the ongoing colonial violence of the state. This present-day state archive directly descends from the imperial archive, including Norman Tindale's genealogical archive that includes photographs taken of Ah Kee's own family on Palm Island in 1938.[28] Use of the same footage as the prosecution shows a reverse incrimination as this evidence 'tainted' in the court system is laid bare to witness the shocking colonial histories and ongoing impacts lived today. The offensive language of the police and intent to 'scare the shit', alongside the visual of firearms, echoes the constant destruction of Indigenous bodies and identities throughout the colonial archives to the present day.

Born in Innisfail, Far North Queensland, Ah Kee is a member of the Yidindji, Kuku Yalandji, Waanji, Koko Berrin and Gugu Yimithirr Peoples. In his series *Fantasies of the Good* (2004), Ah Kee creates work in response to photographs of his relatives that his grandmother carried around in her purse. Having grown up with these images, he discovered while researching historical depictions of Aboriginal Peoples, that these 'family photos' were in fact reproductions of colonial photographs taken by ethnographer Norman Tindale. These images emerged from a time of eugenics with theories that Aboriginal people, as a dying race and inferior species, would become extinct. The extent of Tindale's collection, held in the South Australian Museum archives, evokes the earlier definition of archives as manifesting through obsessive classification. His journals recorded over five decades of notes, sounds and film recordings, maps, and genealogies that include information on approximately 50,000 Indigenous Peoples.[29] The photographs of Ah Kee's family are part of a collection of thousands of such photographic portraits.

In response to these archives, Ah Kee creates his own family portraits, enlarged in scale and drawn in charcoal. These deeply profound portraits speak back to the practices of 'scientific' documentation integral to studying the 'other' as objects to be measured and observed with blood samples extracted. The eyes in Ah Kee's portraits embody the oppositional gaze. Ah Kee speaks to the power of humanising through art:

> I use my own family to demonstrate the depth and complexity of modern Aboriginal life…I'm expanding the idea of what it means to be Aboriginal and what it means to be human. A lot of the problem this country has with Aboriginal people is that it struggles to see Aboriginal people as fully human.[30]

A profile piece on Ah Kee describes how:

> Sometimes he will turn out the lights in his studio and sit in silence among portraits he is working on, surrounded by the eyes of his family, an experience he finds comforting. 'My portraits are beautiful because I want the subject, Aboriginality, to be a beautiful thing'.[31]

The reclamation of beauty and humanity in a time of war is a powerful decolonising manoeuvre and one that Ah Kee explicitly engages. *The Tall Man* and his portraits address the same subject. This subject, the ongoing colonial war, is the vital connection across his *oeuvre*. The series title *Fantasies of the Good* captures how his artistic interventions bear witness to the evidence of ongoing trauma and continuous Indigenous Sovereignty. Ah Kee writes:

> Australia, as a country, as an idea, as an ideal, as a social-political system, thinks of and believes itself, despite its history of racism and exclusion, to be essentially good; I of course disagree. These drawings and what they represent are my evidence.[32]

This is epitomised in one work in particular: the portrait of his son, a child's face staring out from the paper with the archetypal burning intensity of Ah Kee's signature 'eyes'. Next to his child intrudes the rod and tag inscribed with the documenting data of Tindale's anthropological archive.

Bleeding the Archives as *Testimony*: Yhonnie Scarce

Yhonnie Scarce, a descendant of the Kokatha people of the Lake Eyre region and the Nukunu from around Port Augusta in South Australia, uses glass as a weapon against colonial archives. She is one of many Indigenous women artists who put 'their bodies on the line' to present the, 'violation, theft and destruction of bodies and cultures…through the maze of colonialised methods, from scientific research, anthropological projects, academia, art and the profits of museums'.[33]

Like Ah Kee, Scarce uses Tindale's photographs of her family to decolonise his archive. In *N0000 N2359 N2351 N2402* (2014),

Scarce places images of her ancestors taken from the Tindale collection under glass domes. They are labelled by the index numbers Tindale gave each image after he photographed and examined her family on their home at the Koonibba mission in South Australia. In this work, the glass domes are visual metaphors for the institutional and archival containment of Aboriginal Peoples.

Scarce's family were moved from their traditional lands into the enclosed and controlled space of the mission and then subjected to the intrusions of archivists such as Tindale who visited to record, collect, quantify and categorise. Scarce says Tindale was particularly interested in her Granny Melba Coleman. He measured her tongue and pronounced her five-eighths Aboriginal.[34] Tindale's photograph of her appears under a dome, along with those of two other family members.

Scarce considers herself, along with artists such as Julie Gough, as 'artistic archivists' utilising 'documentation and objects relating to death, memory, time and identity in order to activate the processes of remembering'. By 'artistic archivists' she means artists whose interventions 'unsettle' the dominant historical narratives of official archives.[35] Such intervention, Scarce believes, is

> a tool for expressing the ongoing damage that is related to the colonisation of Australia through the eyes of Aboriginal people like myself…I am interested in how the modes of perception were, and still are, used as underlying weapons of colonial power to keep colonised people submissive to the hierarchy of colonial rule.[36]

Scarce and Gough are part of a cohort of Indigenous artists who can be seen to be providing 'testimonial arts' promoting Indigenous cultural memory. These testimonial forms not only document the genocidal and ethnocidal practices of the colonial war, they also aim to deconstruct the logic of state archives from which national histories are written.[37] She literally incarnates her ancestors in fruits from the desert country they were dispossessed from, such as the bush banana or silky pear *(Marsdenia australis)* and desert or long yam *(Ipomoea costata)*[38]. *Bleeding* the archive is an apt description for Scarce's practice, given the fluid shimmering movement captured in the reflective surfaces of the dark glass yams/bodies she creates as she piles them together en masse. Liquid yet static, these piles evoke the corporealised truths of massacre uncovered and exposed. These fruits, she says, represent 'Aboriginal culture, bodies, traditions',[39] and Scarce is keenly aware of how the properties of glass speak to her subject:

> The fragility and strength of blown glass makes it especially appropriate in relation to Australia's post-colonial history, as it conveys the vulnerability and persistence of Aboriginal people and their culture despite the consequence of colonisation.[40]

Scarce's glass works, often situated within found objects, are the outcome of research into colonial archives and discovering the experiences of her family and her own historical situatedness as an Indigenous woman. *The Collected* (2010) is an installation of almost translucent glass yams layered into wooden drawers, reminiscent of the classificatory apparatus of the colonial museum archive. As monolithic storage sites – archives for the empire's fantasies – such museums are '...institutional scrapbooks of nature and culture, presenting the newly conquered globe in microcosm'.[41] The direct reference of *The Collected*, however, is the widespread museum practice of collecting Indigenous bodies. The drawers represent these spaces and the barbaric practices of these institutions in collecting the human remains of Indigenous Peoples, a practice described as 'the violent movement of the frontier across nineteenth-century Australia converging with the intellectual frontier of contemporary science'.[42] Each glass yam represents a nameless, dispossessed body. The archival style box they are held in, reminiscent of the drawer of a nineteenth-century cabinet, is now their 'coffin'.[43]

Scarce's experiences delving into the official archival records of her family triggered a fascination with eugenics and the colonial science of race. Her practice reflects *embodied* knowledge, as a fair-skinned Aboriginal person in a society where her identity is constantly interrogated. *Black White Other (04.02.1973–19.07.2011)* (2011), brings this into sharp focus. Thirty-eight hand blown glass depictions of black bush bananas, representing her thirty-eight years of life, lie in a row, each engraved with 'black', 'white' or 'other'– testimony to how this categorisation of the 'other' endures in her own everyday experiences. In cataloguing the violence of the settler-colonial state and its archives, Scarce and Ah Kee impel viewers to witness the continuity and impact of colonisation.

James Hatley's work *Suffering Witness: The Quandary of Responsibility after the Irreparable* (2000) elaborates on this connection to opening ethical dialogue between past and present trauma, arguing that the onus is then on the audiences:

> one is summoned to attentiveness, which is to say, to a heartfelt concern for and acknowledgment of the gravity of violence directed toward particular others. In this attentiveness, the wounding of the other is registered in the first place not as an objective fact but as a subjective blow, a persecution, a trauma. The witness refuses

> to forget the weight of this blow, or the depth of the wound it inflicts.[44]

Karen Till describes the work of the artist-activist as 'a socially engaged form of memory-work through site-specific (re)makings of a traumatized region' that, 'animate the multiple spacetimes of memory'.[45] While her focus is on physical locations in the landscape, this can be applied to the 'space' and place of the archives. The imperial archives document 'wounded places' – bodies and sites where violence has occurred. Wounded places are understood to be 'present to the pain of others and to embody difficult social pasts'.[46] Connection with these places through 'the silent acts of witnessing and listening...allow individuals and groups to begin the process of mourning the past and loss'. Bearing witness is the first step to critical dialogue and the potential for healing where 'social networks and possible futures can be created, imagined and inhabited'.[47] Deborah Bird Rose writes:

> If the purpose of violence was to extinguish certain people, knowledges and perspectives, then memory continues to resist that violence. Thus the moral burden of the past in the present includes this refusal to succumb to the world of violence and amnesia; witnessing promotes remembrance and works against death and the comfort of monologue.[48]

Julie Gough describes Indigenous artists who delve into the nation's past as 'agents of memory' who are obsessed with 'the past as *not*-history' but as an 'entity' within us.[49] In bleeding imperial archives, Indigenous artists decolonise powerful reservoirs of oppressive representations, transforming the war-zone of Australia's contemporary race relations.

Notes

1 H. Perkins & J. Jones (eds), *Half Light: Portraits from Black Australia*, Art Gallery of NSW, Sydney, 2009, p. 13.

2 S. Muecke, *No Road: Bitumen All the Way*, Fremantle Arts Centre Press, Perth, 1997, p. 227.

3 D. B. Rose, *Reports from a Wild Country: Ethics for Decolonisation*, UNSW Press, Sydney, 2004, p. 21.

4 A. Curthoys, F. Peters-Little & J. Docker, *Passionate Histories: Myth, Memory and Indigenous Australia*, ANU ePress, Canberra, 2010, p. v.

5 G. Jones, 'Vernon Ah Kee: Sovereign Warrior', *Artlink*, vol. 30, no. 1, 2010, website, viewed 7/5/2015, <https://www.artlink.com.au/articles/3361/vernon-ah-kee-sovereign-warrior/>.

6 L. T. Smith, *Decolonising Methodologies: Research and Indigenous Peoples*, Zed Books, New York, 1999, p. 28.

7 ibid., pp. 150–1.

8 ibid., pp. 153–4.

9 ibid., pp. 241–2.

10 E. Tuck & K. W. Yang, 'Decolonization is not a metaphor', *Decolonization: Indigeneity, Education & Society*, vol. 1, no. 1, 2012, pp. 1–40.

11 S. Keenan, 'Moments of Decolonization: Indigenous Australia in the Here and Now', *Canadian Journal of Law & Society*, no. 29, 2014, pp. 163–80 at 164.

12 ibid., p. 167.

13 J. Biddle, *Breasts, Bodies, Canvas: Central Desert Art as Experience*, University of NSW Press, Sydney, 2007, p. 39.

14 A. Maxwell, *Colonial Photography and Exhibitions*, Leicester Press, London, 1999, p. 2.

15 ibid., p. 42.

16 C. Nicholls, 'Re-Take: Contemporary Aboriginal and Torres Strait Islander Photography, a National Gallery of Australia Travelling Exhibition', *Journal of Australian Studies*, vol. 24, no. 64, pp. 110–16 at 110–11.

17 ibid., p. 111.

18 S. Tibbetts, 'Tom Hudson's Archive – Methodologies of Intervention', *Journal of Writing in Creative Practice*, vol. 7, no. 3, 2014, pp. 533–44 at 534.

19 J. Schwartz & T. Cook, 'Archives, Records and Power: The Making of Modern Memory', *Archival Science*, no. 2, 2002, pp. 1–19 at 4.

20 T. Richards, *The Imperial Archive: Knowledge and the Fantasy of Empire*, Verso, London, 1993, p. 6.

21 S. Tibbetts, 'Tom Hudson's Archive', p. 534.

22 F. Fanon, *Black Skin, White Masks*, Pluto, London, 1952, p. 112.

23 S. Newell, 'Postcolonial Masculinity and the Politics of Visibility', *Journal of Postcolonial Writing*, vol. 45, no. 3, 2009, pp. 243–50 at 243.

24 H. Perkins & J. Jones, *Half Light*, p. 22.

25 C. Hooper, *The Tall Man: Death and Life on Palm Island*, Penguin, Melbourne, 2009, p. 10.

26 A. McQuire, 'Palm Island Death In Custody Cop Chris Hurley Investigated By Queensland Police', *New Matilda*, 22 May 2015, viewed 2 July 2015, <https://newmatilda.com/2015/05/22/palm-island-death-custody-cop-chris-hurley-investigated-queensland-police#sthash.2YhLE3Sa.dpuf>.

27 P. Timms, 'Coroner delivers Open Finding', ABC News 14 May 2010, viewed 20 July 2015, <http://www.abc.net.au/pm/content/2010/s2899983.htm>.

28 M. Ludgate, 'Transforming Tindale Exhibition Strips Away Scientific Method to Show Humanity', *The Courier Mail*, 24 September 2002, viewed 21 July 2015, <http://www.couriermail.com.au/questnews/north/transforming-tindale-exhibition-strips-away-scientific-method-to-show-humanity/story-fn8m0rl4-1226478995682>.

29 29 Norman Barnett Tindale Collection, Memory of the World, National Committee of Australia, viewed 21 July 2015, <http://www.amw.org.au/register/listings/norman-barnett-tindale-collection>.

30 Vernon Ah Kee interview with R. Sorenson, 'The Face: Vernon Ah Kee', *The Australian*, 12 July 2008, viewed 21 July 2015, <http://www.theaustralian.com.au/arts/the-face-vernon-ah-kee/story-e6frg8n6-1111116855996>.

31 Vernon Ah Kee interview with R. Sorenson.

32 Vernon Ah Kee cited by Museum of Contemporary Art, Sydney, viewed 20 July 2015 <http://www.mca.com.au/collection/work/2006111/>.

33 M. Clarke & O. Kelada, 'Bodies on the Line: Repossession and "Talkin Up"', *Artlink*, vol. 33, no. 3, 2013, pp. 37–9 at 39.

34 Y. Scarce, artist talk, Ausglass Conference, Adelaide, August 2015.

35 Y. Scarce, Masters of Fine Arts thesis, Monash University, 2010, pp. 20–1.

36 ibid., p.1.

37 R. Kennedy, L. Bell & J. Emberley, 'Decolonising Testimony: On the Possibilities and Limits of Witnessing', *Humanities Research*, vol. 15, no. 3, 2009, pp. 1–10 at 2.

38 L. Slade, 'In Spite of Colonisation: Yhonnie Scarce', *Broadsheet*, vol. 42, no. 2, 2013, pp. 101–3 at 101.

39 Y. Scarce, artist talk.

40 Y. Scarce, Masters of Fine Arts thesis, pp. 1–2.

41 T. Griffiths, *Hunters and Collectors: The Antiquarian Imagination in Australia*, Cambridge University Press, Cambridge, 1996, p. 18.

42 P. Turnbull, 'Ramsay's Regime: The Australian Museum and the Procurement of Aboriginal Bodies, C. 1874–1900', *Aboriginal History*, vol. 15, no. 1/2, 1991, pp. 108–11 at 109.

43 Y. Scarce, artist talk.

44 J. Hatley, *Suffering Witness: The Quandary of Responsibility after the Irreparable*, SUNY Press, New York, 2000, p. 3.

45 K. Till, 'Artistic and Activist Memory-Work: Approaching Place-based Practice', *Memory Studies*, vol. 1, no. 1, 2008, pp. 102–3.

46 ibid., p. 108.

47 ibid., p. 108.

48 D. B. Rose, *Reports from a Wild Country*, p. 30.

49 J. Gough, *Transforming Histories*, p. 89.

15

ANACHRONIC ARCHIVE: TURNING THE TIME OF THE IMAGE IN THE ABORIGINAL AVANT-GARDE

Khadija von Zinnenburg Carroll

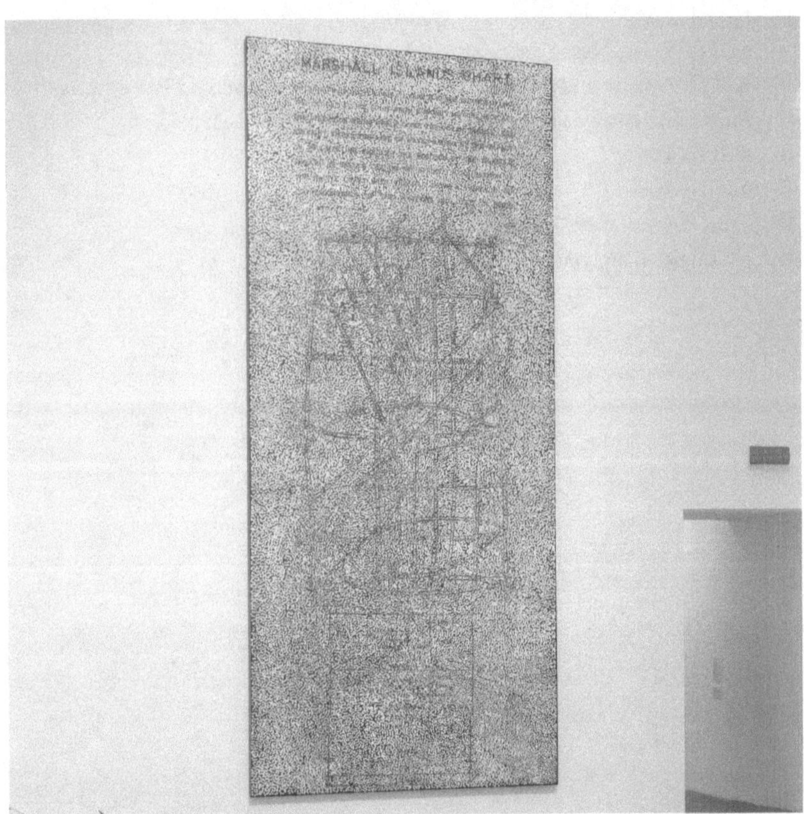

Figure 15.1: Daniel Boyd, Untitled TI3, *2015, Oil, charcoal and bookbinding glue on polyester 56th International Art Exhibition – la Biennale di Venezia,* All the World's Futures. *Photo by Andrea Avezzù. Courtesy: la Biennale di Venezia.*

Daniel Boyd's *Untitled T13* (2015) is not an Aboriginal acrylic dot painting but dots of archival glue placed to match the pixel-like form of a reproduction from a colonial photographic archive. Archival glue is a hard, wax-like material that forms into lumps – the artist compares them to lenses – rather than the smooth two-dimensional dot of acrylic paint. As material evidence of racist photography, Boyd's paintings in glue at the 2015 Venice Biennale exhibition physicalised the *leitmotiv* of archives.

In Boyd's *Untitled T13* the representation of the Marshall Islands' navigational charts is an analogy to the visual wayfinding of archival photographs. While not associated with a concrete institution, Boyd's fake anachronic archive refers to institutionalised racism – thus fitting the Biennale curator Okwui Enwezor's curatorial interest in archival and documentary photography, which he argues was invented in apartheid South Africa.[1]

In the exhibition he curated in 2008, *Archive Fever: Uses of the Document in Contemporary Art*, Enwezor diagnosed an 'archival fever' that had afflicted the art of modernity since the invention of photography. The invention, he believed, had precipitated a seismic shift in how art and temporality were conceived, and that we still live in its wake. Photography, argued Enwezor, was an inherently archival activity that sought to rescue a lost past: 'Here we witness firsthand how archival legacies become transformed into aesthetic principles, and artistic models become historicising constructs'.[2] These principles, which are essentially 'mnemonic strategies', operate as the distinctive medium of art in the previous 100 years. A persistent question haunts this archival logic of our times: 'the relationship between temporality and the image, or, rather, the object and its past'.[3] Thus, he concluded, the contemporary artist:

> serves as the historic agent of memory, while the archive emerges as a place in which concerns with the past are

> touched by the astringent vapours of death, destruction, and degeneration. Yet, against the tendency of contemporary forms of amnesia whereby the archive becomes a site of lost origins and memory is dispossessed, it is also within the archive that acts of remembering and regeneration occur, where a suture between the past and present is performed, in the indeterminate zone between event and image, document and monument.[4]

Enwezor's project was concerned with photographically based art, but his analysis had wider implications, as it implied that the invention of photography was such a paradigmatic epistemological shift that it marked all art whatever its medium. This is readily apparent in Hal Foster's analysis of an 'archival impulse at work internationally in contemporary art'.[5] Foster focused on three artists who worked across a range of media. While acknowledging that archivalism had been pervasive in modernist art throughout the last 100 years, he identified a distinctive current emergent in recent times that was relational (aimed at eliciting discussion) and charged with affect, utopian rather than subversive and geared to a world in which cultural memory and the symbolic order was failing. Indeed, the fetish for bureaucracy and accumulation is aestheticised in many postcolonial archive projects the world over. Zarina Bhimji and Emily Jacir, for instance, document and accumulate, respectively.

These themes also circulate in various ways in the work of Aboriginal contemporary artists most keyed to the international art that interests the likes of Enwezor and Foster – that is, urban-based artists who have trained in university art schools and/or are familiar with the discourses of the contemporary art world. However, these artists also bring a distinctive thematic to bear on the archive that directly addresses their collective colonial history, one which, to follow Enwezor, positions itself 'against the tendency of contemporary forms of amnesia whereby the archive becomes a site of lost origins and memory is dispossessed', but 'also within the archive' as if here 'acts of remembering and regeneration occur'.[6] This distinctive Aboriginal thematic, I argue, is theoretically grounded in an anachronistic temporality.

In broadest terms, anachronism describes the act of understanding the past through the terms of another period. In this context, the interpretation of the past from the perspective of the present is anachronistic. Such a perspective, I argue, is the necessary precondition to decolonise the official discourse of Australian history. This official discourse constructed a totalising temporal model of teleological linear progression – the historicist chronology of civilisation's advance – in which the continent is progressively de-Aboriginalised as it is Europeanised. In this context Aboriginal art history can only be produced anachronically, or against the temporality of the teleological assumptions of the colonial archive that organise the memory of colonialism, and which official Australian histories use to memorialise white Australia.

While the archival impulse in contemporary art is often if not overwhelmingly anachronistic – the tendency has been evident at least since Manet's engagements with the history of Western painting and is the mainstay of postmodernist appropriation – Aboriginal artists tend to practice an engaged or tendentious anachronism, one that plunges into the past in order to imagine a new postcolonial future geared to an Aboriginal sovereignty. This chapter will test the thesis that Aboriginal art invented an anachronic archival turn. It will have to twist time to bend it to such a claim of precedence. Such an anachronistic history of art is not based on a strict linear teleology of the archival turn from the avant-garde to the present. Its method enables a set of questions to be asked: Does the archival turn undermine or seek to draw on the historical power and temporal authority of the non-Indigenous archive? How would an Aboriginal archive collect and classify differently than the colonial that still marks most institutional archives? Why is the *un*archiving of colonial record keeping part of the archival art project for Aboriginal artists, and how does it undermine rather than replicate the government archive?

The necessity of anachronic histories – of histories written against the grain of historicism's chronologies – is evident in other disciplines. The agency in anachrony, Jacques Rancière argues, comes from the necessity of subjects acting 'against their time' to create change.[7] Feminist historian Caroline Arni uses Sigfried Kracauer's challenge to historicism's temporal teleology to define historical subjectivities and their strategic anachronism.[8] Art historians, such as Georges Didi-Huberman, Keith Moxey, Alexander Nagel and Christopher Wood, have also begun recently to theorise productive anachronism.[9]

First I need to justify the use of this cumbersome historical terminology in what should be an argument that steers us away from the dominance of chronological frameworks in canonical art history. For the traditional historian or 'anti-anachronist', trying to encounter the past objectively or 'on its own terms', anachronism is to be stringently avoided. Thus, for example, anti-anachronists judge it impossible to use contemporary Aboriginal culture as a means of mediating work produced by Europeans and Aboriginal people during the nineteenth century.[10] 'That is "not history" but "art"', they protest. However, a productive anachronism has been at the core of much contemporary postcolonial and Aboriginal art that engages with the colonial archive and the colonial record.

Contemporary art contributes productively to the revision of history that has been standardised by political interests.

The ephemerality of much Aboriginal visual material from the nineteenth century (works on bark, performances, body art, organic ephemera) demands creatively associative methods of restoration. Contemporary Aboriginal art, in particular, is working with the colonial archive to re-imagine or rediscover such lost material. The ways in which an anachronic archival impulse ignites the sparking distances between the historical and the contemporary also amplifies the struggles in art history against normative categories of time. Postcolonial artists are intervening distinctively in the colonial record to decolonise Australian art history and produce Aboriginal art history.

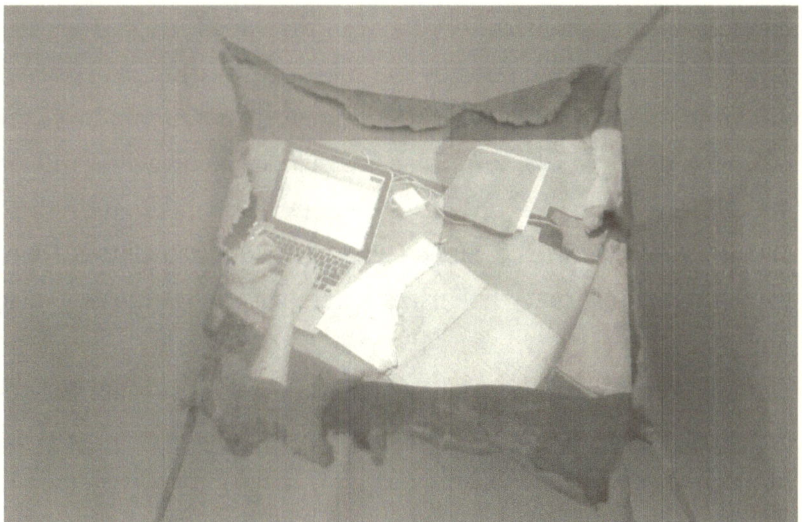

Figure 15.2: Julie Gough, TAHO LC347, *HDMI video, Tasmanian Bennett Wallaby skins, sheep skins, 2013. Courtesy of Julie Gough.*

Other artists more directly engage with the archive by capitalising on the potential of revisionist history writing in the material aspects of archival practice and its representational politics in the institutional environment. Such approaches in contemporary art are typically related to postmodernist exercises in appropriation and institutional critique that often cite the writings of Michel Foucault and Walter Benjamin.[11] In the video *TAHO LC347* (2013) Julie Gough films from a tripod over her shoulder the act of typing archival records, accompanied by the bureaucratic noises of the archive.

The name refers to the boxes of loose-leafed, uncatalogued police magistrate reports (LC347) from Northern Tasmania held in the TAHO Tasmanian Archives and Heritage Office in Hobart. These records, which date from the early 1820s, archive stories involving Aboriginal people and the Aboriginal community's sealer/sailor ancestors. As the everyday in the archives for Gough unfolds on film, the banality of evil in the violent encounters she is transcribing is heightened by the subtle mimicry in her gesture: the artist digitising a copy of a document that was produced in the same cool, deadly vein. The Tasmanian archives are full of the most gruesome descriptions of the mistreatment of Aboriginal people by settlers in the nineteenth century. It is a physical violence that haunts the whole island archipelago and the few that survived it.

The eerily barren sites of colonial Tasmania are also epitomised in Ricky Maynard's landscape photographs of important Aboriginal sites on the island, as if he is making his own counter archive to the official colonial record of Aboriginal Tasmania. The series *Portrait of a Distant Land* (2007) includes *The Healing Garden* in Wybalenna on Flinders Island in Tasmania. Also a Tasmanian Aboriginal artist, Maynard was inspired to become a photographic artist in the early 1980s after working in the photographic archive of AIATSIS (Australian Institute of Aboriginal and Torres Strait

Islander Studies) in Canberra, engaged in historical research in his photographic practice.

Archive Acupuncture

As Enwezor explored in his 2008 exhibition referred to previously, archivally oriented contemporary art takes historical evidence both literally and metaphorically, and thus highlights the often indeterminate lines between documentation and fiction in the archive. Addressing the archive as a medium or paradigm, postcolonial artists work through its materiality in order to rethink the temporality of the postcolony. Amongst those working anachronistically on the archive, we can count such celebrated artists as Samson Kambalu, Simryn Gill, Tom Nicholson, Judy Watson, Susan Hiller, Christian Boltanski, Mark Dion, Tacita Dean, Taryn Simon, Thomas Hirschhorn, Walid Raad, William Kentridge, Doris Salcedo, Kara Walker, Georges Adéagbo, Sammy Baloji, Samuel Fosso, Marlene Dumas, Shigeyuki Kihara, Kent Monkman, Jeffrey Thomas and Doris Salcedo.

Such is the proliferation of artists these days working with the archive or in an archival manner, that the genre is evident in many of the works in the 2015 Venice Biennale. In urban Aboriginal art geared to postcolonial themes in particular, the genre may be seen to be dominant to the point of being hegemonic, as if a postcolonial future cannot be imagined without first dismantling the colonial archive. The anthropologist of archive-art, Ferdinand de Jong, speaks of a 'context of postcolonial fatigue, in which many postcolonial subjects have abandoned the project of decolonising the imagination and have resigned themselves to what the anthropologist Charles Piot has termed "nostalgia for the future"'.[12] A new impulse to rethink postcolonial futures is required. Such an impulse may be found in the archival work of those artists whose critique of the archive yields a decolonised subjectivity. I am thinking of those artists who act on the clenched muscle of time like the acupunctural needle does, diving into just a precise spot and from there enlivening the whole body of material again. In one such strain there is an intense focus on one or a few items from an archive that open out into an artwork, as in cultural revival projects such as the possum skin cloaks and mourning rituals in which Clarke has been engaged.

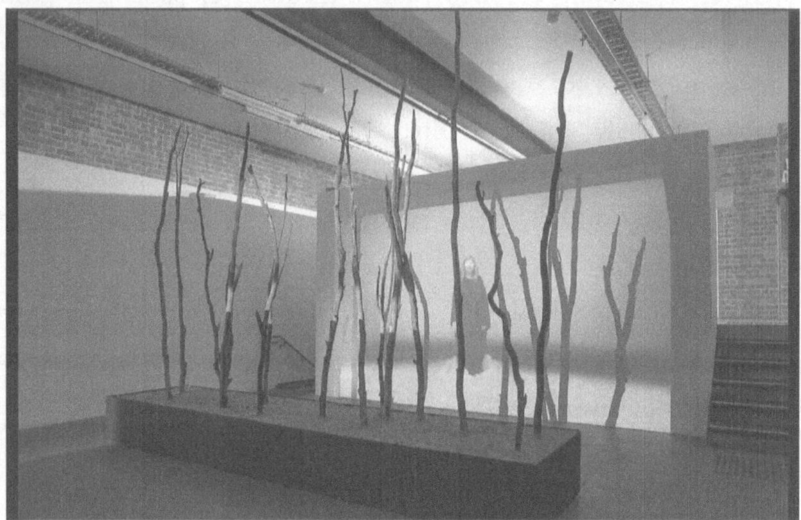

Figure 15.3: Maree Clarke, Born of the Land, *2014, sculptural video installation, dimensions variable, duration 1:48 minutes, video produced by SW Production. Courtesy the artist and Vivien Anderson Gallery, Melbourne. Photography by Kirsty Milliken.*

Inspired by images in the encyclopedia of 1860 by Wilhelm von Blandowski, Clarke began to remake mourning skull caps. Clarke's research revealed that the dead were given a clay digging stick (made from the same 'Kopi', the white gypseous clay that occurs naturally around Mildura in Victoria) to dig their way out of a possum skin cloak and grave to become one of the stars in the night sky.[13] While painting bodies with this white clay, Clarke was continually confronted with her communities' fear of the ghosts of the dead. The archival image was taken deadly seriously and re-enacting it was seen as a potential danger. The magic of the image was very much seen to be potentially effective, and borrowing even just the gestures of the archival ancestor could wake in the living the same fate as the long dead.

Brook Andrew has also approached taboo topics surrounding death through the same archive. For him the engraving of the burial mound near the Budda River in Blandowski's archive represents the ongoing recuperation of archives of disappeared Aboriginal people. Particularly perturbed by the protocols and taboos that now limit access to and use of ethnographic collections, Andrew recuperates precisely those 'images of death, sexuality and evidences of colonial wars [that] are thought not to exist and are therefore erased or hidden from the public eye, without witness or assessment'.[14]

Andrew's screen-print *The Island*, on 2.5 m x 3 m cloaks of Belgian linen, is so large that one enters the work as the only human figure, surrounded by dendroglyphs, facing a life-size burial mound. Around the burial mound is a flattened path in a circle with two approaches, one from the central foreground and a second obscured and leading out at 180 degrees on the far side. Through the trees that rise above the mound is a forest of eucalypts. The surface of *The Island* is ruptured, the red paint cracked to reveal a silver underground. The artificiality of the colours makes the landscape more alien and unbelievable. It is as if the colour repressed in the prints and photographs from the 1850s returns in Andrew's screen prints.[15] His images appear, as Andrew said of his interpretation of Blandowski, to be a 'science fiction' of a civilisation refracted back through time.[16]

Andrew's growing personal archive, from which he sources found materials for his art works, is an example of an artist's archive – a not uncommon practice amongst contemporary artists. Indeed, it is an age-old practice: Dürer had his own cabinet of curiosities and Picasso and Matisse were famous for their collections of Indigenous art. However, Andrew's work shows how acts of archiving can be violent displacements of meaning. The artist's intervention in archives is not a peaceful or conciliatory act. Nor does he shy away from the allure of the archive, its nostalgia and fetishistic nature evident in the ambivalence that pervades his work.

The archive is a place of visibility and invisibility. Its revelations or visibilities are enacted through its strategic management of invisibilities. It is not just the obscurity of the classification system that makes archives difficult to penetrate, but the willed concealment on the part of curators who see them as their own and, even more, the epistemologies in which they work. Thus the histories of museum displays are palimpsests of the shifting reception and extension of control and power in debates about Aboriginal culture. Adjudication of proper and anachronistic reuses of culture is also still the domain of anthropology. Baldwin Spencer's social evolutionism, in which all Aboriginal contact with Europeans produced cultural degeneration (rather than creative engagement) may no longer carry much weight, but few yet accepted that Aboriginal artists of the nineteenth century who anachronistically appropriated European material culture were ahead of their time. Only now are critics beginning to see that to deconstruct a mission blanket for thread rather than use it whole was a creative rather than ignorant act. Some change in the reception of 'entangled objects' – a term coined by the anthropological historian Nicholas Thomas as a way to re-imagine Indigenous cross-cultural engagements as creative endeavours – evidences a celebration of anachronistic reuse.[17]

Anthropologists following Nicholas Thomas are debating the terms of 'entanglement' between Indigenous and modern, thereby looking at the mutual entanglements of people around objects rather than a hierarchical coloniser–colonised relationship of exchange. Shawn Rowlands argues that to analyse entanglement, as Thomas did, is to define it as a synthesis of desire. This, Rowlands argues, omits close analysis of material entanglements. Although the study of entangled objects is primarily an anthropology of material culture, the archival impulse in contemporary art urges us to question what cultural entanglements mean when the archive reconstitutes culture for community, not just for the art scene, salvage ethnographers, or history writers.

The possum skin cloaks are an example of this and have been written about and remade from many different perspectives.[18] The 'old ways' maintain that the possum skin cloak was a medium used by Indigenous people in south-east Australia before contact to signify kin. This is reinforced by identifying the features of country represented on the cloaks. However, now that the revival of a ritual object has been realised in its fabrication, it is all the more difficult to move again beyond the object, which does not yet carry the culture of rituals and country that once surrounded it. The recent success in the difficult task of remaking possum skin cloaks in suburban twenty-first-century Australia is held as hope for cultural revival.[19]

Let me give an example of the material entanglements in the possum skin cloaks. Len Tregonning plans to chew the fat off the kangaroo tail that can today be bought fresh at the Victoria Market in Melbourne, in order to prepare sinews that will be the thread to sew together the skins. Every day the tails available from the butcher shop prove too rotten, so Vicki Couzens, Maree Clarke and Lee Darroch have to use commercially bought thread instead.

With a mixture of old and new tools – mussel shells and possum jaws, thread rather than kangaroo sinew and with a herringbone blanket stitch – they have refashioned a family tradition.[20] Along with Couzens' stitching together of methods comes not only a fresh set of designs, but a revitalisation of familial ties sung in whatever lists of language can be found.[21] Mourning songs for the cloaks when they are hung over a coffin, and naming songs for specific days and stories, are accompanied with clap-sticks.

Inventing 'Art' From the Archive

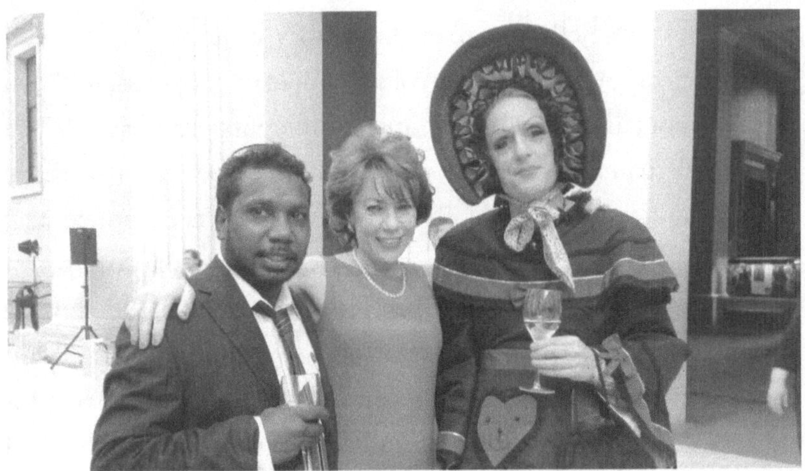

Figure 15.4: Ishmael Marika, Kathy Lette and Grayson Perry at the opening of Enduring Civilisation *at the British Museum, London, in April 2015. Photo: John Carty.*

Australian art historian Ian McLean's thesis that Aboriginal Australians invented contemporary art has stimulated justifications in many directions, and contemporary artist Grayson Perry recently articulated a provocative mutation of the thesis.[22] Perry is a celebrity transvestite potter, the Dame Edna of the London art world and trustee of the British Museum. Transvestism does not preclude conservatism, and Perry's careful choice of a Victorian costume to the opening of the *Enduring Civilisation* exhibition at the British Museum in 2015 was an absurd picture of the colonial among the Aboriginal elders the evening was supposed to spotlight.

Positioned at the entrance of the opening of the *Enduring Civilisation* exhibition at the British Museum, Perry reiterated to me his inversion of McLean's thesis, which he gave in the prestigious Reith Lectures on BBC radio.

> I went to the 'Australia' show recently at the Royal Academy and that's got quite a lot of Aborigine art, and they're very beautiful and powerful objects, but are they art? Because the original bark paintings were kind of spiritual maps and their relationship with the universe and the landscape and they're powerful ethnic items, but are they contemporary art? You know they look like abstract expressionist paintings, but are they, you know, because do they know about the contemporary art world? I don't know.
>
> But then I read this story about this 81-year-old white artist in Australia called Elizabeth Durack who painted Aborigine style paintings under the pseudonym of Eddie Burrup and put them into an Aborigine art show, and there was outrage that she should borrow their special otherness – you know, the fact that they *weren't* artists. She was borrowing the power. And yet there was outrage at that and yet there wasn't outrage about the Aboriginal artists borrowing the power of being a contemporary artist somehow. It was an interesting point about, you know, is it art if it's not done by someone who sort of acknowledges themselves as an artist.[23]

In this way, Perry inverts the 'Aborigines invented contemporary art' idea. He clarified this to me in conversation by saying Aboriginal people who claim they are contemporary artists steal his identity as white, male, British Museum Trustee and fixture of the London art establishment. *They are not artists, I am*, he says, before launching into a lecture about how Duchamp made a toilet an artwork because he was Duchamp. The artist is artist because the self-referential art scene judges it to be so. The parody-come-pandering-to-the-market that Perry excels at is supposed to justify his claim that Aboriginal artists are fakes and intruders. What it doesn't take into account is the way in which Aboriginal art has far surpassed in quality, innovation and even economic success anything a dealer could have come up with on their own, and it has enabled artists to stay, self-determined, on country.

The British Museum is only now beginning to conceive of the future existence of an Australian gallery. As Perry says, 'all the best stuff is already on display', and 'when you see what's going on in Syria you think maybe it's safer here'. The Museum's Director 'Neil MacGregor takes the sting out the great storehouse of stuff that has been taken from around the world'.[24] Yet in his television programs Perry plays with the utter construction of identity. Is not the successful invention of an Aboriginal contemporary art just the kind of manoeuvre in the market that is embraced by the fickle and fast-moving art scene? For Perry is also saying Aboriginal Australians invented contemporary art, fabricating it from history, as historian Keith Windschuttle would argue. Stephen Muecke, citing Bruno Latour, recently responded to Windschuttle by writing that good fabrication is a sign of understanding the material.[25] A cleverly invented art that fabricates the claims of contemporaneity is contributing to the essence of making art and history.

Muecke deals a deft blow to the authenticity problem. Perry, on the other hand, says: 'old, poor, dirty things always seem more authentic, that's why people go to old, poor, dirty places on holiday...[These are the] tropes associated with authenticity'. Perry's problem with Aboriginal artists anachronistically inventing contemporary art is not a problem at all. Perry claims in his BBC interview that Aboriginal artists seek to draw on the power of contemporary artists, just like white settler artists (Gauguin, Picasso, Matisse and the rest) have sought the cache of the Aboriginal archive in primitivism.

Conclusion

As Howard Morphy recently urged, it is not all of Aboriginal art that is anachronistic in its dealings with the archive.[26] This discussion focuses on a particular range of Aboriginal artists that use avant-garde strategies from institutional critique, performance, and ethnographic conceptualism. There are many different strategies that artists working archivally have used in Australia. Some stage a performative institutional critique (as in the Julie Gough example of TAHO), while others like Brook Andrew create their own archive. Yet another contemporary strategy makes the biography of one previously invisible protagonist stand for 'the devastatingly incomplete archive'.[27] Take, for example, reconfigurations of archival photographs such as Daniel Boyd's pixel-like three-dimensional dots made of oil and archival glue on canvas in the *Untitled T13* (see figure 15.1), based on a photograph of a Marshall Islands Chart given to author Robert Louis Stevenson. Like many of his works in this series of ambivalent black and white history paintings, black and white relations are metaphorically reproduced and restructured through the lens of concave blobs of archival glue. The details of the historical moment, the artefacts and captions being represented are blurred by the very medium that is intended as fixture of archival photographs to their mounts – here a metaphor for the epistemological limits of the archive. Black and white is both signifier and signified in the semiotic play on Boyd's canvas. It fractures the colonial photograph through the vocabulary of contemporary conceptual painting. The photograph's meanings in the archive change as it recirculates as an appropriated artwork. There are shifts in the potential meanings of photographs that document institutionalised racism, and when these images are materially and anachronistically re-worked they also become critical and reflexive.

I have discussed examples of Julie Gough, Brook Andrew, Daniel Boyd and Maree Clarke's work because they use anachronism not to condemn or ironically attack those artist-historians who transport themselves into the terms of the past and ventriloquise from there – they have moved beyond this – but to show a more creative alternative use of the archive. Rather than treat the archive as a mute object to be mined, with its visibilities and invisibilities taken as a given, they make it into a subject that can reveal and speak back its secrets and invisibilities, and somewhat paradoxically they do this by adopting the procedures of the archive. Their contemporary and thus anachronistic use of the colonial archive shows how effective a strategy for decolonisation it is to wrench colonial artefacts from the terms in which they were once cast and let them unsettle the settler discourses about Australian art history.

Notes

1 O. Enwezor, *Rise and Fall of Apartheid: Photography and the Bureaucracy of Everyday Life*, Munich, Prestel, 2013.

2 O. Enwezor, 'Archive Fever: Photography between history and the monument', in O. Enwezor (ed.), *Archive Fever: Uses of the Document in*

Contemporary Art, International Centre of Photography, New York, 2008, pp. 11–52 at 21–2.

3 ibid., p. 23.

4 ibid., pp. 46–7.

5 H. Foster, 'An Archival Impulse', *October* vol. 110, Autumn 2004, pp. 3–22 at 3.

6 O. Enwezor, 'Archive Fever', p. 47.

7 C. Arni, '"Moi seule", 1833: Feminist Subjectivity, Temporality, and Historical Interpretation', *History of the Present*, vol. 2, no. 2, 2012, pp. 107–21 at p. 117.

8 S. Kracauer, *History: The Last Things Before the Last*, Paul Oskar Kristeller (ed. and trans.), Markus Wiener, Princeton, 1995, pp. 139–63.

9 G. Didi-Huberman, 'Before the Image, Before Time: The Sovereignty of Anachronism', in Claire Farago (ed.), *Compelling Visuality: The Work of Art in and Out of History*, University of Minnesota Press, Minneapolis, 2003, pp. 31–44 at 42; K. Moxey, *Visual Time: The Image in History*, Duke University Press, Durham, 2013; A. Nagel & C. Wood, *Anachronic Renaissance*, Columbia University Press, New York, 2002.

10 I recall here as examples especially a response from Nicholas Jardine at the University of Cambridge, History of Science Senior Seminar. Nicholas Jardine defines vicious anachronism as a 'historically incoherent interpretation of past deeds and works' in which the conditions of production that determine meaning are denied. See N. Jardine, 'Uses and Abuses of Anachronism in the History of the Sciences', *History of Science*, no. 38, 2000, pp. 251–70 at 252.

11 For example see *Visual Resources: An International Journal of Documentation*, Special Issue: Following the Archival Turn: Photography, the Museum, and the Archive, C. Simon (ed.), vol. 18, no. 2, 2002.

12 F. de Jong, Introductory address to *At Work in the Archive* conference, Sainsbury Institute for Art, University of East Anglia (UEA), 8 May 2014. The framework and discussions at the conference de Jong organised at UEA is the source of many of the reflections in these paragraphs and I am grateful to all the participants, especially Alexandra Dodd, Paul Basu, Ferdinand de Jong, Rania Jaber, Nadine Siegert, Angela Briedbach, and Brenton Maart.

13 Maree Clarke has made *Kopi: Connected to Country* in a range of exhibitions including the 2016 Sovereignty exhibition at ACCA.

14 B. Andrew, 'Come in to the Light', viewed 11 December 2015, < http://maa.cam.ac.uk/the-island-catalogue/>.

15 W. Garden, 'Ethical Witnessing and the Portrait Photograph: Brook Andrew', *Journal of Australian Studies* vol. 35, no. 2, June 2011, pp. 251–64.

16 B. Andrew, 'Remember How we See: *The Island*', in H. Allen (ed.), *Australia: William Blandowski's Illustrated Encyclopaedia*, Aboriginal Studies Press, Canberra, pp. 165–8 at 166.

17 S. Rowlands, 'Entangled Frontiers: Collection, Display and the Queensland Museum, 1878–1914', *Journal of Australian Colonial History*, vol. 13, 2011, pp. 183–206.

18 F. Edmonds with M. Clarke, *Sort of Like Reading a Map: A Community Report on the survival of Aboriginal Art in Southeastern Australia since 1834*, website accessed 15 April 2015, <http://www.lowitja.org.au/sites/default/files/docs/Sort-of-like-reading-a-map-amended.pdf>; F. Edmonds, '"Art is Us": Aboriginal Art, Identity and Wellbeing in Southeast Australia', PhD dissertation, University of Melbourne, 2007.

19 For hope as a method see the various chapters of J. McDonald & A. M. Stephenson (eds), *The Resilience of Hope*, Rodopi, Amsterdam, 2010.

20 J. L. Comaroff & J. Comaroff, *Ethnicity Inc*, Chicago University Press, Chicago, 2009.

21 Ivan Couzens (Vicki's father) has written a dictionary of the Kirrae Wurrong language in which there are many words related to possum skins, evidencing how important they are to that culture. *Teen Yoolonteeyt* (old female possum), *Takoort weentat* (young possums) and *Weeyan* (possum cry) are just a few examples. Vicki Couzens works for the aboriginal Language Corporation, see the Dictionary of Australian Artists Online (DAAO) entry for Vicki Couzens.

22 I. McLean (ed.), *How Aborigines Invented the Idea of Contemporary Art,* Power Publishing, Sydney, and Institute of Modern Art, Brisbane, 2011 and 2014.

23 G. Perry, 'Playing to the Gallery' and 'Beating the Bounds', Reith Lectures 2013, Liverpool, 22 October 2013, pp. 12–13. See website, viewed 2 October 2015, <*downloads.bbc.co.uk/radio4/transcripts/reith-lecture2-liverpool.pdf*>. Thank you to Helen Idle for guiding me to this source.

24 All quotations unless otherwise stated are taken from an interview published as: Khadija von Zinnenburg Carroll, 'My Big Ugly Art World: Grayson Perry on Aboriginal art and how to be undiplomatic in the history wars', *Art Monthly Australia*, no. 285, November 2015, pp. 38–41.

25 S. Muecke, 'A diplomat for the history wars', *Text*, no. 28, April 2015, viewed 2 October 2015, <http://www.textjournal.com.au/speciss/issue28/Muecke.pdf>.

26 Howard Morphy in response to Khadija von Zinnenburg Carroll, Art in the Time of Colony and The Importance of Being Anachronistic, public lecture, Australian National University, Centre for Heritage and Museums, Canberra, 5 June 2015.

27 E. Smith, 'Obsolescence and Ephemera in Postcolonial History: the Work of Julie Gough', in K. von Zinnenburg Carroll (ed.), 'The Importance of Being Anachronistic: Contemporary Aboriginal Art and Museum Reparations', *Discipline* and *Third Text*, Melbourne, 2016, p. 148.

16

ABORIGINAL TRANSFORMATIONS OF THE PHOTOGRAPHIC ARCHIVE

Jane Lydon

Photographs of Australian Aboriginal people are powerful objects. Produced from the 1840s, when the camera first arrived in the continent's nascent white settlements, such images are now invested with new meanings, becoming a rich resource for Indigenous families, history-telling and culture. The intersection of imperialism, science and popular curiosity generated a vast body of imagery of Indigenous peoples now held within the archive. This chapter assesses Australian Aboriginal photographic archives as an instrument of past power inequalities, but also asking whether such archives might nevertheless be 'democratised' in the present. I first trace the production and circulation of such images beginning during the nineteenth century, before turning to their more recent transformations in the hands of Aboriginal people, examining the Indigenous significance of historical photographs as revealed through research with relatives and descendants of the images' subjects. I conclude by exploring the ways that Aboriginal photo-media artists have engaged with this rich and vast archive.

Archival Practices: Collecting, Sorting, Displaying

The so-called 'archival turn' in art and critical practices has brought increased scrutiny to the practices of collecting, collating and classifying photographs and artefacts – procedures that are now sites of contested histories.[1] Until recent years, the photographic archive relating to Australian Aboriginal people was interpreted in totalising and instrumentalist ways, as inevitably constituting a tool of colonial surveillance and control. However, new approaches to the archive emphasise its 'recodability', as these artefacts of the past are framed by new meanings. It is important to understand their origins within the often traumatic and profoundly unequal relations of colonial invasion and dispossession – yet their performance in the present, in the hands of Indigenous relatives and descendants, may counter colonial amnesia and express Aboriginal views.

What is the Aboriginal photographic archive? The 'archival turn' evident during the 1990s saw fresh scholarly and artistic attention given to those material traces of the past: photographs, artefacts and the institutional forms in which they have been preserved, and from which they are now liberated.[2] Collections held across Australia and around the world reflect the history of engagement between white photographer and black subject, and increasing control over representation by Aboriginal people themselves. Photography was introduced to Australia in 1841 under the sponsorship of the influential Paris-based *la Société d' Encouragement pour l'Industrie Nationale.* This experiment was quickly followed by the arrival of photographers catering to curiosity about foreign sights and peoples, as well as a local desire for domestic portraits.[3] Australian Aboriginal people had been the subject of Western theories since first contact, with some observers arguing that they represented an earlier stage of humankind's development.[4] Following the publication of Charles Darwin's (1859) *The Origin of Species by Means of Natural Selection*, evolutionism became scientific orthodoxy and such ideas only strengthened. Applied to sociology, the social evolutionist paradigm was used to rationalise the ill effects of invasion and dispossession upon Indigenous people. The general public took a great interest in these debates during the nineteenth century, and the market for images of Indigenous people included a large general audience.

As photographic technologies developed, they recorded diverse cross-cultural relationships around the continent – moving from 1840s daguerreotype portraits of the Kulin Nations of Port Philip, to 1860s *carte de visites* from the Brisbane region, to Aboriginal people's own use of the cheap and mass-produced Kodak from at least the 1930s. As a result of the growing belief that the Aboriginal 'race' was doomed to extinction, photographers sought to record what was believed to be a disappearing way of life. They followed the 'frontier', seeking to find Aboriginal people apparently untouched by change – seemingly 'primitive', 'authentic' subjects, stripped of signs of European civilisation such as clothing. By contrast, humanitarians such as missionaries sought to show Aboriginal people as essentially the same as Western observers, dressed elegantly with signs of 'civilisation' and Christianity such as the Bible.[5] During the 1850s the invention of the wet-plate collodion process allowed photographers to move from the studio to outdoors, and some of the first photographs of Indigenous people away from the settlements were produced, such as William Stanley Jevons' 1859 group view on the Braidwood goldfields, the first images of NSW Aboriginal people. These relatively early series show the colony's Indigenous people still living on traditional country, and adjusting to white incursion.

With the emergence of the cheap, palm-sized *carte de visite* in the mid-1850s, portraiture became an international craze, and permitted collectors to obtain examples, or 'types', of different peoples from around the world. Over the last decades of the nineteenth century, notions of the socio-biological difference of Aboriginal people became increasingly accepted, justifying tightening control in southern Australia where images recorded people living on government institutions. Northern and north-western Australia remained a 'frontier' and a source of 'authentic', 'primitive' views of tradition. By the early twentieth century, however, cheap Kodak cameras started to become widely available, allowing Aboriginal people to adopt the medium for their own purposes. As a storekeeper on the Birdsville Track wrote to a friend in 1933, 'Nearly all the young [Aborigines] today go through a Kodak stage. I have three box Brownies left here for repairs by young [Aborigines] who have had the craze.'[6]

From the 1920s, distance from the frontier conditions of the north enabled a southern, urban audience to be shocked by revelations of ill-treatment conveyed by new visual media. Indigenous activists themselves began to campaign for reform, and deplored the power of racist media representations. Activists took up photography as a form of witness to past injustice and as the basis of demands for rights in the present.[7] When the movement for Indigenous rights gained momentum during the 1970s, Indigenous and non-Indigenous photographers seized upon the medium as a means to express an explicitly Indigenous perspective; their political project was frequently driven by an intense desire to counter degrading historical imagery.[8] Aboriginal people recognised that the visual archive offered evidence for their historical experience, and might be reframed by Indigenous narratives in order to counter colonial, often documentary-based, history.

Interpretation: From Surveillance to Heritage Resource

During the early 1980s, an Indigenous art photography movement began to emerge that began to represent Aboriginal culture, identity and political claims from an explicitly Aboriginal perspective. A range of young Aboriginal photographers emerged, including Tracey Moffatt, Brenda L. Croft and Michael Riley.

The Bicentennial year was a particularly important landmark that focused attention on the nation's unresolved past and galvanised Indigenous photographers – for example Peter McKenzie's image of a protest at La Perouse against the First Fleet re-enactment of January 1788.[9] These oppositional projects took issue with the celebration of the Bicentennial, rejecting the triumphalist tone of most commemoration.

At this time, dominant theoretical approaches tended to emphasise photography's role in exploiting and distancing its Indigenous subjects. These interpretations emerged in conjunction with poststructuralist critiques of modernism that emphasised the entanglement of knowledge, vision and power. In 1988, for example, John Tagg influentially drew upon Foucauldian notions of surveillance and control in arguing that the social and political context in which the image is embedded organises the viewer's experience and gives the image its meaning – and so is profoundly implicated in structural inequalities of race, class and gender.[10] This interpretive tradition also shaped exhibitions of colonial Australian photography throughout the 1980s and 1990s, *as* historians of photography showed how ideas of primitivism had structured the ways that photos of Aboriginal people were circulated and viewed during the nineteenth century.[11] However, in arguing that subaltern groups 'were represented as, and wishfully rendered, incapable of speaking, acting or organising for themselves', John Tagg articulates a view of photographic meaning as *wholly* determined by norms, and of photographic subjects as passive victims.[12] In such readings, the power relations inherent in colonialism have already decided the truth of these images. Indeed, the distancing effects of such images continue to evoke anger and grief from Indigenous people today. Writing in 1997, artist and writer Brenda L. Croft, of the Gurindji/Malngin/Mudpurra/

Bilinara peoples and Anglo-Australian/German/Irish heritage, termed anonymous anthropological subjects 'ghosts deprived of rest', their images used to control and oppress their own people in an almost dehumanising way.[13] However, Croft also pointed to the ambivalence and radical potential of the photographic archive to be reworked and re-evaluated by Indigenous relatives and descendants of their subjects.

Over recent years a shift has occurred in ways of seeing photographs as a renewed interest has emerged in their diverse cultural *uses.* Where interpretation once focused on the meaning contained with the frame, as representation, much recent analysis has explored the role of photographs as social actors within distributed networks of people and things that make up the social – sometimes glossed as a shift from what images *mean* to what they *do*.[14] Ethnographies of the archive have begun to focus on exploring the photograph's multivalency in different cultural contexts, and the ways that the archive constitutes and is constituted by 'a history materially performed by things', including the institutional structures around objects and their dynamic social lives.[15] Archival practices work to establish meanings over time, and against a single or dominant reading, as the photograph's 'infinite recodability' is activated by shifting relations of the material object.[16]

We now acknowledge that photographs are given diverse meanings and uses within specific cultural traditions and historical contexts. Cross-cultural encounters between Europeans and Indigenous people have great analytical significance, for preconceptions from both sides of the encounter were brought into dialogue, and ultimately mutual transformation.[17] The resulting form of the archive may owe much to an Indigenous agenda, as choices made by photographers in recording Indigenous peoples depended on culturally specific relationships. Christopher Morton, for example, has argued that differences within the photographic work of anthropologist Edward Evans (E. E.) Evans-Pritchard in Central Africa may be attributed to the interests and reactions of his subjects, rather than to disciplinary frameworks.[18] Conversely, the 1993 Brisbane exhibition *Portraits of Our Elders* showed that some photographs were explicitly produced for Aboriginal purposes, such as early twentieth-century studio portraits; as curator Michael Aird noted, 'the more recent photographs are obviously of paying customers with total control over the situation. They display the absolute confidence and dignity of people who have succeeded, who have earned the respect of the community'.[19]

These interpretive shifts have intersected with Indigenous demands for restitution and return of cultural heritage, signalling a shift to acknowledge Indigenous rights in a wide range of material and intangible culture, and by extension photographs.[20] Many cultural institutions across Australia and overseas now house large collections of photographs documenting Aboriginal lives and history. Since the 1970s, a growing international literature has examined the process and effects of returning photographs to source communities.[21]

Stolen Generations

For many Aboriginal people, old photographs may be used to help reconnect family and connections to place torn apart by official assimilation policies known now as the Stolen Generations. In New South Wales, for example, the NSW Aborigines Protection Board increasingly implemented policies of child removal from the end of the nineteenth century.[22] The *Aborigines Protection Act 1909* (NSW) gave the board the power to 'assume full control and custody of the child of any Aborigine' if a court found there was neglect, but by 1915 the board could take Aboriginal children from their homes without a court hearing. From 1912 to 1938 more than 1,400 children – from an Indigenous population of fewer than 10,000 – were taken from their parents in New South Wales.[23] In 1997, the *Bringing Them Home* report presented the findings of a national inquiry into the separation of Aboriginal and Torres Strait Islander children from their families. It revealed that the impact of these policies was devastating, leaving very few families untouched by their effects, which are still felt painfully in the present in the form of broken family ties, sad childhood memories, or persisting anger and grief. In this context, many Aboriginal individuals and communities eagerly seek to reclaim photographs of relatives and ancestors lost through these historical processes.

Many projects have established digital points of contact between communities and archives, such as the landmark *Ara Irititja*, which means 'stories from a long time ago' in the language of Anangu (Pitjantjatjara and Yankunytjatjara people) of central Australia. This project was begun in 1994 by Anangu in partnership with a team led by John Dallwitz, and has transformed records of the past into valuable cultural heritage for descendants by returning 'lost' material including photographs, films, sound recordings and documents. It states, 'These are the cultural sources for the stories of land, of self, of the present, the past and the future. They provide for the celebration of cultural identity, and allow also for focus on family and kinship'.[24] Another important initiative is the Buku-Larrnggay Mulka project, a production house and archive, housed in the art centre at Yirrkala in north-eastern Arnhem Land. The Mulka Project ('Mulka' means a sacred but public ceremony, and, to hold or protect) aims to sustain and protect Yolngu cultural knowledge under the leadership of Yolngu people.[25] Again, in 2000 the University of Western

Australia's Berndt Museum initiated a project titled *Bringing the Photographs Home*, which was funded by the Aboriginal and Torres Strait Islander Commission (ATSIC) in response to the *Bringing Them Home* inquiry.[26]

Aboriginal people have begun to explain the importance of recovering such images in their quest to reconnect with family and place. As Shauna Bostock-Smith's account of discovering her Great-Great Grand-Aunt's photo through a television documentary suggests, this is an emotional but often healing process. The documentary explored Australia's most famous nineteenth-century photographer John William Lindt, whose acclaimed 1872–73 series *Australian Aboriginals* comprised portraits of Gumbaynggirr and Bandjalung peoples of the lower Clarence River.[27] Bostock-Smith writes, that she 'gasped aloud' when she heard that Lindt's well-known image of 'Mary Ann of Ulmarra' was identified as Mary Ann Cowan:

> I have been researching my family history for the last few years, and I knew that Mary Ann Cowan was my Great-Great Grand-Aunt. This exciting news had such a profound effect on me. It is as though this lovely photograph taken last century has spiritually reached through time and altered my perception of her today. She has now magically transformed from being an abstract entity…a name on her marriage and death certificates, into a real life, flesh and blood, beautiful young woman.[28]

The image manifested Bostock-Smith's years of family research, and embodied a physical link with her ancestor that became the occasion to build further family connections, and to revisit Mary-Ann's traditional country with her relatives.

For artists such as Brenda L. Croft, this theme resonates with personal experience, as she explored in her landmark 1998 series, *Colour Blind*. She tells the intensely personal yet emblematic story of her father's removal from his family as a child, and his subsequent reunion as an adult with his mother, just once, shortly before she died. Croft maps her father's and her own experience of loss on to the wider damage experienced by most Aboriginal families as a result of the Stolen Generations. These works are palimpsests of family snapshots, Croft's own photographs of childhood home, and official images, including a 'eugenicist' line-up of women grading from 'white' to 'black'. This image recurs, functioning like a brand or tattoo – for example stamped across a photograph showing her father briefly reunited with his mother. In these works, the conflation of historical, assimilationist and family images, inscribed with remembered scraps of 'hearsay' ('they said she had given him away', 'they told him that she was dead'), summons up a tragic story of yearning and waste. Croft uses this technique of multiplicity and simultaneity to prompt other family narratives which illustrate widespread tales of discrimination. Her visual palimpsest brings past policy into the present, showing its effects; the superimposed words pass judgement. From personal loss she constructs a pictorial metaphor for Aboriginal people's historical loss of identity, land, and culture; pain in the present suffuses the earlier imagery to reveal the trauma of assimilation.

Politically, this work of remembering and reconstruction challenges conservative forces within Australian society that continue to resist acknowledgement of the harm caused Aboriginal people by past policy. Croft's conflation of a personal and a wider Indigenous bereavement is paralleled by her conflation of present and past in approaching the colonial archive. As an Aboriginal person searching for 'the spaces in the shadows that facts don't allow us to see', she experiences these images as 'fragile "mirrors", reflecting every indigenous person who views them'; memories of her father project themselves, 'shadow-like', behind all nineteenth-century portraits. [29]

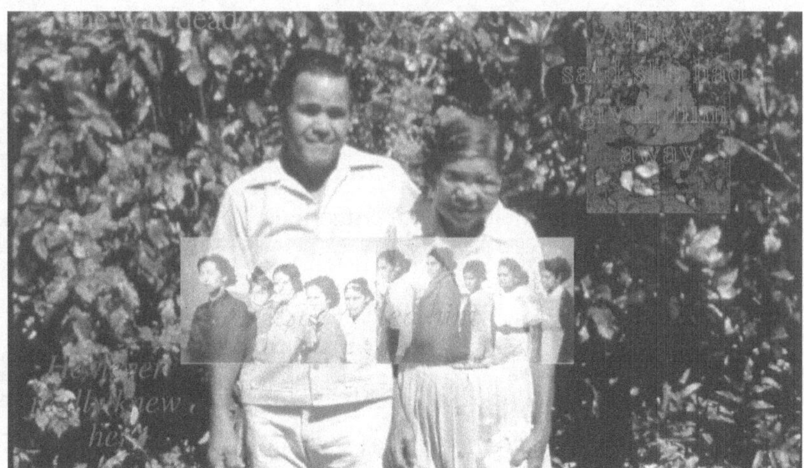

Figure 16.1: Brenda L. Croft, She Called Him Son, *1998, 49 cm × 75 cm, from the series Colour B(l)ind, Ilfochrone print, 1998. Courtesy of the artist.*

Croft's work exemplifies the way that the photographic archive has been plundered, reassembled and cross-pollinated by Aboriginal artists who challenge its colonial meanings. Through seemingly simple techniques of recontextualisation – over-writing, inscription, layering, enlargement and resurfacing – the historical image may be literally transformed. Wiradjuri artist Brook Andrew for example has deliberately attacked a legacy of invisible violence by retrieving photographs that bear traces of colonial trauma from the archive as evidence for the forgotten or concealed tragedies of dispossession. While he is careful to respect the distinction between these disturbing historical images and traditionally restricted secret-sacred subjects, Andrew argues that 'they should be brought into the light, aroused in the public domain'. Through enlargement, over-writing and printing on gleaming metallic foil, these overlooked fragments of evidence become 'unmanageable', swelling out from the archive, beyond our control.[30]

Another strategy responds tangentially to the archive, producing new, Aboriginal-authored images. Some choose to recreate or re-imagine extant historical photographs – and even to cast themselves as re-imagined subjects or heroes and heroines.[31] One such engagement with the colonial archive is Christian Thompson's 2012 series *We Bury Our Own*, in which he has responded to the collection held by the Pitt Rivers Museum at Oxford University, where he was a postgraduate student. *We Bury Our Own* deploys Thompson's trademark self-portraits to displace the historical markers of identity central to colonial photography – especially the anthropometric mug shot. Here *he* is the photographer who chooses how to see the Indigenous subject. Instead of the Australian flora of his earlier work, he has introduced roses and chrysanthemums, alluding to his new environment, the domestic flower gardens of England. He wears the formal dress of an Oxford student. In some self-portraits a scatter of crystals is arranged carefully across his eyes, or forms a tiara – perhaps a means of connecting the spiritual with the corporeal, suggests Christopher Morton, Senior Curator of Photography at the Pitt Rivers Museum. Morton uses Thompson's own phrase, 'spiritual repatriation', to refer to a process of engaging with these images' colonial heritage in imaginative and allusive ways. However, instead of returning the bodies of war victims, as originally denoted by the term 'repatriation', or even the original photo-object, Thompson creates an emotional, affective tie with the archive. During the nineteenth century, Indigenous bodies were in a sense captured by photographs that sought to reduce their humanity to an essential corporeal truth. Thompson, by contrast, shows us new forms of a cosmopolitan, hybrid Indigenous identity that transcends this literal return. The beauty, clarity and formality of these portraits convey a sacred process of acknowledgment of ancestral forces with great dignity and emotion.

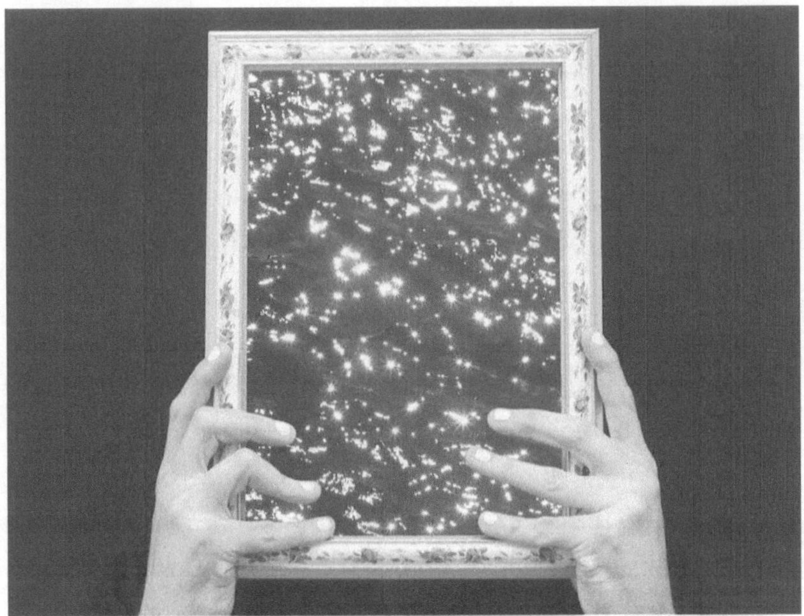

Figure 16.2: Christian Thompson, Danger Will Come, *2012, 100 cm × 100 cm, from the* We Bury Our Own *series. Courtesy of the artist.*

Transforming Tindale

Another recent landmark that has reclaimed the archive was the 2012 exhibition *Transforming Tindale,* curated by Michael Aird and based on the work of Vernon Ah Kee. Ah Kee is an artist from North Queensland, and a founding member of the Brisbane-based proppaNOW artists collective, who identifies as an 'urban Aboriginal artist'.[32] This project drew upon genealogical information and photographs amassed by anthropologists Norman Tindale and Joseph Birdsell in 1938, at the Queensland Aboriginal communities of Yarrabah, Cherbourg, Mona Mona, Palm Island, Woorabinda, Bentinck Island, Doomadgee and Mornington Island. Tindale (1900–93) was an Australian anthropologist, archaeologist, entomologist and ethnologist. From 1919 he was an Entomologist's Assistant at the South Australian Museum, obtaining qualifications in science from the University of Adelaide. From 1938 he collaborated with Joseph Birdsell of Harvard University in studying Aboriginal 'hybrids', seeking to explore race-crossing and classify Aboriginal people into racial types. Together they undertook anthropological surveys in 1938–39 and again in 1952–54 on Aboriginal missions across Australia.

After WWII Birdsell and Tindale abandoned their framework of racial classification in favour of population dynamics.[33] In addition, toward the end of their careers both became supporters of Aboriginal self-determination and the land-rights movement. Nonetheless, their substantial mission collections were made within a framework of racial classification, and they collected anatomical measurements and took standardised photographs as records of the physical form of the Aboriginal residents. It was not always a pleasant experience for the Aboriginal people involved: when Tindale and Birdsell went to Point Pearce Mission (Burgiyana) on the Yorke Peninsula in 1939, Narungga Elder Lewis O'Brien, who was nine years old at the time of the visit recalled:

> We had to line up in the school and have our heads and bodies measured with callipers. We didn't know what was going on, but I remember feeling out of sorts about the whole business.[34]

However, As Vernon Ah Kee's blog noted, at the launch of *Transforming Tindale* at the State Library of Queensland in

September 2012, Elder Marshall Bell said: 'It doesn't matter whether Tindale was good or bad. It doesn't matter whether what he did was right or wrong. Those photos are real'.[35] Ah Kee had first encountered these photographs when he was young because his grandmother had carried some around in her purse. He discovered many years later that the originals contained much more detail than the cropped 'mugshots' she had owned.[36] He studied the archival images, using them as the basis for large-scale charcoal portraits of his relatives, in the process also learning about his great-grandparents, such as George Sibley, photographed on Palm Island, off Townsville, in 1938.[37] *Transforming Tindale* comprised large format photographic prints plus Ah Kee's drawings which responded to them.

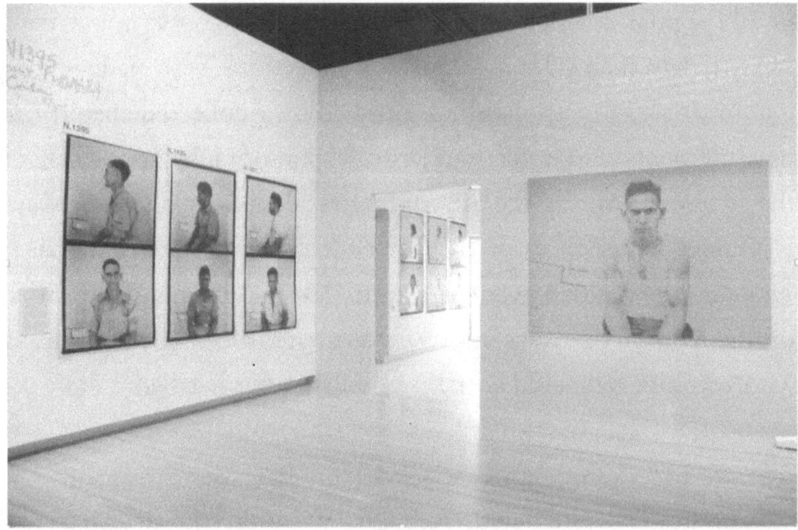

Figure 16.3: Michael Aird, photograph of Transforming Tindale *exhibition, 2012.*

When I look at these juxtapositions, both the enlarged photos and Ah Kee's detailed, intricate, human lines that mimic, but also soften and transform them, I see intimacy and a kind of visual regeneration, in a wider context of community ties and history.

The exhibition was based on extensive discussion with the relatives of the photographic subjects, and the process leading up to this exhibition is inseparable from its final form, fulfilling the goal of reconnecting relatives with these photos, as well as the genealogies and field notes Tindale collected.[38] This is an emotional and often painful journey that forces descendants to confront the oppression of the past. Curator Michael Aird notes:

> I learnt how powerful words can be when attached to photos. I have always known that, but the words in this exhibition were the most powerful words I have ever worked with. (I spent a lot of time crying while I was transcribing)'.[39]

Ultimately, however, Aird suggests that

> The *Transforming Tindale* exhibition was about the journey that Aboriginal people have been through to discover and connect with these images. As Vernon would always say 'the name Tindale might be in the title of the exhibition, but it is not about Tindale'. Instead it was all about a set of photos that Tindale played a part in producing and how people today relate to those photos.[40]

Conclusion

In southern Australia, first invaded and longest settled by white colonists, colonial images have also assumed powerful new meanings in the context of colonial dispossession and loss. Photos help constitute technologies of Indigenous memory through a range of practices that construct the past in the present, including by revealing unknown ancestors lost during the displacements of colonialism, and substantiating Indigenous stories and experiences formerly hidden from view. As Gaynor Macdonald argues of the Wiradjuri people of New South Wales, 'photos of kin link one to ancestors and to one's children's children when myth and history cannot'.[41] But these ties are not based only on kinship bonds, or on an anthropological notion of cultural tradition, but extend to include the historical experience of communities since invasion, countering the 'non-writing of the past, the secret and silent histories, and the past distorted by imperial histories'. [42] For Aboriginal artists, photographic archives offer a rich source of history, and a means to explore many issues that remain in the present. Despite the ambivalence and doubt that has always surrounded claims for photographic truth, archival images are tangible and powerful relics that provide a link with the past, and bring it concretely into our time. This is the power of photographs: to address absence, to reconnect relatives with each other and to country, and to heal: as Wiradjuri scholar Lawrence Bamblett argues, photos link people in the present, as well as connecting them to places and the past; they 'fit into the joyful scene of people telling stories'.[43] The history of broken families, and the dispossession and control of Aboriginal people, remain contested and often absent from national stories, but these silences are filled by the solidity and presence of people recorded in photographic portraits.

Notes

1 E. Edwards & C. Morton, 'Introduction', in E. Edwards & C. Morton (eds), *Photography, Anthropology and History: Expanding the Frame,* Ashgate, Farnham, Surrey, 2009, pp. 1–24 at 9.

2 C. I. Simon, 'Following the Archival Turn', *Visual Resources*, no. XVIII, pp. 101–7.

3 R. D. Wood, 'The Voyage of Captain Lucas and the Daguerreotype to

Sydney', in A. Foucrier (ed.), *The French and the Pacific World, 17th–19th Centuries: Explorations, Migrations and Cultural Exchanges,* Ashgate and Variorum, Aldershot and Burlington, VA, 2005, pp. 69–79.

4 See for example, P. Cunningham, *Two Years in New South Wales,* Henry Colburn, London, 1827, p. 46; P. Turnbull, 'Savages Fossil and Recent: Gerard Krefft and the Production of Racial Knowledge, ca. 1869–73', in M. Crotty, J. Germov & G. Rodwell (eds), *Race for a Place: Eugenics, Darwinism and Social Thought and Practice in Australia, Proceedings of the 2000 History and Sociology of Eugenics Conference,* University of Newcastle, Newcastle, 2000, pp. 133–40; B. W. Butcher, 'Darwinism, Social Darwinism and the Australian Aborigines: a Reevaluation', in R. MacLeod & P. F. Rehbock, *Darwin's Laboratory: Evolutionary Theory and Natural History in the Pacific,* University of Hawaii Press, Honolulu, 1994, pp. 371–94.

5 J. Lydon (ed.), *Calling the Shots: Aboriginal Photographies,* Aboriginal Studies Press, Canberra, 2014.

6 Cited in P. Jones, *Images of the Interior,* Wakefield Press, Adelaide, 2011, pp. 48–69.

7 J. Lydon, *The Flash of Recognition: Photography and the Emergence of Indigenous Rights,* NewSouth Books, Sydney, 2012.

8 ibid.

9 One landmark was the Bicentennial *After 200 Years* project, coordinated by Penny Taylor and the Australian Institute of Aboriginal and Torres Strait Islander Studies, which brought together twenty-one photographers (of whom eight were Indigenous) who visited nineteen communities to document the diversity of Indigenous life in Australia. P. Taylor, 'Introduction' in *After 200 Years: Photographic Essays of Aboriginal and Islander Australia Today,* Australian Institute of Aboriginal Studies, Canberra, 1988, pp. xv–xix.

10 See especially J. Tagg, *The Burden of Representation: Essays of Photographies and Histories,* University of Minnesota Press, Minneapolis, 1993; A. Solomon-Godeau, *Photography at the Dock: Essays on photographic history, institutions, and practices,* University of Minnesota Press, Minneapolis, 1991, p. 176; M. Rosler, *Three Works,* Nova Scotia College of Art and Design, Halifax, 1981; A. Sekula, *Photography against the grain: essays and photo works 1973–1983,* Nova Scotia University Press, Halifax, 1984.

11 See for example J. Faris, *Navajo and Photography: A Critical History of the Representation of an American People,* University of Utah Press, Salt Lake City, 2003.

12 Tagg, *The Burden of Representation,* p. 11.

13 B. L. Croft, 'Laying Ghosts to Rest', in C. Cooper & A. Harris (eds),

Portraits of Oceania, Art Gallery of New South Wales, Sydney, 1997, pp. 15–21.

14 Prompted by studies of scientific communities and cultures such as B. Latour, *Reassembling the Social: An Introduction to Actor-Network-Theory*, Oxford University Press, Oxford, 2005, and the anthropology of art such as A. Gell, *Art and Agency: An Anthropological Theory*, Clarendon, Oxford, 1998.

15 Igor Kopytoff coined the term 'object biographies' for this approach. See I. Kopytoff, 'The Cultural Biography of Things: Commoditization as Process', in Arjun Appadurai (ed.), *The Social Life of Things*, Cambridge University Press, Cambridge, 1986, pp. 64–94; E. Edwards & C. Morton, *Photography, Anthropology and History*, p. 10.

16 E. Edwards, *Raw Histories: Photographs, Anthropology and Museums*, Berg, Oxford and New York, 2001, p. 13. See also E. Edwards & C. Morton, *Photography, Anthropology and History*; P. Joyce & T. Bennett, 'Introduction', in T. Bennett & P. Joyce (eds), *Material Powers: Cultural Studies, History and the Material Turn*, Routledge, London and New York, 2010, pp. 1–21.

17 M. Jolly & S. Tcherkézoff, 'Oceanic Encounters: A Prelude', in M. Jolly, S. Tcherkézoff & D. Tryon (eds), *Oceanic Encounters: Exchange, Desire, Violence*, Australian National University e-Press, Canberra, 2009, pp. 1–36 at 2; B. Smith, *European Vision and the South Pacific*, Clarendon Press, Oxford, 1960.

18 C. Morton, 'Double Alienation: Evans-Pritchard's Zande and Nuer Photographs in Comparative Perspective', in R. Vokes (ed.), *Photography in Africa: Ethnographic Perspectives*, Boydell and Brewer, Woodbridge and Rochester, 2012. See also A. Herle, 'John Layard Long Malakula 1914–15: The Potency of Field Photography', in E. Edwards & C. Morton, *Photography, Anthropology and History*, pp. 241–64.

19 M. Aird, *Portraits of Our Elders*, Queensland Museum, Brisbane, 1993, p. vii.

20 For an overview of repatriation in Australia see M. Green & P. Gordon, 'Repatriation: Australian Perspectives', in J. Lydon & U. Rizvi (eds), *Handbook to Postcolonialism and Archaeology*, World Archaeological Congress, LeftCoast Press, San Francisco, 2011, pp. 257–65. For an overview with respect to photography see J. Lydon, 'Return: The photographic archive and technologies of Indigenous memory', *Photographies*, vol. 3, no. 2, 2010, pp. 173–87.

21 See for example contributions to R. Vokes (ed.), *Photography in Africa: Ethnographic Perspectives*, Woodbridge, New York, 2012; L. Peers & A. K. Brown (eds), *Museums and Source Communities: A Routledge reader*, Routledge, New York, 2003; E. Edwards & J. Hart (eds), *Photographs, Objects, Histories: On the Materiality of Images*, Routledge, New York, 2004;

L. Peers & A. K. Brown with members of the Kainai Nation, *'Pictures bring us messages': Sinaakssiiksi aohtsimaahpihkookiyaawa: photographs and histories from the Kainai Nation,* University of Toronto Press, Toronto, 2006. Formal guides to ethical research practices include the Aboriginal and Torres Strait Islander Library and Information Resources Network (ATSILIRN) Protocols for Libraries, Archives and Information Services, viewed 29 June 2015, <http://atsilirn.aiatsis.gov.au/protocols.php>.

22 H. Goodall, *Invasion to Embassy: Land in Aboriginal politics in New South Wales, 1770–1972,* Allen and Unwin, Sydney, 1996.

23 '*Timeline – History of Separation of Aboriginal and Torres Strait Islander Children from Their Families*', Australian Human Rights Commission, viewed 12 June 2015, <https://www.humanrights.gov.au/timeline-history-separation-aboriginal-and-torres-strait-islander-children-their-families-text>.

24 Aṟa Irititja website, viewed 28 June 2015, <http://www.irititja.com/about_ara_irititja/index.html>; M. Hughes & J. Dallwitz, 'Aṟa Irititja: Towards Culturally Appropriate Best Practice in Remote Indigenous Australia,' in L. E. Dyson, M. Hendriks & S.Grant (eds), *Information Technology and Indigenous People,* Information Science Publishers, Hershey, pp. 146–58; S. Thorner, 'Imagining an Indigital Interface: Aṟa Irititja Indigenizes the Technologies of Knowledge Management', *COLLECTIONS: A journal for Museums and Archives Professionals*, vol. 6, no. 3, 2010, pp. 125–46.

25 Mulka Project website, viewed 28 June 2015, <http://www.yirrkala.com/themulkaproject>.

26 J. E. Stanton, 'Snapshots of the Dreaming: Photographs of the past and present', in L. Peers & A. K. Brown (eds), *Museums and Source Communities: A Routledge reader,* Routledge, New York, 2003, pp. 136–51 at 139.

27 *The John William Lindt Collection: Grafton Regional Gallery*, Grafton Regional Gallery, Grafton, 2005, p. 4; K. Orchard, 'J. W. *Lindt's* Australian Aboriginals (1873–74)', *History of Photography*, vol. 23, no. 2, 1999, pp. 163–70.

28 S. Bostock-Smith in J. Lydon (ed.), *Calling the Shots: Aboriginal Photographies,* Aboriginal Studies Press, Canberra, 2014, pp. 61–5. See also M. Briggs, J. Lydon & M. Say, 'Collaborating: Photographs of Koories in the State Library of Victoria', *La Trobe Journal*, no. 85, 2010, pp. 106–24.

29 B. L. Croft, *In My Father's House, In conjunction with Postcards from Mummy, Destiny Deacon*, Australian Centre for Photography, Paddington, NSW, 1998, pp. 8–14.

30 B. Andrew, 'Come into the light', in *The Island Catalogue*, Museum of Archaeology and Anthropology, Cambridge, 2007.

31 C. Parsley, 'Christian Thompson and the art of indigeneity', *Discipline*, no. 1,

2011, viewed 29 June 2015, <http://discipline.net.au/Discipline/Issue_1_files/Connal%20Parsley%20-%20Christian%20Thompson.pdf>; R. Butler, 'Margaret Preston and the history wars', *Australian Graffiti,* exhibition catalogue, Gallery Gabrielle Pizzi, Melbourne 2008, p. 1.

32 G. Jones, 'Vernon Ah Kee: Sovereign Warrior', *Artlink*, vol. 30, no. 1, 2010, pp. 46–53. See also *Borninthisskin: Vernon Ah Kee,* exhibition catalogue, Institute of Modern Art, Brisbane, 2009.

33 W. Anderson, *The Cultivation of Whiteness: Science, Health, and Racial Destiny in Australia*, Duke University Press, North Carolina, 2006.

34 A. Roberts, M. Fowler & T. Sansbury, 'A report on the exhibition "Children, Boats and Hidden Histories": Crayon drawings by Aboriginal children at Point Pearce Mission (Burgiyana) (South Australia), 1939', *Bulletin of the Australasian Institute for Maritime Archaeology*, no. 38, 2014, pp. 24–30. The researchers' wives, Dorothy Tinsdale and Bee Birdsell, supervised children's crayon drawings – these have now formed the basis for a permanent exhibition, *Children, Boats and Hidden Histories* and constitute a heritage resource for Aboriginal communities, documenting them in ways that have now been given new meanings.

35 *Transforming Tindale* website, viewed 29 June 2015, <http://vernonahkee.blogspot.com.au/2012/09/transforming-tindale.html>.

36 G. Barkley, interview with Vernon Ah Kee, in *Borninthisskin: Vernon Ah Kee,* exhibition catalogue, Institute of Modern Art, Brisbane, 2009, pp. 11–23 at 21.

37 ibid. This 2004 work was titled *Fantasies of the Good.*

38 G. Macdonald, 'Photos in Wiradjuri biscuit tins: negotiating relatedness and validating lives', *Oceania*, vol. 73, no. 4, 2003, pp. 225–42 at 239. Heather Goodall has also written of north-western NSW where Tindale worked in 1938 at Brewarrina: 'It is not only traditional or even biological kinship which has generated the most complex and active readings, it has been the historical and lived experiences which these people had shared and which continue to link their descendants'. In H. Goodall, 'Karroo-Mates: Communities Reclaim their Images', *Aboriginal History*, no. 30, 2006, pp. 48–66 at 65.

39 Personal communication with Michael Aird, 2015.

40 ibid.

41 G. Macdonald, 'Photos in Wiradjuri biscuit tins', pp. 225–42.

42 ibid.

43 L. Bamblett, 'Picture Who We Are: Representations of Identity and the Appropriation of Photographs into a Wiradjuri Oral History Tradition', in J. Lydon (ed.), *Calling the Shots: Aboriginal Photographies,* Aboriginal Studies Press, Canberra, 2014, pp. 76–100.

17

KEPT IN SILENCE - AN ARCHIVAL TRAVELOGUE

Brook Andrew and Katarina Matiasek

The following chronology retraces and reflects the itinerary of Australian Aboriginal ancestral remains from their expropriation and archiving to their repatriation. Our artistic research revolving around the Australia collection of Viennese anthropologist and multi-media documenter Rudolf Pöch (1870–1921) can be seen as a case study of obsessive colonial collection practices that reduced Aboriginal people and their culture to mere collectibles in the name of 'science' and the colonial project. The ensuing silent trading, collecting and archiving in mainly European museums has distressing effects for communities and families to this day, not to mention the legacy of trauma these collections still vibrate and permeate. The *Kept in Silence* project is situated in our convergent artistic, community and research practice. At times, artists are criticised for taking these themes to the art world and its spectators, as if they would create an elitist product from such harrowing legacies of colonialism. Though, let us remember that the stories of natural disasters, massacres, dictatorships and legacies of the disappeared told by artists such as Jenny Holzer, Alfredo Jarr, Ai Weiwei and Christian Boltanski do exist in a place called Australia. And it is in this vein that we follow the path from Australia to Austria and back again. Rudolf Pöch's expeditions emulate those of many other anthropologists and photographers that similarly affected many cultures and thousands of lives. And now is the time that Australia joins the list of countries that break the silence of their difficult pasts so that the young do not forget.

15th November 1892

Grafton, New South Wales, Australia

The Clarence and Richmond Examiner *reports that an area of 200 acres about 9 miles north from Grafton is allotted by the Government for the establishment of an 'Aborigines Home' for those 'which have dwindled down by the encroachments of civilisation to a mere handful'. While the article presents the 'Home' as an improvement of Indigenous living conditions, it deplores the poor quality of its land as being swampy, hardly fertile or level.*[1] *This discloses the real purpose of the 'Grafton Home' that starts out with twenty-two inhabitants – an Aborigines Protection Board experiment to replace traditional food practices for an English agricultural re-education.*

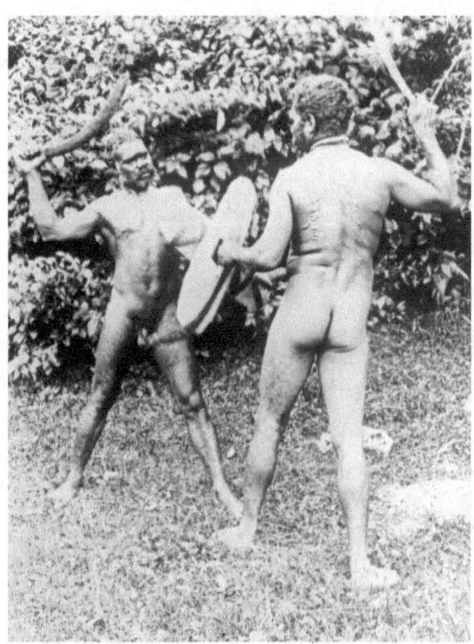

Figure 17.1: George Savidge, Australians fighting with boomerang and parrying shield, *1895. Image courtesy the Department of Anthropology, University of Vienna.*

1895

Copmanhurst near Grafton, New South Wales, Australia

George Savidge (1859–1932), a correspondent of the Australian Museum,[2] *takes a photograph of Coby, a 27-year-old 'Kumbudok' man of the Copmanhurst hills near Grafton with another unknown man. Ten years later, Savidge offers this photograph of a staged fight to visiting Viennese explorer Rudolf Pöch, for 'scientific evaluation'.*[3]

20th February to 1st May 1897

Bombay, India

Allegedly, it is photography that brings Rudolf Pöch (1870–1921), a 27-year-old medical doctor of Vienna's II. University Hospital, on a first overseas journey that will spur his interest in anthropology. His professional photographic training under the eminent pioneer of scientific photography, Josef Maria Eder (1855–1944),[4] *qualifies Pöch to participate in the official Austrian Plague Expedition to Bombay in 1897. The Plague Commission returns from this journey not only with Pöch's 'rich photographic yield… of this important disease',*[5] *but also with the pathogen itself – eventually causing Vienna's last three plague deaths in the following year.*[6]

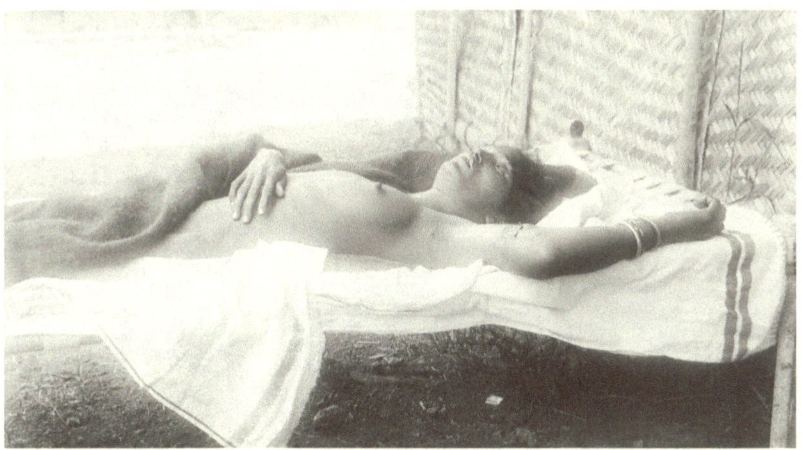

Figure 17.2: Rudolf Pöch, Plague Patient at the Arthur Road Hospital in Bombay, *1897. Image courtesy the Department of Anthropology, University of Vienna.*

1st January 1901
Centennial Park, Sydney, Australia

With the Royal Assent of Queen Victoria (1819–1901), six former self-governing colonies collectively proclaim the Commonwealth of Australia. Its constitution states that 'in reckoning the numbers of people…Aboriginal natives shall not be counted' and also that the Commonwealth would legislate for any race except Aboriginal people.[7] *This restricts Aboriginal voting rights in federal elections.*

16th March to 6th June 1902
Hamburg, Germany to the coast of Senegambia and Upper Guinea, West Africa

Contracted by the Institute for Tropical Hygiene in Hamburg, Rudolf Pöch boards a steamer of the German Woermann shipping line to survey the high incidence of malaria on the company's trading route down the West

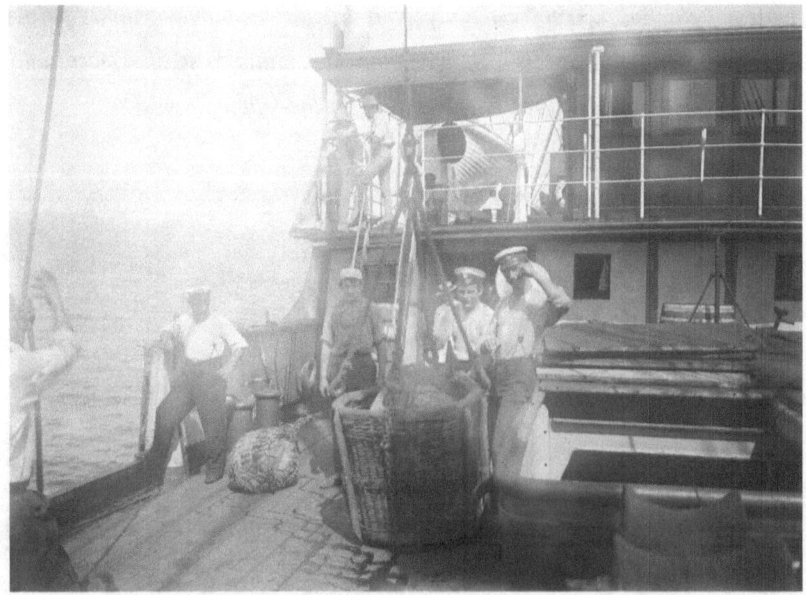

Figure 17.3: Rudolf Pöch, Aboard the SS *Ella Woermann, 1902. Image courtesy the Department of Anthropology, University of Vienna.*

African coast. He meticulously experiments with prophylactic measures for the crew, chronicling quinine administrations and fever curves, counting mosquitoes aboard and blood cells in an improvised laboratory, as well as inventing different mosquito netting techniques.[8] *Yet Pöch will contract malaria on his next journey himself – a condition that will eventually lead to his premature death in 1921.*

25th March 1905
Namatanai, Papua New Guinea
In a letter from the Bismarck Archipelago, Rudolf Pöch reports an unscheduled interception of his first own expedition – a biennial journey to Papua New Guinea – to the Imperial Academy of Sciences in Vienna. The Burns Philp shipping company's cancellation of all services to then German New Guinea forces the well-travelled physician to reach the British parts of New Guinea by 'taking the detour of Australia'. Rudolf Pöch intends to make use of this occasion though and announces anthropological investigations 'also on the Australian Aboriginal' to his patrons,[9] *stressing the importance of 'every investigation of an ethnic group whose existence will have ceased in the foreseeable future'.*[10]

21st June to 6th September 1905
New South Wales, Australia
The first entry in Rudolf Pöch's travel notebook from New South Wales lists nine Australian Indigenous remains bought during his first weeks in Sydney.[11] *Consecutively labelled with 'cranial numbers', these were later complemented by two further remains acquired on site, among them the skeleton of a child. Pöch refers to these as 'reference material' to his anthropological measurements, type photographs and facial casts taken during a tour of the Clarence River district in the third week of July 1905 – a region recommended to him by curator Robert Etheridge jun. (1847–1920) of the Australian Museum for the 'racial purity' of its Indigenous population.*[12]

22nd July 1905
Copmanhurst to Grafton, Australia

On a small steamboat, Rudolf Pöch travels about 8 miles downstream from Copmanhurst to Grafton to visit the 'Grafton Home' that he describes as an 'Asylum created by the State of New South Wales'.[13] *It will become the site where he takes most of his anthropometric and ethnographic photographs during his explorations of the Clarence River district – among them his first stereo photographs.*[14]

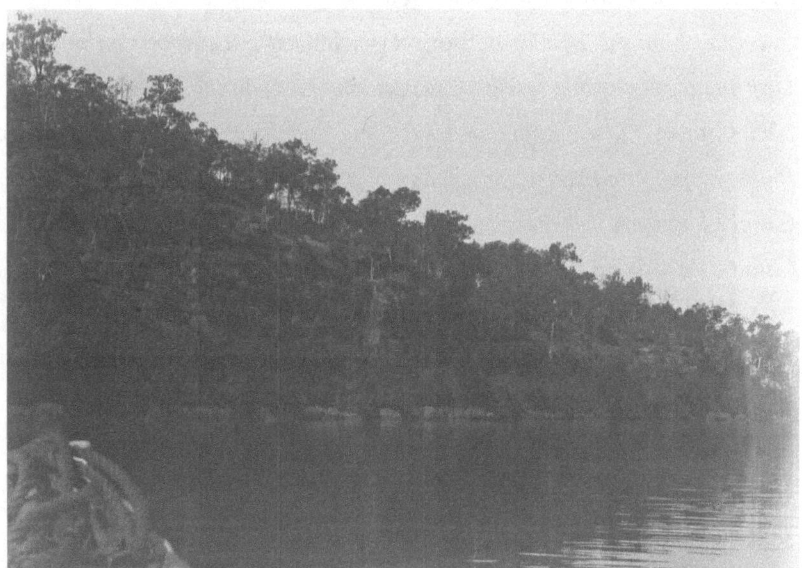

Figure 17.4: Rudolf Pöch, Travelling downstream from Copmanhurst to Grafton, *1905. Image courtesy the Department of Anthropology, University of Vienna.*

5th November 1905
Cape Nelson, Papua New Guinea

After having again taken up his main itinerary in Papua New Guinea, Rudolf Pöch uses his new Lancaster stereo camera recently acquired in Sydney[15] *to document the procedures of anthropometric photography. It shows Resident Magistrate Guy Owen Manning (1881–1915) photographing*[16] *an Indigenous man at the Government Station in Cape*

Nelson where Pöch had taken fixed quarters in October.[17] *This stereograph plastically documents what usually remains outside the picture frame: that anthropological documentation was largely carried out within the administrational confinements of the colonial apparatus.*[18] *These restrictive structures can be seen to have extended into the standardised protocol of anthropometric photography – allowing Manning, a native of New South Wales, to indeed support Pöch's work 'in every way'.*[19]

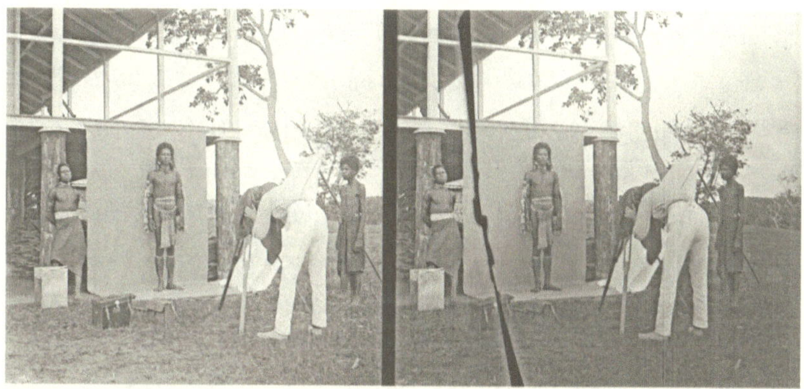

Figure 17.5: Rudolf Pöch, Mr Manning taking photographs, *1905. Image courtesy the Department of Anthropology, University of Vienna.*

12th November 1906
Vienna, Austria

In 1906, the year of his return and before he had 'overlooked his observations and documentations' from Papua New Guinea,[20] *Pöch is assigned to a new two-year expedition to South Africa by the Imperial Academy of Sciences of Vienna.*[21] *His proposal to study the Khoe-San people of the Kalahari Desert – again under the premise of his previous expedition that small stature is a 'primitive' feature indicative of evolutionary proximity to a primordial human stage*[22] *– is immediately granted funding.*

6th November 1907 to 8th December 1909
South Africa

Rudolf Pöch summarises his South Africa expedition in his travel notebook: '2 years, 1 month; 6.000 km off the tracks; 1.000 BM [Khoe-San] seen; 300 measurements; 2.000 photos; 1.000 m cinemat[ic] film; 50 phonogr[aphic] rec[ordings]; 200 cold-blooded animals; 150 mammalian objects; 1.500 letters written; 30 postal parcels; 100 crates sent; 10 different BM [Khoe-San] languages (5 orderly) recorded; 100 skeletons; 25 single skulls; 50 [plaster] casts of living people; hair samples; foot and hand prints'.[23] *This list does not include about 1,000 artefacts, nor does it mention the exhumation of two recently deceased, a man and a woman from Gamopedi.*[24] *Both his overseas journeys will establish Pöch's long-standing reputation as a pioneer in anthropological fieldwork and multimedia documentation – an affirmative view that will become subject to critical revision around the turn of the millennium.*[25]

16th August 1917 to 18th October 1918
Wünsdorf, Germany and Turnu Magurele, Romania

At the instigation of the Anthropological Society in Vienna,[26] *Rudolf Pöch headed a study commission for anthropological surveys on a large scale in the Austro-Hungarian prison camps of World War I between 1915 and 1918. Pöch, meanwhile promoted to the rank of associate professor of anthropology and ethnography at the University of Vienna,*[27] *echoed his patron's concern that the war situation with prisoners from all European and Asian parts of Russia offered science 'a non-recurring research opportunity' that should not be passed up.*[28] *Now Pöch and his main assistant, Josef Weninger (1886–1959), extend the project to include the German camp of Wünsdorf near Berlin and the Romanian camp of Turnu Magurele then under German occupation.*[29] *Pöch claims to be prepared by his previous overseas expeditions for investigations on a 'large and important exotic mixture' of African and Indian colonial soldiers from the western front imprisoned there.*[30] *Among them is Pan-Africanist Paul Panda Farnana (1888–1930), a prominent critic of colonial policies in his native Congo.*[31] *In its promise of anthropological knowledge on a panoply of geographic sites, the endeavour can be considered a streamlined Ersatz expedition that substituted the 'unpredictable' anthropological field for the controlled conditions of the camp. During World War II Pöch's students will use his methods established during World War I in their work during the era of National Socialism, surveying detained Jews and, again, thousands of prisoners-of-war.*[32]

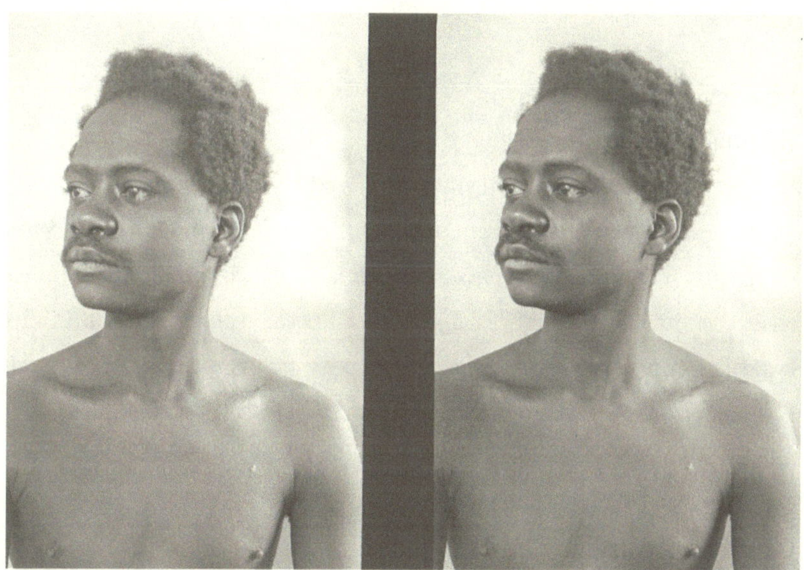

Figure 17.6: Rudolf Pöch, Anthropometric Portrait of Paul Panda Farnana, *1905. Image courtesy the Department of Anthropology, University of Vienna.*

4th March 1921

Innsbruck, Austria

After the war, in 1919, Rudolf Pöch had become a regular professor on the newly established University Chair for Anthropology and Ethnography, a corresponding member of the now Austrian Academy of Sciences, and a married man.[33] *His unexpected death in Innsbruck only two years later leaves Pöch's extensive anthropological and ethnological 'collections' and documentations in a largely unevaluated state. His* Studies on Indigenous people from New South Wales and on Australian Skulls – *which had earned the trained physician a second doctoral degree from the Philosophical Faculty of the University of Munich in 1913,*[34] *entitling him to the venia legendi for both anthropology and ethnography*[35] *– remains his only in-depth study. He equally bequests his young widow and student, anthropologist Hella Pöch-Schürer (1893–1976), and the Austrian Academy of Sciences with his scientific legacy and considerable earmarked funds to organise its posthumous scientific evaluation.*[36]

January 1922
Vienna, Austria
A 'Pöch Commission' is appointed by the Austrian Academy of Sciences for the publication and dissemination of Rudolf Pöch's anthropological 'collections' from his expeditions to Oceania, South Africa and the prisoner-of-war camps.[37] *Between 1927 and 1962, a twelve-volume* Rudolf Pöchs Nachlass *series will be published. Except for two ethnological studies, all volumes of the series are based on the prisoner-of-war documentations.*[38]

1st August 1925
Grafton, Australia
The Brisbane Courier *announces that the 'throwing open of what was originally the Aborigines Home' causes 'the greatest interest amongst land seekers'. The former grounds of the 'Home' have been cut into three blocks of about 100 acres each, and set apart as homestead farms. On the first day the land is available, hundreds of applications are received for an upcoming ballot at the Grafton Court House.*[39]

12th September 1926

Salzburg, Austria

At 8am Hella Pöch presents the partially dissected corpses of two Khoe-San, a man and a woman, at the morgue of Salzburg's St. Johann Hospital. She gives a detailed account on how her late husband had ordered the married couple's exhumation on the 4th October 1909 in Gamopedi, just one month after they had died of a fever within a short time of each other. Hella Pöch elaborates on gruesome details of their conservation in formaldehyde bandages or their forcing into salt-filled barrels for transport.[40] *The research of two historians from South Africa, Martin Legasick and Ciraj Rassool, will lead to their identification as Claas and Trooi Pienaar,*[41] *and to their eventual repatriation to South Africa for reburial from the Anthropological Department of the Museum of Natural History in 2012.*

25th September 1931

Vienna, Austria

The Municipal Cultural Committee names a street in Vienna's 14th district after Rudolf Pöch.

1939

Vienna, Austria

The annexation of Austria into the German Third Reich and the ensuing National Socialist 'alignment' policies have fundamentally altered Vienna's university and museum structures after March 1938. In the Museum of Natural History, a respective exhibition on The Physical and Mental Appearance of the Jews *is staged on the basis of confiscated holdings of Vienna's Jewish Museum and of mug shots provided by the Police Directorate*[42] *in 1939. The second and central special exhibit of the year entitled* Ostmark Germans as Explorers and Collectors in our Colonies[43] *resorts to earlier expedition inventories, especially those of*

Rudolf Pöch within the topical framework of colonial revisionism, and calls for an 'own sphere of influence in our robbed colonies'.[44]

3rd March 1941
Vienna, Austria
The Reich Ministry of Education approves the funding of a joint initiative of Hella Pöch and her second husband, Georg, with the Anthropological Department of the Museum of Natural History, to make use of the Nazi occupation of the Netherlands.[45] *Owing to Hella's good relations with Reich Commissioner-in-charge, Arthur Seyss-Inquart (1892–1946), under whose chancellorship the Austrian 'Anschluss' was implemented in 1938, the way seems paved for the project of anthropologically surveying Sephardic Jews from Amsterdam now interned at Ommen concentration camp in the Dutch province. Yet these plans will be postponed indefinitely – most likely by the incipient deportations to the Nazi death camps of Poland.*[46]

10th August 1943
Vienna, Austria
In a report to the Reich Governor in Vienna, the Anthropological Department of the Museum of Natural History announces the completion of a concerted effort with the University's Institute for Anthropology to evacuate the city's anthropological collections to rural Schönborn castle.[47] *With the former Austrian territory coming into the reach of allied air raids during World War II, Nazi authorities start implementing an earlier order by Adolf Hitler to evacuate the holdings of Viennese Museums and other cultural heritage, including expropriated artworks, to the countryside to protect them against war damage.*[48] *Rudolf Pöch's anthropological 'collections' are transported to Schönborn together with valuable art and natural history collections, among them the* Providentia Fountain, *a Baroque masterpiece by Georg Raffael Donner (1693–1741).*

30th June 1945
Schönborn-Mallebarn, Austria

Museum ornithologist Moriz Sassi (1880–1967), entrusted with the supervision of the major evacuation site Schönborn castle in Mallebarn,[49] *reports a 'black day'. After an initial inspection of the site right after the end of World War II had found the hidden holdings intact, Sassi finds that the Soviet occupying forces have started moving things, while Countess Schönborn is found dead in her bed.*[50] *Sassi writes increasingly alarmed letters to the Federal Monument Office, eventually stating that Schönborn castle has become a 'child of sorrow', with not a single evacuation box remaining in place.*[51]

23rd September 1945
Obermallebarn, Austria

A local farmer writes to the Head of the Institute for Anthropology, Pöch's former main assistant Josef Weninger, that he has found further inventories from their collection at a nearby dump, soiled from the heavy dew, rain and wind that had scattered them over the fields. He asks for packing material for 'skulls, plaster casts, skeletal parts' which he has collected with his wife and stored in their attic, as the 'objects' would further suffer during a transport back to Vienna over streets full of potholes.[52]

7th February to 28th May 1946
Viendorf and Schönborn-Mallebarn, Austria

During an inspection of Schönborn castle, considerable holdings from the Institute for Anthropology, with human skeletons and skulls from the 'collection' of Rudolf Pöch among them, are found in a ruined state at the gravel quarry of Viendorf near Schönborn castle.[53] *With the imminent withdrawal of the Soviet occupying forces three months later, an appeal from the Schönborn castle's Forestry and Goods Directorate goes out to the mayors of the region to see to the recollection of evacuation goods, and to stop further lootings of the castle and its surroundings. The call states that even the most unassuming items from greater art or natural history collections are of immense value, yet only within their original context.*[54]

25th September 1946
Salzburg, Austria

According to an official survey of the Salzburg city council, Hella Pöch is reported to have relocated to an unknown place without cancelling her official Salzburg residency registration.[55] *Having both catered to the Nazi regime's racial policies, Hella and Georg Pöch were among those successfully going underground after its collapse in 1945. They will eventually flee to the remote Indonesian island of Sumbawa Besar where Hella continues her 'racial studies' and Georg takes up medical practice again.*[56] *Their former mentor, Seyss-Inquart, is found guilty of crimes against humanity as a 'compliant executive' and sentenced to death during the Nuremberg trials in 1946.*[57]

1962
Adelaide, Australia

Andrew Arthur Abbie (1905–76) from the Department of Anatomy at the University of Adelaide deplores that 'the name of Rudolf Pöch is scarcely known in Australia'. Abbie claims that even a brief reference of Pöch's published studies on the Aborigines of New South Wales, on a Tasmanian skull and on the 'blondness' in Tasmanians, 'suffices to establish Pöch's importance to the physical anthropology of Australia'.[58]

11th December 1964
Munich, Germany

Ferdinand Wagenseil (1887–1967), former Director of the Anatomical Institute at the University of Giessen, presents a special print of a dissection protocol to the Austrian Academy of Sciences in Vienna.[59] *With their financial support, he had 'investigated' the mimic and masticatory musculature on the prepared heads of two Melanesian men, both between thirty and thirty-five years old, which had been sent to Vienna on behalf of Rudolf Pöch in the course of his Oceania expedition from 1904–6. Wagenseil, rated a 'racial scientist of moral integrity' by his biographer,*[60] *refers to a third preserved head of a man from the Baining mountains of the same provenance that had been dissected back in 1935.*[61] *The dubious conclusion of Wagenseil's own observations is the 'co-existence of both primitive and progressive conditions'.*[62]

27th May 1967

Australia

The Holt Government accepted revisions to the Australian Constitution relating to Indigenous Australians. This was a national vote on Constitution Alteration (Aboriginals) 1967. Following the result's extraordinary outcome from six states of a positive 90.77%, the referendum became law on 10th August 1967. As a consequence, the Federal Government and state governments, were responsible for making laws for Indigenous Australians, and Indigenous Australians would from now on be officially included in the census.

1st November 1976

Vienna, Austria

After having returned to Austria in the mid-1960s and undisturbedly taken up 'racial studies' again,[63] *Hella Pöch dies at the age of 83.*

1980

Vienna, Austria

To mark Rudolf Pöch's 110th birthday, a commemorative exhibition is staged in the domed hall of the Museum of Natural History. His research 'material' is presented in eight vitrines and on thirty wall charts.[64] *Echoing their 1939 exhibit, the museum's much-cited accompanying publication presents Pöch as an uncontested national hero.*

17th December 1982

Vienna, Austria

The general conference of the Austrian Academy of Sciences proposes 'not to activate the Pöch Commission anymore' and entrusts its presidium with the administration of the remaining funds.[65] *Having survived capital depreciation, the legacy is effective to this day.*

1996

Sydney, Australia

Brook Andrew accesses the photographic archives of the Mitchell Library and creates the work Sexy & Dangerous, *which will be awarded the RAKA award in 1998. This work is created during times when fellow artists Rea and Leah King-Smith are interested in new light shed on ethnographic representations, largely orphaned images of Aboriginal people taken during colonial times. They and other artists begin to interrogate Australia's photographic documentation of Aboriginal people. Following important debates during the next few decades, formal guidelines are developed to assist communities, researchers and collections to access and identify these orphan images, not all of which have to this day been identified.*

1996

Exeter, United Kingdom

Supported by his first Australia Council grant, Brook Andrew travels for his first international residency to the Royal Albert Memorial Museum, as part of the larger touring exhibition Abstracts: New Aboriginalities. *In preparation for his inaugural international museum intervention, he was informed that all Aboriginal human remains had been repatriated to Australia. During this residency, Brook first located the 'Mammals*

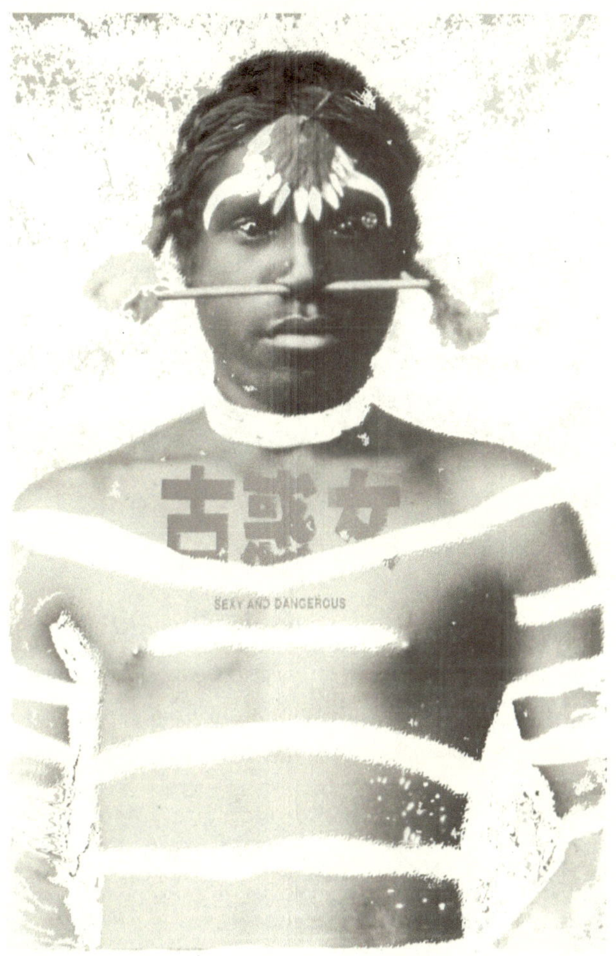

Figure 17.7: Brook Andrew, Sexy & Dangerous, *1996. Image courtesy the artist and Tolarno Galleries, Melbourne.*

Register' containing Aboriginal and other non-human remains such as whales and monkeys. The collections manager informs Brook that all Aboriginal human remains had been repatriated or returned to Australia. Whilst then following the accession number to empty boxes once containing human remains, he then opens one box that reveals a skull. This has a profound impact on Brook who immediately contacts his family and fellow artist Rea for support, who at the time creates work specifically on the Aboriginal human remains trade. Consequently, this discovered skull will not be repatriated due to its status of being an Aboriginal skull 'of unknown New South Wales provenance'.

1998

Sydney, Australia

Brook Andrew came across a nineteenth-century document during research for his first museum intervention in Australia, Black Beauty, *at the djamu gallery, Australian Museum. Published at the Australian Museum, it outlined a recipe on how to prepare Aboriginal human remains and other mammals for the removal of tissues to extract the skeleton.*

2004

Sydney, Australia

Brook Andrew is granted his first Australia Council Fellowship to collect research from elders of NSW. Conducted through Gandangarra Elders Land Council, the Elders of this community were engaged in workshops

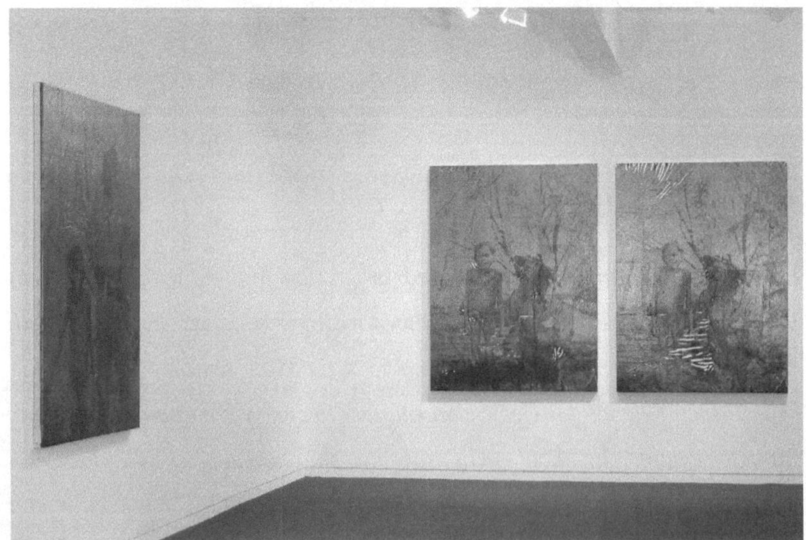

Figure 17.8: Brook Andrew, Gun-metal Grey, *2007. Image courtesy the artist and Tolarno Galleries, Melbourne.*

that included topics on the visibility of ethnographic Aboriginal people and the Elders' thoughts on the existence of these photographs, of which many were not aware existed. The outcome was the photographs Kalar Midday *in 2003/04 and mixed-media works* Gun-metal Grey *in 2007.*

24th October 2007

Vienna, Austria

The Australian embassy invites the members of a scientific research project on Rudolf Pöch, directed by Maria Teschler-Nicola of the Anthropological Department of the Museum of Natural History and Harald Wilfing of the University's Department of Anthropology, to participate in a workshop to discuss repatriation issues with an Indigenous committee that has come from Australia. Having started two years earlier in 2005, the research project aimed at a re-evaluation of Pöch's legacy that lays scattered over several Viennese institutions to this day.[66] *Katarina Matiasek, having critically reviewed Pöch's status as a media pioneer on this project,*[67] *will embark on an archival research of several years after the workshop at the Australian embassy. With just a loose typescript on Pöch's 'Craniological Collection' dating from after 1911, she will set out to identify Australian remains among the largely orphaned holdings of the Department of Anthropology.*

2010

Sydney, Australia

In light of missing official monuments to Aboriginal loss and conflict such as the frontier wars which some argue raged into the twentieth century, Brook Andrew will create Jumping Castle War Memorial *exhibited in the 17th Biennale of Sydney:* THE BEAUTY OF DISTANCE – Songs of Survival in a Precarious Age. *This large soft-sculpture was a response to the lack of memorials dedicated to the frontier wars and to the immense removal of Aboriginal human remains during international colonial projects.*

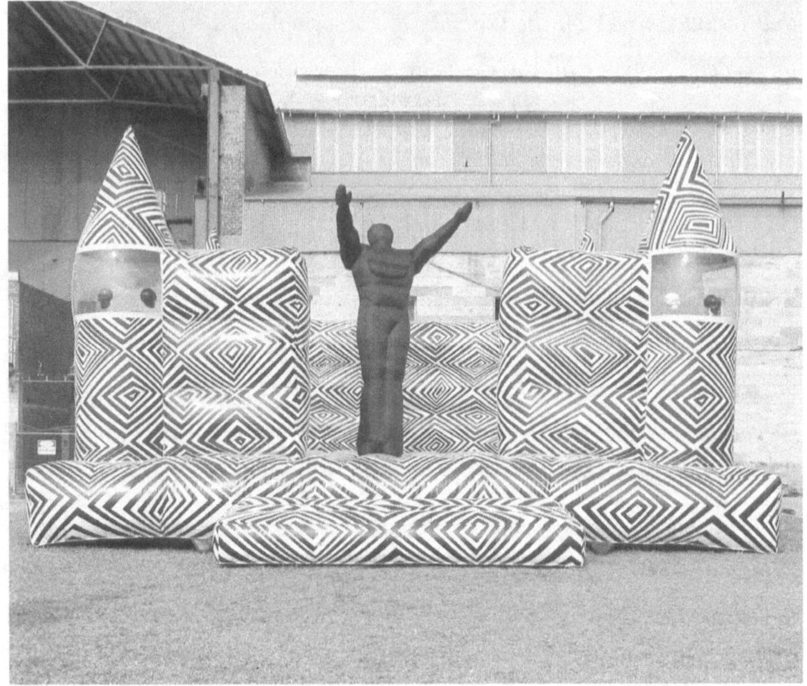

Figure 17.9: Brook Andrew, Jumping Castle War Memorial, *2010. Image courtesy of the artist and Tolarno Galleries, Melbourne.*

30th June 2011
Vienna, Austria

Bill Risk, Elder and custodian of the Larrakia nation from the Northern Territory, leads a Smoking Ceremony in the portico of the Austrian Academy of Sciences. Coordinated by the Australian embassy in Vienna, the institution formally returns thirty Australian Indigenous remains acquired by Rudolf Pöch during his 'detour' to Australia and after. A delegation of five traditional owners from New South Wales, Queensland and the Northern Territory[68] *have travelled across the globe to accompany their ancestors home for repatriation and reburial after more than 100 years in archival exile at the University Department of Anthropology in Vienna. While Katarina Matiasek's research enabled this repatriation, the fate of further Aboriginal remains from Rudolf Pöch's 'collection' remains unclear.*

10th February 2012
Melbourne, Australia

Before Brook Andrew and Katarina Matiasek know of each other, Brook acquires for his personal archive a vintage special print of Rudolf Pöch's Studies on Indigenous people from New South Wales and on Australian Skulls, *as published with the Proceeding of the Anthropological Society in Vienna in 1915.*[69] *This work, covering the Indigenous remains repatriated to Australia in 2011, also gives examples of Pöch's photography in the Clarence River district.*

17th April 2013
Vienna, Austria

Brook Andrew and Katarina Matiasek meet for the first time after an introduction by Simon Rees, currently curator at the MAK, Vienna. Having attended the Smoking Ceremony, Simon knows of Katarina's deep wish to find a form to commemorate the silent history surrounding this repatriation and suggests that Brook may share this interest.

17th September 2013
Vienna, Austria

A historical transcript on Rudolf Pöch's 'Skeletal Collection' incidentally turns up in the archives of the Department of Anthropology at the University of Vienna, complementing documents found earlier by Katarina Matiasek in the course of her archival research. Three people can now be identified that sent out or brought in further Australian Indigenous remains to Vienna after Pöch's return: Walter Richard Harper (1873–1942), amateur anthropologist and Secretary of the Anthropological Society in Sydney[71]*, Clifford Coles (1876–1949), dealer in furs, ethnological and natural history items in Sydney, and Emil Hansel, Secretary of the Austro-Hungarian Consulate in Sydney, who has published the autobiographical account,* Oben und Unten, *of his years in Australia under the pseudonym of Hans von Lippa.*[72]

7th November 2013
Paris, France

Brook Andrew creates the sculpture Anatomie de la mémoire du corps: au-delà de la Tasmanie *for an exhibition at Galerie Nathalie Obadia, Bourg-Tibourg, Paris. This sculpture displays a human skeleton probably from the sub-continent c. 1920 used for medical teaching practices, and objects from the artist's personal archive – including the original print of Rudolf Pöch's New South Wales studies. Brook re-presented the work at Madrid's Museo Reina Sofia for his installation* Splinters of Monuments: A Solid Memory of the Forgotten Plains of our Trash and Obsessions *as part of the WHW curated exhibition* Really Useful Knowledge *in 2014. This new installation reflected on British, Spanish and European colonial histories and cultural identities, and included work beyond the artists immediate archive from the collections of the Museo Reina Sofia, the Museo de América and the Museo Nacional de Antropología.*[70]

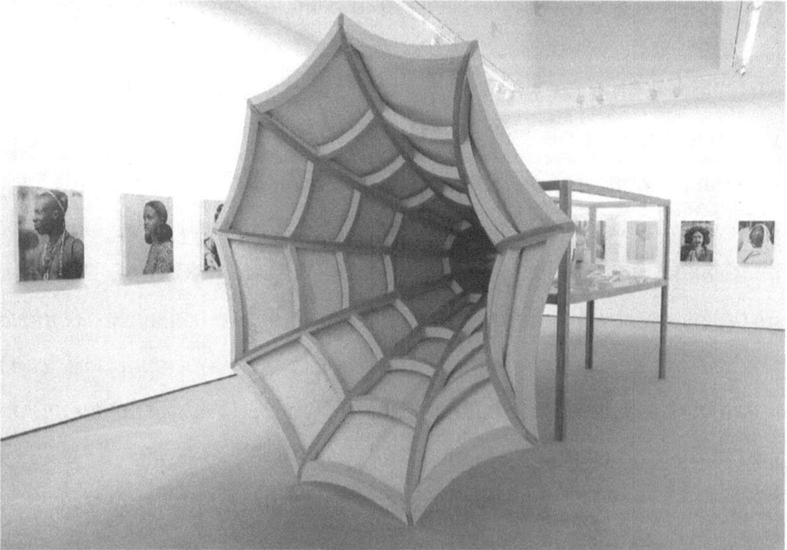

Figure 17.10: Brook Andrew, Anatomie de la mémoire du corps : au-delà de la Tasmanie, *2014. Image courtesy the artist and Galerie Nathalie Obadia, Paris and Brussels.*

8th November 2013
Paris, France

Brook Andrew and Katarina Matiasek meet to discuss ways of breaking the silence that usually shrouds acts of posthumous displacement. Sharing a belief in the significance of remembering history and in the transforming potency of conceptual art, they decide to create a book serving as a lieu de mémoire to the people once objectified to 'scientific' collectibles. Brook and Katarina agree on a visual travelogue across the century that juxtaposes ephemeral archival traces with strong contemporary opinions and actively engages the reader in the process of restoring a voice to the dead.

19th May 2014
Vienna, Austria

Brook Andrew has arrived in Vienna to start the research for the Kept in Silence *project with Katarina Matiasek. Over the next days, they browse Rudolf Pöch's original glass negatives and vintage prints taken during his tour of New South Wales in 1905. Despite their originally anthropometric setting, these images now radiate an immense beauty that temporarily alleviates the weight of history on the artists. They decide to make the repatriation of these little known photographs to the Aboriginal communities whose ancestors were portrayed an integral part of their project.*[74]

June 2014
Vienna, Austria

According to the final report of a research team appointed by the University and the city of Vienna to research and contextualise the naming of Vienna's streets since 1860, Rudolf Pöch exhibited problematic collecting activities. Due to his unlawful export of robbed remains of Indigenous Australians and of South African Khoe-San during his scientific expeditions, nurturing 'racial research' in Vienna, the street name Rudolf-Pöch-Gasse is rated as a 'case that necessitates discussion'.[73]

10th to 12th October 2014

Madrid, Spain

Between installing times of his Splinters of Monuments: A Solid Memory of the Forgotten Plains of our Trash and Obsessions *at Museo Reina Sofia, Brook Andrew contacts his mother. Veronica Andrew, a Wiradjuri woman, agrees to help locate community Elders of the Grafton area for consultation regarding the repatriation of the Pöch photographs. Katarina Matiasek compiles a list of all known persons and places from various archival sources she had researched during the inventorying of the different photographic media and sends it on to Madrid and Australia. Brook suggests making some enquiries into families who are related to the people on the list before sending a digital copy of the set of images to the community.*

4th June 2015

Melbourne, Australia

Brook Andrew writes to Vienna and to Grafton to introduce Roberta Skinner, a Gumbaynggirr woman from South Grafton that he has just talked to about the 'Grafton Home' photographs taken by Rudolf Pöch in 1905. Brook sends a small set of images to Roberta that she has never seen before. Roberta has been researching Aboriginal genealogy since 1995, and has been instrumental in a project that identified ancestors portrayed in the photographs of John William Lindt (1845–1926) held in the collection of the Grafton Regional Gallery. German born Lindt photographed the Clarence River and its local people three decades before Pöch. Still using the wet-plate process, Lindt produced iconic photographic albums in 1875 and 1876.[75]

22nd June 2015

Vienna to Viendorf and Obermallebarn, Austria

On a sunny day, Brook Andrew and Katarina Matiasek travel to Schönborn castle, the evacuation site where most of Rudolf Pöch's anthropological 'collection' had survived World War II. Today, the castle's grounds have been converted into a golf course, while the current Count Schönborn still resides behind the closed wooden shutters of the main building. Brook and Katarina travel the surrounding villages of Viendorf and Obermallebarn, knocking on doors of local homes to enquire about the sites where Vienna's hidden collections were scattered after their looting under Soviet occupation in the immediate after-war years. Finally, both Brook and Katarina stop the car and stand in front of an undulating, slightly sloping field filled with potato crops – it could just as easily have been here where five Indigenous remains from Australia's Northern Territory and one from New South Wales were lost. One of the skulls was still filled with eucalyptus bark – possibly originally looted from a traditional Aboriginal grave.

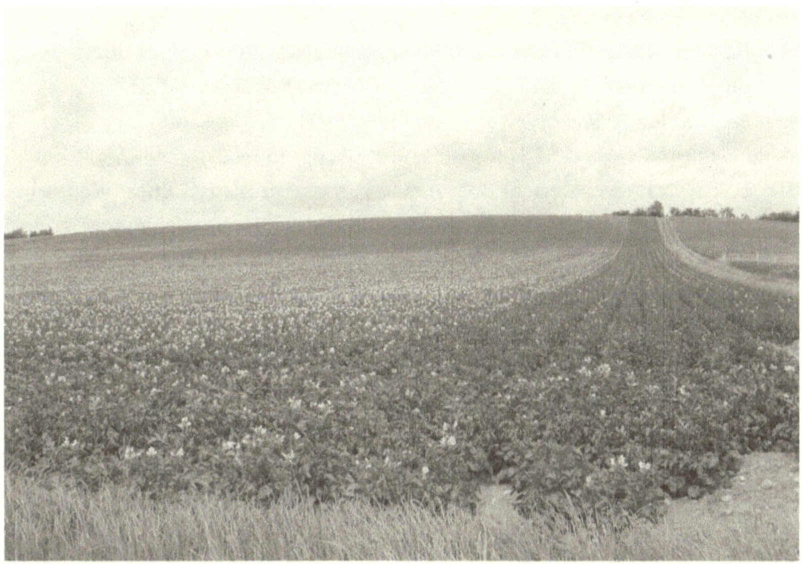

Figure 17.11: Katarina Matiasek, Field in Obermallebarn, *2014. Image courtesy of the artist, Vienna.*

Notes

1 *The Clarence and Richmond Examiner*, 15 November 1892, p. 8.
2 R. Etheridge, 'Ethnological notes made at Copmanhurst, Clarence River. I.

An aboriginal rock-shelter with an inscribed rockface. II. Disarticulation of one of the little finger joints', *Records of the Australian Museum*, vol. 5, no. 5, 1904, p. 271.

3 R. Pöch, 'Studien an Eingeborenen von Neu-Südwales und an australischen Schädeln', *Mitteilungen der Anthropologischen Gesellschaft in Wien*, vol. 45, 1915, pp. 18–19.

4 R. Pöch, 'Die Methoden der anthropologischen Photographie', *Photographische Korrespondenz*, vol. 54, no. 679, 1917, p. 137.

5 J. Weninger, 'Das Denkmal für Rudolf Pöch an der Wiener Universität', *Mitteilungen der Anthropologischen Gesellschaft in Wien*, vol. 63, 1933, p. 260.

6 M. Teschler-Nicola, 'Die Wiener Pest-Expedition 1897 – Rudolf Pöchs erste Forschungsreise', *Mitteilungen der Anthropologischen Gesellschaft in Wien*, vol. 136/137, 2006–07, pp. 75–105.

7 See Australian Museum website, viewed 22 November 2015, http://australianmuseum.net.au/indigenous-australia-timeline-1901-to-1969.

8 R. Pöch, 'Ergebnisse einer Reise längs der Küste von Senegambien und Oberguinea', *Archiv für Schiffs- und Tropenhygiene*, vol. 7, no. 3–4, 1903, pp. 125–46; pp. 153–72.

9 R. Pöch, 'Erster Bericht von meiner Reise nach Neu-Guinea über die Zeit vom 6. Juni 1904 bis zum 25. März 1905', *Sitzungsberichte der kaiserlichen Akademie der Wissenschaften in Wien, Mathematisch-Naturwissenschaftliche Klasse*, vol. 114, 1905, pp. 452–53.

10 R. Pöch, 'Dritter Bericht über meine Reise nach Neu-Guinea (Neu-Süd-Wales, vom 21. Juni 1905 bis 6. September 1905, Britisch-Salomonsinseln und Britisch-Neu-Guinea bis zum 31. Januar 1906)', *Sitzungsberichte der kaiserlichen Akademie der Wissenschaften in Wien, Mathematisch-Naturwissenschaftliche Klasse*, vol. 115, 1906, p. 603.

11 R. Pöch, *Notizbücher der Forschungsreise nach Neu-Guinea* (handwritten travel notebooks), Anthropological Department of the Museum of Natural History, Vienna (Inv. no. 14.036), 'Kleines Heft', no. 12, 1904–06, p. 2.

12 R. Pöch, 'Dritter Bericht über meine Reise nach Neu-Guinea', p. 603.

13 R. Pöch, 'Studien an Eingeborenen von Neu-Südwales und an australischen Schädeln', p. 13.

14 R. Pöch, 'Kleines Heft', no. 12, 1904–06, pp. 5–9.

15 R. Pöch, 'Kleines Heft', no. 13, 1904–06, p. 17.

16 ibid., p. 25.

17 R. Pöch 'Dritter Bericht über meine Reise nach Neu-Guinea', p. 601.

18 See also B. Lange, *Die Wiener Forschungen an Kriegsgefangenen 1915–1918. Anthropologische und ethnografische Verfahren im Lager*, Austrian Academy of Sciences, Vienna, 2011, pp. 87–91.

19 R. Pöch, 'Dritter Bericht über meine Reise nach Neu-Guinea', p. 601.

20 Letter by R. Pöch (manuscript, dated 12th November 1906), Archive of the Austrian Academy of Sciences, *Subventionen der mathematisch-naturwissenschaftlichen Klasse* (862/1906), p. 9.

21 E. Oberhummer, 'Rudolf Pöch (Obituary)', *Mitteilungen der Anthropologischen Gesellschaft in Wien*, vol. 51, 1921, p. 99.

22 See grant applications by R. Pöch 'Ansuchen um eine Subvention für eine Reise nach Süd-Afrika zum Zwecke des anthropologischen und ethnologischen Studiums der Buschmänner' (manuscript folder, dated 25 October 1906), Archive of the Austrian Academy of Sciences, *Subventionen der mathematisch-naturwissenschaftlichen Klasse* (862/1906).

23 R. Pöch (1907–1909) *Notizbücher der Forschungsreise nach Südafrika* (handwritten travel notebooks), Anthropological Department of the Museum of Natural History, Vienna (Inv. no. 14.037a), 'Kleines Heft', no. 12, p. 1110.

24 M. Teschler-Nicola, 'Rudolf Pöchs osteologische Lehr- und Forschungssammlung im Spannungsfeld von Wissenschaft und Ethik', *Mitteilungen der Anthropologischen Gesellschaft in Wien*, vol. 141, 2011, pp. 60–1.

25 See M. Legassick & C. Rassool, *Skeletons in the Cupboard: South African Museums and the Trade in Human Remains 1907–1917*, South African Museum and McGregor Museum, Cape Town & Kimberley, 2000; M. Teschler-Nicola, 'Rudolf Pöchs osteologische Lehr- und Forschungssammlung im Spannungsfeld von Wissenschaft und Ethik', pp. 51–66.

26 M. Berner, 'Die "rassenkundlichen" Untersuchungen der Wiener Anthropologen in Kriegsgefangenenlagern 1915–1918', *Zeitgeschichte*, vol. 30, no. 3, 2003, p. 125.

27 G. Ziegelmayer, 'Pöch, Rudolf (1870–1921)', in F. Spencer (ed.), *History of Physical Anthropology: An Encyclopedia*, vol. 2, M–Z, Garland, New York & London, 1997, p. 825.

28 R. Pöch, 'I. Bericht über die von der Wiener Anthropologischen Gesellschaft in den k. u. k. Kriegsgefangenenlagern veranlassten Studien', *Mitteilungen der Anthropologischen Gesellschaft in Wien*, vol. 45, 1915, p. 219.

29 M. Berner, 'Die "rassenkundlichen" Untersuchungen der Wiener Anthropologen in Kriegsgefangenenlagern 1915–1918', p. 126; B. Lange, *Die Wiener Forschungen an Kriegsgefangenen 1915–1918. Anthropologische und ethnografische Verfahren im Lager*, p. 110.

30 Grant application by R. Pöch (dated 2 July 1917), Archive of the Austrian Academy of Sciences, *Subventionen der mathematisch-naturwissenschaftlichen Klasse* (461/1917).

31 We wish to thank Anette Hoffmann, University of Fort Hare, South Africa, and Margit Berner, Museum of Natural History, Vienna, for their inquiry regarding Paul Panda Farnana that led to our discovery of his photograph in the Archive of the Department of Anthropology, University of Vienna.

32 M. Berner, 'Forschungs-"Material" Kriegsgefangene: Die Massenuntersuchungen der Wiener Anthropologen an gefangenen Soldaten 1915–1918', in H. E. Gabriel and W. Neugebauer (eds), *Vorreiter der Vernichtung? Eugenik, Rassenhygiene und Euthanasie in der österreichischen Diskussion vor 1938*, Böhlau, Vienna, 2005, p. 193.

33 G. Ziegelmayer, 'Pöch, Rudolf (1870–1921)', p. 825.

34 See R. Pöch, *Studien an Eingeborenen von Neu-Südwales und an australischen Schädeln: Inaugural-Dissertation zur Erlangung der Doktorwürde der hohen philosophischen Fakultät, II. Sektion der Königlich bayerischen Ludwig Maximilians-Universität zu München, am 23. Juni 1913 vorgelegt von Dr. med. Rudolf Pöch*, W. Hamburger, Munich and Vienna, 1915.

35 I. Ranzmaier, 'Ein Stolperstein für die Etablierung der Anthropologie und Ethnologie an der Universität Wien', in T. Brandstetter, D. Rupnow & C. Wessey (eds), *Sachunterricht. Fundstücke zur Wissenschaftsgeschichte*, Löcker, Vienna, 2008, pp. 31–5.

36 Testament of R. Pöch (dated 6th August 1920), Archive of the Austrian Academy of Sciences, *Pöch-Kommission*, Folder 1 (201/1921).

37 See Archive of the Austrian Academy of Sciences, Box *Pöch-Kommission*.

38 M. Berner, 'Die "rassenkundlichen" Untersuchungen der Wiener Anthropologen in Kriegsgefangenenlagern 1915–1918', p. 127.

39 *The Brisbane Courier*, 1 August 1925, p. 16.

40 H. Pöch, 'Beitrag zur Kenntnis des Muskelsystems und einiger Rassenmerkmale der Buschmänner', *Mitteilungen der Anthropologischen Gesellschaft in Wien* (Sitzungsberichte), vol. 57, 1926–7, pp. 108–12.

41 M. Legassick & C. Rassool, 'South African human remains, Viennese museums, and the politics of repatriation: Reconsidering the legacy of Rudolf Pöch', *The Life of the Corpse, WISER Symposium*, University of the Witwatersrand, Johannesburg, 2008.

42 K. Taschwer, '"Anthropologie ins Volk". Zur Ausstellungspolitik einer anwendbaren Wissenschaft bis 1945', in H. Posch & G. Fliedl (eds), *Politik der Präsentation: Museum und Ausstellung in* Österreich *1918–1945*, Turia & Kant, Vienna, 1996, pp. 248–51.

43 See V. Pietschmann, *Führer durch die Sonderschau 'Ostmarkdeutsche als Forscher und Sammler in unseren Kolonien': Ein Anteil der Ostmark an der Erforschung und Erschliessung der deutschen Kolonialgebiete*, Waldheim-Eberle, Vienna, 1940.

44 J. Wastl, 'Neu-Guinea, Land und Leute. Mit einer Lebensbeschreibung

des ostmärkischen Forschers Rudolf Pöch', in H. Kummerlöwe (ed.), *Wissenschaft ins Volk*, no. 1, p. 2, 1940.

45 B. Fuchs, *'Rasse', 'Volk', Geschlecht: anthropologische Diskurse in* Österreich *1850–1960*, Frankfurt am Main and New York: Campus, 2003, pp. 291–2.

46 B. Fuchs, 'Pöch, Hella', in B. Keintzel and U. Korotin (eds), *Wissenschafterinnen in und aus Österreich. Leben – Werk – Wirken*, Böhlau, Vienna, 2002, p. 589.

47 Archive of the Federal Monuments Office, *Restitutionsmaterialien*, Box 4/2 'Wiener Museen N–V', Folder 7 'Naturhistorisches Museum 1942–1949' (5470/1943), p. 31a.

48 H. *Haupt , Jahre der Gefährdung. Das Kunsthistorische Museum 1938–1945*, Private Publishing, Vienna, 1995, p. 19.

49 A. Keve & G. Rokitansky, 'Hofrat Dr. Moriz Sassi 1880–1967 (Obituary)', *Annalen des Naturhistorischen Museum Wien,* vol. 73, 1969, p. 7.

50 Archive of the Federal Monuments Office, *Restitutionsmaterialien*. Box 2 'Bergungen Niederösterreich R–T', Folder 66 'Schönborn' (2114/1945), p. 69.

51 Archive of the Federal Monuments Office, *Restitutionsmaterialien*. Box 2 'Bergungen Niederösterreich R–T', Folder 66 'Schönborn' (2013/1945), p. 60 and (31201/1946), p. 41.

52 Letter from Richard Oberlohr to Josef Weninger, Head of the Institute for Anthropology (dated 23 September 1945), Archive of the Department of Anthropology, University of Vienna.

53 Archive of the Federal Monuments Office, *Restitutionsmaterialien*. Box 2 'Bergungen Niederösterreich R–T', Folder 66 'Schönborn' (288/1946), p. 46.

54 Archive of the Federal Monuments Office, *Restitutionsmaterialien*. Box 2 'Bergungen Niederösterreich R–T', Folder 66 'Schönborn' (31413/1946), p. 36.

55 See 'Meldezettel Dr. Pöch, Hella' (issued 30 April 1940, officially cancelled 17 April 1947), Magistrate of the City of Salzburg, *City Archive and Statistics*.

56 B. Fuchs, 'Pöch, Hella', p. 589.

57 B. Fuchs, *'Rasse', 'Volk', Geschlecht: anthropologische Diskurse in Österreich 1850–1960*, p. 355.

58 A. A. Abbie, 'Rudolf Pöch', *Oceania*, vol. 33, 1962, pp. 128–30.

59 See special print offered by F. Wagenseil (dated 11 December 1964), Archive of the Austrian Academy of Sciences, *Pöch-Kommission*, Folder 3 (1661/1964).

60 See M. Unger, *Der Anatom Ferdinand Wagenseil (1887–1967). Integrer Rassenforscher und Bewahrer der Medizinischen Fakultät Giessen*, Wilhelm Schmitz, Giessen, 1998.

61 A. Harrasser, 'Die Gesichtsmuskulatur eines Melanesiers in ihren Beziehungen zu Innervation und Gefässverlauf', *Verhandlungen der Gesellschaft für Physische Anthropologie*, vol. 7, 1935, pp. 12–27.

62 F. Wagenseil, 'Die mimische und Kau-Muskulatur zweier Melanesier', *Anthropologischer Anzeiger*, vol. 27, 1964, pp. 143–61.

63 Grant application by H. Pöch (dated 1968), Archive of the Austrian Academy of Sciences, *Subventionen der mathematisch-naturwissenschaftlichen Klasse* (106/1968).

64 J. Szilvássy, P. Spindler and H. Kritscher, 'Rudolf Pöch: Arzt, Anthropologe und Ethnograph', *Annalen des Naturhistorischen Museums in Wien*, vol. 83, 1980, p. 743.

65 Archive of the Austrian Academy of Sciences, *Pöch-Kommission*, Folder 3 (1306/1982).

66 See the research project 'Rudolf Pöch: A Scientific Pioneer' under the direction of Maria Teschler-Nicola and Harald Wilfing, funded by the Austrian Science Fund (FWF P17761-G6, 2005–2007).

67 K. Matiasek, 'Die Pionierfrage – Rudolf Pöchs Einsatz von Bildmedien' in M. Teschler-Nicola, T. Ballhausen & K. Matiasek (eds), *Archivhorizonte – Wissenslandschaften und Perspektivgrenzen im multimedialen Nachlass des Anthropologen und Forschungsreisenden Rudolf Pöch*, Löcker, Vienna, in print.

68 The delegation was composed of Reverend Lenore Parker, Elder of the Yaegl Community, Chrissy Doherty, Traditional Owner of the Butchulla and the Woppaburra, Bill Risk, Elder and custodian of the Larrakia nation, Elaine Ohlsen, Elder and custodian of the Wangaaypuwan and Ngiyampaa nations, and Narelle Lyons, Wiradjuri custodian for the Eora nation.

69 See R. Pöch, 'Studien an Eingeborenen von Neu-Südwales und an australischen Schädeln', pp. 12–94.

70 See the exhibition catalogue What, How and for Whom (ed.), *Really Useful Knowledge*, Museo Nacional Centro de Arte Reina Sofia, Madrid, 2014.

71 We wish to thank David Kaus of the National Museum of Australia in Canberra for helpful biographical information on Walter Richard Harper.

72 See H. von Lippa, *Oben und Unten – Zwanzig Jahre in Australien*, Carl Konegen, Vienna, 1912.

73 P. Autengruber, B. Nemec, O. Rathkolb & F. Wenninger, *Umstrittene Wiener Strassennamen: Ein kritisches Lesebuch*, Pichler, Vienna, 2014, p. 52.

74 We wish to thank Harald Wilfing, Head of the Department of Anthropology at the University of Vienna for his institutional and personal support of this project, and also for his permission to reprint Rudolf Pöch's photographs in the present publication.

75 See V. Frost, 'Lindt, John William (1845–1926)', in D. Pike (ed.), *Australian*

Dictionary of Biography, vol. 5, Melbourne University Press, Melbourne, 1974, pp. 89–90.

18

AFTERWORD: DIAGRAMMATIC AND DATABASE DREAMINGS

Darren Jorgensen

When the nineteenth-century Australian artist Tommy McRae filled drawing books with pictures of dancing, fishing and hunting in the nineteenth century, he told his colonial collectors and commissioners what to write on them so that his subjects would not be misunderstood. It is tempting to read McRae's titles, such as *Aborigine chasing Chinese man*, as eyewitness accounts of his times, pictures of life in nineteenth-century Australia. The colonial Chinese, however, with their braided hair and shouldered buckets, were unlikely to have been chased across the landscape by axe-wielding Aboriginal men.

Carol Cooper and James Urry argue that these caricatures were designed to appeal to a European sense of humour,[1] but this was surely a shared joke, invented in a cross-cultural dialogue between McRae and his collaborator. In this collaboration, McRae inaugurated a genre of annotation that would be taken up by ethnographers and art advisors in the twentieth century. The shift from ethnography to art took place when Geoffrey Bardon entered into a shared joke with the artists at the Papunya settlement when he asked for 'children's learning stories' to assist his own education in the Dreaming.[2] Bardon documented the paintings on separate pages, moving information off the item itself to inaugurate a new genre of Dreaming, in annotated diagrams that schematised the painting's designs.[3] Such handwritten and carefully drawn and typed archives guide the eye into what Nancy Munn called a 'system of denotative signs' among desert people.[4]

Since the bloom of art centres across the Australian desert, the enthusiasm of artists and art advisors alike has left us a body of annotated diagrams and stories explicating the paintings of remote Australia. This period of diagrammatic Dreaming came to an end around 1998, when a second period of digital archiving commences with the arrival of computers in remote communities. These new systems combine text, photographic images and sometimes video footage, but do not have space for the hand-drawn diagrams that were once customary in the documentation of paintings. Instead, these databases established a standard set of Dreamings that are cut and pasted across multiple documents. The digital Dreamings of this latter period of art centre history are impoverished compared to the earlier, interpersonal diagrammatic period, as databases freed artists from having to explain each painting in turn. They were no longer obliged to create iconic, informational paintings, and the twenty-first century is marked by the rise of abstract paintings instead.

The first, diagrammatic period of documenting Dreamings began with ethnographers travelling through remote Australia. Many had taken paper and crayons with them to open a visual window onto the world of the Dreaming. Some of the Papunya artists saw these ethnographers at work. In the 1930s, young boys who would go on to become artists with Bardon at Papunya saw Norman Tindale commission drawings on brown paper at Mt Leibig (Yamunturrngu), near the present-day settlement of Haasts Bluff.[5] In the 1960s, Papunya artist Dinny Nolan Tjampitjinpa was in the Warburton Ranges when the archaeologist Richard Gould recruited a group of men to draw for him, and his drawings are annotated with the names of each site on the Tingarri Tjukurrpa

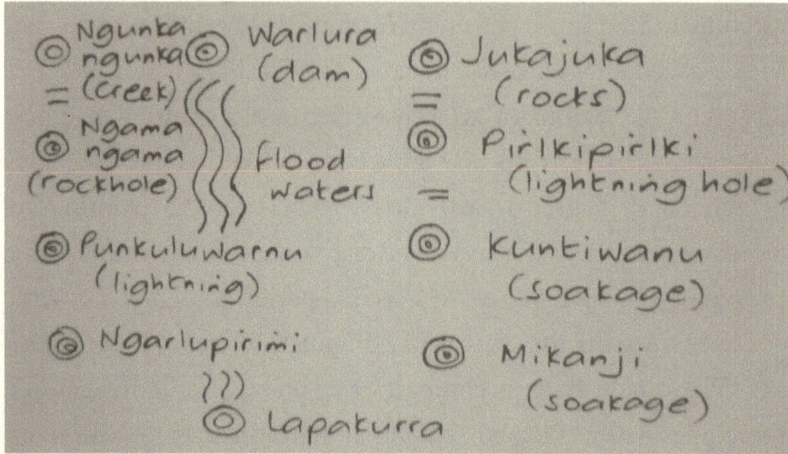

Figure 18.1: A typical diagram from a Warlukurlangu certificate of authenticity, including diagrams of parallel sinewy lines here meaning 'flood waters'.

as it extends south, along the route that the men had just walked. Gould, like many other ethnographers, was careful to annotate Nolan's diagrams with arrows and transliterations in tiny letters on the drawing paper.

The history of ethnographic diagramming in the Australian desert culminates with the publication of Nancy Munn's study *Walbiri Iconography: Graphic Representation and Cultural Symbolism in a Central Australian Society* (1973). Here Munn generalised desert designs into a system of graphic language. Munn is careful not to be too specific about what desert icons represent, and instead emphasises the way that graphemes can convey multiple meanings. A line might signify a spear, fighting stick, digging stick, or a person lying down.[6] She knew that the context for these drawings was significant in constructing their meaning, as their elements functioned amidst a greater story, a complex ethnic context.

Munn's interpretations emphasise the communal nature of visual language, the way that designs were shared in a co-operative organisation of kin.[7] With the coming of art coordinators rather than ethnographers, such communalism would give way to increasing individualism, as artists modified a shared graphic language through a developing body of work, an *oeuvre* that stood apart from other artists.

The beginnings of an art centre in the Warlpiri capital of Yuendumu in the mid-1980s shows how designs are constituted individually as much as communally, and how these designs come into being in a diagrammatic relationship with art coordinators. The earliest art coordinator for Warlukurlangu Artists was Felicity Wright, who documented an assortment of meanings for several motifs that the artists had in common. The most distinctive of these motifs is made up of sinewy parallel lines, that snake across many of these early compositions. In Munn's iconographic system, this motif is described in terms of a storm, meaning rain, lightning and rainbow.[8] However, at Warlukurlangu the meaning of these lines varies both within an artist's *oeuvre*, and between artists.

In Judy Napangardi Watson's earliest documented painting, *Janyinki Jukurrpa/Janyinki Dreaming* (1986), the archives at Warlukurlangu inform us that the sinewy line 'represents paths taken by women between sites'. In a second painting, *Karnakurlangu Jukurrpa* (1986), Watson clarifies the way that these lines are in fact *ngalyipi*, the snake vine that women gather as they travel. To these meanings of sinewy lines, we can add the fact that Walpiri women use *ngalyipi* to make shoulder straps to help carry *ngami* (water carriers) and *parraja* (food carriers). So that across and within Watson's work these lines hold all of these meanings at once.

Other artists working in the early years of Warlukurlangu also use the motif, including Paddy Nelson, Shorty Jangala Robertson, Paddy Japaljarri Sims and Paddy Stewart Japaljarri, and for each of these artists they signify different things. Robertson is the most consistent in describing his lines as water of one kind or another, yet even here the precise meaning of this water is multiple, as it stands for both *ngawarra* or flooded waters and the track of the *Ngapa Tjukurrpa* (Water Dreaming).

For Sims's work, the earliest meaning of the sinewy line is fire, specifically fire that drives *liwirringki* (burrowing skinks) from their holes to be killed for food. These fires burn through snake plain country, so that the sinewy line also represents the movement of snakes. The motif distinguishes Warlukurlangu from other art centres of this time, including the Papunya artists, many of whom who had by then moved to Kintore to the south-west.

In distinguishing art from its information, Bardon reified desert expressions into a beauty unburdened by knowledge. The object became privileged above and beyond its significations, and defined the place of the art advisor or coordinator on remote communities. So that at Walayirti Artists at Balgo, John Carty goes so far as to argue that the artists thought of themselves '*working for* the art coordinator' rather than for the distant network that supports and sells their paintings.[9] So too in the early years of Warlukurlangu in Yuendumu, Francoise Dussart reports that artists saw the art coordinator serving 'as *de facto* stand-in for non-indigenous audiences and more broadly the state'.[10]

The artists in Papunya in 1971 and 1972 had similar ideas about Bardon, going so far as to hold him responsible when money was not forthcoming from sales.[11] Such relationships could be intense and intimate. Bardon's successor John Kean recalls watching the Papunya artist Johnny Warangula Tjupurrula as he performed in order to document a painting, which comes to life as 'extravagant gestures and the signs on the canvas to which he referred'.[12] So it was that the paintings, as important as they were in themselves, also anticipated this intimate relationship, this collaborative documentation, this diagrammatic relationship to the work of art.

It is then no wonder then that the early Papunya paintings have become renowned for their powerful designs. Constituted in anticipation of becoming a diagram of themselves, schematised in anticipation of their own schematisation, the diagram is constitutive of their form.

This is to reverse the assumption that these diagrams were created to explain the paintings and their subjects, to act as prostheses for the works of art. Instead, the diagram does not explicate but double, dissimulating what it describes and creating another, distinct order of being.[13] So it was with the early Papunya paintings, whose icons were diagrammed out from their place on bodies, rocks and sand, and diagrammed once more into Bardon's documentation. Their diagrams were doubled and then tripled, their designs resonating though repetition.

Artworks

Catalog No	Category	Artwork Size	Title	Description	Status	Artwork
09-1288	Painting	61 x 80 cm acryl	The Seven Sisters	This is a popular dreamtime story of seven ladies being chase	Sold	
09-1130	Painting	60 x 90cm; acryl	The Seven Sisters	This is a popular dreamtime story of seven ladies being chase	Sold	
09-1097	Painting	65 x 65cm; acryl	The Seven Sisters	This is a popular dreamtime story of seven ladies being chase	Sold	
09-1022	Painting	50 x 83.5cm; ac	The Seven Sisters	This is a popular dreamtime story of seven ladies being chase	Sold	
09-999	Painting	60 x 101cm; acr	The Seven Sisters	This is a popular dreamtime story of seven ladies being chase	Sold	
09-929	Painting	50 x 83.5cm; ac	The Seven Sisters	This is a popular dreamtime story of seven ladies being chase	Sold	
09-893	Painting	76 x 51cm; acryl	The Seven Sisters	This is a popular dreamtime story of seven ladies being chase	Sold	
09-810	Painting	45.5 x 152cm; a	The Seven Sisters	This is a popular dreamtime story of seven ladies being chase	Sold	
09-770	Painting	100 x 100cm; ac	The Seven Sisters	This is a popular dreamtime story of seven ladies being chase	Sold	
09-758	Painting	40 x 49cm; acryl	The Seven Sisters	This is a popular dreamtime story of seven ladies being chase	Sold	

Figure 18.2: A listing of artworks on the Stories Art Money database.

This period of diagrammatic Dreaming came to an end across the desert after 1998, as art centres adopted computer-based databases as archiving and documenting systems. Of these new systems the most common was the Artists Management System (AMS). First developed at Warlayirti Artists in Wirrimanu (Balgo) in 1998, it was subsequently licensed across the country, and has since undergone a revamp to become known as Stories Art Money (SAM). These digital systems no longer accommodated the diagram, marking the end of the diagrammatic period of remote desert art, and the particular quality of collaborative relationships between artists and ethnographers, artists and art coordinators.

The second reason behind the loss of diagrams in the twenty-first century lies in a boom in the production of paintings, as the number of artworks from art centres increased around fifty per cent.[14] With pressures on artists and art coordinators alike, databases of Dreaming stories became the *de facto* titles and explications of paintings, a virtual repository from which predetermined genres of painting were actualised. Whatever they painted, artists knew that their work would become a part of the Dreaming, digital fields populated by predetermined text. At Warlukurlangu the 'Title' field of the archive was replaced by a 'Dreaming' field, literally merging the database with the Dreaming.

In the absence of secondary diagrams, there was no need for artists to explicate the individual elements of their paintings, no need to emphasise iconography on the canvas. This is why paintings across the desert, from Balgo to Yeundumu, tended toward abstraction in the twenty-first century.

Take, for example, the painting movement at Balgo, where comprehensive studies were undertaken in both the 1990s and in the 2000s. Christine Watson's *Piercing the Ground* (2003), based on fieldwork undertaken during the 1990s, is illustrated with an extensive guide to the icons of these artists.[15] Watson remains a scholar of the diagrammatic, but by the twenty-first century John Carty's doctoral thesis, 'Creating Country' can no longer rely on iconography in Balgo paintings, and instead traces the emergence of abstraction in the twenty-first century.[16]

This shift to more abstract painting coincides with digital documentation among Ngaanyatjarra painters, too. While the Warburton Arts Project of the late 1980s and early 1990s is marked by its detailed transcription of Dreamings, in the 2000s the founding of Ngaanyatjarra art centres brought about a shift to dotted abstractions. The first Aboriginal artist to be acclaimed for her abstraction, although not the first abstract Aboriginal artist, was one who worked with minimal documentation, and whose designs were never diagrammed. Painting through the early 1990s, Emily Kame Kngwarreye was free from the conditions that bound many other artists to an archive. Working without the support of an art centre, and for a variety of agents whose documentation was often scant, Kngwarreye anticipated the boom of abstract rather than iconographic painting in the deserts of Australia. So it is that Carty's argument that abstraction emerged at Balgo as a part of a formal development of family styles is one that can also be understood in terms of the more general conditions within which artists are working.

The consequences of this shift to digital documentation is not only implicit in Carty's study. Jennifer Biddle's *Breasts, Bodies, Canvas* (2007) is an analysis of *kuruwarri*, a Warlpiri term that describes mark making in sand, on bodies and on canvas among Warlpiri artists.[17] It grapples with many of the social features of life in the desert that both Munn and Watson theorised before her, but Biddle's study departs from iconographic analysis. Instead, Biddle inscribes *kuruwarri* into a phenomenology of affect that wants to capture the 'pre- or extra-linguistic level, prior to, or outside the normative and structured constraints of language, discourse, history, culture'.[18]

This shift away from reading signs while firmly grounded in ethnography and a visual analysis of Warlpiri arts can be read as a product of the digital era, characterised by what Mark Poster calls 'underdetermination', in which the relationship of subject to object, of people to information, is so immensely complex our means of understanding it can only be vague.[19] So it is that Biddle is critical of an 'overdetermined signified, of *kuruwarri* signs being the literal cartographic country itself'.[20]

Poster proposes that instead of this sort of literalism, objects in the twenty-first century 'do not direct agents into clear paths; they solicit instead social construction and cultural creation'.[21] So it is that Biddle's use of 'affect' recreates the Dreaming as sensual abstraction. As paintings have become less about their signification, less oriented to their secondary documentation, their aesthetic has become more obtuse, their precise subject more difficult to discern. The stories that accompany the paintings come to assume a character of solicitation rather than explanation. The Dreaming becomes extra-linguistic, extra-iconographic, and the relationship between painting and Dreaming can only be made, to borrow Biddle's terms, in a 'chiasmatic meeting' in which the two are intertwined, but are not the same thing.[22]

Art centre databases are certainly representative of this underdetermination of the Dreaming, as vague accounts of the Seven Sisters, the Tingarri or other Dreamings come to stand for a raft of paintings by different artists, and each of which relate to different sites. These stories constitute a kind of meta-Dreaming, as their generality rises from the desert like Hellenic myths, with characters playing out epochal, world creating actions that condemn them to live forever embedded within the country. The art centre database is recursive, an engine by which these meta-Dreaming stories reproduce themselves.

The tension between the underdetermined and overdetermined, meta-Dreamings and their more particular manifestation in personalities and the land itself, played itself out in a recent dispute over the documentation of the Ngintaka Dreaming by the Songlines of the Western Desert project.[23] Songlines is a cultural mapping exercise that includes art making and exhibitions.

The controversy revolved around an exhibition and book about the Ngintaka, a cheeky lizard that steals a grinding stone and is pursued across the desert.[24] One custodian of the Ngintaka story refused to be a part of the Ngintaka project, keeping his part of the story out of this synthesis of the Dreaming, and initiating legal action against Ananguku Arts for its part in the project.[25] Here the Yankunytjatjara statesman Yami Lester assumes the cheeky pose of the Ngintaka itself, for as he explains in his autobiography:

> I'm a *ngintaka*...I was born at Walyatjata, near the waterhole there, Wallatina Waterhole. They hold me, maybe if I want to, I might be *malu*, that kangaroo, because it's close by. But the more they thought about it, they said, that *ngintaka* was mine. Me. It was like that.[26]

Here Lester explains that he does not represent the *ngintaka*, but that he himself is this Dreaming, that he performs it in being himself. So it is that the *ngintaka* character recreates itself in this cheeky legal move. Lester also illuminates the way that the Dreaming is created and recreated in each of its iterations. His opposition to the project performs a kind of poststructuralism of the *tjukurrpa*, as he highlights the way that the Dreaming is constituted by internal differences as much as continuities.

Yet there are also historical reasons why Lester is opposed to the very creation of such a meta-Dreaming. For he has been a central player in the Land Rights movement of South Australia, and has seen the ways in which what Jacques Derrida calls the 'archive fever' of Western society, the push to document desert culture, entails the destruction of this Dreaming archive's authority.[27] As he writes:

> Sometimes I wonder why Aboriginal people always have to justify themselves, prove themselves to white people. Not just with land rights, but on all kinds of things. You know, I think life is more easy for white people. They don't have to try and prove who they are, where they come from, what language they speak.[28]

The interest in archiving Aboriginality, whether it be in documenting the Dreaming in the Native Title process or recording oral testimony of massacres or the experience of Stolen Generations, has led to disputes as to the authority of Aboriginal accounts. In each case, the development of archives around Dreamings and Aboriginal histories have proved Derrida's point that the impulse to archive, 'archive fever', erases the authority of that which is in the archive.

Derrida argues that the unconscious of the 'archive drive' is a death drive that wants to erase the authority of the knowledge that it also represents. For the archive is constructed from a process of selection, of radical finitude, that in constructing its limits subjects itself to the aggression of the infinite.[29] This was certainly the case for Sigmund Freud, whose writings Derrida is addressing, and who listened to the accounts of his patients only to erase their own voices to establish his own ideas about what they were saying, to the infinite possibilities of the unconscious. In archiving their testimony, Freud erased the authority of these voices.

Derrida's most troubling example around remembering and archiving these memories is the state of Israel, which establishes its identity on the imperative not to forget historical wrongs, yet in this act of remembering erases the authority that these wrongs afford it.[30] As he writes: 'The gathering into itself of the One is never without violence, nor is the self-affirmation of the Unique, the law of the archontic, the law of *consignation* which orders the archive'.[31]

Such is the paradox that Lester and other Aboriginal activists face. In consigning to the archive, they erase the very authority that the archive presumes to give them. In Derrida's terms, they subject their assignation to a consignation, to the infinite regress of meaning that takes place in the archival text.[32]

So it is that Lester stands as Australia's equivalent of the historian poet Homer, who thought that the universe was a domain ruled by the passions of the Gods. Homer stands before the era of the great Greek philosophers, Socrates and Plato, who wanted to rise above the oral culture of mythology to reason out the ethical terms for a good society. Ultimately, it was Plato who created a template for classical thinking with his ideal world, of which our world is but a fallen version.

Art is even further down the line of simulations for Plato, a simulation of third degree, a copy of a copy.[33] Lester turns this classical philosophy on its head, echoing Gilles Deleuze's critique of Platonic idealism, arguing that although one thing might look like another, their divergence is more fundamental than their likeness. Deleuze compares this kind of simulation of the same to Nietzsche's eternal return, as the arrival of the same comes about only because of its difference from what came before.[34] So that rather than describing a continuity, the recurrence of the *Ngintaka* Dreaming testifies to its difference from itself.

Such differences are at play within the artworks in the *Ngintaka* exhibition itself. Among the works in the *Ngintaka* exhibition was Billy Wara's only known painting, *Ngintaka–Perentie Lizard* (2007), as well as examples of his *punu*, his carving. Wara was a fine carver, not only of *ngintaka*, but of snakes, spears and spearthrowers. To make his carvings, Wara looked at the trees growing in the desert, and picked specially shaped roots that already look like the animals themselves. His snakes are distinct because they are so complex in shape, arching around themselves as if they are in motion. His *ngintaka* are similarly invested with life, their heads often raised like the animal itself, peering from sightlines in the landscape to tease hungry desert people with its presence. So it is that, in Platonic terms, there is this ideal character of a lizard, whose personality embodies many anthropomorphic shapes.

Yet Wara's carvings come from the ground itself, each piece of wood being different from the other, and each manifestation of *ngintaka* expressing a difference in itself. They are also produced out of the material of the ground itself, the resemblance of wooden shapes to the lizard a resemblance without repetition. In the various *ngintaka*, Wara expresses a transcendental immanence, as ideal forms arise from within the material world.

Wara illuminates how it is that the Dreaming acts to break the tense deadlock between its generalisation its local manifestations. For the Dreaming cannot be turned into a Platonic ideal or kept secret by any one custodian. The archive of the Dreaming lies, for Wara, in the trees, which are slowly but surely changing around him in the landscape. And like the trees, the stories of the Dreaming are all different from each other, appearing and disappearing in a landscape of information.

So it is that the digital Dreamings of art centres, in which Dreamings are repeated through multiple certificates of authenticity, multiple authorities, come to represent no authority at all. In Nietzschean terms they do not represent a difference that is sufficient to stage a true return of the Dreaming. They are instead a simulacra whose original and originality they erase, their enunciation not concealing or revealing through expression, but obfuscating and undifferentiating in simulation.[35] For if the archive determines the possibilities of what can be said, it does so not because possibility of saying is finite, but because what is said exists in a differential relation to what has already been said.

These are the differences at work in the era of diagrammatic documentation, during the 1970s, 1980s and 1990s, in which the transformation of each document testified to the differences at work in personalities and places, the way that the *tjukurrpa* appears and reappears in all of its complexity and variety. In the twenty-first century the Dreaming goes from being iconographic to abstract, from handwritten archive to the database, from diagrammatic to chiasmic. As engines of art practice, the diagram and database dissimulate the Dreaming in historically distinct ways, creating different orders of the archive. While the first was tied to ethnographic entanglements and iconographic idiosyncrasies, the second tends to create meta-Dreamings that gloss over the complexities of the *tjukurrpa.*

However, this second digital archive has also freed desert painting from its iconography, allowing a less determinate relationship between desert painting and Dreaming, and enabling artists a freedom of expression that neither conceals nor reveals.

It has, then, been the ultimate irony of the digital that rather than clarifying the tjukurrpa, the digital has turned it into a vast metaphysics that bears little relation to its details. This, not only in relation to the rise in abstract painting, but also in the rise of a political, decolonising art of the twenty-first century, the art explored in the fourth section of this book. Here too the digital archive does not clarify but makes murky the relations of Aboriginality to its representations, the archive to history. The traffic of figures, signs and remains appears as unreal as any abstraction, yet this is a dream from which we are yet to awaken, as the metaphysics of race and the archive play themselves out across the centuries.

Acknowledgements

With thanks to Cecilia Alfonso, manager of Warlukurlangu Artists Aboriginal Corporation, for her generosity and hospitality in the writing of this paper. Thanks too to Clive Scollay for introducing me to the work of Billy Wara, and to David Brooks, with whom I have worked through many of the ideas in this paper but who is not responsible for them.

Notes

1 C. Cooper & J. Urry, 'Art, Aborigines and Chinese: a nineteenth century drawing by the Kwaltkwat artist Tommy McRae', *Aboriginal History* 5.1, pp. 81–8 at 85–6.

2 G. Bardon & J. Bardon, *Papunya: A Place Made after the Story: The Beginnings of the Western Desert Painting Movement,* Lund Humphries, Aldershot, UK, 2006, p. 64.

3 See ibid. for the most extensive reproduction of this documentation.

4 N. Munn, *Walbiri Iconography: Graphic Representation and Cultural Symbolism in a Central Australian Society*, Cornell University Press, Ithaca, 1973, p. 4.

5 J. Kean, 'Johnny Warangula Tjupurrula: history, landscape and La Niña', this volume, p. 145.

6 ibid., p. 64.

7 ibid., pp. 89–90.

8 ibid., p. 170.

9 J. Carty, 'Creating Country: Abstraction, Economics and the Social Life of Style in Balgo Art', PhD, Australian National University, Canberra, 2011, p. 191.

10 F. Dussart, 'Canvassing Identities: Reflecting on the acrylic art movement in an Australian Aboriginal settlement', *Aboriginal History,* no. 30, pp. 156–68 at 159.

11 G. Bardon, *Papunya Tula: Art of the Western Desert,* McPhee Gribble, Melbourne, 1991, pp. 43–5.

12 J. Kean, 'Johnny Warangula Tjupurrula: history, landscape and La Niña',

essay this volume.

13 G. Deleuze & F. Guattari, *A Thousand Plateaus*, trans. B. Massumi, University of Minnesota Press, Minneapolis, 1987, pp. 141–8.

14 T. Acker & A. Woodhead, 'Art Economies Value Chain Report: Artists and Art Centre Production', report for Ninti One Cooperative Research Centre for Remote Economic Participation, Adelaide, 2014, p. 15.

15 C. Watson, *Piercing the Ground*, Fremantle Arts Centre Press, Fremantle, 2003.

16 J. Carty, 'Creating Country: Abstraction, Economics and the Social Life of Style in Balgo Art'.

17 J. Biddle, *Breasts, Bodies, Canvas: Central Desert Art as Experience*, UNSW Press, Sydney, 2007.

18 ibid., p. 16.

19 M. Poster, *What's the Matter with the Internet?*, University of Minnesota Press, Minneapolis, 2001, pp. 1–20.

20 J. Biddle, *Breasts*, p. 59.

21 M. Poster, *What's the Matter*, p. 17

22 J. Biddle, *Breasts*, p. 104.

23 S. Rintoul, 'Songline at heart of secret men's business', *The Australian*, 19 May 2012.

24 The *Ngintaka* exhibition was held at the South Australian Museum in 2014. The book is the catalogue for the exhibition, D. James & E. Tregenza (eds), *Ngintaka*, Wakefield Press, Adelaide, 2014.

25 See the Songlines documentation of this case and associated meetings, viewed 15 December 2015, < http://archanth.anu.edu.au/heritage-museum-studies/songlines-western-desert/cultural-governance>.

26 Y. Lester, *Yami: The Autobiography of Yami Lester*, IAD Press, Alice Springs, 2000, p. 9.

27 J. Derrida, *Archive Fever: A Freudian Impression*, trans. Eric Prenowitz, Chicago, University of Chicago Press, 1998.

28 Y. Lester, *Yami*, p. 143.

29 J. Derrida, *Archive Fever*, p. 19

30 ibid., pp. 76–7.

31 ibid., pp. 78–9.

32 ibid., p. 81.

33 Plato, *The Republic*, trans. Benjamin Jowett, 1892, Book 10, viewed 23 October 2015, <http://classics.mit.edu/Plato/republic.11.x.html>.

34 G. Deleuze, 'Plato and the Simulacrum,' trans. R. Krauss, *October no. 27*, Winter 1983, pp. 45–56 at 54.

35 See M. Foucault on concealing and revealing in *The Archaeology of*

Knowledge and the Discourse on Language, trans. A. M. Sheridan Smith, New

York, Pantheon Books, 1972, pp. 128–30.

BIBLIOGRAPHY

Abbas, B. & R. Abou-Rahme, 'The Archival Multitude: Basel Abbas and Ruanne Abou-Rahme (in Conversation with Tom Holert)', *Journal of Visual Culture*, vol. 12, no. 3, December 2013.

Abbie, A. A., 'Rudolf Pöch', *Oceania*, vol. 33, 1962.

Acker, T. & A. Woodhead, 'Art Economies Value Chain Report: Artists and Art Centre Production', report for Ninti One Cooperative Research Centre for Remote Economic Participation, Adelaide, 2014.

Ah Kee, V., Interview with R. Sorenson, 'The Face: Vernon Ah Kee', *The Australian*, July 12 2008, <http://www.theaustralian.com.au/arts/the-face-vernon-ah-kee/story-e6frg8n6-1111116855996>.

Ah Kee, V., Interview with G. Barkley, in *Borninthisskin: Vernon Ah Kee*, exhibition catalogue, Institute of Modern Art, Brisbane, 2009.

Aird, M., *Portraits of Our Elders*, Queensland Museum, Brisbane, 1993.

Akerman, K., 'The Renascence of Aboriginal Law in the Kimberleys', in R. and C. Berndt (eds), *Aborigines of the West; their past and present*, University of Western Australia Press, Perth, 1979.

Akerman, K., untitled catalogue entry for 'Lot 42' and 'Lot 43', *Mossgreen Auction Catalogue: The Marc and Elena Pinto Collection, Melbourne 20 May 2015*, Mossgreen, Melbourne, 2015.

Akerman, K. & J. Stanton, *Riji and Jakuli: Kimberley pearl shell in Aboriginal Australia*, Northern Territory Museum of Arts and Sciences, Darwin, 1994.

Albrecht, F. W., 'Hermannsburg from 1926 to 1962', in E. Leske (ed.), *Hermannsburg: A Vision and a Mission*, Lutheran Publishing House, Adelaide, 1977.

Altman, J., 'John Mawurndjul: Art and Impact', *Art Monthly Australia*, no. 225.

Anderson, W., *The Cultivation of Whiteness: Science, Health, and Racial Destiny in Australia*, Duke University Press, North Carolina, 2006.

Andrew, B., 'Come into the light', in *The Island Catalogue*, Museum of Archaeology and Anthropology, Cambridge, 2007.

Andrew, B., 'Remember How we See: The Island', in Harry Allen (ed.), *Australia: William Blandowski's Illustrated Encyclopaedia*, Aboriginal Studies Press, Canberra, 2010.

A<u>r</u>a Irititja, '*Nganampa warka*: Annual Report to Pitjantjatjara Council, APY and all Anangu', December 2015.

A<u>r</u>a Irititja, 'Who are we?', <http://www.irititja.com/about_ara_irititja/who_are_we.html>.

Archive of the Austrian Academy of Sciences, *Pöch-Kommission*.

Archive of the Austrian Academy of Sciences, *Pöch-Kommission*, Folder 3 (1306/1982).

Archive of the Federal Monuments Office, *Restitutionsmaterialien*, Box 4/2 'Wiener Museen N–V', Folder 7 'Naturhistorisches Museum 1942–1949' (5470/1943).

Archive of the Federal Monuments Office, *Restitutionsmaterialien*. Box 2 'Bergungen Niederösterreich R–T', Folder 66 'Schönborn' (288/1946).

Arni, C., '"Moi seule", 1833: Feminist Subjectivity, Temporality, and Historical Interpretation', *History of the Present*, vol. 2, no. 2, 2012.

Art and Soul, documentary, dir. Warwick Thornton, Screen Australia and Hibiscus Films, 2010.

Australian Museum, website, http://australianmuseum.net.au/indigenous-australia-timeline-1901-to-1969.

Autengruber, P, B. Nemec, O. Rathkolb & F. Wenninger, *Umstrittene Wiener Strassennamen: Ein kritisches Lesebuch*, Pichler, Vienna, 2014.

Bamblett, L., 'Picture Who We Are: Representations of Identity and the Appropriation of Photographs into a Wiradjuri Oral History Tradition', in J. Lydon (ed.), *Calling the Shots: Aboriginal Photographies*, Aboriginal Studies Press, Canberra, 2014.

Bardon, G., *Aboriginal Art of the Western Desert*, Rigby, Adelaide, 1979.

Bardon, G., *Papunya Tula: Art of the Western Desert*, McPhee Gribble, Melbourne, 1991.

Bardon, G. & J. Bardon, *Papunya, A Place Made After the Story: the beginnings of the Western Desert Painting Movement*, Miegunyah Press, Carlton, 2004.

Barrett, J. & J. Millner, *Australian Artists in the Contemporary Museum*, Ashgate, Farnham Surrey, 2014.

Battarbee, R., *Modern Australian Aboriginal Art*, Angus & Robertson, Sydney, 1951.

Batty, P. (ed.), *Colliding Worlds: First Contact in the Western Desert 1932–1984*, Museum Victoria Publishing, Melbourne, 2006.

Batty, P., 'The Gooch Effect. Rodney Gooch and the art of the art advisor', in *Gooch's Utopia: Collected works from the Central Desert*, exhibition catalogue, Flinders University City Gallery in collaboration with Riddoch Art Gallery, Mt Gambier, 2008.

Batty, P., '"Primitive Blacks Face White Man's Laws": The 1932 Anthropological Expedition to Mt. Liebig, Central Australia', in A. Bell, A. K. Brown & R. J. Gordon (eds), *Recreating First Contact: Expeditions, Anthropology, and Popular Culture*, Smithsonian Institution Scholarly Press, Washington DC, 2013.

Bell, R., 'Bell's Theorem: Aboriginal Art – it's a white thing!', 2002, <http://www.kooriweb.org/foley/great/art/bell.html>.

Benjamin, R. & Andrew C. Weislogel (eds), *Icons of the Desert: Early Aboriginal*

Paintings from Papunya, exhibition catalogue, Herbert F. Johnson Museum of Art Cornell University, Ithaca, 2009.

Benterrak, K., S. Muecke & P. Roe, *Reading the Country: Introduction to Nomadology*, Fremantle Arts Centre Press, Perth, 1984.

Bergson, H., *The Creative Mind*, trans. M. L. Andison, The Citadel Press, New York, 1992.

Berner, M., 'Die "rassenkundlichen" Untersuchungen der Wiener Anthropologen in Kriegsgefangenenlagern 1915–1918', *Zeitgeschichte*, vol. 30, no. 3, 2003.

Berner, M., 'Forschungs-"Material" Kriegsgefangene: Die Massenuntersuchungen der Wiener Anthropologen an gefangenen Soldaten 1915–1918', in H. E. Gabriel & W. Neugebauer (eds), *Vorreiter der Vernichtung? Eugenik, Rassenhygiene und Euthanasie in der österreichischen Diskussion vor 1938*, Böhlau, Vienna, 2005.

Biddle, J., *Breasts, Bodies, Canvas: Central Desert Art as Experience*, UNSW Press, Sydney, 2007.

Blocker, J., 'Repetition: A Skill which Unravels', in A. Jones & A. Heathfield (eds), *Perform, Repeat, Record: Live Art in History*, Intellect, Bristol, 2012, *ebook*.

Borninthisskin: Vernon Ah Kee, exhibition catalogue, Institute of Modern Art, Brisbane, 2009.

Bostock-Smith, S., in J. Lydon (ed.), *Calling the Shots, Calling the Shots: Aboriginal Photographies*, Aboriginal Studies Press, Canberra, 2014.

Bourriaud, N., *Relational Aesthetics*, Les Presses du réel, Paris, 2002.

Briggs, M., J. *Lydon* & M. *Say*, 'Collaborating: Photographs of Koories in the State Library of Victoria', *La Trobe Journal*, no. 85, 2010.

Brody, A., *The Face of the Centre: Papunya Tula Paintings, 1971-84,* National Gallery of Victoria, Melbourne, 1985.

Brody, A., *Utopia Women's Paintings. The First Works on Canvas. A Summer Project 1988–89, The Robert Holmes à Court Collection*, Heytesbury Holdings Ltd., Perth, 1989.

Brody, A., *Utopia. A Picture Story: 88 silk batiks from The Robert Holmes à Court Collection*, Heytesbury Holdings Ltd, Perth, 1990.

Brooks, D., 'What Impact the Mission?', in V. Plant & A. Viegas (eds), *Mission Time in Warburton: An Exhibition Exploring Aspects of Warburton Mission History 1933–1973*, Warburton Arts Project, Warburton, 2002.

Brooks, D., cited in N. Rothwell, *Another Country*, Black Inc, Melbourne, 2007.

Brooks, D. 'An Emerging Present: A Short History of the Ngaanyatjarra Lands', in T. Acker & J. Carty (eds), *Ngaanyatjarra: Art of the Lands*, University of

Western Australia Publishing, Perth, 2012.

Bullen, C., 'Ngipi Ward', in *Western Australian Indigenous Art Awards 2013*, exhibition catalogue, Art Gallery of Western Australia, Perth, 2013.

Butcher, B. W., 'Darwinism, Social Darwinism and the Australian Aborigines: a Revaluation', in R. MacLeod & P. F. Rehbock (eds), *Darwin's Laboratory: Evolutionary Theory and Natural History in the Pacific*, University of Hawaii Press, Honolulu, 1994.

Butler, R. 'Margaret Preston and the history wars', *Australian Graffiti,* exhibition catalogue, Gallery Gabrielle Pizzi, Melbourne 2008.

Campbell, N., 'Nola Campbell', in T. Acker & J. Carty (eds), *Ngaanyatjarra: Art of the Lands*, University of Western Australia Publishing, Perth, 2012.

Carty, J., 'Creating Country: Abstraction, Economics and the Social Life of Style in Balgo Art', PhD, Australian National University, Canberra, 2011.

Carty, J., 'Bold Abstractions' in T. Acker & J. Carty (eds), *Ngaanyatjarra: Art of the Lands*, University of Western Australia Publishing, Perth, 2012.

Carty, J., 'Maruku Arts and Crafts', in *Ngaanyatjarra: Art of the Lands*, T. Acker & J. Carty (eds), University of Western Australia Publishing, Perth, 2012.

Carty, J., 'Rethinking Western Desert Abstraction', in Nils Nadeau (ed.), *Crossing Cultures*, exhibition catalogue, Hood Museum of Art, New Hampshire, 2012.

Carty, J. with E. Circuitt, 'Warakurna Artists' in T. Acker & J. Carty (eds), *Ngaanyatjarra Art of the Lands*, University of Western Australia Publishing, Perth, 2012.

Chatwin, B., *The Songlines*, Picador, London, 1987.

Choo, C., *Mission Girls: Aboriginal women on Catholic missions in the Kimberley, Western Australia, 1900–1950,* University of Western Australia Press, Perth, 2001.

Clarke, M. & O. Kelada, 'Bodies on the Line: Repossession and "Talkin Up"', *Artlink*, vol. 33, no. 3, 2013.

Comaroff, J. L., & J. Comaroff, *Ethnicity Inc*, Chicago University Press, Chicago, 2009.

Cooper, C. & J. Urry, 'Art, Aborigines and Chinese: a nineteenth century drawing by the Kwaltkwat artist Tommy McRae', *Aboriginal History* 5.1.

Corke, D., 'Aviation: The adventures of Love Bird and Diamond Bird', <http://www.australiangeographic.com.au/topics/history-culture/2010/02/aviation-the-adventures-of-love-bird-and-diamond-bird/>.

Corrin, L. G. (ed.), *Mining the Museum: An Installation by Fred Wilson*, The New Press, Baltimore & New York, 1994.

Crawford, I., 'Late Pre-historic Changes in Aboriginal Cultures in Kimberley, Western Australia', PhD thesis, University of London, 1969.

Cribbin, J., *The Killing Times: the Coniston Massacre 1928*, Fontana/Collins, Sydney, 1984.

Croft, B. L. 'Laying Ghosts to Rest', in C. Cooper & A. Harris (eds), *Portraits of Oceania*, Art Gallery of New South Wales, Sydney, 1997.

Croft, B. L., *In My Father's House, In conjunction with Postcards from Mummy, Destiny Deacon*, Australian Centre for Photography, Paddington, NSW, 1998.

Cunningham, P., *Two Years in New South Wales,* Henry Colburn, London, 1827.

Curthoys, A., F. Peters-Little & J. Docker, *Passionate Histories: Myth, Memory and Indigenous Australia*, ANU E press, Canberra, 2010.

Dayman, K., 'Authentication: The role of art centres', in *Proceedings of the Art Crime Conference: Protecting Art, Protecting Artists and Protecting Consumer*, Australian Institute of Criminology, Sydney, 1999.

Deakin, H., 'The Unan Cycle: A study of social change in an Aboriginal community', PhD thesis, Monash University, Melbourne, 1978.

Deakin, H., 'Some Thoughts on Transcendence in Tribal Societies', in E. Dowdy (ed.), *Ways of Transcendence: insights from major religions and modern thought,* Australian Association for the Study of Religions, Adelaide, 1982.

Deleuze, G., 'Plato and the Simulacrum,' trans. R. Krauss, *October* no. 27, Winter 1983.

Deleuze, G., *The Logic of Sense*, trans. Charles Stivale, Columbia University Press, New York, 1990.

Deleuze, G. & F. Guattari, *A Thousand Plateaus: Capitalism and Schizophrenia*, trans. B. Massumi, University of Minnesota Press, Minneapolis, 1987.

Derrida, J. 'Archive Fever: A Freudian Impression', trans. E. Prenowitz, *Diacritics*, vol. 25, no. 2, 1995.

Derrida, J., *Archive Fever: A Freudian Impression*, trans. Eric Prenowitz, University of Chicago Press, Chicago, 1995.

Dessau, O., 'Against the Archive', *Flash Art International*, vol. 46, no. 292, 2013.

Didi-Huberman, G., 'Before the Image, Before Time: The Sovereignty of Anachronism', in Claire Farago (ed.), *Compelling Visuality: The Work of Art in and Out of History*, University of Minnesota Press, Minneapolis, 2003.

Djalkiri: we are standing on their names, Blue Mud Bay, documentary, Nomad Art Productions, Darwin, 2010.

Donaldson, M., 'The *Gwion* or Bradshaw art style of Australia's Kimberley region is undoubtedly among the earliest rock art in the country – but is it Pleistocene?', *IFRAO Congress, Symposium: Pleistocene art of Australia (Pre-Acts)*, 2010.

Dussart, F., 'Canvassing Identities: Reflecting on the acrylic art movement in an Australian Aboriginal settlement', *Aboriginal History*, no. 30, 2006.

Edmond, M., *Battarbee and Namatjira*, Giramondo Publishing Company, Artamon, 2014.

Edwards, E., *Raw Histories: Photographs, Anthropology and Museums*, Berg, Oxford and New York, 2001.

Edwards, E. & J. Hart (eds), *Photographs, Objects, Histories: On the materiality of images*, Routledge, London & New York, 2004.

Edwards, E. & J. Hart, 'Introduction: Photographs as Objects', in E. Edwards & J. Hart (eds), *Photographs, Objects, Histories: On the Materiality of Images*, Routledge New York, 2004.

Edwards, E. & C. Morton, 'Introduction', in E. Edwards & C. Morton (eds), *Photography, Anthropology and History: Expanding the Frame*, Ashgate, Farnham Surry, 2009.

Edmonds, F., '"Art is Us": Aboriginal Art, Identity and Wellbeing in Southeast Australia', PhD dissertation, Melbourne University, 2007.

Edmonds, F. with M. Clarke, *Sort of Like Reading a Map: A Community Report on the survival of Aboriginal Art in Southeastern Australia since 1834*, <http://www.lowitja.org.au/sites/default/files/docs/Sort-of-like-reading-a-map-amended.pdf>.

Eickelcamp, U., *Don't Ask for Stories: the women from Ernabella and their art*, Aboriginal Studies Press, Canberra, 1999.

Eldin, S., *Mapping the Present: Heidegger, Foucault and the Project of a Spatial History*, Continuum, London, 2001.

Enwezor, O., 'Archive Fever: Photography between History and the Monument', *Archive Fever: Uses of the Document in Contemporary Art*, International Center of Photography, New York, 2007.

Enwezor, O., *Rise and Fall of Apartheid: Photography and the Bureaucracy of Everyday Life*, Munich, Prestel, 2013.

Escobar, A., 'Culture sits in Places: Reflections on Globalism and Subaltern Strategies of Localization', *Political Geography*, no. 20, 2001.

Etheridge, R., 'Ethnological notes made at Copmanhurst, Clarence River. I. An aboriginal rock-shelter with an inscribed rockface. II. Disarticulation of one of the little finger joints', *Records of the Australian Museum*, vol. 5, no. 5, 1904.

Eyerman, Ron, 'Social theory and trauma', *Acta Sociologica*, vol. 56, no. 1, 2013.

Fanon, F., *Black Skin, White Masks*, Pluto, London, 1952.

Faris, J., *Navajo and Photography: A Critical History of the Representation of an American People*, University of Utah Press, Salt Lake City, 2003.

Foley, F., 'When the Circus came to Town', *Art Monthly Australia*, no. 245, 2011.

Fortescue, E., *Art of Utopia, Volume 1*, Boomerang Art, Adelaide, 2008.

Foster, H., 'The Artist as Ethnographer', in J. Fisher (ed.), *Global Visions: Towards a new internationalism in the visual arts*, Kala Press in association with The Institute of International Visual Arts, London, 1994.

Foster, H., 'An Archival Impulse', *October*, no. 110, Autumn, 2004.

Foster, W., 'Why is Ara Irititja Important?', <http://www.irititja.com/about_ara_irititja/index.html>.

Foucault, M., 'Fantasia on the Library', *Language, Counter-Memory, Practice*, D. F. Bouchard (ed.), trans. D. F. Bouchard & S. Simon, Cornell University Press, Ithica, 1967.

Foucault, M., *Archaeology of Knowledge*, trans. S. Smith, Pantheon Books, New York, 1972.

Foucault, M., 'The Subject and Power', *Critical Inquiry*, vol. 8, no. 4, 1982.

Foucault, M., *The Order of Things: An Archaeology of the Human Sciences*, Vintage Books, New York, 1994.

French, A., *Seeing the Centre: The Art of Albert Namatjira 1902–1959*, National Gallery of Australia, Canberra, 2002.

Fried, M., 'Jules Olitski (1966–67)', *Art and Objecthood*, University of Chicago Press, Chicago, 1998.

Frost, V., 'Lindt, John William (1845–1926)', in D. Pike (ed.), *Australian Dictionary of Biography*, vol. 5, Melbourne University Press, Melbourne, 1974.

Fuchs, B., 'Pöch, Hella', in B. Keintzel & U. Korotin (eds), *Wissenschafterinnen in und aus Österreich. Leben – Werk – Wirken*, Böhlau, Vienna, 2002.

Fuchs, B., *'Rasse', 'Volk', Geschlecht: anthropologische Diskurse in Österreich 1850–1960*, Frankfurt am Main and New York: Campus, 2003.

Galatis, E., 'Yuwa Walkumunu Telephonepa – lampatju (Hello, I've got a mobile phone)', *Artlink*, vol. 34, no. 2, 2014.

Garden, W., 'Ethical Witnessing and the Portrait Photograph: Brook Andrew', *Journal of Australian Studies* vol. 35, no. 2, June 2011.

Gell, A., *Art and Agency: An Anthropological Theory*, Clarendon Press, Oxford, 1998.

Georgeff, S., 'Kimberley Painters in Legal Bind', *The Australian*, 14 August 1998.

Gil, T., 'A Dictionary of the Pela Language used by the Natives of the Coastal Regions of East Kimberley in W.A.', held at AIATSIS, Canberra, 1934.

Gil, T., 'Concise Catechism of Christian Doctrine Written in the Pela Language (Drysdale River Mission)', held at AIATSIS, Canberra, 1934.

Gil, T., 'Translation into Pela of Short Life of Our Lord', held at AIATSIS, Canberra, 1934.

Glaskin, K., 'Claim, Culture and Effect; property relations and the Native Title process', in B. Smith & F. Morphy (eds), *The Social Effects of Native*

Title; recognition, translation, coexistence, Research Monograph no. 7, Centre for Aboriginal Economic Policy Research, ANU, ANU ePress, Canberra, 2007.

Goodall, H., *Invasion to Embassy: Land in Aboriginal politics in New South Wales, 1770–1972,* Allen and Unwin, Sydney, 1996.

Goodall, H., 'Karroo-Mates: Communities Reclaim their Images', *Aboriginal History,* no. 30, 2006.

J. Gough, 'The Possessed Past. Museums: Infiltration and Outreach and *The Lost World (Part 2)*', in Khadija von Zinnenburg Carroll (ed), *The Importance of Being Anachronistic: Contemporary Aboriginal Art and Museum Reparations,* Discipline in collaboration with *Third Text* Publications, an affiliate of Third Text journal, Australia, 2016.

Graber, C., 'Aboriginal Self-determination vs the Propertisation of Traditional culture: the case of the sacred Wanjina sites', *Australian Indigenous Law Review,* vol. 13, no. 2, 2009.

Green, J., *Utopia Women, Country and Batik,* Utopia Women's Batik Group, Alice Springs, 1981.

Green, M., & P. Gordon, 'Repatriation: Australian Perspectives', in J. Lydon & U. Rizvi (eds), *Handbook to Postcolonialism and Archaeology,* World Archaeological Congress, LeftCoast Press, San Francisco, 2011.

Greene, G., 'Dispute Over Control of Outback Art', *The Age,* 30 May 1998.

Greene, G., 'Doctors Dispute Agreement signing away artist's rights', *The Age,* 9 June 1998.

Gregg, M. & G. J. Seigworth, 'An Inventory of Shimmers' in M. Gregg & G. J. Seigworth (eds), *The Affect Theory Reader,* Duke University Press, Durham, 2010.

Griffiths, T., *Hunters and Collectors: The Antiquarian Imagination in Australia,* Cambridge University Press, Cambridge, 1996.

Grimshaw, A., *The Ethnographer's Eye: Ways of Seeing in Anthropology,* Cambridge, Cambridge University Press, 2001.

Hadjinicolaou, N., *Art History and Class Struggle,* trans. L. Asmal, Pluto Press, London, 1978.

Hardy, J., 'Visitors to Hermannsburg: An essay in cross-cultural learning', in J. Hardy, V. S. Megaw & M. R. Megaw (eds), *The Heritage of Namatjira: The Watercolourists of Central Australia,* William Heinemann Australia, Port Melbourne, 1992.

Hardy, J., J. V. S. Megaw & R. Megaw (eds), *The Heritage of Namatjira,* William Heinemann, Melbourne, 1992.

Harrasser, A., 'Die Gesichtsmuskulatur eines Melanesiers in ihren Beziehungen zu Innervation und Gefässverlauf', *Verhandlungen der Gesellschaft für*

Physische Anthropologie, vol. 7, 1935.

Hart, D., *Fred Williams: Infinite Horizons*, National Gallery of Australia, Canberra, 2011.

Hatley, J., *Suffering Witness: The Quandary of Responsibility after the Irreparable*, SUNY Press, New York, 2000.

Haupt , H., *Jahre der Gefährdung. Das Kunsthistorische Museum 1938–1945*, Private Publishing, Vienna, 1995.

Healy, J., 'A Fragile Thing: Marketing Remote Area Aboriginal Art', PhD thesis, University of Melbourne, 2005.

Henson, B., *A Straight-out Man: Pastor F. W. Albrecht and Central Australian Aborigines*, Melbourne University Publishing, Carlton, 1995.

Herle, A., 'John Layard Long Malakula 1914–15: The Potency of Field Photography', in Morton & Edwards (eds), *Photography, Anthropology and History.*

Hernández, T., 'Social Organization of the Drysdale River Tribes, North-west Australia', *Oceania,* vol. 11, no. 3, 1941.

Hernández, T., 'Children among the Drysdale River Tribes', *Oceania*, vol. 12, no. 2, 1942.

Hernández, T., 'Myths and Symbols of the Drysdale River Aborigines', *Oceania,* vol. 32, no. 2, 1961.

Holt, D., 'The History of Delmore Gallery', <http://www.delmoregallery.com.au>.

Holt, D. & J. Holt, *Emily Kngwarreye: Paintings*, Craftsman House, Sydney, 1998.

Holt, J., 'Emily Kngwarreye at Delmore Downs 1989–1996', in J. Isaacs (ed.), *Emily Kngwarreye paintings*, Craftsman House and Arts International, Sydney, 1998.

Hoogenraad, R. & B. Thornley, *Aboriginal languages of Central Australia and the places where they are spoken*, Jukurrpa Books, Alice Springs, 2010.

Hooper, C., *The Tall Man: Death and Life on Palm Island*, Penguin, Melbourne, 2009.

Hooper Greenhill, E., *Museums and the Shaping of Knowledge*, Routledge, London & New York, 1992.

Hughes, M. & J. Dallwitz, 'A͟ra Irititja: Towards Culturally Appropriate Best Practice in Remote Indigenous Australia,' in L. E. Dyson, M. Hendriks & S. Grant (eds), *Information Technology and Indigenous People,* Information Science Publishers, Hershey.

Isaacs, J., *Desert Crafts: Anangu Maruku Punu*, Doubleday, Sydney, 1992.

Isaacs, J., *Spirit Country: Contemporary Aboriginal Art*, Hardie Grant Books, Melbourne, 1999.

Jacobs, J., *Edge of Empire: Postcolonialism and the city*, Routledge, London, 1996.

James, D. & E. Tregenza (eds), *Ngintaka*, Wakefield Press, Adelaide, 2014.

Jardine, N., 'Uses and Abuses of Anachronism in the History of the Sciences,' *History of Science*, no. 38, 2000.

Jebb, M. A., *Blood, Sweat and Welfare: A history of white bosses and Aboriginal workers*, UWA Press, Nedlands, 2002.

Jensen, M., *Photographs of Indigenous artists, Papunya, 1972*. Digital Pictures Collection, National Library of Australia website, <http://nla.gov.au/nla.pic-vn3301193>.

Johnson, V., *Lives of the Papunya Tula Artists*, IAD Press, Alice Springs, 2008.

Johnson, V., *Once Upon a Time in Papunya*, University of New South Wales Press, Sydney, 2010.

Johnson, V., *Streets of Papunya: the re-invention of Papunya painting*, New South Publishing, Sydney, 2015.

Jolly, M., & S. Tcherkézoff, 'Oceanic Encounters: A Prelude', in M. Jolly, S. Tcherkézoff & D. Tryon (eds), *Oceanic Encounters: Exchange, Desire, Violence*, Australian National University e-Press, Canberra, 2009.

Jones, G., 'Vernon Ah Kee Sovereign Warrior', *Artlink*, vol. 30, no. 1, 2010, <https://www.artlink.com.au/articles/3361/vernon-ah-kee-sovereign-warrior/>.

Jones, P., *Images of the Interior*, Wakefield Press, Adelaide, 2011.

Jones, P., *Ochre and Rust: Artefacts and Encounters on Australian Frontiers*, Wakefield Press, Adelaide, 2007.

Jorgensen, D., 'Nowhere Man: The Countryside of Fred Williams after Western Desert Painting', *EMAJ: Electronic Melbourne Art Journal*, issue 6.

Joyce, P., & T. Bennett, 'Introduction', in T. Bennett & P. Joyce (eds), *Material Powers: Cultural Studies, History and the Material Turn*, Routledge, London and New York, 2010.

Kean, J., *East to West: Land in Papunya Tula Painting*, [Tandanya] Aboriginal Cultural Institute, Adelaide, 1990.

Kean, J., 'Johnny Warangula Tjupurrula: painting in a changing landscape,' *Art Bulletin of Victoria*, no. 41, 2001.

Kean, J., 'Papunya, Place and Time', in *Papunya Painting: out of the desert*, exhibition catalogue, National Museum of Australia Press, Canberra, 2007.

Kean, J., 'Johnny Warangkula Tjupurrula', in J. Ryan & P. Batty (eds), *Tjukurrtjanu: Origins of Western Desert Art*, exhibition catalogue, National Gallery of Victoria, Melbourne, 2011.

Kean, J., 'Lot 50', *Sotheby's Australia, Important Australian art, Sydney 13 May 2014*, Second East Auction Holdings, Melbourne, 2014.

Keenan, S., 'Moments of Decolonization: Indigenous Australia in the Here and Now', *Canadian Journal of Law and Society*, no. 29, 2014.

Kennedy, R., L. Bell & J. Emberley, 'Decolonising Testimony: On the Possibilities and Limits of Witnessing', *Humanities Research*, vol. 15, no. 3, 2009.

Keve, A. & G. Rokitansky, 'Hofrat Dr. Moriz Sassi 1880–1967 (Obituary)', *Annalen des Naturhistorischen Museum Wien,* vol. 73, 1969.

Kimber, R., 'Papunya – the dialogue of the country', in N. Amadio & R. Kimber (eds), *Wildbird Dreaming: Aboriginal Art from the Central Deserts of Australia*, Greenhouse, Melbourne, 1988.

Kimber, R. G., 'Walawurru, the Giant Eaglehawk: Aboriginal Reminiscences of Aircraft in Central Australia 1921-1931', *Aboriginal History*, vol. 6, 1982.

Kofod, F., 'My Relations, My Country-Language, Identity and Land in the East Kimberley of Western Australia', in *Proceedings of the 7th Foundation for Endangered Languages Conference*, Broome, 2003.

Kolig, E., 'A Sense of History and the Reconstitution of Cosmology in Australian Aboriginal Society: the case of myth versus history', *Anthropos,* vol. 1, no. 3, 1995.

Kompridis, N., 'Introduction: Turning and Returning: The Aesthetic Turn in Political Thought', in Nikolas Kompridis (ed.), *The Aesthetic Turn in Political Thought*, Bloomsbury, London, 2014.

Kopytoff, I., 'The Cultural Biography of Things: Commoditization as Process', in Arjun Appadurai (ed.), *The Social Life of Things*, Cambridge University Press, Cambridge, 1986.

Kracauer, S., *History: The Last Things Before the Last*, ed. and trans. Paul Oskar Kristeller, Markus Wiener, Princeton, 1995.

Kramer, E., *Report on the Western Tour 1932,* PRG–1322 Series 1-11 Kramer Family, Mortlock Library, Adelaide.

Lampshed, M., 'Expedition Leaves to Study World's Last Prehistoric Race', *The News*, Thursday, 4 August 1932.

Lane, R., 'To Hold and Protect: Mulka at Yirrkala', *Artlink*, vol. 31, no. 2, 2011.

Lange, B., *Die Wiener Forschungen an Kriegsgefangenen 1915–1918. Anthropologische und ethnografische Verfahren im Lager*, Austrian Academy of Sciences, Vienna, 2011.

Langton, M., 'Religion and Art from Colonial Conquest to Post-Colonial Resistance', *The Oxford Companion to Aboriginal Art and Culture,* in S. Kleinert and M. Neale (eds), Oxford University Press, Melbourne, 2000.

Latour, B., *Reassembling the Social: An Introduction to Actor-Network-Theory,* Oxford University Press, Oxford, 2005.

Laverty, C. & E. Laverty (ed.), *Beyond Sacred: Recent paintings from Australia's remote Aboriginal communities*, Hardie Grant Books, Melbourne, 2008.

Lawlor, L. & V. M. Leonard, 'Henri Bergson', in E. N. Zalta (ed.), *The Stanford Encyclopedia of Philosophy*, <http://plato.stanford.edu/archives/win2013/entries/bergson/>.

Lefebvre, H., *The Production of Space*, trans. D. Nicholson-Smith, Blackwell Publishing, Cambridge, Mass., 1991.

Legassick, M. & C. Rassool, *Skeletons in the Cupboard: South African Museums and the Trade in Human Remains 1907–1917*, South African Museum and McGregor Museum, Cape Town & Kimberley, 2000.

Legassick, M. & C. Rassool, 'South African human remains, Viennese museums, and the politics of repatriation: Reconsidering the legacy of Rudolf Pöch', *The Life of the Corpse, WISER Symposium*, University of the Witwatersrand, Johannesburg, 2008.

Lepecki, A., 'The Body as Archive: Will to Reenact and the Lives of Dances', *Dance Research Journal*, vol. 42, no. 2, 2010.

Lester, Y., *Yami: The Autobiography of Yami Lester*, IAD Press, Alice Springs, 2000.

Lewis, D., 'Observations on Route Finding and Spatial Orientation among the Aboriginal Peoples of the Western Desert Region of Central Australia', *Oceania*, vol. 46, no. 4, June 1976.

Lippa, H. von, *Oben und Unten – Zwanzig Jahre in Australien*, Carl Konegen, Vienna, 1912.

Lockard, R. A., 'Outside Boundaries: Contemporary Art and Global Biennales', *Art Documentation: Journal of the Art Libraries Society of North America*, vol. 32, no. 1, 2013.

Lommel, A., *Die Unambal: A tribe in Northwest Australia*, Takarakka Nowan Kas Publications, Brisbane, 1997.

Lowish, S., 'Ara Irititja: adding more value to Aboriginal art through education', *SangSaeng*, no. 20, 2008.

Lucich, P., 'Ethnographic Survey of the North-West of Australia Part I: the Northern Kimberley', held at AIATSIS, Canberra, 1963.

Ludgate, M., 'Transforming Tindale Exhibition Strips Away Scientific Method to Show Humanity', *The Courier Mail*, 24 September 2002, <http://www.couriermail.com.au/questnews/north/transforming-tindale-exhibition-strips-away-scientific-method-to-show-humanity/story-fn8m0rl4-1226478995682>.

Lydon, L., 'Return: The photographic archive and technologies of Indigenous memory', *Photographies*, vol. 3, no. 2, 2010.

Lydon, J., *The Flash of Recognition: Photography and the Emergence of Indigenous*

Rights, NewSouth Books, Sydney, 2012.

Lydon, J. (ed.), *Calling the Shots: Aboriginal Photographies,* Aboriginal Studies Press, Canberra, 2014.

Macdonald, G., 'Photos in Wiradjuri biscuit tins: negotiating relatedness and validating colonial histories', *Oceania*, vol. 73, no. 4, 2003.

Mahood, K., 'Why the Martu Don't Need a Map', in *We Don't Need a Map: A Martu experience of the Western Desert*, exhibition catalogue, Fremantle Arts Centre, Perth, 2013.

Manovich, L., *The Language of New Media*, MIT Press, Boston, 2001.

Marika, W., *Wandjuk Marika: Life story*, University of Queensland Press, Brisbane, 1995.

Massumi, B., *Parables for the Virtual: Movement, Affect, Sensation*, Duke University Press, Durham, 2002.

Matiasek, K., 'Die Pionierfrage – Rudolf Pöchs Einsatz von Bildmedien' in M. Teschler-Nicola, T. Ballhausen & K. Matiasek (eds), *Archivhorizonte – Wissenslandschaften und Perspektivgrenzen im multimedialen Nachlass des Anthropologen und Forschungsreisenden Rudolf Pöch*, Löcker, Vienna, in print.

Maughan, J. et al., *Dot and Circle: A Retrospective Survey of the Aboriginal Acrylic Paintings of Central Australia*, Communications Service Unit, Royal Melbourne Institute of Technology, Melbourne, 1986.

Maxwell, A., *Colonial Photography and Exhibitions*, Leicester Press, London, 1999.

McDonald, J. & A. M. Stephenson (eds), *The Resilience of Hope*, Rodopi, Amsterdam, 2010.

McGrath, P., 'Hard Looking: A historical ethnography of photographic encounters with Aboriginal families in the Ngaanyatjarra lands, Western Australia', PhD thesis, Australian National University, Canberra, 2010.

McGrath, P., 'The Past is Everywhere: Ngaanyatjarra History Paintings' in T. Acker & J. Carty (eds), *Ngaanyatjarra Art of the Lands*, University of Western Australia Publishing, Perth.

McLean, I., 'Aboriginal Modernism in Australia', in K. Mercer (ed.), *Exiles, Diasporas and Strangers*, INIVA and MIT Press, Cambridge, 2008.

McLean, I., 'Aboriginal Cosmopolitans: A Prehistory of Western Desert Painting', in J. Harris (ed.), *Globalization and Contemporary Art*, Wiley-Blackwell, West Sussex, 2011.

McLean, I., 'The Gift that Time Gave: Myth and History in the Western Desert Painting Movement', in Jaynie Anderson (ed.), *The Cambridge Companion to Australian Art*, Cambridge University Press, Cambridge, 2011.

McLean, I., (ed.), *How Aborigines Invented the Idea of Contemporary Art,* Power Publishing, Sydney, and Institute of Modern Art, Brisbane, 2011 and 2014.

McNiven, I. & L. Russell, '"Strange Paintings" and "Mystery Races"; Kimberley rock art, diffusionism and colonialist constructions of Australia's Aboriginal past', *Antiquity*, vol. 71, 1997.

McQuire, A., 'Palm Island Death In Custody Cop Chris Hurley Investigated By Queensland Police', *New Matilda*, 22 May 2015, <https://newmatilda.com/2015/05/22/palm-island-death-custody-cop-chris-hurley-investigated-queensland-police#sthash.2YhLE3Sa.dpuf>.

Mollison, J., *A Singular Vision: the Art of Fred Williams,* Australian National Gallery, Canberra, 1989.

Morphy, H., *Ancestral Connections: Art and an Aboriginal System of Knowledge,* University of Chicago Press, Chicago, 1991.

Morphy, H., 'The Aesthetics of Communication and the Communication of Cultural Aesthetics: A Perspective on Ian Dunlop's Films of Aboriginal Australia', *Visual Anthropology Review*, vol. 21, nos 1–2.

Morphy, H., 'Art as a Mode of Action: Some Problems with Gell's Art and Agency', *Journal of Material Culture*, vol. 14, no. 1, March 2009.

Morphy, H., 'Recursive and Iterative Processes in Australian Rock Art: an anthropological perspective', in J. McDonald & P. Veth (eds), *A Companion to Rock Art,* Wiley-Blackwell, Hoboken, New Jersey, 2012.

Morton, C., 'Double Alienation: Evans-Pritchard's Zande and Nuer Photographs in Comparative Perspective', in R. Vokes (ed.), *Photography in Africa: Ethnographic Perspectives*, Boydell and Brewer, Woodbridge and Rochester, 2012.

Morton, C., 'Spiritual Repatriation and the Archive in Christian Thompson's "We Bury Our Own"', <https://www.prm.ox.ac.uk/christianthompson.html>.

Morton, J., 'Country, People, Art: The Western Aranda 1870–1990', in J. Hardy, J. V. S. Megaw and M. R. Megaw (eds), *The Heritage of Namatjira: The Watercolourists of Central Australia*, William Heinemann Australia, Port Melbourne, 1992.

Moxey, K., *Visual Time: The Image in History*, Duke University Press, Durham, 2013.

Muecke, S., *No Road: Bitumen All the Way*, Fremantle Arts Centre Press, Perth, 1997.

Muecke, S., 'A diplomat for the history wars', *Text*, no. 28, April 2015, website, <http://www.textjournal.com.au/speciss/issue28/Muecke.pdf>.

Munn, N., *Walbiri Iconography: Graphic Representation and Cultural Symbolism in a Central Australian Society*, Cornell University Press, Ithaca, 1973.

Murray, J., 'Utopia Batik: The Halycon Days 1978-82', in J. Ryan and Robyn Healy (ed.), *Raiki Wara – Long Cloth from Aboriginal Australia and the Torres*

Strait, exhibition catalogue, National Gallery of Victoria, 1998.

Murray, J., 'Drawn Together: The Utopia Batik Phenomenon', in J. Ryan (ed.), *Across the Desert – Aboriginal Batik from Central Australia*, exhibition catalogue, National Gallery of Victoria, Melbourne, 2008.

Myers, F., *Pintupi country, Pintupi Self: Sentiment, place and politics among Western Desert Aborigines*, Smithsonian Institution Press and Australian Institute of Aboriginal Studies, Washington and Canberra, 1986.

Myers, F., *Pintupi Country, Pintupi Self: Sentiment, Place, and Politics among Western Desert Aborigines*, University of California Press, Berkeley, 1991.

Myers, F., 'Ways of Place Making', *La Ricerca Folklorica*, no. 45, 2002.

Myers, F., *Painting Culture – The Making of an Aboriginal High Art*, Duke University Press, Durham, 2002.

Myers, F., 'Graceful Transfigurations of Person, Place, and Story: The Stylistic Evolution of Shorty Lungkarta Tjungurrayi', in R. Benjamin & A. C. Weislogel (eds), *Icons of the Desert: Early Aboriginal Paintings from Papunya*, Herbert F. Johnson Museum of Art, Cornell University, Ithica, 2009.

Myers, F., 'Emplacement and Displacement: Perceiving the Landscape through Aboriginal Australian Acrylic Painting', *Ethnos*, vol. 78, no. 4, 2013.

Nagel, A. & C. Wood, *Anachronic Renaissance*, Columbia University Press, New York, 2002.

Nakambala Tjungurrayi, W., 'Big Trouble came to Papunya' & M. Nelson Tjakamarra, 'Every Friday was ration day' in M. Bowman (ed.), *Every hill got a story: we grew up in country / men and women of Central Australia and the Central Land Council,* Hardie Grant Books, Richmond Victoria, 2015.

Naparrula, P. & J. Nakamarra, *Mamulama Ngalyananyi,* Papunya Literature Production Centre, Papunya, 1987.

Neale, M., *Yiribana*, Art Gallery of New South Wales, Sydney 1994.

Neale, M. (ed.), *Emily Kame Kngwarreye. Alhakere: Paintings from Utopia*, exhibition catalogue, Queensland Art Gallery, Art Gallery of New South Wales and National Gallery of Victoria, 1998.

Neale, M., 'Colourism' in M. Neale (ed.), *Utopia: The Genius of Emily Kame Kngwarreye*, exhibition catalogue, National Museum of Australia, Canberra, 2008.

Neale, M., 'Marks of meaning: the genius of Emily Kame Kngwarreye', in M. Neale (ed.), *Utopia: the Genius of Emily Kame Kngwarreye*, National Museum of Australia Press, Canberra, 2008.

Neale, M. (ed.), *Utopia: The Genius of Emily Kame Kngwarreye*, exhibition catalogue, National Art Centre and The Yomiuri Shimbun, Osaka and Tokyo, 2008.

Neale, M., 'God Lives in the Dreaming; Aboriginal treasures in the Vatican', *Artlink,* vol. 31, no. 2, 2011.

Neale, M. & T. Keenan, 'Talking around Songlines: Kungkarangkalpa and Ngintaka', *Goree*, vol. 9, issue 2, November 2012.

Newell, S., 'Postcolonial Masculinity and the Politics of Visibility', *Journal of Postcolonial Writing*, vol. 45, no. 3, 2009.

Newstead, A., *The Dealer is the Devil: an Insider's History of the Aboriginal Art Trade*, Brandl and Schlesinger, Sydney, 2014.

Ngaanyatjarra, Pitjantjatjara and Yankunytjatjara (NPY) Women's Council, '2010–11 Director's Report', 2011.

Ngaanyatjarra, Pitjantjatjara and Yankunytjatjara (NPY) Women's Council, 'Janet Inyika, NPY Women's Council Director 2011–2013', <http://www.npywc.org.au/about-npywc/directorate/janetinyika/>.

Nicholls, C., 'Ronnie and Co: The making of the Gooch Collections,' in *Gooch's Utopia: Collected works from the Central Desert*, exhibition catalogue, Flinders University City Gallery in collaboration with Riddoch Art Gallery, Mt Gambier, 2008.

Oberhummer, E., 'Rudolf Pöch (Obituary)', *Mitteilungen der Anthropologischen Gesellschaft in Wien*, vol. 51, 1921.

Olsen, J., *Drawn from Life*, Duffy & Snellgrove, Sydney, 1997.

Orchard, K., 'J. W. *Lindt's* Australian Aboriginals (1873–74)', *History of Photography*, vol. 23, no. 2, 1999.

Parks and Wildlife Service, Northern Territory: *A Management Program for the Dingo (Canis lupus dingo) in the Northern Territory of Australia, 2006-2011,* Parks and Wildlife Service Department of Natural Resources, Environment and the Arts, Darwin, 2006.

Parsley, P. 'Christian Thompson and the art of indigeneity', *Discipline*, no. 1, 2011, <http://discipline.net.au/Discipline/Issue_1_files/Connal%20Parsley%20-%20Christian%20Thompson.pdf>.

Peers, L. & A. K. Brown (eds), *Museums and source communities: a Routledge reader,* Routledge, New York, 2003.

Peers, L. & A. K. Brown with members of the Kainai Nation, *'Pictures bring us messages': Sinaakssiiksi aohtsimaahpihkookiyaawa: photographs and histories from the Kainai Nation,* University of Toronto Press, Toronto, 2006.

Perez, E., *The Benedictine Mission and the Aborigines, 1908–1975,* Kalumburu Benedictine Mission, via Wyndham Western Australia, 1977.

Perez, E., *Kalumburu War Diary,* R. Pratt & J. Millington (eds), Artlook Books, Western Australia, 1981.

Perkins, H. & H. Fink (eds), *Papunya Tula Genesis and Genius,* exhibition catalogue, Art Gallery of New South Wales, Sydney, 2000.

Perkins, H. and J. Jones (eds), *Half Light: Portraits from Black Australia*, Art Gallery of N.S.W., Sydney, 2009.

Perniola, M., *Enigmas*, trans. C. Woodall, Verso, London, 1995.

Perry, G., 'Playing to the Gallery' and 'Beating the Bounds', Reith Lectures 2013, Liverpool, 22 October 2013, *<downloads.bbc.co.uk/radio4/transcripts/reith-lecture2-liverpool.pdf>*.

Petri, H., *The Dying World in Northwest Australia*, Hesperion Press 2011 facsimile edition, Carlisle, WA, 1954.

Pidgeon, W. E., 'New look at old scenes', *The Sunday Telegraph*, Sydney, 20 April 1975.

Pietschmann, V., *Führer durch die Sonderschau 'Ostmarkdeutsche als Forscher und Sammler in unseren Kolonien': Ein Anteil der Ostmark an der Erforschung und Erschliessung der deutschen Kolonialgebiete*, Waldheim-Eberle, Vienna, 1940.

Plant, V. & A. Viegas, 'Re-membering the Past', in Vikki Plant & Albie Viegas (eds), *Mission Time in Warburton*, Tjulyuru Regional Arts Gallery, Warburton, WA, 2001.

Plato, The Republic, trans. Benjamin Jowett, 1892, Book 10, <http://classics.mit.edu/Plato/republic.11.x.html>.

Pöch, H., 'Beitrag zur Kenntnis des Muskelsystems und einiger Rassenmerkmale der Buschmänner', *Mitteilungen der Anthropologischen Gesellschaft in Wien* (Sitzungsberichte), vol. 57, 1926–27.

Pöch, R., 'Ansuchen um eine Subvention für eine Reise nach Süd-Afrika zum Zwecke des anthropologischen und ethnologischen Studiums der Buschmänner' (manuscript folder, dated 25 October 1906), Archive of the Austrian Academy of Sciences, *Subventionen der mathematisch-naturwissenschaftlichen Klasse* (862/1906).

Pöch, R., 'Ergebnisse einer Reise längs der Küste von Senegambien und Oberguinea', *Archiv für Schiffs—und Tropenhygiene*, vol. 7, nos. 3–4, 1903.

Pöch, R., *Notizbücher der Forschungsreise nach Neu-Guinea* (handwritten travel notebooks), Anthropological Department of the Museum of Natural History, Vienna (inv. no. 14.036), 'Kleines Heft', no. 12, 1904–06.

Pöch, R., 'Erster Bericht von meiner Reise nach Neu-Guinea über die Zeit vom 6. Juni 1904 bis zum 25. März 1905', *Sitzungsberichte der kaiserlichen Akademie der Wissenschaften in Wien, Mathematisch-Naturwissenschaftliche Klasse*, vol. 114, 1905.

Pöch, R., 'Dritter Bericht über meine Reise nach Neu-Guinea (Neu-Süd-Wales, vom 21. Juni 1905 bis 6. September 1905, Britisch-Salomonsinseln und Britisch-Neu-Guinea bis zum 31. Januar 1906)', *Sitzungsberichte der kaiserlichen Akademie der Wissenschaften in Wien, Mathematisch-Naturwissenschaftliche Klasse*, vol. 115, 1906.

Pöch, R., *Notizbücher der Forschungsreise nach Südafrika* (handwritten travel notebooks), Anthropological Department of the Museum of Natural History, Vienna (inv. no. 14.037a), 'Kleines Heft', no. 12, 1907–09.

Pöch, R., 'Studien an Eingeborenen von Neu-Südwales und an australischen Schädeln', *Mitteilungen der Anthropologischen Gesellschaft in Wien*, vol. 45, 1915.

Pöch, R., Archive of the Austrian Academy of Sciences, *Subventionen der mathematisch-naturwissenschaftlichen Klasse* (461/1917).

Pöch, R., 'Die Methoden der anthropologischen Photographie', *Photographische Korrespondenz*, vol. 54, no. 679, 1917.

Poster, M., *What's the Matter with the Internet?*, University of Minnesota Press, Minneapolis, 2001.

Radford, R., 'Director's Foreword: Fred Williams: Infinite Horizons', in D. Hart (ed.), *Fred Williams: Infinite Horizons,* exhibition catalogue, National Gallery of Australia, Canberra, 2011.

Ranzmaier, I., 'Ein Stolperstein für die Etablierung der Anthropologie und Ethnologie an der Universität Wien', in T. Brandstetter, D. Rupnow and C. Wessey (eds) *Sachunterricht. Fundstücke zur Wissenschaftsgeschichte*, Löcker, Vienna, 2008.

Rappaport, R., *Ecology, Meaning, and Religion*, North Atlantic Books, Berkeley, 1979.

Redmond, A., '"Alien Abductions", Kimberley Aboriginal rock paintings, and the speculation about human origins: on some investments in cultural tourism in the northern Kimberley', *Australian Aboriginal Studies* no. 2, 2002.

Reid, M., 'Aboriginal Art', *The Australian Art Market Report,* no. 8, 2003.

Richards, T., *The Imperial Archive: Knowledge and the Fantasy of Empire*, Verso, London, 1993.

Rifkin, A., 'Dancing Years, or Writing as a Way Out', *Art History*, vol. 32, no. 4, 2009.

Rintoul, S., 'Songline at heart of secret men's business', *The Australian,* 19 May 19, 2012.

Roberts, A., M. Fowler & T. Sansbury, 'A report on the exhibition "Children, Boats and Hidden Histories": Crayon drawings by Aboriginal children at Point Pearce Mission (Burgiyana) (South Australia), 1939', *Bulletin of the Australasian Institute for Maritime Archaeology*, no. 38, 2014.

Robin, L., R. Heinsohn & L. Joseph (eds), *Boom and Bust, bird stories for a dry country*, CSIRO Publishing, Collingwood, Vic, 2009.

Robins, C., *Curious Lessons in the Museum*, Ashgate, Farnham Surrey, 2013.

Rogoff, I., 'Hit and Run – Museums and Cultural Difference', *Art Journal*, vol. 61, no. 3, 2002.

Rose, D. B., *Reports from a Wild Country: Ethics for Decolonisation*, UNSW Press, Sydney, 2004.

Rosler, M., *Three Works*, Nova Scotia College of Art and Design, Halifax, 1981.

Rothwell, N., 'Lines Shimmer into Shape: Desert Mob 2005', *The Australian*, 13 September 2005.

Rothwell, N., 'Colour Fades into Shadow', *The Australian*, 22 June 2007.

Rothwell, N., 'Quicksilver: Reflections', <http://nicolasrothwell.com/quicksilver-reflections/>.

Rowlands, S., 'Entangled Frontiers: Collection, Display and the Queensland Museum, 1878–1914', *Journal of Australian Colonial History*, vol. 13, 2011.

Rowse, T., *White Flour, White Power: From Rations to Citizenship in Central Australia*, Cambridge University Press, Melbourne, 2002.

Rubuntja, W. & J. Green, *The Town Grew Up Dancing: The Life and Art of Wenten Rubuntja*, Jukurrpa Books, Alice Springs, 2002.

Rumsey, A., 'The dreaming, human agency and inscriptive practice', *Oceania*, vol. 65, no. 2, 1994.

Ryan, J., 'Aesthetic Splendour, Cultural Power and Wisdom: early Papunya painting', in J. Ryan and P. Batty (eds), *Tjukurrtjanu: Origins of Western Desert Art*, exhibition catalogue, National Gallery of Victoria, Melbourne, 2011.

Ryan, J. & K. Akerman, 'Shadows of Wandjina: Figurative Art of the North-west and Central Kimberley', in J. Ryan with K. Akerman (eds), *Images of Power: Aboriginal Art of the Kimberley*, National Gallery of Victoria, Melbourne, 1993.

Ryan, J. & P. Batty (eds), *Origins of Western Desert Art Tjukurrtjanu*, exhibition catalogue, National Gallery of Victoria, Melbourne, 2011.

Saunders, S. 'Isolation: the development of leprosy prophylaxis in Australia', *Aboriginal History*, vol. 14, no. 2, 1990.

Scarce, Y., Artist Talk, Ausglass Conference, Adelaide, August 2015.

Schmidt, C., 'Utopia: The Genius of Emily Kame Kngwarreye', exhibition review, *ReCollections* vol. 4, no. 1, 2009, <http://recollections.nma.gov.au/issues/vol_4_no1/exhibition_reviews/utopia>.

Schmidt, C., 'Rodney Gooch's Role and Influence in the Development of the Utopia Art Movement: A History of the Art Movement and Rodney Gooch's Role within it', *International Journal of the Arts in Society*, vol. 5, no. 6, 2011.

Schmidt, C., '"I Paint for Everyone" – the making of Utopia art', PhD thesis, Australian National University, Canberra, 2012.

Schwartz, J. & T. Cook, 'Archives, Records and Power: The Making of Modern Memory', *Archival Science*, no. 2, 2002.

Sekula, A., *Photography against the grain: essays and photo works 1973–1983*, Nova Scotia University Press, Halifax, 1984.

Serventy, V., *The Desert Sea: The Miracle of Lake Eyre in Flood*, Macmillan, South Melbourne, 1985.

Simon, C. (ed.), *Visual Resources: An International Journal of Documentation*, Special Issue: Following the Archival Turn: Photography, the Museum, and the Archive, vol. 18, no. 2, 2002.

Simon, C. I. 'Following the Archival Turn', *Visual Resources*, XVIII.

Simpson, M. G., 'Charting the Boundaries: Indigenous models and parallel practices in the development of the post-museum', in S. J. Knell, S. MacLeod & S. Watson (eds), *Museum Revolutions: How Museums Change and are Changed*, Routledge, London and New York, 2007.

Slade, L., 'In Spite of Colonisation: Yhonnie Scarce', *Broadsheet*, vol. 42, no. 2, 2013.

Smith, B., *European Vision and the South Pacific*, Clarendon Press, Oxford, 1960.

Smith, E. 'Obsolescence and Ephemera in Postcolonial History', in K. von Zinnenburg Carroll (ed.), *The Importance of Being Anachronistic*, Discipline, Melbourne, in press.

Smith, L. T., *Decolonising Methodologies: Research and Indigenous Peoples*, Zed Books, New York, 1999.

Smith, M., *Peopling the Cleland Hills: Aboriginal History in Western Central Australia, 1850-1980*, Aboriginal History Inc., Canberra, 2005.

Smith, P., 'Station Camps: legislation, labour relations and rations on pastoral leases in the Kimberley region, Western Australia', *Aboriginal History*, no. 24, 2000.

Smith, T., 'Kngwarreye woman abstract painter' in J. Isaacs (ed.), *Emily Kame Kngwarreye Paintings*, Craftsman House, Sydney, 1998.

Smith, T., 'Contemporary art and Contemporaneity', *Critical Inquiry*, vol. 32, no. 4, 2006.

Smith, T., 'Emily Kngwarreye's practice of painting: an international perspective', presentation at *Emily: 'Why do these fellas paint like me?'*, 23 August 2008, < http://www.nma.gov.au/audio/transcripts/emily/NMA_Smith_20080823.html>.

Solomon-Godeau, A., *Photography at the Dock: Essays on photographic history, institutions, and practices*, University of Minnesota Press, Minneapolis, 1991.

Spear, T., 'Neo-Traditionalism and the Limits of Invention in British Colonial Africa', *The Journal of African History*, vol. 44, no. 1, 2003.

Stanton, J. E., 'Snapshots of the Dreaming: Photographs of the past and present', in L. Peers & A. K. Brown (eds), *Museums and Source Communities: A Routledge reader,* Routledge, New York, 2003.

Steve, S. et al., *Desert Lake: Art, Science and Stories from Paruku*, CSIRO Publishing, Melbourne, 2013.

Strehlow, T. G. H., 'From 1941 Diary, Haasts Bluff Population Census, Taken Patrol Officer, T. G. H. Strehlow, 1941', Strehlow Research Centre, Alice Springs.

Strehlow, T. G. H., 'The Art of Circle, Line and Square', in R. Berndt (ed.), *Australian Aboriginal Art*, Ure Smith, Sydney, 1964.

Strehlow, T. G. H., 'Culture, Social Structure and Environment in Aboriginal Central Australia', in R. Berndt (ed.), *Aboriginal Man in Australia*, Angus & Robertson, Sydney, 1965.

Strehlow, T. G. H., 'Geography and the Totemic Landscape in Central Australia: A Functional Study', in R. Berndt (ed.), *Australian Aboriginal Anthropology: Modern Studies in the Social Anthropology of the Australian Aborigines*, Published for the Australian Institute of Aboriginal Studies by the University of Western Australia Press, Nedlands, 1970.

Strocchi, M., *Ikuntji: Paintings from Haasts Bluff, 1992–1994*, IAD Press, Alice Springs, 1995.

Sutton, P., 'Aboriginal Maps and Plans', in D. Woodward & G. Malcolm Lewis (eds), *Cartography in the Traditional African, American, Arctic, Australian, and Pacific Societies*, University of Chicago Press, Chicago, 1998.

Sutton, P., 'Icons of Country: Topographic Representations in Classical Aboriginal Traditions', in D. Woodward & G. Malcolm Lewis (eds), *Cartography in the Traditional African, American, Arctic, Australian, and Pacific Societies*, University of Chicago Press, Chicago, 1998.

Swain, T., *A Place for Strangers*, Cambridge University Press, Melbourne, 1993.

Tagg, J., *The Burden of Representation: Essays of Photographies and Histories*, University of Minnesota Press, Minneapolis, 1993.

Taschwer, K., '"Anthropologie ins Volk". Zur Ausstellungspolitik einer anwendbaren Wissenschaft bis 1945', in H. Posch & G. Fliedl (eds), *Politik der Präsentation: Museum und Ausstellung in Österreich 1918–1945*, Turia and Kant, Vienna, 1996.

Taylor, P., 'Introduction', *After 200 Years: Photographic Essays of Aboriginal and Islander Australia Today*, Australian Institute of Aboriginal Studies, Canberra, 1988.

Teschler-Nicola, M., 'Die Wiener Pest-Expedition 1897 – Rudolf Pöchs erste Forschungsreise', *Mitteilungen der Anthropologischen Gesellschaft in Wien*, vol. 136/137, 2006–07.

Teschler-Nicola, M., 'Rudolf Pöchs osteologische Lehr- und

Forschungssammlung im Spannungsfeld von Wissenschaft und Ethik', *Mitteilungen der Anthropologischen Gesellschaft in Wien*, vol. 141, 2011.

The John William Lindt Collection: Grafton Regional Gallery, Grafton Regional Gallery, Grafton, 2005.

Thompson, C., 'Artist Statement', *We Bury Our Own*, 2012, exhibition website <https://www.prm.ox.ac.uk/christianthompson.html>.

Thorner, S., 'Imagining an Indigital Interface: A<u>r</u>a Irititja Indigenizes the Technologies of Knowledge Management', *COLLECTIONS: A journal for Museums and Archives Professionals*, vol. 6, no. 3, 2010.

Thorner, S., & J. Dallwitz, 'Storytelling Photographs, Animating Anangu', in J. Decker (ed.), *Technologies and Digital Initiatives*, Roman and Littlefield, New York, 2015.

Tibbetts, S., 'Tom Hudson's Archive – Methodologies of Intervention', *Journal of Writing Creative Practice*, vol. 7, no. 3, 2014.

Till, K., 'Artistic and Activist Memory-Work: Approaching Place-based Practice', *Memory Studies*, vol. 1, no. 1, 2008.

Timms, P. 'Coroner delivers Open Finding', ABC News 14 May 2010, <http://www.abc.net.au/pm/content/2010/s2899983.htm>.

'Tjanpi at the 2015 Venice Biennale', <http://www.npywc.org.au/2015/06/tjanpi-at-the-2015-venice-biennale/>.

Transforming Tindale website, <http://vernonahkee.blogspot.com.au/2012/09/transforming-tindale.html>.

Tuck, E., & K. W. Yang, 'Decolonization is not a metaphor', *Decolonization: Indigeneity, Education and Society*, vol. 1, no. 1, 2012.

Turnbull, P., 'Ramsay's Regime: The Australian Museum and the Procurement of Aboriginal Bodies, c1874–1900', *Aboriginal History*, vol. 15, no. 1/2, 1991.

Turnbull, P., 'Savages Fossil and Recent: Gerard Krefft and the Production of Racial Knowledge, ca. 1869–73', in M. Crotty, J. Germov & G. Rodwell (eds), *Race for a Place: Eugenics, Darwinism and Social Thought and Practice in Australia, Proceedings of the 2000 History and Sociology of Eugenics Conference*, University of Newcastle, Newcastle, 2000.

Unger, M., *Der Anatom Ferdinand Wagenseil (1887–1967). Integrer Rassenforscher und Bewahrer der Medizinischen Fakultät Giessen*, Wilhelm Schmitz, Giessen, 1998.

Vasari, G., *Lives of the Most Eminent Painters, Sculptors and Architects*, trans. Gaston du C. De Vere, 10 vols., Macmillan and Co. and the Medici Society, London 1912.

Vinnicombe, P., *Women's Sites, Paintings and Places: Warrmarn Community Turkey Creek (A project with Queenie Mckenzie)*, Aboriginal Affairs Department, formerly Department of Aboriginal Sites, Western Australian Museum,

Perth, 1995–6.

Vokes, R. (ed.), *Photography in Africa: Ethnographic Perspectives*, James Currey, Rochester and Woodbridge, 2012.

Wagenseil, F., 'Die mimische und Kau-Muskulatur zweier Melanesier', *Anthropologischer Anzeiger*, vol. 27, 1964.

Walsh, G. L., *Bradshaws: ancient rock paintings of north-west Australia*, Édition Limitée, Geneva, 1994.

Ward, G. & M. Crocombe, 'Port Keats Painting: revolution and continuity', *Australian Aboriginal Studies*, no. 1, 2008.

Ware, V., *Supporting Healthy Communities Through Arts Programs*, Closing the Gap Clearinghouse, Resource sheet no. 28, Australian Institute of Health and Welfare, 2014.

Wastl, J., 'Neu-Guinea, Land und Leute. Mit einer Lebensbeschreibung des ostmärkischen Forschers Rudolf Pöch', in H. Kummerlöwe (ed.), *Wissenschaft ins Volk*, no. 1, 1940.

Watson, C., *Piercing the Ground*, Fremantle Arts Centre Press, Fremantle, 2003.

Weninger, J., 'Das Denkmal für Rudolf Pöch an der Wiener Universität', *Mitteilungen der Anthropologischen Gesellschaft in Wien*, vol. 63, 1933.

West, M., J. Green and K. Petyarr, 'Kathleen Petyarr in Conversation', in H. Perkins (ed.), *One Sun One Moon – Aboriginal Art in Australia*, Art Gallery of New South Wales Press, Sydney, 2007.

What, How and for Whom (ed.), *Really Useful Knowledge*, Museo Nacional Centro de Arte Reina Sofia, Madrid, 2014.

Wood, R. D., 'The Voyage of Captain Lucas and the Daguerreotype to Sydney', in A. Foucrier (ed.), *The French and the Pacific World, 17th–19th Centuries: Explorations, Migrations and Cultural Exchanges*, Ashgate and Variorum, Aldershot and Burlington, 2005.

Worms E. A. & H. Petri, *Australian Aboriginal Religions*, Nelen Yubu Missiological Series no. 5, Spectrum Publications/Nelen Yubu Missiological Unit, Sydney, 1998.

Wright, F. *The Art and Craft Centre Story, Volume One Report*, Aboriginal and Torres Strait Islander Commission, Canberra, 1999.

Young, D., 'Dingo Scalping and the Frontier Economy in North-West of South Australia', in I. Keen (ed.), *Indigenous Participation in Australian Economies: Historical and Anthropological Perspectives*, ANU e-Press, Canberra, 2010.

Ziegelmayer, G., 'Pöch, Rudolf (1870–1921)', in F. Spencer (ed.), *History of Physical Anthropology: An Encyclopedia*, vol. 2, M–Z, Garland, New York and London, 1997.

www.ingramcontent.com/pod-product-compliance
Lightning Source LLC
LaVergne TN
LVHW050951080826
845145LV00005B/1471